ACCLAIM FOR ANDREW BURSTEIN'S

THE PASSIONS OF ANDREW JACKSON

"Excellent. . . . A must-read for anyone interested in the presidency or early American history."   —*The Flint Journal*

"Impressive. . . . Persuasive. . . . Argues that the times shaped Jackson and thrust him into the White House as the first 'commoner' elected president because he so personified the young nation's bold, brash spirit and sense of destiny."   —*The Baltimore Sun*

"In his ably drawn portrait . . . [Burstein] studies Jackson from many angles: as the orphan of the American Revolution, the self-taught orator . . . and as the lanky husband who loved his stocky wife, Rachel, touchingly and fiercely."
—*The New York Times Book Review*

"Well-researched and well-written. . . . Burstein, with his long-standing interest in the American mind, wants to show how we pick our national heroes."   —*Chicago Tribune*

"Burstein's subtle analysis of Jackson's complex personality helps explain the man as well as the times in which he lived."
—*Richmond Times-Dispatch*

"Rewarding. . . . Consistently illuminating. . . . Burstein skillfully reveals the complex central figure in his narrative while also conveying the upheaval taking place in the country during the era of western expansion."   —*BookPage*

Andrew Burstein

THE PASSIONS OF ANDREW JACKSON

Andrew Burstein is the author of three previous books on American political culture, including *America's Jubilee: How in 1826 a Generation Remembered Fifty Years of Independence* and *The Inner Jefferson*. A graduate of Columbia University, he earned his Ph.D. at the University of Virginia. Burstein is currently professor of history and coholder of the Mary Frances Barnard Chair at the University of Tulsa.

THE PASSIONS OF ANDREW JACKSON

The Passions of

ANDREW JACKSON

❯❯❯❯❯❯·❮❮❮❮❮❮

Andrew Burstein

VINTAGE BOOKS

A DIVISION OF RANDOM ROUSE, INC.

NEW YORK

FIRST VINTAGE BOOKS EDITION, APRIL 2004

Copyright © 2003 by Andrew Burstein

All rights reserved under International and Pan-American Copyright
Conventions. Published in the United States by Vintage Books,
a division of Random House, Inc., New York, and simultaneously in
Canada by Random House of Canada Limited, Toronto. Originally
published in hardcover in the United States by Alfred A. Knopf,
a division of Random House, Inc., New York, in 2003.

The Library of Congress has cataloged the Knopf edition as follows:
Burstein, Andrew.
The passions of Andrew Jackson / Andrew Burstein.—1st ed.
p. cm.
Includes bibliographical references (p.) and index.
1. Jackson, Andrew, 1767–1845. 2. Jackson, Andrew, 1767–1845—Psychology.
3. Presidents—United States—Biography. I. Title.
E382.B96 2003
973.5'6'092—dc21
[B] 2002016258

Vintage ISBN: 0-375-71404-9

Author photograph © Josh Burstein
Book design by Peter A. Andersen
Map by David Lindroth, Inc.

www.vintagebooks.com

Printed in the United States of America
10 9 8 7 6 5 4 3 2 1

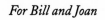

For Bill and Joan

Never did captive with a freer heart
Cast off his chains of bondage and embrace
His golden uncontrolled enfranchisement,
More than my dancing soul doth celebrate
This feast of battle with mine adversary.
                              —Shakespeare, *Richard II*

I have set my life upon a cast,
And I will stand the hazard of the die.
                              —Shakespeare, *Richard III*

His heart's his mouth.
What his breast forges, that his tongue must vent;
And, being angry, does forget that ever
He heard the name of death.
                              —Shakespeare, *Coriolanus*

CONTENTS

❯❯❯❯❯❯❯❯❯❯·❮❮❮❮❮❮❮❮❮❮

ILLUSTRATIONS

❦❦❦❦❦❦❦❦❦·❧❧❧❧❧❧❧❧❧

INTRODUCTION

❯❯❯❯❯❯❯❯❯·❮❮❮❮❮❮❮❮❮

Andrew Jackson (1767–1845), seventh president of the United States (1829–1837), is one of those figures in the pantheon of larger-than-life Americans past whose real personality has all but vanished. Once flesh and blood, he seems two-dimensional now, and perhaps even irrelevant to what America has become. But that should not be, because Jackson embodies American defiance and American bravado. He combined aggressiveness with a belief in his own benevolence, and he made an indelible mark on his country.

Jackson's life reads very much like that of a Shakespearean subject. He was the ultimate opportunist, born poor and orphaned young, who rose as a popular champion and captivated the public. Settling in frontier Tennessee in 1788, he burst from obscurity and into a series of self-made controversies. Without fighting experience, he fought to be named a general. And from that point on, he made sure that no one would ever silence him. He awakened a whole generation, an expectant generation with a great weight on its collective shoulders, for it contained the children of the republic's founders. Jackson symbolized nationalism and pride in ways the original Revolutionaries had not predicted. He envisioned America as a military giant.

It was the Battle of New Orleans, grand finale to the War of 1812, that brought the outspoken General Andrew Jackson a lifetime of renown. The eighth of January, 1815, was a day of siege and slaughter in one of the most active ports on the continent. It came at the end of two and a half years of fruitless fighting from Lake Erie to the Chesapeake Bay, and after the pointless pillage of Washington, D.C. In the midst of a thick, early morning fog, British forces, thousands of them, gallantly, recklessly marched across a vast, muddy plain toward the tall staff at the center of Jackson's lines that held the American flag. The British expected victory, and to be living it up in the merry Mississippi River city by day's end. Rockets whistled. Cannonballs pounded the earth. An unprecedented fusillade of musket shot poured into columns of the advancing, red-coated soldiers. By eight o'clock in the morning, two hours after fighting commenced, it was done. The red line had crumbled. Men lay thickly strewn across the field for two hundred yards. The local civilian population exulted, and Jackson gained, once and for all, the heroic stature he sought. His rough-hewn army had stopped the proud British, with insignificant losses of their own.[1]

After New Orleans, he became known to a grateful public as a man of endurance, unwavering will, and resolute action. Over the years, as the public got to know him better, they realized alternative meanings for endurance, will, and action: obstinacy, fierceness, and self-absorption. Which was Jackson? they pondered. Brave or unbalanced? Or both? Was he steel wrought in a fiery furnace, or an uncontrollable monster irresponsibly unleashed into the political world? Was he the ultimate democrat or the ultimate despot?

That sense of duality is as close to the historic Jackson as the modern record comes. It is striking that this most passionate symbol of a ripening republic could have become so emotionally empty in the historic memory of twenty-first century Americans. "The man of to-day is no longer agitated by the same passions which distracted the man of yesterday," wrote Adam Smith in 1759.[2] In our own time, Andrew Jackson is an amorphous figure, and to a majority of Americans no more than the sharp-eyed, romantically gazing, stormy-haired presence on the redesigned twenty-dollar bill. The nobly constructed George Washington; the newly appreciated John Adams; the ever-scrutinized Thomas Jefferson; and the soulful, melancholy Abraham Lincoln all continue to command attention as men whose personalities are somehow comprehensible to the modern mind. Jackson, in spite of the many cities and counties named for him, arouses far less curiosity. Yet in opinion polls, he consistently ranks as one of the "greatest" presidents.

For decades after his death, he remained controversial. Into the twentieth century he was reviled by Indians for his central role in the dispersal of thousands of families on the lethal "Trail of Tears." During the Depression, the mere thought of Andrew Jackson once caused the amiable radio and film personality Will Rogers, part Cherokee, to launch into an unbridled condemnation of a man who had died more than fourscore years before.[3]

Among white Americans, the name *Jackson* was for a long time a synonym for courage, and "Old Hickory" an unsurpassed war hero who walked among ordinary people. To others of the nineteenth century, who considered themselves genteel, the general was a rude and grossly overblown man of meager understandings. Like one of his presidential predecessors, the eloquent partisan Jefferson, he was ardently loved and fiercely hated. Even more than Jefferson, he became, for the rest of the world, the popular symbol of an "American" personality, one that claimed honor in commonness.

His death at seventy-eight, in 1845, inspired the faithful to remark upon his character and worth. Mourners were told that his most striking feature was "an irresistible energy." One of his eulogists, historian George Bancroft, asserted, "No public man of this century ever returned to private life with such an abiding mastery over the affections of the people." Jackson's was, he proclaimed, "the last great name, which gathers round itself all the associations that form the glory of America." He was frequently compared to Washington, the essential founder.[4]

Modern historians generally concur that the Jackson phenomenon was an advertisement for his countrymen's sense of their own rise to respectability relative to Europe. When Americans of his day, proud of their simple impulses, declaring their wishes pure and strong, elevated Jackson to the highest political office, they were presenting him to history as a symbol of themselves. He was, and they were, enterprising and self-satisfied, a might-makes-right caricature reflecting the awkwardness of cultural transition in the preindustrial age. This brash man of common stock, aphoristic and intangible, was as intimidating as many in America liked to imagine their young nation.[5]

Those who adored the plebeian leader and those who feared or despised him all thought they knew him. I submit, however, that the historical Jackson, a man often described, is intensely difficult to find. This book is an attempt to make him more knowable. The collected correspondence of Andrew Jackson; the papers of his friends and public associates; strangers' chance encounters; vicious attacks; campaign biographies—all of the above were written when the subject was alive or recently remembered. To venture a judicious study from so great a cultural distance as the twenty-first century, one must sift through these and also the records of previous historians to find what Jackson's biographers have missed—documents that were overlooked, events oversimplified, quotations misapplied, relationships undervalued—to separate offhand assumptions from more persuasive evidence, finally to be left with those materials from which to speculate forthrightly.

In three previous books, my particular quest has always been an attentive dissection of language, and it is the same here: I aim to identify those sources that most plausibly open Jackson to us. It is a subjective enterprise, because every life is secretive. No historical personage is adequately self-revealing. Nonetheless, a new perspective on Jackson-as-communicator is called for.

Most crucial to this study are Jackson's first fifty years or so, the years before he became a candidate for president. Indeed, as richly rewarding as a study of his presidency is, the long chapter I give to it cannot do full justice to the complex interactions among the Congress, the Executive, and the states. Thus my emphasis remains, there and throughout, on my subject's character and impulses.

Jackson spent very few of his formative years anywhere near the center of national politics, and so the ways he behaved as president only make sense in the context of what preceded. His decisions are best understood in light of a bitter and hard-fought experience. To say that he was prosecutor, state judge, congressman, and U.S. senator—all before he rose in stature as a victorious major general during the War of 1812—is to explain little or nothing about Jackson's appeal or even his ambition. To answer the question "Who was he?" requires that we look at building blocks, and separate the individual's lean years, his struggle to achieve respectability, from his subsequent political fashioning.

I have found over the course of research that careless compositions often tend to be the most revealing texts, beautiful sentiments the most superficial. The hardest but assuredly the most exciting part of doing archival research is to fathom meaning from handwritten letters and drafts of letters, from unceremonious communications and newspaper commentary. I have tried to lift the veil of society and manners, to disclose literary styles, tropes and habitual phrases.

It sounds good. But humans, while often predictable, are as often confoundingly unpredictable. Jackson's great nineteenth-century biographer James Parton knew this. Writing just before the outbreak of the Civil War, he expressed many concerns about his craft. He had scoured the country interviewing those who claimed to have known the late president intimately, including one aged woman who recalled him as an infant. But even after his extensive travels, and his painstaking research, his meetings with prominent political figures and Jackson's ordinary neighbors, Parton confessed:

Andrew Jackson, I am given to understand, was a patriot and a traitor. He was one of the greatest of generals, and wholly ignorant of the art of war. A writer brilliant, elegant, eloquent, without being able to compose a correct sentence, or spell words of four syllables. The first of statesmen, he never devised, he never framed a measure. He was the most candid of men, and was capable of the profoundest dissimulation. A most law-defying, law-obeying citizen. A stickler for discipline, he never hesitated to disobey a superior. A democratic autocrat. An urbane savage. An atrocious saint.[6]

Though he embellished and editorialized freely in the conversational style of nineteenth-century writing, Parton's degree of critical detachment makes him unusual for a biographer of his day. Writing an earlier biography, a controversial life of the reputedly amoral Aaron Burr, had challenged Parton to see good as well as bad in a man who was generally repugnant to his readership. With Jackson, he maintained a romantic attachment to his prose while pronouncing a relative objectivity toward his subject. His years as a New York journalist are evident in his work.[7]

Several twentieth-century works deserve mention. Marquis James won the 1938 Pulitzer Prize in biography for his two-volume study, copious in its endnotes yet too loosely poetic for the discriminating historian. The original book jacket for the "complete in one volume" edition proclaims *The Life of Andrew Jackson* "a colorful human story"—which it is—and terms Jackson "a true Knight of the Frontier," which is excessive. James's book is a case of chivalry taken too far.

Over the last half century or so, more has been written about Jackson's impact than about Jackson the man. Arthur M. Schlesinger Jr. won the 1946 Pulitzer Prize in history for *The Age of Jackson*, which was fittingly blurbed by Marquis James as "a landmark in American historical literature." Schlesinger's work is lively and provocative, but it is more about the vitality of democracy than about Andrew Jackson, emphasizing the president's role in the effort to combat the consolidation of capital.[8] John William Ward's *Andrew Jackson: Symbol for an Age* (1953) is a highly literate examination of the way history made Jackson into a hero. Ward's clever reading of imagery and nineteenth-century language captures Jackson's mystique at least as well as some of his vaunted biographers. *The Jacksonian Persuasion* (1957), by Marvin Meyers, is another coherent, original study in political culture that addresses Jackson's psychological impact on his times. James C. Curtis wrote a short, synthetic biography in 1976, with much to commend it, that undertook to humanize a Jackson who, surrounded by death, "spent his life in trying to prove his right to survival."[9]

Harry L. Watson's well-read *Liberty and Power* (1990) offers a skillful analysis of partisanship in the time of Jackson. Watson looks past Jackson's private passions, in making sense of the politics of a pained democracy.

As to modern scholarship, no one has done more in an effort to popularize Jackson than Robert V. Remini. A prolific scholar, Remini matched Parton with a three-volume biography (published between 1977 and 1984), and far exceeded his predecessor in output of articles and spin-offs on "the Hero," as Jackson was often designated in his lifetime. Schlesinger praised Remini's trilogy as "superb professional history that moves boldly beyond the scholar's monograph." Other historians consider Professor Remini to be "obsessed with explicating Jackson's perspective."[10]

Comprehensive as his work is, one must read Remini discerningly. His imaginary encounter with schoolboy Andrew suggests a time-bending acquaintance, more intimate than it ought to be: "A tall, extremely slender boy, whose most distinguishing features were his bright, intensely blue eyes—how they blazed when passion seized him!" During the Creek War of 1813–14, the stalwart Jackson is made to stand nearly alone against the enemy, while his weary troops conspire to desert him: "Audible grumbles greeted the command [to stay and fight]. . . . As the mutineers approached Jackson presented quite an awesome sight. A shaft of implacable determination stretched high on the saddle of his horse, eyes flashing, grizzled hair bristling on his forehead, Jackson roared a threat to kill any man who defied him. To brave this fury was madness." This kind of creative storytelling suffuses Remini's writings on Jackson. There are times when he appears to have imbibed too well the campaign biographies and other works by Jackson's closest associates.[11]

A knowledgeable reviewer of Remini's trilogy, Donald B. Cole, credited him with producing a well-documented analysis of Jackson's career, while pointing to the author's "excess emotion" and the occasional "overblown interpretation." I agree in large measure with Cole's assessment of Remini's "pardonable hyperbole." The problem, as I see it, is one of literary method: Remini has styled an heroic saga that places the individual before all other historical forces, privileging "greatness" over more useful (and more critical) measures of politics and culture.[12]

Writers are accountable for what they write. I have written this book as dispassionately as possible, while writing about passion. I would not single out Professor Remini for criticism except that he is the reigning Jackson authority, and his single-minded emphasis on "greatness" limits the kinds of questions he asks. His ideological inclinations are ultimately a matter of taste, but they have served to polarize. Among students of the presidency, no less than among his contemporaries, one hears Andrew Jackson hailed as a great democrat and upbraided by an equal number as an ill-educated hothead and the "butcher" of Indians.[13] Less often has he been examined without concern for the life of his legacy.

Regardless of my intent, I fully expect to annoy those readers who already have fixed perceptions of the kind of leader Jackson was, based on Remini's traditional formula. In touring the Hermitage, Jackson's Nashville home, one is treated to an idyllic picture of a robust past. It is at once irresistible and insidious, irresistible as a story based on fact — on historic accounts and archaeology — and insidious because it cannot possibly be true. Even the blemishes, the defects (most notably slavery) are assiduously made tasteful, because all heroes must be retrievable. This is not to criticize the modern management of Jackson's historic house and grounds either, but rather to recognize in the public consciousness a need to feel good about ourselves. We gauge our prospects as a people by locating a past from which we can draw hope and pride. Heroes become necessary in such an enterprise. The Hermitage is a wonderful place to visit: *it* is not the problem.

There is another way to say this. Biography is never a faithful record. It is a construction, a clandestine effort to refashion memory, to create a new tradition, or sanction yet another myth about what is past. In the interest of writing an exciting or inspiring book, too many popular biographers refuse to confront the problems of their own pretense and ideology, the problems inherent in how they relate to their subject. As the social critic Hannah Arendt has noted, the storyteller consciously and unconsciously intrudes, revealing his or her mounting desire to reach a particular conclusion.[14] I know that I, too, risk such a critique in undertaking this study. I prefer to think of what follows as a provisional portrait of the historic Jackson, designed not so much to ask whether he was truly great or exaggerated in stature — these are emotional determinations — but whether and to what extent we, so far removed from the values of his day, can take his measure.

It is for this reason that I emphasize what previous scholars have not: Jackson's friendships. They shed new light on his populism (what others might call demagoguery), his heated suspicions, his clear sense of victimization. Edward Livingston, John Henry Eaton, Sam Houston, Richard Keith Call, and William Carroll were prominent political figures. Though unknown to all but a handful of American historians today (with the obvious exception of Houston), these were Jackson's handpicked favorites, and they all rose along with him. They did not subsume their public personalities into his (at least, not permanently), nor did they necessarily compromise their careers just to advance his interests. Still, they interacted in important ways with Jackson amid his public and private battles.[15]

What happened over the course of these friendships explains much about Jackson's inner drive. These five individuals and others, for and against him, whose impulses are nearly as important as Jackson's in this book, help us to resolve key questions: At the gut level, with whom did Jackson identify and why? What led this notably suspicious man to trust? Ambition climbs only with others' help and encouragement, and so the web of relationships matters a great deal if this study is to present a deliberative, demythologized view of Andrew Jackson.

Memory is always subjective, ideologically informed, fancified, and even, at times, delusive. In that sense, the goal of this book is to help critical readers tunnel through the politics of memory—for the politics of memory is, in a phrase, what history really is when we anoint heroes or presume to categorize an entire age. Passion is integral to the art of persuasion that defines politics (or the politics of memory). Thus examining the language of passion, amid the pursuit of ambition, will disclose a good part—but only part—of what spawned the momentous controversies in which Jackson was cast as a lead actor. *The Passions of Andrew Jackson* is not meant to make the past "familiar" or more venerable or less venerable, but to make it tempting.

I wish to thank the following individuals and institutions for contributing in substantive ways to my research. At the American Antiquarian Society, for some years now a summer haven of contemplative study for me, I salute again the supportive and highly professional staff. At the Tennessee State Library and Archives, Susan Gordon was absolutely instrumental as a guide to a rich repository. Similarly, the staff of the Hermitage, home of Andrew Jackson, was quite helpful and forthcoming. I am as grateful to have had access to collections at the libraries of Princeton University, the University of Texas at Austin, the University of Virginia, the Virginia Historical Society, the New York Public Library, and the Manuscript Division of the Library of Congress.

At the University of Tulsa, funding generously provided through the Mary Frances Barnard chair endowment has made the research process particularly easy and productive. Everyone at McFarlin Library has been diligent, and interlibrary loan prompt and effective. Talented colleagues— I begin with the generous James Ronda—Christine Ruane and Joseph Bradley, Andrew Wood, Paul Rahe, Amy Carreiro, Thomas Buckley, Thomas Buoye, Thomas Horne, and Robert Donaldson, have all gone out of their way to create a scholarly community and to sustain an environment where talk is meaningful. They—and department secretary Toy Kelley—have contributed enormously to this book. For help with Shakespearean sensibilities, I am in debt to Lars Engle. And for his patient reading and critical eye, special thanks to Keith Howells. Many historians of the early American republic have prompted me with keen questions and solid ideas; among these I wish to point to Matthew Dennis; Saul Cornell; Douglas Egerton; David Waldstreicher; and the adviser whom I can never adequately thank, Peter Onuf, for their particular insights.

I am most fortunate, once again, to have experience guiding the production of this book: Gerard McCauley as my literary agent and Ashbel Green as my editor. My son Josh, with all the subtlety of a teenager, has helped me to expunge vocabulary that only stuffy historians use. My partner, and with me coholder of the Mary Frances Barnard chair, Nancy Isenberg, knows precisely what her contribution has been, and how that special affinity works.

Explanatory note regarding Jackson's orthography: The reader should be aware that the spellings in this book adhere to the standards in cited materials. The published *Papers of Andrew Jackson,* an ongoing series covering the period 1788–1824, adopts Jackson's unorthodox style, while the earlier *Correspondence of Andrew Jackson,* incomplete though it encompasses the period up to 1845, alters Jackson's spelling to conform to modern standards. When quoting from originals or the microfilm edition of the *Andrew Jackson Papers* at the Library of Congress, which comprises handwritten materials, I follow the actual text as closely as possible. This is the case, too, for citations from other nineteenth-century manuscripts identified in the endnotes.

THE PASSIONS OF ANDREW JACKSON

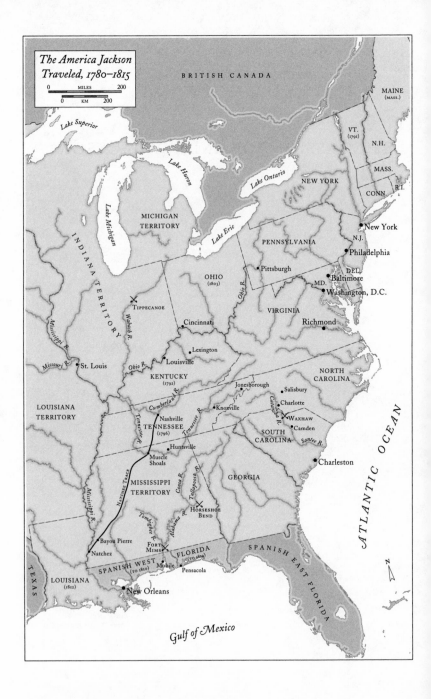

The America Jackson
Traveled, 1780–1815

0 — MILES — 200
0 — KM — 200

BRITISH CANADA

Lake Superior

Lake Huron

Lake Michigan

Lake Ontario

Lake Erie

MAINE
(MASS.)

VT.
(1791)

N.H.

MASS.

CONN.

R.I.

NEW YORK

New York

N.J.

Philadelphia

DEL.

MICHIGAN
TERRITORY

INDIANA
TERRITORY

Mississippi R.

Missouri R.

St. Louis

LOUISIANA
TERRITORY

Wabash R.

TIPPECANOE

OHIO
(1803)

Ohio R.

PENNSYLVANIA

Pittsburgh

Baltimore

MD.

Washington, D.C.

VIRGINIA

Richmond

Cincinnati

Lexington

Louisville

Ohio R.

KENTUCKY
(1792)

Cumberland R.

Tennessee R.

NORTH
CAROLINA

Jonesborough

Salisbury

Charlotte

Catawba R.

Knoxville

Tennessee R.

Waxhaw

Camden

Nashville

TENNESSEE
(1796)

SOUTH
CAROLINA

Santee R.

Huntsville

Muscle
Shoals

MISSISSIPPI
TERRITORY

Coosa R.

Tallapoosa R.

Alabama R.

GEORGIA

Charleston

Natchez Trace

Tombigbee R.

HORSESHOE
BEND

Bayou Pierre

Natchez

Mississippi R.

FORT
MIMS

FLORIDA
(TO 1819)

SPANISH EAST FLORIDA

SPANISH WEST
(TO 1810)

Mobile

Pensacola

ATLANTIC OCEAN

TEXAS

LOUISIANA
(1812)

New Orleans

N

Gulf of Mexico

CHAPTER ONE

The Formative Frontier

*Tarlton passed thro the Waxhaw settlement to the cotauba nation
passing our dwelling but all were <u>hid out.</u> Tarleton passed within a
hundred yards of where I & cousin crawford, had concealed ourselves.
I could have shot him.*

> —fragment in Jackson's hand, probably written
> late in life for the benefit of a biographer

Of the many controversies that envelop the turbulent world he occupied,
Andrew Jackson's birthplace is one dispute with local repercussions only:
both North and South Carolina have claimed him. The site of his nativity,
"the crossing of the Waxhaw," as Jackson referred to it, had little to recom-
mend it beyond a creek, red earth, a modest church, and proximity to the
post road. The two Carolinas merged at this fairly nondescript place, and
exemplify for us the difference between the words *frontier* and *border*. The
first is amorphous, unregulated, and in the minds of some, even mysterious; the second is marked and fixed. Suffice it to say that the two colonies
were still negotiating jurisdiction of the area at the time of Jackson's birth
on March 15, 1767, and that Jackson himself placed his origin within the
bounds of South Carolina.

In 1824, the year of his first presidential run, Jackson received a letter at
his Hermitage estate outside Nashville, Tennessee, from the respected car-
tographer Robert Mills of Columbia, South Carolina. Mills had fought
under General Jackson at the Battle of New Orleans nine years earlier. His
letter contained a map of the border district where the western country's
famed general was born, but which he had not seen, at this point, for forty
years. Jackson wrote back to Mills with a mix of nostalgia and fatalism: "A
view of this map pointing to the spot that gave me birth, brings fresh to
my memory many associations dear to my heart, many days of pleasure

with my juvenile companions: but alas, most of them are gone to that bourne where I am hastening & from whence no one returns." As much as Jackson was known to communicate with unsparing directness, he could also affect this style, which was perceived, in his time, as "chaste" and generous. *Nostalgic, fatalistic, chaste,* and *generous* are all good words for describing Andrew Jackson.[1]

Scotch-Irish had colonized the Waxhaws, which bore the name of the Indians who had previously lived there. Early in the eighteenth century, the Catawba tribe battled the Waxhaw tribe, killed their best warriors, and drove away the survivors. By the time of Jackson's birth, the Catawbas were themselves much reduced in number, dependent upon the colonists for food and protection, and sufficiently wary of their non-Indian neighbors to have requested formal settlement on a reservation. That reservation, about ten miles square, straddled the future state border and stopped just above the Jacksons' community.[2]

Yet a Catawba had only recently played a pivotal role in the unfolding drama of America's history. The Indian "Half King" Tanaghrisson was born into the South Carolina tribe before its undoing. His tumultuous life demonstrates the confused allegiances of frontier peoples of all sorts. When young, he was captured and adopted into the marauding Seneca tribe of western New York, and eventually became an agent of the Iroquois confederacy in the Pennsylvania-Ohio backcountry, helping to maintain a delicate balance between interior peoples and colonial governments. In 1754, Tanaghrisson accompanied twenty-two-year-old George Washington on the Virginian's first (and rather catastrophic) military expedition. When he used his hatchet to tear open the skull of a French emissary before the eyes of the inexperienced Major Washington, the Catawba literally had a hand in fomenting the French and Indian War.[3]

The declining Catawbas were the first Indians Andrew Jackson knew. A good number of them joined the Revolutionary cause when and where Jackson, at the age of thirteen, did. They tasted combat, and bled on behalf of the newly independent United States. In later years, the larger Indian nations of the South and Southwest—Cherokees, Creeks, Choctaws, and Seminoles—would, each in turn, be awed by the inflexible Gen. Andrew Jackson. By then, the Catawbas he knew as a child were long since an invisible presence in the Carolinas, a servile, impoverished people, found by mapmaker Robert Mills to be "depraved" and "immoral."

This was one way that Jackson, too, thought generically of Indians. Their struggle to survive never seemed to move him. Like so many other tribes before and since, the eighteenth-century Catawbas had made practical choices: they tried to accommodate growing numbers of whites. Separateness may have appealed to them initially, but in the 1760s, as a means to achieve economic self-sufficiency, they began renting out land within their reservation to white settlers. Known around mid-century as a sometimes "insolent" and "mischievous" people who trespassed and stole, the Catawbas were decimated by smallpox in a 1759 epidemic, and were termed "harmless and friendly" neighbors during Jackson's childhood, when they numbered only in the hundreds. They were often seen as peddlers of moccasins, basketware, and pottery along the southbound post road to Camden and Charleston.[4]

No one can say with certainty what Jackson's first encounters with Indians augured. But it is worth depicting the Catawbas of his earliest years, as a means of setting forth the terms for understanding this quintessential rough-and-ready American reared in Revolutionary times and destined to be the first U.S. president to have sprung from a modest space, from outside the social elite. To approach him, we must recover his physical as well as emotional environment, and learn enough to speculate about what it was that caused him to grow up so brash and ambitious, with an uncompromising will. This much is clear: distinguishing himself from the dissipated Indians, Jackson wanted credit for all he did, credit for his moral energy.

Moral energy. No other term so manifestly embodies Jackson's self-image. If he had not constantly proclaimed his potential, and backed up his claims with an abundant militancy at a time when battlefield victories were direly needed, he might never have been able to justify himself to eastern power and pretension. Were it not for the way America's identity was increasingly tied to conflict and settlement in the West, he might—like the Catawba—have festered and died, unnoticed by posterity, in the backwoods.

His rise was nothing short of phenomenal. He was not learned, nor particularly bright. Until 1815, when his martial triumphs rocked the nation, he had a marginal impact on government. Arriving in the national capital of Philadelphia in December 1796, as Tennessee's very first congressman, Jackson appeared to his prominent colleague, western Pennsylvania's Albert Gallatin, as "a tall, lank, uncouth-looking personage, with long locks of hair hanging over his face, and a queue down his back tied in an eel skin."[5] It was the way whites typically described the untutored Indian. To his detractors in polite society, Jackson's raw experience made him seem "savage." To others, reacting with excitement against traditional symbols of privilege, he was to become favored as an uncommon commoner—rebellious, heroic, earthy, masculine. In the 1820s, such qualities held romantic appeal.

Ironically, this destroyer of Indian cultures (for that was how he first achieved national prominence) was judged by urban Americans as one who had borrowed something of the Indian. The historian James Parton, himself a nineteenth-century man, writes of the last decade of the eighteenth century, when Jackson became a Tennessean: "The western man of the olden time had much of the Indian in him. He caught the Indian's stealthy footstep; imbibed something of his passion for revenge; abandoned himself like him to the carouse." It is a rather unambiguous characterization.[6]

The stereotypes presented by late-eighteenth-century writers combined Indian ruthlessness with primitive virtue. A portrayal of Indians by the novelist Tobias Smollett is representative: they were "too tenacious of their own customs to adopt the modes of any nation whatsoever. . . . they were too virtuous and sensible to encourage the introduction of any fashion which might help render them corrupt and effeminate." This depiction sounds strangely Jacksonesque, for he was certainly tenacious, and he came to see himself as a virtuous warrior.[7]

The frontier fermented in American opinion makers' imaginations. The Indian, deemed "wild" or "savage," was as often praised for exhibiting bravery and stoicism, and ennobled for his resistance to the corruptions of civilization. His uninvited neighbor, the white settler, could be a doubt-conquering builder or a simple degenerate. To the philosophic critics who rendered these judgments, a man like Jackson existed near to the primitive state and lacked the rational capacity of his learned counterpart back east. Thus Jackson, like the Indian, was suspected of wanting that inner control and self-restraint on which a workable republic thrived. He fought on behalf of the civilizing power, but his boasted familiarity with the Indian manner made him dangerous.

Being a representative western man was a double-edged sword for the civilizer-warrior in this case. The wilderness was a part of him. He was as comfortable with destruction as with cultivation. He was "Indian-like" insofar as he was bluff, direct, and resistant to all forms of seductive softness—in modern terms, one who could always "take it like a man." But could he rule a civilized people?

Any such ambiguity was in the minds of others. Jackson would have regarded these comparisons as mean-spirited, if not ludicrous. He was American through and through. The needs of Indians were, to him, fairly trivial. Yet the irony persists: acutely aware of his reputation, captive of a myth, he fought, with an Indian's supposed fury, to be non-Indian, to be a discernibly republican gentleman. And what was that? "Republican gentleman" was a known quality, associated in Jackson's day with writing and speaking skills and an abundance of sympathy and fellow feeling. It was a term of acceptance employed by the recognized leaders of post-Revolutionary America, and it was not automatically accorded to a temperamental man with a backwoods vocabulary.

The way for Jackson would not be easy. Acceptance required that he adapt and adhere to demands set forth by the national power structure. He made efforts to do so over his career, without ceasing to be himself: a frontier American.

"The mark of which he bears to this hour"

There were two routes that immigrants and their wagons took to the Waxhaws, one across Virginia and North Carolina over the "Catawba Path" and one from the port of Charleston. In 1765, Andrew Jackson Sr., sailing from Carrickfergus, near Belfast, Northern Ireland, likely came by the former route, with his wife, Elizabeth Hutchinson, and their two young sons, Hugh and Robert. Elizabeth's sister and her husband, James Crawford, accompanied them across the Atlantic and to the Carolina uplands, where numerous of their compatriots had previously settled. The surrounding landscape was a mix of piney woods, cornfields, and fenced-in areas for hogs and cattle.[8]

Andrew Jackson Sr. died in 1767, very shortly before or shortly after the birth of his third son and namesake.[9] The first authorized biography of "the Hero" of the Battle of New Orleans, which was begun by Jackson's closest aide, John Reid, after the War of 1812, and completed by another Jackson protégé, John Henry Eaton, after Reid's death, predictably described the widow Jackson as "an exemplary woman" who saw that her youngest son received an education at "a flourishing academy at the Waxsaw meetinghouse." That "flourishing academy" was a log cabin.[10]

There is no account to suggest that Jackson was studious then or at any time during his formative years. On the contrary, all have emphasized his sportiveness and recklessness. Parton, in particular, cites the reminiscences of Jackson's early schoolmates, in reporting that the youth was "fond of running foot-races" and enthusiastic about wrestling; that he slobbered, was easily offended, quick-tempered, and generally, in the words of one, "difficult to get along with." His speech was countrified, as suggested in the pronunciation of *development* as "devil-*ope*-ment" and *sublime* as "*soo*-blime."[II]

When the American Revolution came to the interior, Jackson did all he could to take part. His eldest brother, Hugh, had ridden with patriot and Princeton graduate Col. William Richardson Davie of North Carolina, only to die, it is said, of heat exhaustion after the Battle of Stono Ferry, near Charleston, in the summer of 1779.[12] From that point, the British onslaught continued unabated. Conquering Charleston in May 1780, Lord Charles Cornwallis and the notoriously brutal Lt.-Col. Banastre Tarleton proceeded to launch attacks on rebels in the backcountry, and they directed Tory militia to consolidate their gains. Tarleton was a greatly feared enemy, a twenty-six-year-old terrorist who dressed the part of a dandy, in tight breeches and tall black boots, and directed his men to slash and stab and spare no one. Late in life, Jackson recalled having observed the marauding Tarleton from a hundred yards away. Claiming "I could have shot him," Jackson is either telling us that had he a musket, he was within range; or, in more grandiose terms, that he was prepared, at a tender age, to become a patriot-hero. It is impossible to interpret which way he meant himself to be understood.[13]

At the Waxhaw meetinghouse, wounded patriots were nursed by Elizabeth Jackson and her two remaining sons, Andrew and Robert. The family was forced into hiding when another army of invaders arrived at their settlement. At the beginning of August 1780, an American force led by Colonel Davie engaged the enemy at Hanging Rock, some fifteen miles to the south, and Andrew and Robert Jackson assisted the troops, if they did not actually fire muskets. It was a momentary success for the Americans, marred by "plundering and carousing."[14]

In all, the war did not go well for the Revolutionaries in the Carolina piedmont. General Horatio Gates was defeated at nearby Camden the week after the Battle of Hanging Rock, placing the Waxhaw settlement again in the way of the redcoats' northerly march. Cornwallis himself occupied the house of militia officer Robert Crawford, brother of Jackson's uncle by marriage. The Jackson family headed for sanctuary near Charlotte, North Carolina, and was able to return home only four months later.[15] It was after these disruptions and aggravations that an easily provoked Andrew Jackson tasted what a political appointee much later termed his "baptism of blood," as if it were meant to be, a fated life adventure consistent with the lad's heritage: "The martyr blood of Scotland blended with that of the Emerald Isle."[16]

Here is the story, which Jackson told his early biographers, and not even the most skeptical historian has disputed. One day in April 1781, unwelcome guests suddenly called upon the Waxhaw settlers. It was a day when no hostile forces were thought to be in the area. A vanguard of inconspicuously dressed Tories approached, ahead of a party of British mounted light dragoons and infantry. The Waxhaw patriots were surprised, eleven prisoners were taken, and brothers Andrew and Robert Jackson narrowly escaped into the underbrush of a small creek. The next morning, seeking food from a neighbor, they were spotted by Tories and captured. In a defining moment, a British officer faced fourteen-year-old Andrew Jackson and ordered him to clean his muddied boots. The youth refused, demanding proper treatment as a prisoner of war, and the imperious officer slashed at Jackson's head with his sword. Instinctively, the disobedient prisoner thrust his left hand into the air, possibly saving his own life in the act. "He received a severe wound," the Reid-Eaton biography warrants, "the mark of which he bears to this hour."[17]

Robert was less fortunate. After the same officer gave him the same order, he refused, and was struck on the head. Next, the Jackson brothers were transported forty miles to Camden, where they were separated and penned with other prisoners. They were "treated with marked severity," and Robert weakened. Elizabeth Jackson was successful in arranging for her boys' release as part of a prisoner exchange, but Robert, age sixteen, died just days later.[18]

The gash on his head and hand represented the first of three serious wounds that Andrew Jackson was to suffer for his principled insolence. The second would result from an affair of honor, a frontier duel; and the third from a quarrel arising from someone else's duel.

Among the Pathfinders of Middle Tennessee

Shakespeare offers a military metaphor in one of his aphorisms, that sorrows come not in single spies but in battalions. The dutiful Elizabeth Jackson survived her unfortunate son Robert by a few months at best. Andrew, the last of her children, battling smallpox in the Waxhaws, left no record of how he grieved for his kin during the autumn of 1781. That was as Cornwallis hunkered down on the Yorktown peninsula and the American Revolution neared its end. At fourteen, Jackson was left without any immediate family, and without sufficient funds to insure his future. As one of his eulogists pronounced in 1845, the Revolution was a "joyous era for America and for humanity! But for him, the orphan boy, the events were full of agony and grief." Without blood ties, Jackson was "bound the more closely to collective man." This was one way to craft the history of a selfless hero.[19]

Though most every chronicler of his life has endeavored to project the influence of his earliest wartime experience on his mature temperament, we do not in fact know what Jackson's convictions were at this time, nor what models of behavior, if any, he looked to. Parton (like many others before and since) made the point that Jackson was of the Scotch-Irish or North-of-Ireland temperament, "a tenacious, pugnacious race . . . , often angry, but most prudent when most furious . . . , when excited by anger or warped by prejudice, incapable of either telling, or remembering, or knowing the truth; not taking kindly to culture, but able to achieve wonderful things without it." It is an exaggerated stereotype that serves again to introduce an easily exaggerated personage.[20]

While still in his teens, he took to gambling in Charleston, and he drank.[21] He may have taught rural school briefly, where erudition was unnecessary. At some point around 1784–85, Jackson severed his connection with the past and traveled to the secluded town of Salisbury, North Carolina. Here he received instruction in the law from the well-regarded Spruce McCay, who seven years earlier had trained William R. Davie. Here young Jackson was said to have played practical jokes; and, here, on the later testimony of one of the townsfolk, the future horse breeder was "more in the stable than in the office." Here, too, he met John McNairy, who had better social connections in the state and who, just two years later, was to offer Jackson a job and change the course of his life.[22]

The period during which Jackson trained in the law is shrouded in local legend and too unreliable to retell at length. These were, in any event, emotionally trying times for the new republic. In the country Jackson had recently vacated, lost markets and crop failures occurred when slaves defected to the enemy during the Revolution; backcountry South Carolinians went on a postwar rampage, snatching slaves at will, while other dislocated whites turned to vagrancy and plunder. With alarm, newspapers began reporting on Americans' diminishing dignity, of a people who had proclaimed themselves morally superior to the British but who, soon after Independence, grew faithless and dissolute. Did Jackson, while under McCay's tutelage in Salisbury, pick up on this mood? Did he ruminate at all on the potential consequences of continued political division? Or did he see his prospects as the exceptionally optimistic Thomas Jefferson did at this time: that it was in the American character "to consider nothing as desperate; to surmount every difficulty by resolution and contrivance"? All we really know is that the orphaned Jackson, in his late teens and not far removed from a dissolute detour in Charleston, was beginning to test his fortitude in a North Carolina town, as he contemplated the opportunities for a young lawyer.[23]

The confederated states did not yet constitute a nation. While Jackson was haphazardly pursuing a legal career, the pioneering North Carolinian Daniel Boone was being celebrated as a trailblazer, heralded for his wartime escape from Indian captivity, and now enticing thousands to settle in Kentucky.[24] Chances lay west. In Philadelphia, in May 1787, a proposed federal constitution came under vigorous debate. Resurgent patriots wrote more evocatively of America as "an asylum for the oppressed." At least in the papers of the major coastal towns, a sense of optimism revived. That summer, the shrewd, philosophic framers offered an energetic government to their widening constituency, preserving elite influence while appearing to entrust self-rule to an unpredictable populace.

Did the government really represent "the people"? The United States in 1787 was as protean, as alterable, as its expanding frontier. Anything might happen. The early American poet Joel Barlow, son of a modest farmer, pronounced in his Fourth of July oration that year, "The natural resources of this country are inconceivably various and great; the enterprising genius of the people promises a most rapid improvement in all the arts that embellish human nature." To the social liberals who conceived it, the new government could only mean greater happiness for the multitude.[25]

Around this time, too, the long-faced, rawboned Andrew Jackson reached his adult height of six feet and one inch. At the end of 1787, his friend McNairy received appointment as Superior Court judge for the Western District of North Carolina, encompassing much of what eventually became the state of Tennessee. McNairy had the power, in turn, to appoint a public prosecutor for the sparsely populated Western District, and so he took the twenty-year-old Jackson along with him, granting that "the Said Andrew Jackson from proper credentials to me produced appears to be of an unblemished Moral character, and from a previous examination before me had likewise appears to possess a competent degree of law Knowledge." That measure of competence in "law knowledge" was, of course, relative, and suited for life in an outland.[26]

The way west was as uncertain as it was alluring to fortune-seeking men and their families in the early post-Revolutionary years. Some had professions and speculated in land, while others were small-scale farmers who migrated out of desperation. From their accounts, both classes seemed to believe that the wilderness would grant deliverance to those who endured its hardships. The noble yeoman image, a literary invention describing hardy, self-sufficient American frontiersmen, was already part of a growing national mythology. It marked these people's potential for political society at a time when they had, as yet, little to show for their struggle. The earthbound emigrants were described as free spirits, and given a colorful collective character. Yet, just as this stereotype was imposed on them from without, so would be the "savage" label.

Free spirits or white savages? The first portrait had some effect in encouraging more and more to take to the trail, but there was an equal abundance of socially hostile reportage. Hopeful settlers sought lives in which they could claim economic freedom and, eventually, economic comfort. But cynical observers printed descriptions of crusty adventurers who possessed less dreamy attributes: "an idle, dissolute, quarrelsome, insolent set . . . , too vicious or too poor to live where they were born," wrote one of the western population in 1793. When Jackson traveled with McNairy to Tennessee, he was "experimenting," the 1817 Reid-Eaton biography tells us. "His stay remained to be determined by the advantages that might be disclosed."[27]

Here it becomes possible to reclaim both the rhetoric and reality that the young frontier lawyer was exposed to, and to approach Jackson's formative pioneering experience with greater accuracy.[28] The first whites to settle along the winding Cumberland River of middle Tennessee were people whom Andrew Jackson knew intimately. Indeed, he would marry one of them not long after his arrival, and remain devoted to her for their thirty-eight years together.

Dark-eyed Rachel Donelson (1767–1828) was the daughter of Rachel Stockley (1730?–1801) and John Donelson (1718?–1786). Her father was a Virginia surveyor and land speculator, onetime member of the House of Burgesses, who had already led a party of volunteers to Boonesborough, Kentucky. His intention at that time had been to contribute to the war effort in the western theater, where the intrepid Virginian George Rogers

Clark reigned, most noted for engineering a stunning defeat of British and Indian forces along the Mississippi River. Demonstrating the sense of scale that ambitious men of this time confidently brought to mind, Clark was thinking to secure the near backcountry that Virginia claimed—the future state of Kentucky—when he moved to eliminate any and all enemies from forts and hunting outposts below distant St. Louis.

The adventuresome Colonel Donelson reached the Cumberland with his family in May 1780, after a novel six-month journey by water. So, just as thirteen-year-old Andrew Jackson was seeing, firsthand, the British and Tory invasion of South Carolina, his future wife, also thirteen, was journeying into the unknown. Leading a flotilla of some thirty 100-foot-long flatboats, transporting livestock and fifty families with slaves (some of them destined for Illinois and Kentucky), the Donelsons drifted down the Holsten River, out of southwest Virginia, onto the swollen Tennessee River near present-day Knoxville, then down and up the U-shaped river, past the treacherous waters of Muscle Shoals, Alabama, all the way to the Ohio, finally descending from the northwest to the Cumberland. They landed at French Lick, forerunner to Nashville. Earlier in the eighteenth century, French trappers had been the first non-Indians to lodge there, hence the "French" in French Lick. (A "lick" was a salty spring where animals would lick, or lap up, water.) It was an appealing place to look at, with undulating hills, cedar groves, and a twisting river. When Jackson was president, the compiler of the *Tennessee Gazetteer* would call it "romantic, healthy and flourishing." But to the first white settlers, there was little time to dwell on its romantic possibilities.[29]

The Donelsons were in fact preceded by a smaller overland party, all male, and led by John Donelson's cosponsor of the Cumberland settlement plan, the indomitable James Robertson (1742–1814). Robertson was of Scotch-Irish descent, with roots in both Virginia and North Carolina. In the autumn of 1779, he made his way across the Cumberland Mountains near the trijuncture of Virginia, Tennessee, and Kentucky. He and his men carved out canoes with their hatchets, and in addition to hunting buffalo, subsisted on supplies of salted meat, and flour or cornmeal and maple sugar, blended with jerked meat in the Indian style—pemmican. They found their way to French Lick in December by following some combination of riverways and Indian trails.

Virginia-reared Kaspar Mansker (ca. 1750–1824), who spoke with a German or Dutch accent, first hunted along the Cumberland in 1769. He planted corn and settled permanently twelve miles above the future

Nashville at some point before Robertson arrived on the scene. It was to Mansker's fortified position that Rachel Donelson and her family fled when tormented by Indians in their first year.[30]

The early colonists survived many seasons of bloody skirmishes with Indians before the Cherokees of the region were finally expelled. The Cherokee tribe was automatically perceived by early Tennesseans as their enemy for having joined with the British at the outbreak of the American Revolution. The year 1781 was particularly devastating for the Robertson-Donelson band: hunting, planting, and milking could not be forestalled, though men and women were frequently killed, day or night, when found alone near their homes by stealthy Indians. Sometimes the settlers' dogs warned them in time, and sometimes, in this world of hand-to-hand combat, numbers of horse-stealing Indians were trapped and killed.

It was as violent a world as any American ever inhabited. Men learned to gouge at the enemy's eyes, if suddenly assaulted while unarmed. Hunting dogs were trained to chew on the limbs of attacking Indians. In 1781, the Donelsons stayed at Mansker's Station until one siege ended, then moved to a Kentucky settlement where they felt safer. In the summer of that year, risking his life, James Robertson rode east, hundreds of miles through Indian country, back to North Carolina, there to assert the land claims of his fellow colonists. During the many months away, he could not know whether the crops of those whom the Indians could not kill would be set on fire to make the whites give up, or indeed, whether anyone would be left when he returned. Like the much younger Andrew Jackson, Robertson was a horse lover and, by the time he finally met the new state prosecutor in 1788, a seasoned Indian fighter both feared and respected by the Cherokees. He did not "hate" the Indian. He spent a great deal of time in the woods, wore moccasins, and feasted on bear meat.[31]

Jackson never knew Donelson, who died violently two years before he came to Tennessee, but he knew and respected Robertson. Fully a quarter century Jackson's elder, Robertson had risen to the militia rank of general. He was party to negotiations with the Cherokees from 1776—even before he began to shape the Cumberland settlement. In the first years after Jackson's arrival, Robertson would help conclude the short-lived Holsten Treaty (1791), which President Washington had cautiously urged in order to prevent "unrestrained encroachment on Indian lands" by white settlers. In 1794, however, responsive to the harsh frontier reality, and without federal assistance, Robertson armed the militia and directed what became known as the Nickajack expedition. While Jackson remained behind,

Robertson marched on the Chickamauga of east Tennessee, decisively dispatching those Cherokees who remained hostile. The Nickajack campaign opened the way for mass settlement of the Cumberland.[32]

As peace came to Tennessee in 1794, a new relationship between whites and Indians evolved. During the preceding years of strife, an active trade between settlers and natives was marred by incidents of violence: there is ample evidence that white thieves ambushed Cherokee traders, kidnapped and enslaved the unoffending, and roamed in packs, murdering small parties of Indians for their horses. They may have done this as often as Indians initiated aggressive actions against settlers—the written record, of course, tends to reflect white biases.

Though pioneer families after 1794 proved themselves capable of friendly relations when they enjoyed hunting privileges in Indian territory, whites did not appreciate the emotional cost that formal land transfers had on the male Indian's sense of his personal power. Certainly Jackson would never empathize enough to understand this either. With the constriction of their lands, Indians resorted to violence to stave off an unendurable sense of inadequacy. Recognizing reality, tribal elders often redistributed trade goods to enrich the most militant males. But this could do only so much. The change in status wrought by the white presence could not be prevented, and when the traditional long winter hunt was reduced and narrowed, and game became scarce, Indian men turned to beating their own wives and slaves, something unheard of in their matrilineal societies before the whites' intrusion. In the 1790s, as new westbound settlers passed through Cherokee towns and Indians brought their livestock to the Knoxville market, Indians were sometimes seen drinking with whites in Knoxville taverns; at other times, when the whiskey flowed, white-Indian brawls took place. At no time, of course, was white-Indian accord based on social equality, because the white population was growing fast and the Indians' traditional way of life was becoming harder and harder to sustain.[33]

In an unaccountable contrast to his later exploits, and his authorized early biographers to the contrary, Jackson apparently played no active role in fighting Indians during his first six years in Tennessee, when Cherokees still posed a threat to him and his neighbors.[34] He himself never claimed to have triumphed against Tennessee Indians the way mythmakers subsequently claimed in their renditions of his early years. Still, Jackson was profoundly influenced by this and every aspect of the frontier condition. Late in life, he colorfully recounted the violent possibilities he faced: he said he had crossed the wilderness between Knoxville and Nashville twenty-two times—once alone, "when the Indians were most numerous and hostile." On one journey, in frigid conditions, he read the ground where Indians had recently trod, and urged a party of whites onward because he sensed that they were outnumbered and he feared a bloody confrontation. Those who did not heed him were later found dead.[35]

When it came to the subject of Indians, Jackson's words were transparent, as they would be consistently throughout his career. Armed with his own sense of justice, he remonstrated with nonwesterners over federal Indian policy. He was particularly critical of President Washington's diplomatic efforts in the mid-1790s, insisting in the strongest terms that any political consideration was wasted on Indians. It is arguable that Jackson respected certain individual Indians. It is probable that he felt a humane sympathy for that communal suffering that he attributed both to their cultural incompetence and the mercenary impulses of profit-seeking whites. But he had neither liberal sentiments, nor the slightest desire to nurture tribes toward territorial self-government on land that whites might someday want to exploit. His politics were uncompromising.

As Cumberland prosecutor in 1793–94, Jackson twice exhorted John McKee of Knoxville, agent to the Cherokees and Choctaws, to banish any thought of accomplishing peace through negotiation. In the first appeal he charged that the Indians were sending false signals, pretending to desire an accord while "they Indians has made [use of] this Finesse to Lull the peo[ple to] sleep that they might . . . open amore Easy Road to [Commit] Murder with impunity." Angrily, he asked: "why do we attem[pt] to Treat with [a Savage] Tribe tha[t] will neither ad[here to] Treaties nor the Laws of Nations." Jackson's tone is unmistakable, even if his literary pretensions are few.[36]

In the second letter to McKee, he scarcely needed to allude to Indians' "finesse," or recurrence to devious artifice, anymore. Only military options made sense to an enemy he now saw as a disease. "Constantly infesting our frontier," he wrote, "their Peace Talks are only Delusions." (As a verb, *to infest* was interchangeable with *to plague; delusions* were akin to feverish hallucinations.) Jackson had no doubts: "Does not Experience teach us that Treaties answer no Purpose than opening an Easy door for the Indians to pass [through to] Butcher our Citizens." Scoffing at language that the ill-informed U.S. Congress was using—"some say humanity [dictates] it"—Jackson demanded "an Equal share of humanity [to her own] Citizens," and to "Punish the Barbarians."[37]

Violence and Volatility

It might seem odd that within a few short years of the tentative birth of the Cumberland settlement, a court system was instituted, but this is in fact what occurred. It was needed. The belligerence and litigiousness of whites matched the vaunted ferocity of the Indian. Seen, even by historians who were reared in the age of Jackson, as "idle and thriftless, and almost always too fond of strong drink," the settlers were a people who were in and out of the courtroom, animated in their public feuds.[38]

They fought incessantly, or so it seemed. Though brawling or street fighting was readily associated with the lower sorts, intensifying as it moved from the Atlantic seaboard into the western frontier, many respected citizens were subject to similar feelings. It was a time when an individual's status never seemed quite secure enough, when masculine competition centered upon assertions of honor. Even in the Virginia Tidewater, where the high culture of the South had originated and continued to flourish, poking, biting, kicking, and gouging out eyes were not remarkable events in the life of the community.

Aggressiveness among young men was most persistent on the frontier, where violence begat violence. The formal duel was the most genteel, but not the only, method of resolving a personal dispute. Ceremony and the use of finely manufactured pistols may have separated the planters (as it did the European aristocracy) from the common people; but the ease with which many resorted to potentially deadly encounters suggests a kind of pressure, unrestrained and unrelenting, that Andrew Jackson's contemporaries imposed and that he certainly imbibed. Men of the frontier felt the need to assert their strengths, indulge in profanity, and behave violently in order to conquer or deny their fears of the wilderness condition.[39]

Before he even reached Nashville, Jackson established the tone of his future dealings with public men. It was in the autumn of 1788, on his way west with Judge McNairy on horseback, that he first became embroiled in an affair of honor. At Jonesborough, in eastern Tennessee, Jackson met up with an older and far more accomplished attorney named Waitstill Avery. Jonesborough supported the first court held in Tennessee in the years before statehood; it had been part of "Franklin," a breakaway region of North Carolina, briefly proclaimed independent of its parent state after the future Tennessee was ceded to the new national government. In 1788, when Jackson tarried there, Jonesborough must have been at least as rough-and-

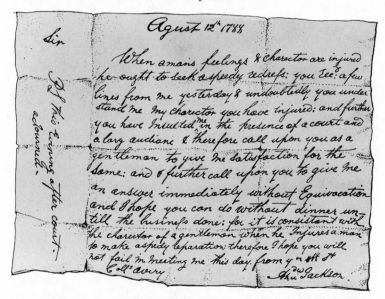

1. The insulted young lawyer seeks "a speedy redress." Facsimile of earliest extant Jackson letter, written to opposing counsel Waitstill Avery, Aug. 12, 1788. Courtesy the Tennessee Historical Society Collections, Tennessee State Library and Archives.

tumble as an imagined "Wild West" town of Hollywood manufacture. Politically distinct from North Carolina, separated from the Cumberland settlements by nearly two hundred miles of unregulated Indian territory, the community was built of log houses. The windowless courthouse was twenty-four feet square, with plank floors and a nine-foot ceiling.[40]

Inside this simple structure, Andrew Jackson found a client to represent—the issue in the case is undeterminable—and tangled with opposing counsel, Avery, who appears to have had a charming capacity to manipulate language. Feeling provoked and insulted in this instance, Jackson composed the first extant letter of his career:

> When a man's feelings and charector are injured he ought to Seek aspeedy redress; you recd. a few lines from me yesterday and undoubtedly you understand me. My charector you have injured; and further you have Insulted me in the presence of a court and larg audianc. I therefore call upon you as a gentleman to give me satisfaction for the Same. . . .[41]

[18]

It was a challenge to duel, a solicitation that only a "gentleman," in recognizing his opposite as a social equal, was willing to accommodate.

Other than Jackson's capitalization of "Insulted," the most interesting word in this letter is *redress*. Redress, a common-law concept, was the same term cited in the Declaration of Independence twelve years earlier in pursuit of justice on a grand scale: "In every stage of these Oppressions We have Petitioned for Redress in the most humble terms." In the final draft of Jefferson's Declaration, the phrase appears immediately after dire reference to the "merciless Indian Savages" who were destroying the lives of "the inhabitants of our frontiers." The word *redress* was used as a noun by both Jefferson and Jackson to differentiate between civilized and uncivilized behavior. It was defined in this historic epoch as "reformation," "relief," or "remedy."[42]

For Jackson, redress was most of all a remedy ("cure of any uneasiness," "means of repairing any hurt") to offset a perceived threat to his as yet undeveloped reputation. During his presidency, when his friend Sam Houston sought to take action against a congressman who had slandered him, Jackson understood the impulse, again insisting that death was preferable to the life that one was left with after swallowing an insult: the "slandered citizen" was, he would say at that time, justified to "seek redress."[43] With Waitstill Avery, the issue was resolved with symbolic action but without bloodshed, both men harmlessly firing into the air.[44]

The frontier was a place of contact, of contingency, of volatility, where face-to-face interactions both challenged and sustained affinities. The Cumberland needed structure. Five years before Jackson's arrival, while Indians were attacking weekly, the North Carolina legislature established the boundaries of Davidson County, in which Nashville was situated. (Gen. William Lee Davidson of North Carolina had been in command of his state's militia in the Revolution, until he was shot by Tories on the Catawba River.) The county encompassed considerable quantities of land that at the time still rightfully lay in Chickasaw and Cherokee hands. Nevertheless, given land hunger, and the numbers of Revolutionary War veterans promised western acreage in payment for wartime service, the Cumberland was immediately opened to larger settlement. North Carolina had promised its volunteer soldiers in 1780 not just 200 acres, but "a prime slave" to help work the land, understanding the uncertainty of life on the frontier and the need for horses, oxen, and farm implements to cultivate land, process produce, and bring surplus to market. Middle Tennessee was an exacting environment.[45]

French Lick was renamed Nashborough after Gen. Francis Nash, a North Carolinian killed at the Battle of Germantown in 1777. In 1785, the town name was shortened to Nashville. The first minister arrived there that year. Also in 1785, Edward Douglas and Thomas Molloy, "real saddle-bag lawyers," entered the settlement. They had never practiced law before, but, as one mid-nineteenth-century memoirist put it, "being of sound practical sense, and possessed of good business talents and of the gift of the gab— good talkers—they soon had clients." Lawyer William Gubbins, with his fine linen shirts and silk vests and books of law and political theory, also opened his practice in 1785, only to be killed by Indians the following year. In 1787, the year before Jackson arrived, thirty-three more settlers were killed by Indians in the Nashville vicinity.[46]

The French botanist André Michaux combed the western country over three years in the mid-1790s and gives us a good sense of how difficult it was, even for an experienced traveler, to endure its privations. In January 1796, a few days out of Nashville, he wrote, "The Roads rough and my horse fell lame. I was obliged to walk. I made 12 miles. I was unable to light a fire because the trees and wood were all frosted. I spent the night nearly frozen." Two days later he was "compelled" a distance of seven miles to shoe his horse, fortunate in having come upon a family "better educated than the common people," who provided civilized hospitality—something, he asserted, "seldom met with in America." Michaux identified the range of wildlife he encountered, which instructs the modern reader in what has changed and what has remained in the two centuries since Jackson commenced his public life: gray squirrels, raccoons, wild turkeys, deer, buffalo, bears, otter, owls, cardinals, and "green Parroquets with yellow heads of the small species" were all plentiful in middle Tennessee. The Frenchman struggled each day with the elements until he happened upon friendly quarters—and then he expressed surprise whenever he encountered any good conversation or a decent meal.[47]

Michaux's son François replicated the journey in 1802, and noted the rapid increase of subsistence farmers, who were renting land from speculators. For home consumption, these new arrivals planted "Indian wheat" (growing ten to twelve feet high) and grew the more lucrative cotton for trade. After a few short years, the most industrious among them acquired one or two slaves. The younger Michaux marveled at the "degree of independence" attainable in the region, so soon after his father described a bleak and rugged and unpredictable frontier.[48]

From a social and economic standpoint, then, the disadvantaged Jackson came to Nashville at the right time. It was a place where people were making adjustments, where they were obliged to invent new rules. Frontier violence and eccentricity may have been indulged, but an Atlantic (more settled) concept of progress and civility was never abandoned. Reputations had various components, ranging from scholarship to bravery. Besides, men told stories. If, on the frontier, they boasted more loudly than people did elsewhere, it was because control was harder to come by. Attempting to explain the nature of a man's ambition on America's fringes, early Jackson biographer Samuel Putnam Waldo wrote in 1818: "Drawn together from different sections of our extensive country, from motives of interest, of power, or of fame, each individual may almost be said to make a province by himself. In such a situation, the most energetic character becomes the object of the greatest popular favour. In this sphere was Jackson exactly calculated to move."[49]

Recognizing the Cumberland as a place of abundance and potential, the first generation of white Tennesseans made value judgments that are hard to reconcile with modern notions. The short career of lawyer William Gubbins and the journals of Michaux *père* and *fils* suggest a way to approach their world. A thriving (if litigious, and thus defective) community was forming amid log houses, active stills, inconstant hospitality, and resilient Indians. No one turned away misfits from the East who were escaping the past by coming to Tennessee. For all these reasons, a philosophical engagement with nature was not the first order of business. Gaining a measure of control, little by little overcoming the barriers to progress and civility, was.

Making a Virtue of Necessity

As he stepped into this world, the resourceful Jackson could not be called refined. At times, he exhibited the raw, stubborn fervor of a venturing troublemaker. But the first chief executive to make his name in the frontier West would inevitably have to contend with men of superior education back east who had imbibed the texts of the Enlightenment, and who *had* found time to worship nature. Like all political aspirants, he would be critically evaluated on the basis of his formal training—his cultural conditioning—which in this era was generally gleaned from one's familiar letters and polished public speech. Whether or not he wholly adapted to metropolitan rules, the frontiersman would be judged by them.

Self-presentation always mattered in early America. Among the low-born (or even highborn) on the American frontier, however, what mattered might not be the same as what mattered in Philadelphia or Boston. Through cultural symbols we learn what was important to people, and how sensitivity was expressed. In Jackson's case, we can extract meaning from an odd reference repeated in his political correspondence over several decades: he took pains, for some reason, to relate the length of a man's hair to individual rights in a republic. In the frontiersman's negotiation between backwoods self-development and metropolitan rules—living in proximity to those who added up scalps in war—it seems that hair counted for something.

The story of Samson and Delilah is well known. Hair has long been allied with masculine power. Jamestown's John Smith found out in the seventeenth century that the Indian's scalp-lock held a potent spiritual value, and to pull it was a grave insult. During the Revolutionary War, recruits to the patriot cause challenged army orders by wearing disorderly locks across their foreheads and "earcurls" that young women found appealing. When it came time to portray Tennessee's gutsy volunteers as the ironic heroes of the War of 1812, it would again be their "long unkempt hair and unshorn faces" that offended "the eyes of the martinet," while symbolizing the raw talent that Jackson recognized when his men made young America prouder in triumph than it had been since 1776. As rebellious youth of the 1960s would much later act out, hairstyle has often enabled society's outsiders to assert their personal freedom while establishing a collective consciousness.[50]

Recall that Jackson appeared in Philadelphia in 1796 with his long hair tied back in eel skin, causing at least one prominent politician to comment on his rusticity. Just a few years later, when he was no longer on the national scene, Jackson was moved to write passionately to President Thomas Jefferson in protest against the court-martial of Col. Thomas Butler, who refused to cut his long hair to conform to U.S. army regulations. Jackson said he perceived enforcement of the short-hair rule as "a tame surrender of a natural right," and he used the rejection of Butler's principled stand as a fixed symbol of tyranny and political corruption. In fact, Jackson would still be bringing up the case of Butler's queue several decades later in his postpresidential retirement.

Unregulated hair meant independence. Jackson upheld the code of military discipline and due subordination, but the short-hair rule was something else to him: To gain power over a person's body in this way was a deviation that he construed as an insult—and in his world, only an apology or a violent confrontation could repair the damage done to one's honor. As it happens, Catawba warriors wore their hair in a ponytail, and a haircut was, in the nineteenth century, perhaps the most obvious sign that an Indian had surrendered something basic to assimilationists. Without reading too much into symbolism, it is worth noting that the artists who painted Jackson's hair in the billowy, windblown style of the day gave him an unauthorized "makeover." Those who described his hair in print paid particular attention to what was most individual about it: it shot up, stayed set, and was not subdued.[51]

Andrew Jackson was, in the most literal sense, representative of the frontier. He knew its hardships, its resistance to unifying administration, and its reliance on lifesaving friendships; he knew it as a breeding ground for independent manhood. The future warrior formed strong opinions and nurtured the same prejudices as his neighbors. Their sense of liberty, like his, arose from an almost fanatical self-confidence. In addition to what he had learned by viewing the weary Catawbas, Jackson adapted his hard-headed Indian policy from those who had preceded him to the Cumberland. He defined his strengths in opposition to Indian qualities (as they were understood), expecting Indians to be either diabolical or pliant, but not suited for citizenship. He distinguished their mobile love of liberty from his own—a liberty that was reflected in the productive calm of a useful, industrious domesticity. A harsh life had to be tempered; and so, while white men traveled, contended, gambled, fought, kicked, bit, dueled, and gouged each other's eyes, their ladies were meant at all times to be protected. Jackson, we can assume, brought these same prejudices to his practice of the law.

Prejudices serve as a means of self-protection and also common protection. Jackson adopted prejudices that proved emotionally, if not physically, necessary for survival in an outland. Tennesseans sought gratification where comforts were few. They were utterly practical. They concluded, for example, that whiskey was a definite social good. In a medically primitive environment, alcohol was prescribed to banish chills after one was caught in a downpour; it cleaned out wounds and cured snakebite. Whiskey was brought out when a neighbor dropped by or a couple married. Jackson's people were proud of their whiskey and increasingly proud of their hardscrabble section.[52]

The frontier shaped him in other ways that are unfamiliar and in some ways abhorrent to modern Americans. Like those who migrated to Tennessee when he did, Jackson was an unapologetic slaveholder. Owning human property, as much as buying land, importing tools, or making whiskey, was a judgment that settlers apparently came to easily as part of their rationale in constituting a new society in a near wilderness. Much later, when the slavery issue occupied center stage during and after Jackson's presidency, thoughtful commentators tried to rationalize his involvement by terming him an indulgent and patient master, or even more defensively, describing him in indefinite terms as one who "was incapable of perpetrating a deed at which humanity would shudder, and from which Christianity would turn weeping away!" Near death, he was said to have gazed on his servants "with tender solicitude," expressing in his final breaths the hope of a reunion in Heaven with both white and black.[53] Even the biographer Marquis James characterized Jackson as "an ideal slave-owner,"[54] as though there could be anything "ideal" in the practice of slavery. Shameful though this sin of the past may be, the fact remains that Jackson lived in a place, and in a century, when it was still possible to be applauded for merely recognizing humanity in one's human property.

That said, Jackson was more active in the slave trade than most. He was shrewd in all his business dealings, stating his price "take it or leave it"; he pursued profit as purposefully whether the commodity was for his country store or for purposes of labor. He was insistent in the belief that liberty-loving white Americans had every right to own slaves, and to prosper from their unpaid exertions. In 1790, he received power of attorney from one James Buchanan to track down five slaves for him. Some years later, advertising to recover a runaway, Jackson offered fifty dollars reward, "and ten dollars extra, for every hundred lashes any person will give him, to the amount of three hundred." He eventually came to see the antislavery movement as "the wicked design of demagogues," who talked about humanity without consulting the "happiness" of the southern states. In this he never wavered.[55]

Some simple statistics demonstrate the character of the early Cumberland's slavery. As of 1790, with a population of 3,459, Davidson County counted 18 free blacks and 659 slaves. Over the next five years, the total population grew only 4.5 percent, while the slave population rose 50.5 percent. In 1800, slaves represented nearly one-third of the county's inhabitants, and in 1810, fully forty percent. During the first years of settlement, slaves were killed, scalped, and held for ransom along with whites. In ensuing years sales of slaves were conducted individual by individual; this meant that slave families were less likely to remain together in Tennessee than in more settled eastern communities. Restraints practiced elsewhere were harder to realize on the frontier.[56]

Jackson's frontier community would not have a newspaper until 1799, eleven years after his arrival. It was a place where force of personality mattered greatly. While learning wilderness routes, he also learned to navigate socially among these people. He felt he understood fairness, as his letters show. But he did not come by polite manners easily. He mingled with soldiers, struggling farmers, and tavern-bred braggarts; absorbed the accents of English, Scotch-Irish (like himself), and German Americans—and, of course, witnessed up close the lives of enslaved blacks. Choosing to improve himself by forging a career in law, he was not taught how to spell by any standard (in which he was not alone among frontier professionals). He had other priorities. To put it plainly, he wished for wealth and was engrossed in its pursuit. He adapted to circumstances, and made a virtue of necessity.

To say it another way, he embodied the *emotional* dimension of frontier life. In the course of his first twenty-five years, he had scarcely seen a city. He was generally surrounded by men who spoke with the grizzled air and constancy of nerve that was demanded of staunch Indian fighters. He also cultivated certain affable men of eastern pretensions who contributed to the population of Knoxville, who dressed and acted with implausible protocol in the backcountry. Jackson met the nation's most privileged and sophisticated men in Philadelphia in the mid-1790s. Did he wish to become more like them? How much did they influence him? These are not simple questions.

On the other hand, we can draw some tentative conclusions about what it was that Jackson wished to possess of the frontier wilderness. We know, in a practical sense, that he wanted to acquire property, develop it, and make a profit. He was a chance-taker, as his encounter with Waitstill Avery demonstrated. He combined the occasional bluster with a zeal for public acceptance. In striving to be regarded by his community as an accepted authority, the young—very young—prosecutor aimed to become more visible. He always desired to be where he could display his energy.

Law and Disorder

Let us return to the beginning of his passage. When a sufficient number of emigrants converged at Jonesborough near the end of 1788, an armed escort brought the twenty-one-year-old Jackson and the others across the adventure-filled western trail to Nashville. There were only a few hundred residents in the town when he arrived, but already there were two taverns and a courthouse. John Donelson had been shot dead—whether by Indians or white settlers was uncertain[57]—and the lanky new arrival came to board with his widow.

Here, in addition to his future wife, Andrew Jackson made a lifelong friend in John Overton (1766–1833), his fellow boarder and fellow lawyer, occasional cocounsel and business partner over the next decade. They complemented each other well: Overton was bookish, judicious, and supportive, unconcerned with political preferment, and content to remain a bachelor (he would not marry until he was in his fifties); Jackson was intellectually diffident, militant, politically sensitive, and desirous of finding a wife.[58]

He got right to work. As a prosecutor, Jackson was extremely busy examining land titles and debt issues, representing to a great degree the interests of merchants and other creditors. From time to time, he dealt with cases of perjury, slander, forgery, assault and battery, rape, and murder. Of seven men brought up on charges of horse stealing, Jackson obtained four convictions. Because he was responsible for a territory that extended to the Kentucky border, he handled cases that obliged him to ride great distances. His job afforded freedom of movement, but with that freedom came very real hazards. The frontier, as we have seen, was not everywhere pristine and could indeed be quite menacing.[59]

In spite of a meager education, there seems little doubt that Jackson was well on the way to establishing his expertise and authority in the first few years after he arrived in Nashville. He argued before judges and juries. He was on excellent terms with the prominent and sympathetic Donelsons. Still in his early twenties, he was keenly aware of the power to be derived from land ownership. It was in Jonesborough, en route to the Cumberland, that he bought his first slave, a young woman. After arriving in Nashville, he acquired an appreciation for the economic importance of Natchez, on the Mississippi (linked directly to Nashville by the Natchez Trace, an old Indian passage). And he soon understood the tie between Natchez and the larger, Spanish-held port of New Orleans, some five hundred miles from the Cumberland. This was the sum of a practical Tennessee education.

Jackson was nothing if not enterprising. We know he started out with little. By 1794, he had taken some role in 476 court cases (nearly half of those recorded); he had traveled the long wilderness road between Nashville and Knoxville many times; and he had, often in partnership with the shrewd and successful John Overton, purchased and worked, and would lease, thousands of cultivated acres. His main residence by this time was at Jones Bend, just a few miles from where the future Hermitage would stand. It was an active farm with eight slaves. By 1798 he would own more than fifty thousand acres in middle and west Tennessee, some of it already worth ten times what Jackson paid for it.[60]

How could he have come so far, so quickly? Self-promotion, sound investment, and constant activity. In Salisbury, North Carolina, under Spruce McCay, he probably learned the law by copying documents and perusing the attorney's collection of bound books and pamphlets, but how much real preparation he had is unclear. He appears to have owned no more than a few law books when he first moved to the Cumberland in 1788. On his journey to Philadelphia in 1797, he would find it desirable to purchase the essential English texts on which the early American legal system was built. These included Sir Edward Coke's three-volume *A Commentary upon Lyttleton,* a seventeenth-century guide that every Revolution-era law student slogged through; John Joseph Powell's *Essay upon the Law of Contracts and Agreements;* and Sir Geoffrey Gilbert's *The Law of Evidence* (1760).

Gilbert offers a credo at the outset of his manual that is consistent with Jackson's oft-revealed faith in himself: "All Certainty is a clear and distinct Perception, and all clear and distinct Perceptions depend upon a Man's own proper Senses." This meant that intuitive knowledge was demonstrable, that judgment was "founded upon the View of our own Senses." Throughout his public career, Jackson would be transported by this article of his faith, for which his frontier legal career prepared him: from a strong inner sense of correctness (more than book learning) he executed judgments. With little else to go on, the prosecutor had to assess the trustworthiness of others. As Gilbert put it, "there is that Faith and Credit to be given to the Honesty and Integrity of credible and disinterested Witnesses." Jackson's choice, from this time forward, was to divide all beings into emotional categories: damnable "villains," who deserved to be undone, and honorable men and women who operated from "conscience."[61]

It is of interest, too, that Jackson bought in Philadelphia Thomas Sheridan's *A Complete Dictionary of the English Language,* first published in 1780. The object of Sheridan's work, as proclaimed on the title page of the edition Jackson almost assuredly owned, was to "establish a plain and permanent standard of pronunciation," and (more subtly) to produce a virtuous society through beautiful speech. We cannot know whether or how often Jackson opened his dictionary, only that he acquired it at the moment he became a national representative.[62]

If the unregimented grammar and spelling of the frontier lawyer seem remote from Sheridan's project of standardizing speech, there are nonetheless clues in his text to literal understandings within Jackson's social circuit. The lexicographer's multiple forms of "honour" thoroughly suited Jackson's evolving sense of human relationships and the basis of a natural hierarchy among men. As a verb, *honour* meant "to regard with veneration"; as a noun, "dignity, reputation," adding the term "honourableness" to mean "eminence, magnificence." It is worth noting that Sheridan's definition of *passionate*—"easily moved to anger"—is typical of late-eighteenth- and early-nineteenth-century dictionaries. The more modern appreciation of passion as a positive emotion—exuberance or enthusiasm—was largely absent from the vocabulary of Jackson and his contemporaries.[63]

The matter of passion, in its most familiar construction, comes headlong into the Jackson story rather soon after his new life in Nashville begins. As a boarder at the Donelsons', sharing the adjacent cabin with John Overton, state's attorney Jackson collided with Rachel Donelson's inconstant husband, Lewis Robards. Rachel had married Robards before her eighteenth birthday, in 1785, after John Donelson had removed his family to Kentucky. Her father returned to Tennessee without her, but when the young couple proved emotionally incompatible, Robards apprised his mother-in-law of his feelings, and Rachel's brother Samuel went and fetched her back. Somewhat later, the contrite husband traveled to Nashville to attempt a reconciliation.

For a while all remained comparatively calm. Not long after Jackson moved in, however, Robards grew jealous of the favored newcomer and accused him of incorrect behavior toward Rachel. According to Overton's testimony many years afterward, Jackson immediately and strenuously denied any impropriety, and on one occasion responded to Robards's angry insinuations by announcing his readiness to give "gentlemanly satisfaction."

Overton was careful to underscore what it was that distinguished Jackson from "every other person with whom I was acquainted." Recurring to the discriminating language of their day, Overton wrote of the Robards incident: "Continually together during our attendance on wilderness courts, whilst other young men were indulging in familiarities with females of relaxed morals, no suspicion of this kind of the world's censure ever fell to Jackson's share." The inference was perfectly clear. He may have been forward, even presumptuous, in other matters, but there was nothing for the world to disapprove of in Jackson's defense of female virtue.[64]

Some have speculated that Jackson, who held the widow Donelson in esteem, saw in her a warm maternal figure, bearing up to the exigencies of raising a large family alone in a frontier environment. In this construction, Jackson's ideal of womanhood related in some way to the memory of his own mother.[65] Whether or not such speculation is warranted, it does suggest the strong possibility that the young man whom the widow Donelson appreciated as a further protector against any prospective Indian attack did all he could to repay her trust, and that his tender regard for her mismatched married daughter met no objection from the mother.

Desertion and Adultery

What really took place between Jackson and the unhappy wife cannot be known in every detail, although a likely explanation emerges: they ran away to be together. The late eighteenth century was a time when self-divorce often supplanted a formal, legal divorce, because the latter required an act of the legislature, which was slow, and hard for most people to obtain. Both American frontier and Scotch-Irish traditions accommodated this reality, bypassing the tedious legal process. In ensuing years, a Tennessean (generally male) might still sometimes publish an ad in the newspaper declaring that he no longer bore economic responsibility for his runaway wife, thus separating their lives in the most practical way. For Rachel Donelson Robards to detach herself from her husband, there were a number of subtle, but public, steps to take.[66]

First, to avoid unseemly appearances, the self-respecting boarder Andrew Jackson moved out of the Donelsons' place, and took lodging at Mansker's Station. Robards delayed some time before returning to Kentucky, never again to set foot in Tennessee. Rachel, the ninth of the Donelsons' eleven children, moved in with a sister, Jane, who had married North Carolina–born Revolutionary War veteran Robert Hays in 1786. This couple is important to the narrative of the romance. They were deeply devoted to Andrew and Rachel, and they would name a daughter Rachel, who went on to marry Jackson's ward and adjutant in the War of 1812.

What happened next? Historians have generally recorded that Andrew Jackson possessed chivalrous intent when he escorted Rachel Robards some 400 miles southwest to Spanish-controlled Natchez. He returned to Nashville alone, and then, on learning (erroneously) that the Robardses' divorce was approved, made the journey to Natchez once again, marrying Rachel there. Back in Tennessee as husband and wife, the Jacksons were later shocked to find out that they were actually bigamists. More than four years after Lewis Robards left his wife, when the divorce finally became fact, they enjoined Robert Hays, now Davidson County justice of the peace, to officiate at their "second" wedding, with Overton present as a witness. This, at any rate, is what we have been asked to believe for nearly two centuries.

However, it is not what really happened. Andrew Jackson and Rachel Robards ran away together—this is what really happened. Let us return to 1789, and set matters straight, based on what can be proven and what must be surmised. In terms of the romantic triangle, the months following the final separation of Lewis and Rachel Robards are hazy. According to Overton's later reconstruction of events, the intemperate, self-exiled Robards made two distinct threats: to "haunt" Rachel, and to return to Tennessee expressly to "take his wife" back to Kentucky. Yet it was also Overton, Jackson's loyal friend, who constructed the accidental bigamy rationale for future generations, claiming that Andrew Jackson and the woman he loved acted modestly and reasonably while they waited for official word from Kentucky on the outcome of Robards's divorce petition.

Did they need to fret over the implications of their "honest mistake"? Not nearly as much as they did in 1828, when Overton was writing on the Jacksons' behalf, and when the moral atmosphere across the nation had thickened. Jackson was seeking the presidency. A vicious newspaper war was raging, and he was baldly accused of having prevailed upon Rachel to "desert" Robards and instead live with him, "in the character of a wife." Rachel was likened to a whore. The political opposition had settled on a new moral imperative, one suited for a different society than the frontier of 1789. It was that moral imperative which necessitated the "honest mistake" explanation that well-intentioned patriots ever since have sympathetically adopted.[67]

Overton's 1828 reconstruction gave the end of 1790 or early 1791 as the time when Rachel left Nashville for Natchez, beyond the reach of Lewis Robards. That was Overton's first miscalculation, because documents show unmistakably that it was one year earlier—the end of 1789 or early 1790—when Andrew and Rachel together left Nashville for Spanish Mississippi. Overton thereby fails to explain the events of the entire year of 1790. Rachel appears to have remained in Mississippi Territory for a good year or more, and Jackson, after resuming his work as a state prosecutor in Tennessee, traveled again to Natchez and spent at least the summer and early autumn of 1790 with her there. When the couple finally returned together to Tennessee sometime during the first half of 1791, Rachel was already known—in legal documents prepared in Nashville on behalf of her family—as Mrs. Jackson. (See the appendix for a full explanation of these and all other details presented here.)

This has to be made very clear: Lewis Robards took the first step in appealing to the Kentucky legislature for a divorce in 1790. He received, on December 20 of that year, permission from the legislature to sue for divorce on the grounds of his wife's desertion and adultery—permission to sue, nothing more. In January 1791, just a few weeks later, Rachel was designated as *Mrs. Jackson* in a legal document prepared in Nashville. Robards was thus aware that the woman who was still technically his wife had already formed an intimate connection with another man. Frontier attorney Jackson, for his part, most assuredly understood that Kentucky was a dependency of Virginia (it achieved statehood only in 1792), and so two legislatures, Kentucky and Virginia, would have to coordinate the Robardses' divorce. Jackson had to know this would take years. Yet in Nashville, Rachel was almost immediately listed as his wife. Because the grounds for Robards's divorce suit were desertion and adultery, it appears that Jackson did little to disguise his intentions after his rival departed Tennessee.

This makes the Jacksons willing adulterers, which sounds harsh, but in fact what they did was reasonable and expedient—and not unheard of on the frontier. The desertion and adultery approach was a well-planned stratagem for people living at such a distance from any state capital; it was the easiest (nearly the only nonviolent) justification for a formal divorce. He and Rachel *needed* to be named as adulterers if she was to be divorced. As prosecutor, Jackson knew the laws of the land well enough to act discreetly to secure his and Rachel's happiness.

Then why did she go to Natchez at all? One could speculate about Robards's temperament or Donelson family property, but no single, overwhelming reason emerges from these facts. Custom—heretofore poorly understood—helps us most in piecing together the couple's choices. First, it is quite plausible that Rachel needed to leave the "Robards" homestead in order to establish desertion, under the law. Second, and more to the point, leaving town preserved anonymity. It was especially important for Rachel to leave town because stricter rules applied to women; her departure from the Cumberland carried greater symbolic weight than Robards's departure did. In essence, she was dissolving the Robards household. Had Andrew and Rachel remained in Nashville, it would have been more difficult to make a break from the past. People would have talked about them and perhaps felt obliged to render a moral judgment upon them. Community surveillance was a feature not just of Puritan Massachusetts, but also, more widely, of the early American social landscape.[68]

A look-the-other-way frontier (or Scotch-Irish) bridal abduction tradition did exist. But it is equally conceivable that to cohabit in the Cumberland would have produced at least a minor scandal, because Andrew Jackson was a state prosecutor, and a man of ambition. The prosecutor and his betrothed were clearly concerned with social reputation; as members of an upwardly mobile group in a growing, shifting society they would have recognized that folk traditions were fine for most ordinary people in their situation, but less than ideal for them. Genteel standards applied. The ambiguity (in Nashville) of what they were doing in Natchez made their situation less of a concern for Jackson and the close-knit Donelson clan alike.

Andrew and Rachel Jackson would be making a "fresh start" upon their reinsertion into the community as husband and wife. But rather than wait years for the legal process to unfold, the roaming attorney Jackson arranged for Rachel and him to remove beyond American governmental authority, to proceed into Spanish-controlled Mississippi, where their status in Tennessee was not jeopardized. From Natchez in 1790, their state of unwedded cohabitation—Rachel's "desertion" and their adultery—could be conveyed to Robards, perhaps through Robert Hays, who was one of the clan still communicating with him. And the divorce would go forward. Another reason why this explanation is plausible is that Robards appears, after 1789, to have been more interested in what he might obtain from the Donelson estate than whether he would ever see his wife again. A "deal" apparently was struck.

Whether or not Andrew Jackson took advantage of the Robardses' crumbling marriage, he and Rachel were unmistakably in love. His earliest known letter to her was sent from Knoxville in 1796. It is entirely conventional in its declarations, though unambiguous in its substance: "My Dearest Heart," it begins. "It is with the greatest pleasure I sit down to write you. Tho I am absent My heart rests with you. With what pleasing hopes I view the future period when I shall be restored to your arms there to spend My Days in Domestic Sweetness with you the Dear Companion of my life, never to be separated from you again during this Transitory and fluctuating life."[69]

In this letter, the wide-ranging attorney, merchant, and land speculator claims that he owns no "ambition" beyond togetherness. Again, the language is entirely conventional. His wife most certainly knew, as any traveler who partook of his hospitality knew, that he was already quite avidly collecting friends in high places: in January 1796, he served as one of five delegates from Davidson County (by now Tennessee had eleven counties) to the Knoxville convention at which the territory voted to apply for statehood. Until that time, Jackson was receiving mail at the somewhat ambiguous address of "Territory south of the River Ohio."

The character of Tennessee was being fashioned. A special census counted 77,000 residents (slaves were designated three-fifths of a person, Indians not counted at all). A constitution was hammered out, by which a white man—any white man—could vote: immediately if a landowner, and after a mere six months' residence if he did not own land. Jackson's role in the constitutional process may have been minimal, but the republican tone of Tennessee politics was readily apparent in the privileges granted to ordinary white settlers.[70]

In March 1796, John Overton traveled to east Tennessee, where he was able to compliment his friend in Nashville: "I must beg leave to congratulate you on your interest and popularity in this country," he wrote. With Tennessee statehood imminent, Overton said he was "certain" that Jackson would be elected to the U.S. House of Representatives, the first member voted in from the sixteenth state.[71]

His was already a remarkable tale of good fortune. The canny Jackson, at twenty-nine, had "won" the wife he desired and, with Overton's support, had done well enough to solidify his place in the rich, protean, western political realm—now Indian-removed. The United States was still described in print as an "infant empire" when its offspring Tennessee was born.

CHAPTER TWO

❦❦❦❦❦❦❦❦❦·❦❦❦❦❦❦❦❦❦

Fraternity and Defiant Honor

Permit me Sir, to request in future, that as far as it respects myself,
you will pay some attention, to the Essential distinction between
observations, involving your political conduct by way of <u>argument</u>,
and such as are malicious and personal.

—Jackson to John Sevier, May 10, 1797

"Take care of my little Rachael until I return," he wrote Robert Hays from Philadelphia.[1] As a legislator, Jackson was not particularly distinguished. Representing the new state of Tennessee from 1796 to 1798, he said little of record on the floor of the House or Senate. The one matter he pursued with vigor was federal reimbursement of the men who had taken part in a Tennessee campaign against the Cherokees in 1793. When it came to defending white settlers against Indians who had waged war on them, Jackson was resolute.[2]

Hugh Lawson White (1773–1840) was a young soldier in the 1793 expedition. He enlisted under Virginia-born John Sevier (1745–1815), brigadier general of the militia and the first governor of Tennessee. White's father was a Revolutionary officer who had helped to settle the town of Knoxville. The son would grow to be a respected judge, U.S. senator, and trusted political ally of Jackson in the 1820s, and he would eventually reject Jackson for, in his mind, abusing power. In 1797, however, young White was a symbol, a test case; his claim for reimbursement became Jackson's cause in Congress as the new representative sought to demonstrate that Tennesseans were zealous peacekeepers and deserving of federal support.[3]

The principle that animated Congressman Jackson was a lifelong one: he believed in soldierly discipline and loyalty, and the uniform acceptance of properly constituted military authority. The troops in the expedition had obeyed their commander's orders and, as his published speech states, "went with full confidence that the United States would pay them." After much effort, Jackson was finally able to advise Governor Sevier at the end of February 1797 that the Ways and Means committee in Congress had decided to include the overdue compensation in a new military appropriation bill.[4]

The first major national issue in which Jackson showed a decided interest was the Jay Treaty. England, at war with Revolutionary France, took advantage of its preeminent position on the high seas by prohibiting neutral shipping from calling on French ports. In 1794, after Congressman James Madison publicly advocated the cessation of trade with England for its having infringed on America's shipping in the French West Indies, President Washington had sent his envoy, Federalist John Jay, to London, to work out a treaty that reduced Anglo-American tensions. The final document, made law in 1796, not only restricted American commerce (preserving British control of the Atlantic), it also allowed the British to continue an independent relationship with Indians who resided within U.S. territory. The result of this omission would bear heavily on the eventual outbreak of war in 1812. The French naturally doubted American resolve as the Jay Treaty took effect, fearing that the Federalists had succeeded in bringing the United States back into the orbit of its former mother country.

Philadelphia's Republican newspaper *Aurora* asserted that the ill-considered treaty had inflicted "national injuries and national insults." With democratic anguish, Jackson had written friendly North Carolina congressman Nathaniel Macon a year before his own election to Congress, stating that the U.S. senators who embraced the Jay Treaty were "aristocratic Nabobs." Unsuccessful in standing for the presidency by agitating against the Jay Treaty, Thomas Jefferson assessed that "our horizon was never so overcast." Thus, by the time he arrived at Congress, Jackson understood that his Federalist colleagues had revealed "their wish to Cultivate a close friendship with Britain at the Expence of awar with the French Republick." He wrote to his trusted friend, his wife's brother-in-law, Robert Hays, and bemoaned the course of events in which "the British are daily capturing our vessels impressing our Seamen and Treating them with the utmost Severity & cruelty." The War of 1812 was still many years in the future, but Jackson's anti-British bias was in full play, and his Jeffersonian affiliation just as obvious.[5]

George Washington was about to leave office after serving two terms. Most in Congress supported a statement (of primarily ceremonial value) being drafted to praise the retiring chief executive for his "obedience to the voice of duty," his "moderation and magnanimity," and his "wise, firm, patriotic administration." Jackson, however, incensed by the apparent U.S. capitulation before British power, sided with the minority who resented all reference to a "wise . . . administration."[6] Notably, it was during this experience that Jackson met the like-minded Congressman Edward Livingston of New York, who had spearheaded the dissent, and Senator Aaron Burr, also of New York, who was a conspicuous supporter of Tennessee statehood when the Federalists had sought to delay admission of the sixteenth state. Both men were destined to play critical roles in Jackson's political education.

Blount Man, Freemason, and State Judge

Andrew Jackson was inelegant and undiplomatic. While he had a strong sense of fair play, the business of the national legislature—both houses— held little allure for him. After a stint in the House from December 1796 to March 1797, he was home briefly before accepting election to the U.S. Senate by the legislature in Knoxville. "I must beg of you," he wrote Robert Hays upon heading east again, "to try to amuse Mrs. Jackson and prevent her from fretting. the situation in which I left her—(*Bathed in Tears*) fills me with woe."[7] Elected for a six-year term, Jackson remained in the Senate but a few months, from December 1797 to April 1798. After his return to Nashville, he was elected by the Tennessee General Assembly as a judge of the state supreme court, a coveted position that he would occupy until 1804. His salary was second only to that of the governor.

There were two important power brokers in the state at this time: Governor Sevier and U.S. senator William Blount (pronounced "blunt"), Jackson's chief backer. Blount was eighteen years Jackson's elder, a Jeffersonian Republican like himself, who had served as territorial governor and superintendent of Indian affairs prior to statehood. He also chaired the 1796 convention that drew up Tennessee's constitution. He was from a wealthy, enterprising North Carolina family, whose vast landholdings were matched only by a craving for more western land. Jackson displayed his loyalty to this unorthodox wheeler-dealer in Tennessee land, and Blount rewarded his Cumberland ally with power and position. Theirs was a perfectly natural alliance: in the 1780s, Blount's surveying partner in western land ventures had been John Donelson, Rachel's father.

In 1797, Blount stumbled. Upon becoming Tennessee's first senator, he concocted an apparent conspiracy to secure the southern and western frontiers for American settlement; he would act independently of federal policy, with not only the might of rugged Americans of the Southwest but with the British fleet and Indian warriors, too, against a perceived French threat to loosely held Spanish dominions—Florida, for one, but most significantly New Orleans. Blount himself would lead a force of Tennessee, Kentucky, and Natchez recruits. But after an incriminating letter to a fellow adventurer fell into government hands, Blount was expelled from the Senate for his "high misdemeanor." Fellow Tennessee senator William Cocke, once an Indian-fighting Virginia colonel and companion of Daniel Boone, voted against him. Jackson stood by him.[8]

Blount retained his influence in Tennessee, and he engineered Jackson's move from the House to the Senate—putting up *his* man to unseat Cocke. Prior to this, Jackson and Cocke had been close, certainly more than just cordial; in one letter, Cocke gushed at "the friendly trust you have been pleased to repose in me." Some months later the thin-skinned Jackson came to suspect that Cocke was smearing his reputation by publicly revealing "a confidence reposed in you." (No doubt their Senate competition and the abuse of a confidence were closely related.) The irate Jackson fired off a letter with almost unprecedented vitriol, accusing Cocke of having selfishly used Jackson's confidential words as a means of reconciling with a former political adversary whom Cocke had previously "view'd with contempt & calumniated in the bitterness of your Soul."[9] How far would Jackson go to show his scorn for Cocke's conduct? Very far.

The letter presents Jackson as a man with ironclad principles, a man easily angered, a man who held back little. As a letter writer, Jackson indulged in hyperbole to a considerable extent. Here is how the letter builds: first, Cocke's betrayal of an "intimate friendship . . . receives my utmost indignation." Next, it confers upon the self-conscious Jackson a "solemn obligation." By his poor choice, Cocke had (Jackson lectures) brought upon himself the "thunderbolt" he had intended for Jackson, one that would backfire and "burst upon your own head." The violence of Jackson's imagery is direct.

Principle and vengeance intertwine. Cocke's "violation" at the "Shrine of malice" did not require Jackson to look for "motives"; it was enough to know that a friendship had been defrauded. Cocke's intentions were "criminal." It was time for the world to judge the betrayer as Jackson already had, to find with him that every public act taken by Cocke up to the point of his latest action would have to be reevaluated, understood as steps toward an unpardonable and disgraceful end. To rub it in, the offended Jackson sneered: "You are now at liberty to shew this letter if you please with the others." His sense of honor (and moral indignation) reached its height.[10]

In designating a former friend an enemy, Jackson was unsparing and, it would seem, irreversible. But that was not always so. He could be persuaded by trusted others to soften, or at least to show some restraint of expression. In the case of Cocke, an exchange of letters seven months later indicated that the coolness between them did not have to be permanent; it appears, too, that Robert Hays and James Robertson were enlisted, along with other notable Tennesseans, to mediate a feud that clearly might otherwise have led to the dueling ground.

Cocke undertook to explain, in language that gentlemen were meant to comprehend, that were he to make an outright concession to the offended Jackson, it "might be considered as an act of timidity." He wished to refrain from digging up the delicate matter, stating: "My honour and your feelings Should both be preserved and Justice Should be rendered to each of us." While protesting that differences existed among honorable men and he should not be branded "the only Culprit in this business," he also allowed that "Our differances Should be Ended on fair Just and honorable terms." Cocke was advancing a spirit of mutual moderation, of subtle give and take.[11]

Jackson responded the same day. "My feelings & honor say Justice must be done me," he began, replacing his previously incendiary language with reference to a vague "odium," an "opprobrium" that needed to be "washed away," a "stigma" that should not remain, a "stain" on "feelings." Such images do not suggest indelibility, but rather variability, mutability; the agent to wash away the blot or taint was near or at hand. Jackson allows, too, that "I have not seen the evidence against you," and notes that Cocke had by this time acknowledged "the publicity of my private letter"—the original charge against him. So there was wriggle room here, if Cocke, in some way, admitted his sin.

What remained, in Jackson's mind, was for the offender to make "an open & publick declaration" that whatever ill he had spoken was "inapplicable . . . upon investigation." Yet Jackson would not be Jackson if he did not make it plain that he was always ready to recur to dueling if means were not found to remove the "stain" and soothe his "wounded feelings." "I wish not the blood of Coll. Cocke," wrote Jackson, "but my reputation is dearer to me than life."[12]

The two never did face each other with pistols as a result of their stunning misunderstanding. The precise negotiations are obscure, but evidence in their letters points to the agreed-upon intercession by "three Brothers"—Masonic brothers, indicating that both Jackson and Cocke were Freemasons, and responsive to the call of a superintending fraternity.[13]

The Masonic brotherhood's construction of social power; its emphasis on loyalty and reciprocity among members; and its designation of staunch, honorable men as symbols of community morals all appealed to Jackson's enlarged sense of honor. The Grand Lodge of North Carolina had sanctioned a western Tennessee lodge as early as 1789, when Jackson was a convivial new member of the Cumberland community. He can be identified as a Mason as early as 1798, and eventually would become grand master of the Grand Lodge of Tennessee in 1822–23, after which this "Most Worshipful Sir and Brother" was heartily commended for his service, and for his "impartiality, judgment, and ability." So it seems quite clear that Jackson early on committed himself to the fraternal order and applauded the efforts of Masons who were called upon to mediate when frontier justice was at an impasse.[14]

Many of the Revolution's most respected leaders—including Washington, Alexander Hamilton, Paul Revere, and the Marquis de Lafayette—were proud of their Masonic identity and took part in such ceremonial acts as laying cornerstones to monuments and public buildings. Jackson's boyhood hero, Revolutionary colonel William Richardson Davie, a Mason, laid the cornerstone of the main building on the University of North Carolina campus in 1798. Davie was thereafter known as the first state university's "father." The Masonic order adopted a variety of paternalistic demonstrations such as these to effect, in its collective mind, social harmony and progress.[15]

Tennessee's political parent, North Carolina, had particularly strong Masonic connections. Davie became governor of the state in 1799; from 1776 to 1836, North Carolina Masons served as governors for forty-eight of the sixty years. Freemasonry was a self-empowered agency that sought to share its vision and "craft" with the world, all to spread "civilization." It claimed to offer society "mental and moral illumination." Its network of trust facilitated political activity; brothers defended one another. As for William Cocke, he was returned to the Senate at the end of 1798, as he and Judge Andrew Jackson buried the matter and went on with their rising careers.[16]

He may have been poorly educated, but everything in the written record says that Jackson was secure in the belief that he knew right from wrong.

More than his service in Congress, it was the judicial gown he wore from 1798 to 1804, plus his Masonic affiliation, that facilitated a strong and growing sense of social obligation. Considerable travel was demanded of Judge Jackson: he ruled from the bench in east as well as west Tennessee, and he heard a wide variety of cases, from divorce and debt to murder. In personal terms, judgeship extended dignity.

The record is minimal, as neither his decisions nor opinions were preserved. Nineteenth-century observers noted that he did not let cases drag on, but reached quick, and some might say snap, decisions. Parton writes: "Tradition reports that . . . his decisions were short, untechnical, unlearned, sometimes ungrammatical, and generally right."[17] During the period of his judgeship, Tennessee's Jackson County received its name.

To provide a general sense of the way justice was meted out in Jackson's court, the trial of Joel Childress is instructive. Childress may have been the Sumner County tavern keeper who was the father of future president James K. Polk's wife Sarah (it is, in any case, the same name). The defendant, described at this time as a hatter, was accused in 1801 of murdering one John Regan by striking him above the left eye with "a certain piece of plank of Oak Wood of the length of three feet six inches, of the Value of One Cent." Childress was found guilty not of murder but of "felonious slaying" and was branded on his hand with the letter M.[18]

It is also worth noting that, in Jackson's juridical experience, jurors, and not judges, were the arbiters of factual questions, and judges were never required to instruct a jury on the finer points of the law. Since juries were drawn from the locality in question, they brought local sentiments to bear on the resolution of disputes and were not expected to justify their verdicts. If a judge disputed a verdict, he could always set it aside, but the extent to which this occurred is not known.[19]

We are thus left with an imperfect idea of Jackson's courtroom. We know more about his decision to leave the bench in 1804: he wanted to devote himself to plantation management, to the business of selling the goods that he and his partners imported from Philadelphia, and to building a military career. He wrote to Robert Hays in 1801, when he was offered and turned down a seat in Congress, that the "Solicitations were so pressing, for me to remain in my present office," suggesting that he was well-regarded as a judge. But his frequently expressed concerns with personal finances during the same period and after suggest as strongly that he had long contemplated other avenues of advancement. He was finally succeeded on the bench by his good friend John Overton.[20]

The Sevier Problem

Gov. John Sevier had long been popular in Tennessee. Even before his triumph over the Indians—not just in 1793–94, but earlier and many times over—"Nolichucky Jack," as he was fondly nicknamed, achieved fame as the audacious border commander who taught the British a lesson at the Battle of King's Mountain in 1780, a major turning point in the Revolutionary War. He was known as a strikingly handsome man, and described as a fancy dresser, but also as the man who popularized the Indian war whoop among backwoods fighters in the Cumberland in the years before Jackson migrated there. He was obliged, like the younger Jackson, to negotiate a public personality that could exist both on the eastern seaboard and in the wild.[21]

He had always personified the independent spirit of the West, defying the North Carolina legislature in 1785 by proclaiming the State of Franklin—in effect seceding—in what would later become east Tennessee. This was not merely the rash action of a megalomaniac: during the tenuous time between the war and ratification of the federal Constitution, pesky Vermonters separated from New York to form the Green Mountain state; unruly citizens with disputed property claims looked warily at other states as all argued boundary demarcations at great length. Fears of what frontier separatists might do shook sections of Virginia and Pennsylvania, as well as the western part of North Carolina, where Sevier operated out of concern for his vast personal landholdings. He had gathered a force to protect his interests, but was eventually obliged to give up, and the land that would be Tennessee was federalized. Despite his secession threat, Sevier retained a strong position in North Carolina, serving as a member of Congress from that state (1789–91) before becoming Tennessee's first governor.[22]

So heroic and self-assured a man as Sevier was someone Jackson had to take very seriously. Of course, their egos were not well matched.[23] Wary of any who would deny him glory or forestall his climb to power in the state, Jackson perceived this older, more experienced version of himself as a potential enemy. Sevier showed him courtesy but little apparent warmth, and treated him as a relatively untested man whose ample ambition and clear expectations were not always appreciated.

Their first tangle of words occurred in 1797, not long after Jackson, as a congressman, had succeeded in securing compensation for Sevier's incursion into Cherokee territory. Sevier had penned a letter to Cumberland dignitary James Robertson, his formidable ally in the recent bloody conflict, in which he referred to Jackson in the most unsympathetic terms. This was an age in which letters tended to make the rounds. Astounded when he learned of the governor's ridicule of him, Jackson asked outright how he could have so contemptuously characterized his efforts as "the Scurrilous Expressions of a poor pitifull petty fogging Lawyer. . . . Those Sir, are Expressions, that my feelings are not accustomed to." The word *scurrilous* had the connotation of buffoonery at this time, and a pettifogger was a "small-rate lawyer." The insult was at once professional and personal.[24]

Jackson addressed his letter to "His Excellency John Sevier," who was staying at that moment at the home of John McNairy in Nashville. Judge McNairy had been Jackson's sponsor in 1788, securing him a livelihood and respectability in the Cumberland, but their relations had cooled considerably by this time (McNairy understood that Jackson had opposed his election to two public offices in the mid-1790s). And so, when the letter was delivered to Sevier at McNairy's, there was already an unpleasant feeling in the air.[25]

The governor replied the same day, accusing Jackson of having pronounced an "unjustifiable attack" on *his* character. "Your public observations of my official conduct was represented to me as unfriendly & illiberal. . . . But Sir the inferance I drew was, that they merited the Epithet Scurrilous, and proceeded from a wish to injure my reputation; which produced in me that spirit of resentment which exists in the breast of every good man." Sevier spoke the same language as Jackson. He proceeded, by the end of his letter, to identify their common sensitivity:

> The voice of calumny has more than once been busied in trying to effect my political Distruction. . . . Sir, Any observations I made in the letters you have quoted, were not bottomed on malice; they were the language of A man who thought himself highly injured, and if it betrayed a little imprudence, I will here add that like yourself when passion agitates my Breast I cannot view things in the calm light of mild philosophy.[26]

Jackson reserved his ire for McNairy. A mutual dislike had already hardened, a sour sarcasm (at least in print) that continued to obscure any possible effort to heal the wound. To Sevier, however, Jackson was generous and entirely guileless: "Facts may be misstated, and it is not improbable that they were. . . . I was neither your political nor private Enemy nor am I yet inclined to be So. . . . It is with pleasure Sir, I now Remark to you, that I think you had no *malicious* design to injure my reputation, and that your Letters proceeded from the warmth of the moment." Two men of honor had spoken.[27]

It is quite possible that Jackson's purity of motive did not fully match his purity of expression. Sevier's power was undeniable, and Jackson could not afford to alienate him at this time, although Sevier had, less than a year earlier, stood in opposition to Jackson's election as major general in the Tennessee militia. The governor plainly thought Jackson to be overreaching. But Jackson, a former congressman and senator, did not yearn for the society of the national metropolis. He wished to use national service as a stepping-stone to further honors within Tennessee. He wanted to be an Indian fighter, and Sevier, unquestionably the best-known Indian fighter in the region, had thwarted him.

It appears that his future in the military was at the forefront of Jackson's mind when the hot exchange of words occurred. A Jackson detractor had used a Sevier letter to show favor to Jackson's competition for the major generalship, the sort of incident one might expect in frontier politics. It angered Jackson, and caused him to feel that Sevier had singled him out for abuse. After the resolution to their misunderstanding, though, he may have begun thinking that Sevier could be induced, in the future, to adopt a neutral position when Jackson sought his high military appointment again. But just in case, Jackson held on to information that cast Sevier's earlier land dealings in a questionable light.[28]

His years in a judicial robe did not make Andrew Jackson any more discreet or any less arbitrary—or for that matter, any less calculating when it came to his own career advancement. While he could at times appear on the verge of detonating, he chose his moments to gamble on the future. These observations are borne out in the wild encounter he finally had with John Sevier in the autumn of 1803, the culmination of a steadily building animosity.

The first sparks had flown through the mails, ignited by rumor and innuendo. A more electrical event between these two belligerents could hardly have been set in motion without a face-to-face encounter. That is precisely what happened one day outside the courthouse in Knoxville. In the intervening years since their Nashville notes resolved a misunderstanding over honor and reputation, Sevier had tacitly approved Jackson's elevation to the bench. He had left the governorship in 1801 because the state constitution required it (after three successive two-year terms, he was obliged to wait two years before seeking the office again). No longer executive, Sevier was, at least for the moment, vulnerable.

In 1802, Jackson contested Sevier for the position of major general of the Tennessee militia. This time Jackson narrowly won. (Parton describes the position at this time as "merely an affair of title, regimentals, and showy gallopings on the days of general muster. There were Indians to be kept in awe. . . .")[29] The gentleman who broke the tie between these two proud rivals was Archibald Roane, who succeeded Sevier as governor and then decided to run for reelection against his predecessor in 1803. Sevier, however, beat him. The interested Judge Jackson had earlier pieced together evidence that Sevier was involved in a scheme to defraud the State of North Carolina by dealing in forged land warrants, selling Tennessee land that he had no right to sell. Jackson had conferred with Governor Roane on the delicate matter, and printed the evidence in the newspapers when it best served their common interests.[30]

After this, while Jackson was holding court in Knoxville, the state capital, and the land fraud issue was in the public view, proud Sevier, cutlass in hand, approached Jackson and challenged him to draw. Weaponless but for his cane (an inferior sword inside), Jackson recoiled at the governor's vulgar allusion to Rachel Donelson (Robards) Jackson, and soon after confronted his antagonist in a private letter: "in the Town of Knoxville did you Take the name of a lady into your polluted lips." Anecdotal history, impossible to verify, says that Sevier had accused Jackson of "taking a trip to Natchez with another man's wife," and Jackson was said to have reacted: "Great God! Do you mention *her* sacred name?"[31]

Jackson fired off a challenge, strident and shrill, laced with acid and marked by disdain. He wrote that Sevier's "gasgonading [grandiose, boastful] conduct" was "in true charactor of your self." Jackson claimed that the governor's acts were blatant; he gave them a name: "the ebulutions [violent internal upheaval] of a base mind," and urged Sevier to respond as a true gentleman was obliged to do. "I only deign to notice you," wrote Jackson, "and call upon you for that satisfaction and explanation that your ungentlemanly conduct & expressions require, and for this purpose I request an interview."[32]

The "interview," from the French *entrevue,* meant "sight of each other." Its literal meaning—a challenge to duel—was more poignantly captured in 1803 than it can be today.[33] Jackson announced his expectation that the two would meet at an agreed-upon place, at an agreed-upon time, with their "friends," or seconds. "I . . . will be armed with pistols," the letter

2. *Excerpt from letter in which Judge Andrew Jackson challenges Governor John Sevier to a duel, October 3, 1803. Courtesy the Tennessee Historical Society Collections, Tennessee State Library and Archives.*

concluded, "you cannot mistake me, or my meaning." Andrew White, brother of Hugh Lawson White, delivered the challenge.

Sevier's reply borrowed Jackson's language—"Your Ungentlemanly and gasconading conduct of yesterday . . ."—and recommended that they "repair" to either North Carolina, Virginia, or Georgia—"all in our Vicinity"—because dueling had been made a criminal offense in Tennessee in 1801. Jackson immediately termed the suggestion of a distant meeting a "subterfuge," and proposed instead that they cross over into "the nearest part of the Indian boundery line" and take care of business there. For the spontaneous challenger, fate could not wait another day. "You shall attone," Jackson decreed.[34]

A week later, nothing had come of Jackson's summons. He wrote Sevier again, indicating that he was about to make good on his threat to "advertise" the governor as a "base coward and poltroon." His message addressed

"For the Publick" was duly printed in the *Knoxville Gazette* and elsewhere. Responding, Sevier continued to protest Jackson's impetuous insistence on an illegal meeting, contending that a judge should know better; he reiterated his willingness to duel—across the state line, in Virginia. According to both Jackson emissary Andrew White and "Veritas," the anonymous author of a subsequent diatribe in the *Tennessee Gazette*, the impatient judge agreed to the Virginia rendezvous. But then Sevier insisted on delaying until he took care of some other (unspecific) pressing business first. "[H]e has created in a short space of time," wrote "Veritas," "more business than fifty honest men could settle in the course of their lives."[35]

Jackson set out for west Tennessee, but he did not get very far. In the company of Dr. Thomas Vandyke, a surgeon's mate from a U.S. army fort southwest of Knoxville on the Cumberland Road, he happened upon Governor Sevier and his son James. The principals in both parties were armed with pistols. According to the affidavit of an observer who was traveling some yards ahead of the governor's party, Jackson dismounted and approached the governor on foot, brandishing his weapon, while they cursed and damned each other. Sevier called to Jackson to "fire away," and yet, "after some parley . . . each of their Pistols were returned to their Holsters."

Before long, Jackson started up again, taunting. Sevier drew his sword, which sudden gesture "freightened his horse." The animal bolted, galloping off with the governor's pistols. As Jackson went for his own pistol, Sevier hid behind a tree, questioning whether Jackson dared "fire on a naked man." (According to Vandyke, however, Sevier did have a pistol at this moment, and Jackson jeered, telling Sevier that "if he was a soldier . . . , to unmark himself and fire." But Sevier would not.) This was when James Sevier entered the picture, drawing his own pistol on his father's tormentor. Vandyke quickly pointed *his* gun at young Sevier, in defense of Jackson, and "after some parley again . . . the pistols was again returned to their Holsters." The awkward dance ended without violence. While Jackson and Sevier argued further about which territory they would stage their "interview" in, the matter was finally left.[36]

It was very possibly the death of William Blount in 1800 that obliged Judge Jackson to begin to act more openly to promote his own career. Sevier was convinced that the upstart Jackson had conspired to "assassinate" him, a charge vehemently denied by Vandyke. (In the vocabulary of dueling, "assassination" was the resort of a non-gentleman.) Whether their meeting on the road was by chance or otherwise, Sevier proceeded to caution James Robertson in Nashville not to believe anything Jackson told him "of My being a rougue, a Coward, and a thousand other things. . . . As to Cowardice, there is thousands who have Witnessed my transactions as a soldier." Jackson, was, he complained, "one of the most abandoned rascals in principle my eyes ever beheld." Not to be outdone, Jackson dispatched a letter to President Jefferson on behalf of his ally Vandyke. Writing from Fort Southwest Point the day after the incident, Jackson offered "the truth" as to Vandyke's honorable part in the affair, in the hope of protecting the army physician from the "little and dishonourable things" that might proceed from the governor's mind.[37]

At the time of their roadside feud, Jackson was thirty-six, in his prime, and Sevier was fifty-eight—past his. But the verbal assaults and challenges that the two engaged in showed a certain similarity in their backgrounds: they were men whose worldviews were built on suspicion, and whose combative approaches relied on an ability to sift out deceit and disguise in others. They were reared for politics.

Qualifying for leadership in their world involved building a reputation for consistency as well as honesty. Jackson had yet to solidify his position by this standard, or at least he still seems to have harbored a certain amount of self-doubt. A man aiming to enhance his social prestige, as he was, had to stand out on public issues, claim a position, and defend the justice of that position. To accomplish this required equally outspoken friends, who might be called upon to debate the counterclaims of someone like Governor Sevier.

What was at stake? The analogy of a "gentleman's" mastery over his landholdings is useful here. Southern men of property were given to display the mask of paternalism, to act kindly toward their slaves, but to maintain a firm hand on the plantation. The very guise, the very vocabulary, that suited the slave owner's pretense of honor worked in demonstrating the same individual's celebrated concern for the public interest. Behavior that made privilege at home seem justified translated into expectations of the public's trust. In both private and public venues, men came to believe that they deserved their power; they were trained in the exhibition of paternalistic (protective, indulgent, benevolent) leadership qualities. A military general, for that matter, was meant to be a "father"—albeit a stern father—to his troops. Thus, a threat to one's reputation incited fear of an entire constructed personality crumbling. Form was not "mere form," but rather a means to convey the authority and future prospects of a man.

If Sevier, and especially Jackson, appears to the modern observer to have been defining honor superficially, or meaninglessly arguing, or recklessly courting destruction, this is because we have a distorted perspective on their society. For them, feelings coincided with more than just ordinary inward pride; feelings were associated with *visibility*. The duel, or other staged confrontation, became a social necessity as it became a *visible* means of manipulating publicity.

By courting death, Jackson in particular was acting so as to exhibit fearlessness, to declare his fearlessness in a most public way. Given the value placed on masculine courage, death was preferable to being unmasked as one not strong enough, and thus unworthy of the public's trust. A leader's word of honor was tangible. The association of "honor" and one's "word" with reputation was literal and viscerally felt; honor was more closely bound with social authority and social harmony than it has since become. As one scholar puts it, the code of southern honor was seen as "a bulwark against social chaos rather than a form of violence."[38]

Here are the interlocking pieces: (1) Jackson felt he had to act to demonstrate that the insult was a lie. (2) Upward mobility or individual prestige was impossible otherwise. (3) Prestige or social respect, gained or regained, fed a sense of self-respect. (4) Self-respect or self-assured honor prospered among friends. (5) Fraternity—such as the Masonic community—supported patriarchy. (6) Patriarchy was the condition of leadership that insulated a man from lies about him, promoted by lesser men, that otherwise could endanger his public reputation. These six conditions demonstrate how the "lie" set off a chain of emotional events that augured a much greater personal calamity than modern observers, not bound to this earlier world, might expect.

There is, finally, a potent explanation for Jackson's reaction to Sevier's dismissive language. If we understand how honor, respect, and approval dominated all relationships involving males, it makes sense that such honor, respect, and approval on the Southwest frontier was first and foremost attainable through battlefield valor, where rank and promotion were especially meaningful and especially visible. But Jackson, anxious for military distinction, had yet to mark himself in this way. That missing element in his résumé, as it were, explains his ardent—or immoderate—solicitation of a confrontation with a proven war hero.

They would each prove to be survivors. Sevier emerged unscathed from the land fraud charges and continued as governor until 1809. After that, he was elected to Congress, serving from 1811 until his death four years later.

The tenor of his remarks over the course of many years suggests that his disregard for Jackson was related to his doubts about the younger man's qualifications as lawyer, judge, and military commander alike. But his disparagement of Jackson was no doubt related as well to his fear of being politically, if not literally, ambushed.

Down to Business

Where but on the frontier would a former congressman, senator, and judge trade in his official robe for a store, tavern, and racecourse? That is what Maj. Gen. Andrew Jackson of the Tennessee militia did in 1804. He had bought goods in Natchez for resale shortly after he took up residence in the Cumberland, and in Philadelphia in 1795 embarked on an ill-fated exchange of land for wholesale products. He unluckily endorsed a promissory note with a wholesaler on behalf of a Philadelphia middleman, a friend of William Blount, who went broke and left Jackson with a financial obligation that took him years to cover. His departure from the U.S. Senate after attendance at only one session was directly connected to the alarming state of his financial affairs.[39]

However, he was not at all averse to risk taking. In 1802, Jackson formed a partnership with two others "for the purpose of Erecting a Store On the plantation of Thomas Watson," with a cotton gin, a distillery, and a stock of goods from Philadelphia and Baltimore.[40] By 1804, he was ready to try again. He and Rachel had been living since 1796 at Hunters Hill, once a property belonging to Lewis Robards; it was located beside the Cumberland River east of Nashville, just two miles north of the future Hermitage. Jackson sold the Hunters Hill plantation, paid his outstanding debts, and moved nearby into a modest log house on a 425-acre plot. The Hermitage that now stands on the site is very much restored. It was not constructed until 1819, and burnt in 1834, so that its real essence during the period when Jackson was on the rise is nearly impossible to recapture.

The name "Hermitage" appears to be nothing fanciful, but rather an expression of Jackson's rhetorical desire—his letters to Rachel serve as evidence of this—to enjoy a relatively carefree domesticity. In Sheridan's *Complete Dictionary* that Jackson had purchased in Philadelphia, *hermitage* is defined as "The cell or habitation of a hermit." It was an old French and English word. Jefferson had briefly called his mountaintop estate "Hermitage," before inventing "Monticello" out of the Italian for "little mountain." It was said that Rachel Jackson chose a low-lying spot for the Hermitage, and that her husband did as she wished. Its foundation was limestone, quarried by slaves; its walls were brick, baked right on the property. The original Hermitage was a square, two-story building, without portico or pretense.[41]

So in 1804, Jackson and Rachel Jackson's nephew John Hutchings, his partner since 1802, joined with a new partner, John Coffee (1772–1833), to enlarge their enterprise by adding a horse racing track and boat landing at Clover Bottom, between the Hermitage and Nashville. Coffee's general store had recently failed, and in falling into Jackson's circle through a business opportunity, he grew to be, along with Jackson's other financially interested but politically untempted friend John Overton, a close confidant. Coffee's business interests were more diversified than Jackson's. He quickly gained a reputation as a fine surveyor, and became the agent of several major Tennessee land speculators. He would marry Rachel's sixteen-year-old niece Mary Donelson in 1809, and distinguish himself at Jackson's side in the Battle of New Orleans.[42]

They must have become fast friends, because when Jackson traveled to east Tennessee in March 1804, and found himself once again boiling over due to repercussions from his encounter with "old Jack," as he now carelessly referred to Sevier, he called upon his new partner to prepare to join him in Knoxville. A newspaper attack emanating from the Sevier camp prompted Jackson to write Coffee: "I mean to punish the author myself if he is any other person but John Sevier—If you can with convenience I wish you to come—least I may have use for a friend." Coffee's bolstering presence ultimately proved unnecessary.[43]

The population of Nashville at this time was still no greater than 500, Davidson County under 5,000. By all accounts, though, the business of Jackson, Hutchings, and Coffee turned a good profit. In 1804, they set out to market Tennessee cotton, and deer and bear skins (provided by Cherokee and Chickasaw hunters), in exchange for "groceries, nails, and steele" obtainable in the principal port cities of Philadelphia, New Orleans, and Baltimore. Relations with their distant correspondents were not problem-free, and money matters never simple, but steady arrangements and assertive methods eventually yielded the desired results. Not surprisingly, Jackson had strong business principles and did not spare any detail in making his positions known. In 1810, he would form a new partnership, with a Natchez connection, to market cotton and tobacco; this short-lived venture grew to include traffic in slaves. If the testimony of Dr. Felix Robertson, son of James Robertson, is reliable, Jackson was "a cool, shrewd man of business."[44]

As a sporting man, Jackson participated in games that involved wagering. At ease in the company of the rough-hewn men of Nashville, he played billiards and cards, and bet on cockfights ("cheering on his favorite birds with loudest vociferation," reports Parton). He did not only compete, but if Fourth of July, 1809, is any guide, organized major cockfights, assisted by Coffee.[45] It was his active involvement in horse breeding and horse racing, however, that led to one of the most remarked upon and controversial episodes of his life.

Jackson Shoots a Man

At the racetrack of Clover Bottom, where years before Rachel Donelson's father had first planted corn, a mile-long course was fixed. Andrew Jackson had bought the racehorse Truxton in Virginia, and brought him back to Nashville to compete. Around the same time, he purchased a slave in his early thirties named Dinwiddie, who ran his stables, trained his horses, and acquired a reputation for his skill as a breeder. A sensational event was planned for November 1805, and because it did not happen on schedule, the sequel, announced repeatedly in the Nashville press in the early months of 1806, was termed "the greatest and most interesting match race ever run in the Western country": six-year-old Truxton versus eight-year-old Ploughboy. Three thousand dollars were at stake.[46]

The owners' initial arrangement included a default clause. If one party had to forfeit, the other would receive $800 in specified notes. When Ploughboy was withdrawn in advance of the November race, Jackson was paid the forfeit. So the matter stood, until the son-in-law of Ploughboy's owner, the twenty-five-year-old attorney Charles Dickinson, was overheard speaking impolitely about Rachel Jackson. Jackson confronted Dickinson, who was a dandy, by all reports, a man given to frolicsome behavior and intemperance in the company of his merry band of friends. Dickinson told Jackson that he intended no insult, that he must have been drunk when he uttered the offensive words. Jackson, we are told, was satisfied by this explanation.[47]

However, there was mischief in the air. Jackson intimate Sam Houston reported many years later that Dickinson subsequently defamed Mrs. Jackson in a tavern again. Otherwise, the story goes that rumors circulated in Nashville as to Jackson's credibility; someone reported that he quibbled over which notes he was willing to accept in payment of the forfeit. Another young lawyer, Thomas Swann, inserted himself in the situation, directly calling Jackson's word of honor into question. Swann published a provocative letter in the local newspaper, the *Impartial Review, or Cumberland Repository,* raising subtle distinctions between what Jackson had said and others had construed with regard to the notes.[48]

The entire issue was absurd, except for the imputation as to Jackson's honor. Jackson wrote to Swann, proud and accusing: "I never wantonly sport with the feelings of innocence." He labeled both Swann and Dickinson (the latter of whom was alleged to have misrepresented his conversation with Jackson) "base, poltroon, and cowardly." Jackson had thought Dickinson was prepared to drop the matter, but now, presuming otherwise, "as he wishes to blow the coal I am ready to light to a blaze that it may be consumed at once, and finally extinguished." Jackson could not walk away from a dispute. It would be settled one way or another.[49]

The issue became simply this: Who had lied? Dickinson, without delay, wrote to Jackson: "Your letter is so replete with equivocation that it is impossible for me to understand you." He cajoled: "Do you pretend to call a Man a *tale bearer* for telling that which is and can be proven to be the truth?" And finally, "As to the word *Coward, I think it as* [appli]cable to yourself as any one." Jackson apparently did not receive this letter for two weeks, by which time Dickinson had left for New Orleans, not to return for three months. The problem festered.[50]

Just two days after Dickinson's letter was dated, before Jackson had even seen it, Swann issued him a challenge; it was published in the *Impartial Review.* "Think not that I am to be intimidated by your threats," he opened the short provocation, demanding "that reparation which one gentleman is intitled to receive of another." To make matters worse, Swann dispatched Nathaniel McNairy, the brother of Jackson's former friend and benefactor — now enemy — John McNairy, to deliver his challenge in person.[51]

Jackson would not give Swann the "reparation" sought. He thought little of Swann, and on the next day, accompanied by John Coffee, entered Winn's Tavern in Nashville aiming to make a visual statement to that effect. Swann walked in the door not long after, and Jackson struck him with his cane — the act of a "gentleman" who will not degrade himself by agreeing to meet a social inferior on the field of honor. According to Coffee's later affidavit, Jackson landed "a very severe blow," and Swann "appeared to stagger forward." Jackson stumbled as he lunged at Swann a second time, and both men went for their pistols. Jackson was quicker, and Swann "withdrew his hand," unwilling to let the drama play out.[52]

In the midst of all this, deeply concerned by what was happening, the old pioneer James Robertson wrote Jackson on February 1, 1806, a letter "from the bottom of my hart." In his marvelously creative English—what he gamely recognized as "incorect scroals [scrawls]"—Robertson indulged Jackson's patience, earnestly requesting that he ignore the flamboyant prose of his enemies' published provocations. He knew Jackson well enough to predict that "the sight of this may Erritate you so as in heat of pation, to do an act, that Sociaty may be deprived of a yousefull member, and on Reflection I am sartain your good senc will dictate to you that no Honer can be attached Ither to the conquered or Conquorer." Think of the loss to your family if you should be killed, he implored. Think of how "misarable" you would be in taking the life of "your Fellow mortal." Robertson pleaded with Jackson not to consider his entreaties trivial. He had heard it said that Aaron Burr had had no "ease in mind" since the "fatal hour" a year and a half before, when he ended the life of Alexander Hamilton.

In speaking out against dueling, Robertson claimed the wisdom that his advanced age bestowed on him: "Will you pardon me my frend when I tell you that I have bin longer in the world than you have, and do heare the fals honer of dueling Redeculed by most of thinking persons." Jackson, he said, needed to realize that he was now a man of "standing," and should therefore maturely ignore the rantings of "young hot heded persons." In Robertson's way of thinking, the victim in any duel rarely was "lemented," rarely retained any "honer," and was always remembered as "imprudant," no matter what more commendable traits he possessed in life. Robertson predicted, accurately, as it turned out, that "if you were to git into a duel I assure you it is my opinion you would have a full sheare of the blame attached to your self."[53]

As simple and compelling as these words from Nashville's foremost founder read, Jackson responded to each and every public taunt. He wrote to the editor of the *Impartial Review,* with point-by-point rebuttals and legalistic rejoinders. He involved his friends in support of each counter-claim. For instance: "But Mr McNairy tells Mr Coffee that the *caning* was the only cause of complaint. Then, why bring the points of veracity and consistancy into view, in the publication?" Once again, Jackson defined his published position as "my proposition for redress."[54]

There was more to come. Swann's friend Nathaniel McNairy and Jackson's friend John Coffee followed up an argument emanating from the events at Winn's Tavern with a reckless duel, across the state line, in Kentucky. On March 1, McNairy fired his pistol before the signal, wounding Coffee in the thigh. Coffee fired ineffectively—ostensibly a jerk coming as a result of being hit. He quarreled with the propriety of such an outcome, but no further exchange of fire occurred, and the two men reached a "compromise," according to one witness.[55]

These twists and turns in controversies over honor demonstrate again the importance of symbols, and of gesture, in defining manhood. To be branded a coward, or to fail to respond to a caning, one in effect acknowledged his social insignificance. This explains the role of trusted messengers—seconds—who represented the offended party in negotiations. In most cases, public quarrels were resolved to the satisfaction of both sides, and balance was restored, generally in the form of a statement printed in the newspaper for all to see. If not, a duel might take place to produce the same result (to achieve "satisfaction"), in which neither duelist really aimed to end the life of his antagonist. Rising to a challenge was enough to sustain honorable status: demonstrating grace and calm, steadiness and fearlessness, helped one's career far more than having to rationalize the technically illegal taking of a life. In episodes wherein one actually set out to kill another in a duel, it was understood that the ritual had devolved into something frowned upon—something less civilized—something frontierlike.[56]

Death of all kinds was a constant topic of conversation. Letters routinely conveyed news of the passing of loved ones; newspapers reported murder plots and covered wars; the natural dangers of the frontier were known to every traveler. On the same day as the Coffee-McNairy duel, Nashville's newspaper printed a satirical poem titled "The Dead Alive," making light of a gruesome affair. It told the concocted tale of a "jovial fellow, full of spunk," who "The other day, by chance got drunk." His drinking buddy decided on the spot to "convert him into money," and wrapped the unconscious drinker in a sack. The enterprising one appeared before a surgeon (who practiced on indigent corpses), and sold the fresh "corpse" for "two guineas." Two guineas for a body? This was a case in which honor was cheapened. The tale proceeds:

> The bargain closed; the corpse began
> To groan, just like a living man!
> Ho s'cried the surgeon, 'what is here,'
> The dead is now alive I fear?

It is no matter,' said the vendor,
You buy the body that I render,
And therefore set your heart at ease,
For you can kill him, when you please.'[57]

The story has no moral, but reveals a state of mind in early Nashville: a capacity for appreciating the absurd while acknowledging the prevalence of death. Across the country, newspapers everywhere lamented human loss in somber verse; in Nashville, as Jackson resolved to go to extremes to defend his honor, not all deaths were proud.

Jackson was being forced to wait for "satisfaction." While Dickinson remained in New Orleans, he found a way to conclude at least one piece of unfinished business—the horse race that had started their very public disagreement. In early April, Jackson was able to write to John Hutchings (who was also in New Orleans on business) that the race between Truxton and Ploughboy took place "in the presence of the largest concourse of people I ever saw assembled, unless in the army." There is a sense here, to begin with, that Jackson relished a crowd; a multitude was on hand to see his surrogate perform, and to see Jackson strut after the victory. Truxton, the noble horse, was a staunch soldier.

As important and symbolic, a Jacksonian principle came into play. Truxton had been hurt prior to the race, his thigh swelling, but Jackson determined that he would run just the same. As he put it in the letter to his business partner Hutchings: "Had it not been for myself, [the injury] would have occasioned the forfeight to have been paid—but this I was determined not to permit. . . . All things prepared, the horses started, and Truxton under every disadvantage beat him." Even lame, the horse had run brilliantly, the winning owner cooed: "Thus ends the fate of ploughboy." Hutchings replied to Jackson's letter with a fantasy he knew would please Jackson: "I am truly sorry that mr. Dickerson [sic] and Capt Wright [a former owner of Ploughboy] left here [New Orleans] befor this pleasing nuse reached me, so I might of had the pleasur of seeing them in their agganey."[58]

The lesson, to Jackson, was that a superior fighter, a winner, had to resist pain and refuse the temptation to sit out an action. On the day he had stood up to the raised cutlass of Jack Sevier in Knoxville in 1803, Jackson himself had been physically weak, recovering from a debilitating fever. In his upcoming interview with Charles Dickinson, he would stand his ground even after receiving a bullet in his chest. And he would endure further privations, nearly as great, in the coming years, when he led an army south to his most heroic victory. That was Jackson's way.

It was May when Dickinson returned to Nashville. As soon as he did, he published a condescending piece in the *Impartial Review* designed to antagonize Jackson. "Andrew Jackson has had several disputes," he noted, referring to the problem with Sevier, while suggesting that Jackson ran off at the mouth too easily. Dickinson turned back the clock a few months. In his published attack on Swann, Jackson had presumed Swann to be a "puppet" of Dickinson, and now Dickinson blithely declared that if Jackson's "epithets" were indeed meant for him, then "I declare him (notwithstanding he is a major general of the militia of Mero District) to be a worthless scoundrel 'a paltroon and a coward.' "[59]

Jackson's predictable reply to Dickinson's letter ritually protested: "You have, to disturb my quiet, industriously excited Thomas Swann to quarrel with me, which involved the peace and harmony of society for a while— You on the tenth of January wrote me a very insulting letter, left the country and caused this letter to be delivered after you had been gone some days. . . ." In sum, Jackson recognized Dickinson's challenge for what it was, and dispatched his second, Revolutionary War veteran Thomas Overton—John Overton's older brother—to work out the logistics for an "affair of honor." It was scheduled to take place one week later, just across the Red River, in Kentucky.[60]

It appears that one of the reasons Jackson so detested Charles Dickinson was that the young lawyer was a dandy: a conceited, spoiled, overconfident fellow who needed to be taught a lesson. Jackson admired a martial bearing, which was why his feud with Dickinson and Swann involved scorn, and his feud with Sevier was a purer contest of masculine egos, in which Jackson felt that he was not being given his due by the hardy governor. Rather differently, it seemed to him that Dickinson was reckless and weak-minded, a public nuisance.

The duel has been narrated by many, and all relate the same details, modeled on Parton's interviews in the 1850s. Dickinson was said to have told his young wife nothing about his deadly mission, merely that he was to be gone on business and back the following night. What Jackson might have said or not said to his wife was not reported. Thomas Overton and a surgeon accompanied him north to the border. In the imagined peace of a bright morning, the parties stood at a distance of twenty-four feet. Jackson wore a loose coat, to conceal the contour of his slender frame. The single word "Fire!" was given, and Dickinson, reputed to be the better shot and egged on by friends, pulled the trigger as Jackson stood, willing to take the first bullet in order to steady his aim—wherever he might be hit—and make certain to strike mortally in his reply.

" 'Great God,' he faltered, 'have I missed him?' " is Parton's rendering of the astonished Dickinson, as Jackson stood, wounded and bleeding but not evincing pain. Overton "saw a puff of dust fly from the breast of his coat," and saw Jackson hold his left arm across his chest. A rib or two were broken, but his vital organs were undamaged. Dickinson was ordered back to the mark by Overton. In an instant, Jackson took aim and shot him. The bullet went through the body, below the ribs, and the young combatant fell to the ground, where he slowly bled to death.[61]

The *Impartial Review* printed its next issue inside black borders, the symbol of mourning for one whose loss was particularly regretted in the community. In the month that Jackson's wound needed to heal, many in Nashville took issue with his having recocked his pistol after he first pulled the trigger without report. While recocking was acceptable practice according to the code of the duel, it had not been specifically incorporated into the terms laid down by the duelists' seconds.[62]

Aftermath of the Duel

Parton remarks that between Dickinson's death and the War of 1812, Jackson's morals were so questioned that he could not have been elected to any office in the state of Tennessee.[63] His correspondence in the wake of the duel makes clear that Jackson felt not the slightest remorse; he treated as enemies those who signed a condolence letter said to have been meant for Dickinson's widow, a letter that was submitted to the newspaper at the same time as a rationalization for its pages to be enclosed in the black borders of public mourning.

Among the signatures to this controversial letter were predictable names like Thomas Swann and several McNairys. But there was also James Robertson's son, the Philadelphia-trained physician Felix Robertson, who had commended Jackson a year earlier for his "unsullied private Character";[64] and French Canadian Timothy Demonbrum, reportedly the first white hunter to settle in west Tennessee, preceding even the crusty Mansker and Robertson.[65] One signatory, Thomas G. Watkins, became a particular target of Jackson, who seemed intent on provoking yet another duel. Watkins had apparently questioned publicly the justification for Jackson's fire, and Jackson was led to understand that it was Watkins who had instigated the offensive consolatory letter.

Watkins wanted no trouble. He claimed to be motivated only by a concern for the feelings of Dickinson's widow. Jackson was not assuaged. "To

CHARLES DICKINSON,
SIR,
Your conduct and expressions relative to me of late, have been of such a nature and so insulting, that it requires and shall have my notice.

Insults may be given by men, and of such a kind that they must be noticed and treated with the respect due a gentleman, altho (as in the present instance) you do not merit it.

You have, to disturb my quiet, industriously excited Tho's Swann to quarrel with me, which involved the peace and harmony of society for a while.

You on the 10th of January wrote me a very insulting letter, left this country, caused this letter to be delivered after you had been gone some days, and viewing yourself in safety from the contempt I held you in—have now in the press a piece more replete with blackguard abuse than any of your other productions. You are pleased to state that you would have noticed me in a different way, but my cowardice, would have found a pretext to evade that satisfaction if it had been called for &c. &c.

I hope for your courage will be an ample security to me that I will obtain speedily that satisfaction due me for the insults offered, and in the way my friend who hands you this will point out—he waits upon you for that purpose, and with your friend will enter into immediate arrangements for this purpose.

I am &c.

Andrew Jackson.

May 23d, 1806.

GEN. ANDREW JACKSON,
SIR,
Your note of this morning is received, and your request shall be gratified. My friend who hands you this will make the necessary arrangements.

I am &c.

Charles Dickinson.

May 23d, 1806.
Gen. Andrew Jackson,
Present.

3. *Jackson's challenge to Charles Dickinson, and Dickinson's terse reply, as reprinted in Nashville's* Impartial Review, or Cumberland Repository *on June 14, 1806, two weeks after the fateful duel.*

dupe the citizens," he charged, "you held out to them that the thing was only intended to console the widow's tears," when in fact "you were preparing in the background to give my reputation a stab." He called Watkins a coward, contrasting his "outward smiles" with "hidden enmity." Though seriously wounded, Jackson felt a righteous indignation that the impertinent Dickinson was being mourned in the same fashion as a Washington. To Watkins: "That I have unrobed you and your whole conduct in this business, shews you to be a hypocritical, cowardly assassin."[66]

The battle for honor had not ended at the dueling ground. Jackson's letter to Watkins is replete with references to "hidden designs" and false gallantry, disguised motives and the lack of a sense of justice. In the end, the wounded man nearly begs Watkins to consent to a duel: "I will receive no communications from you unless a call for satisfaction for the insult I now offer and intend for you." Jackson is at his most peevish and choleric here. He suspects the world and cannot help but perform the role of town bully.

What incensed him most was the apparent inversion of moral principle. Somehow, "a few individuals" had recast the worthless Dickinson as one whose "virtues," as Jackson put it, were "so rare, that he demanded this unusual respect from the Publick." Did you know, he prodded, in a letter to the public, that the deceased had been engaged in "the humane pursuit of purchasing Negroes in Maryland and carrying them to Natchez & Louis[ian]a and thus making a fortune of speculating in human flesh." By branding his victim as a slave trader, Jackson was differentiating between one who bought and sold slaves out of necessity, and one who did so for unreasonable profit. Petulantly, Jackson insisted that Dickinson was goaded into seeking the duel by the villainous Joseph Erwin, Ploughboy's owner, who had been heard to say, with reference to Jackson, "by God, Sir, I think you can kill him."[67]

Whether or not it was an accurate quote, Jackson could not avoid appearing petty, if not desperate, in his struggle for approval. He evidently saw as his last recourse portraying himself as a victim, a man hounded by unprincipled others. Congressman, senator, judge, and major general, he was perhaps not the easiest person to conceive of as having been victimized by the family of the young lawyer he had killed. But Jackson saw only one way: he had done nothing but defend his own inestimable character from wanton attacks. He expected to be vindicated once all the facts were known. He, of course, saw no pettiness, only manliness, in his solicitation of the public.

As part of the melodramatic effort to clear his name, Jackson wrote to the man whose farm was located next to the dueling ground. William Harrison, who had watched Charles Dickinson die, replied by letter that any who might claim that the duel was fought unfairly were dead wrong; the truth was "utterly to the revirce — that yurself and Mr Dickeson both acted like men of furmness." As to the critics who asserted that Jackson was wrong to recock his gun and fire, "them people Could not be a Judge of your fealings at that Time." Jackson's sudden burst of unpopularity had extended into Kentucky, the farmer also reported, where a grand jury convened, and "had me Sworne and very hard attemps made to have you indited," but nothing came of it.[68]

A manly "feast of battle" had turned sour for the victor. The first epigraph to this book, from Shakespeare's *Richard II,* has multiple meanings. It expresses, of course, Andrew Jackson's self-destined celebrity, that extended from the "feast of battle" at New Orleans in 1814–15. But Shakespeare's words are as much meant to describe Jackson's longing for individual confrontation. In *Richard II,* it is Thomas Mowbray who speaks these words, as he prepares for mortal combat with his adversary, Bolingbroke. The two noblemen have accused each other of deceit, and each expects divine justice from their bloody encounter. In the play, the king puts a stop to the hand-to-hand challenge and expels both men from England— Mowbray he banishes forever. After the Dickinson duel, Jackson was, in a sense, banished by his country, held back from further position, punished for his pride. Yet being Jackson, unalterable, and a consummate performer, he would never cease pursuing his highly personalized sense of right.

Insidious rumors persisted into the early fall of 1806. One from Jonesborough reported that Jackson and Swann had finally dueled, killing each other—Jackson falling instantly, with a ball to the head. Jackson was now widely reputed to enjoy shedding blood. "Be assured," wrote John Overton (now Judge Overton) from the source of the latest rumors, "that their slander can do you no harm among your friends."

Overton saw fit to caution his old friend to stop caring about what "*boys, instruments, mere tools of others*" said about him. Jackson's temper was beginning to wear, even on his closest allies. He was making things difficult by failing to distinguish between real threats and minor irritations. "Should any difficulty occur may I ask you as a friend before you do any thing, to consult your friends. Patience, deli[b]eration and bravery will surmount all difficulties." Few dared to address him so forthrightly.[69]

Overton evidently regarded bravery in more passive, self-reflective terms than his friend did. From William Cocke to John Sevier to Charles Dickinson, Jackson had shown that he could recur with ease to vengeful and unrelenting language. He pounced as soon as he concluded that someone desired to prevent him from getting (or holding on to) the stature he craved. William Blount was gone, someone in authority whose goals meshed with his own, whose political rise in the east Jackson had once seemed able to protect by rear-guard action in the west, and who therefore did all he could to protect Jackson.

An old political acquaintance from Jackson's time in Congress arrived at the Hermitage just days after Jackson received John Overton's friendly but cautionary letter from Jonesborough. That old acquaintance, professing friendship on the order of a Blount, was the sociable ex–vice president (and noted duelist) Aaron Burr. Jackson's elder by ten years, Burr was about to lead the Tennessee major general into his next controversial adventure.

Like Blount and Jackson, Burr was growth-minded. He fantasized about acquiring western land and dared to conceive of the power it would accord him. Space, to such men, meant something very personal—yet could be easily translated into national policy, if they were given enough latitude to pursue their common fantasy. Like Blount, like Jackson, Burr talked back to authority and was accused in his time (in the obviously biased words of Alexander Hamilton) of being "a man of extreme and irregular ambition."[70]

To weather the storm that Burr brought to Nashville, Jackson would ultimately have to exercise prudence (if he could), and justify himself on a much larger scale. In focusing on national affairs with renewed energy, he needed to heed Overton's advice and better manage his impulses, which of late had created more problems than solutions for him. But Jackson was not a very self-reflective man.

His problems had arisen, in part, because not everyone believed that the target of his moral outrage was their own. A common foe, a ready opponent, could change everything. That is what the visit of Aaron Burr, in the early autumn of 1806, delivered. The Cumberland turned its attention south, away from the Dickinson duel and its aftermath to the lurking hostility of Spain in the Floridas and maybe even New Orleans—Nashville's lifeline. Burr spoke of impending war.

As Burr stirred things up, Jackson sought to restore his good fortune. By locating an enemy abroad that all could agree upon, the inactive Tennessee militia general began to feel greater cause for optimism. Even so, as things turned out, he would be spending the foreseeable future defending himself.

CHAPTER THREE

➤➤➤➤➤➤➤➤➤·◄◄◄◄◄◄◄◄◄

Judging Character: Burr

As to my letter you may use it as you please—where villainy is con-
cerned I have no secrete & I neither fear the frowns, nor court the
smiles of <u>Genl Wilkeson and his friends—however influential the[y]</u>
<u>may be</u>.
　　　　—Jackson to Congressman John Randolph, c. February 10, 1810

In 1806, as he was nearing forty, Andrew Jackson seemed to relish killing,
or if not, at least flirted with the idea of it often. No doubt Aaron Burr saw
this in him. But to settle for so single-minded an interpretation of language and events is to suggest that there was no nobility in Jackson's
purposes, which would be wrong. It would also be to ignore another phenomenon: the rise of the West, the elevation of the frontier, in American
lore.

The literary frontier of the late eighteenth century, typified by J. Hector
St. Jean de Crèvecoeur's *Letters from an American Farmer* (1782), idealized
the "melting pot," proclaimed America a haven of pacifism, and imagined
a sentimental consensus in praise of pristine nature. In this construct, the
nation was a "refuge," and American power was to transform the world
with morals and without muscle; muscle was for the laboring farmer who
adapted to a nurturing land.

The real frontier, of course, was nothing like Crèvecoeur's pastoral fantasy. As a new century arrived, pioneers moved west in greater numbers,
and Kentucky, Tennessee, and Ohio achieved statehood. Often bitter
political contests reflected an overwhelming hunger for land and influence.
As we have already seen, the trans-Appalachian west was a hodgepodge
that could not be defined simply in glamorous or elegant terms. After
Lewis and Clark traveled from the Mississippi to the West Coast in
1804–6, the ecstasy of natural description may have heightened, but the

practical possibilities of settlement made travelogues more useful, and emigrants' stories more and more literal. Issues of security led to a stronger articulation of national goals.

Language provided early-nineteenth-century Americans with new patriotic means of evaluating the land spread before them. It presented contradictory images as well. The romanticized Daniel Boone was at once a courageous, selfless architect *of* civilization and a gloomy fugitive *from* civilization. He was a child of nature with an intelligent eye, on the lookout for a spot from which to grow a healthy, hardy race. But how noble were his progeny? The West promised camaraderie and adventure; it welcomed families; but it also invited scorn from many opinion makers back east who ridiculed the pioneers as a people lacking both taste and knowledge.

Although the actual frontier was the dangerous, litigious, coarse, and contentious world Jackson experienced, the literary frontier gradually and more consciously provided escape. By the 1820s, it would celebrate a new breed of fiction with the nostalgic works of James Fenimore Cooper, who returned readers to an imagined locale in New York's interior more than half a century earlier. In Cooper's novels, the heroic frontiersman was a perfect blend of chivalry and compassion. He knew the forest as taught to him by model Indians, who were themselves sons of nature and trustworthy friends, imbued with heart and uncorrupted by Euro-American material comforts. It was the opposite of the pursuit of power—the opposite of the real frontier.[1]

Jackson was an authentic frontier figure. He symbolized the real grit of that realm, where bids for power were generally unsubtle. While many proud easterners were to denounce Jackson's rudeness, certain others, established men of the political world who were not "Jacksonian" in background (or as simple in their tastes), came to love him for what he was. Responding differently to the world of print, this latter group saw in him the positive image of Boone, a remarkable, if eccentric, almost whimsical, character.

Among them was one who possessed a rare ability to articulate the passage that Jackson made from backwoods to the national metropolis. He was Levi Woodbury (1789–1851), Dartmouth College graduate, New Hampshire judge, governor, and U.S. senator, who served as President Jackson's secretary of the navy and later as his secretary of the treasury. In retirement, Jackson displayed a bust of his earnest friend and defender at the Hermitage.

Eulogizing his president in 1845, Woodbury revealed a certain amount of candor amid the expected tone of admiration. He began at the beginning, and respected history enough not to embellish as most eulogists did, when the details were hazy. As an intimate, the New Englander over time had heard much of his friend's early career from the lips of Tennesseans. He understood that as a young man Jackson was unsettled but inspired, and that as a young attorney he had shown "inflexible fidelity to the interests entrusted to his care."

"Inflexible fidelity" to a cause was consistently, and from the start, a Jacksonian attribute. Inflexibility, of course, can be read in more than one way. There were "chequered scenes of his middle age," Woodbury acknowledged, that served to "ripen what were only natural impulses in youth," impulses that needed to be "modified, softened." Woodbury's point was that the underlying impulses that drove Jackson were recognizably moralistic, and rooted in a strong sense of personal independence—of will. "Starting life with few strong natural endowments," he explained, "everything beside was, with him, self-made." Jackson's "lot in life" was "cast" amid "agitating circumstances." And so it took time for him to learn to rely on "practical sense" to arrive at practical solutions to those problems that stood in his way.

These observations accurately capture Jackson's progress up through 1806. Viewed beyond the ornamental, Woodbury's eulogy recognized much in Jacksonian firmness that was imperfect. While noting that Jackson's moralism had inspired him with self-confidence, the admiring friend went on to clarify that as such confidence built, as he developed his leadership style, Jackson felt increasingly impelled to "enforce" his sense of right. Here Woodbury paused to reflect that Jackson was a man "subject to human frailties"—he said this unabashedly—"because indiscriminate eulogy is not worth the breath that utters it."

No one with Jackson's record could have been governable. He played outside the rules, because the rules generally did not take into account the way the world had spread itself before Jackson's eyes: for him, a government of reason did not always offer satisfactory means to deal with a range of perceived injustices. And so, Jackson very often recurred to his own, highly emotionalized, inner sense of right and resolve. But, Woodbury wanted to stress, impetuosity began to soften as Jackson matured: "With whatever correctness he may, at times, have been charged with rashness, under the feverish impulses of youth, it is certain that his judgment seldom forsook the helm in advanced life, and under the highest provocation; *in the very tempest of his passion,* he was remarkably wary and watchful." The italics are Woodbury's.[2]

A Jacksonian Vocabulary Lesson:
A Worthy Officer Battles Engines of Despotism

Woodbury knew Jackson as a man of advanced years, but gleaned much of his earlier life through conversation. We, on the other hand, have been assessing Jackson's character in large measure on the basis of what he wrote and how his language comported with the western frontier of his time. The object of studying his written expression is to discover what history can possess of him beyond the merely anecdotal.

Much is said about Jackson's lack of scholarly narration, and it is meant to minimize the significance of his writing. It is easy to say that he was a man of action, period. But this is not so. Though his attempts at crafting a literary personality invariably collapse into clichés, Andrew Jackson, as we have seen, used verbs, adjectives, and nouns in distinctive ways that reveal a clear sensibility.

His familiar letters contain an emotive quality. They inform us how it was that he sustained friendships, and how he roundly assailed those whom he identified as depraved adversaries. He judged character constantly as he endeavored to assert his own. His lack of subtlety, of course, quickly relegated some people into Jacksonian oblivion; but this lack also attracted many people who respected a clear-cut, no-nonsense man with undisguised purposes. Therein lies the key to appreciating Jackson's passion.

Here we return to the contest over military hairstyle that so inflamed Jackson. Col. Thomas Butler was fifty years old in 1804. He had been studying the law in Philadelphia in 1776, when he abruptly left that pursuit to join the Continental Army. He was a hero of the Battle of Monmouth in 1778, and became acquainted with Jackson while serving as commander of the U.S. Army fort at Southwest Point, below Knoxville, from 1797 to 1802. At that time, he was transferred to Mississippi Territory. Butler insisted on wearing his hair in a queue, in the Revolutionary style, and received from Gen. James Wilkinson an exemption from the 1801 general order requiring short or "cropped" hair. That exemption was later rescinded to uphold the general's stiffening desire to enforce military discipline.

When he embraced the cause of Colonel Butler, Jackson conceived a bipolar world of friends and foes. He applied the same dramatic words that he brought to bear in correspondence relating to his own injured honor. To President Jefferson, in emphasizing the wrongheaded absolutism inherent in the order to cut hair, Jackson identified "sufficient evidence of ill will" on the part of the commanding general. Hoping to persuade, he insisted that the president was "not informed truly of the sensibility of both officers of the army."

What "sensibility" was he describing? There was the one party, Butler, whom Jackson depicted as honorable, decent, and direct; and the other, Wilkinson, whom he labeled insensitive, and whose purposes were dark and secretive. Jackson felt that Wilkinson was entranced by the "power . . . to oppress . . . and keep his conduct shielded from investigation." This was the same kind of misdirection he had ascribed to Dickinson's friends when they were seeking to protect the reputation of a bloated, self-aggrandizing slave trader. In both instances, it was owing to an indecent manipulation of facts that someone of worth was "doom'd to persecution." In Butler's case, the injustice went even further, at least rhetorically: for now, "the citizens feelings are roused, and they think they see the buds of Tyranny, arising out of it."

Jackson's disputes invariably centered on character assessment—and character assassination. He foresaw social disharmony where the corrupt were wrongly entrusted with power. He lectured Jefferson: a "meritorious officer" would be foiled if his only appeal for "redress" was "thro the organ of the oppressor." Jackson reached next for still stronger terms: "we think an old and valuable officer [is] driven to be the Victim to satiate the spleen and revenge of the Genl." He used harsh images and countenanced strong measures: the Jacksonian moral economy endorsed "punishment," in order to stop the vicious and malicious from advancing.[3]

To the maltreated Butler, Jackson expressed his sympathetic outrage. He called Wilkinson's "a base and vindictive mind" that any "brave and virtuous mind would shudder at." Note that the crime ("ill will") emanated from a perverted "mind." And the solution, as well, lay in the mind: Butler had to retain "firmness and fortitude," to "ride triumphant over your enemies—and May the engines of Despotism be hurled from their offices with *disgrace*." Clearly, Jackson saw the cropped hair issue as high tragedy, requiring a sublime justice reminiscent of the days of chivalry. As if he were cataloguing and publishing charges against an opponent who had issued an insult, eliciting a challenge to duel, Jackson urged Butler to "collect all the charges against him, and lay them before the President." As Jackson's military position grew secure, his avowal of punishment for crimes of the mind, of "ill will," would more readily involve violent acts for society's benefit.[4]

In a toast he delivered on the Fourth of July, 1805, Jackson applauded the long-harassed, long-haired officer: "Colo. Thomas Butler—may private worth and virtue rise triumphant over persecution." He lifted his hopes along with his glass. But at Butler's court-martial later that month, Wilkinson was upheld and the veteran colonel found guilty of the charges against him. Not only was Jackson's satisfaction delayed, his frustration would soon turn a more melancholy hue; for by the time Wilkinson had confirmed Colonel Butler's sentence—a year's suspension from duty, rank, and pay—Butler had already died.[5]

All Jackson ever wanted to do was to restore the moral order when he saw it under attack. He had emphasized "redress" in the 1788 letter to Waitstill Avery (Jackson's first extant attempt to justify a challenge to a duel); he had repeated in the 1804 letter to Jefferson that redress had been denied to the subverted Colonel Butler. Again "redress" was to be invoked—in the familiar context of "the right of nature"—when Jackson went head to head in 1812 with a federally appointed Indian agent, Silas Dinsmore.

In this curious and revealing episode, Jackson made a federal case out of his personal crusade to punish a man who operated a checkpoint on the road between Nashville and New Orleans and who had been undertaking to inspect whites traveling with nonwhites through Indian country. Part of the problem, in Jackson's mind, was that the federal Indian agent had a disturbingly *unsuspicious* regard for Indians. But what fired him up most directly was Dinsmore's insistence on demanding papers from whites to prove that their accompanying slaves were not runaways. The agent was ostensibly trying to prevent fugitive bondmen from stealing their way into Choctaw territory. For Jackson, though, Dinsmore's authority represented "lawless tyranny."

Faced with an enterprising adversary, the aggressive Jackson prevailed on his friend and fellow Freemason, Tennessee congressman George Washington Campbell, to induce the secretary of war to intervene. The government, he asserted, had to fulfill its obligation to relieve its distressed citizens, "the people who have so often complained without redress." And again, "If redress is not afforded, I would despise the wretch that would slumber in qu[i]et one night before he cutt up by the roots the invader of his solem rights." This last, dramatic metaphor calls up the hallowed image of Jefferson's Declaration, of a people at war driven to extreme measures in defense of their natural right to liberty. Except Jackson was defining liberty as the "free and unmolested use" of a road.

Jackson pressed the congressman much in the way he had pressed Jefferson in the Butler matter, citing the "indignation of our citizens . . . , only restrained by assurances" that government would act as soon as notified of the "unwarrantable insult" posed by Dinsmore. As for punishment—

Jackson increasingly required punishment—nothing less than dismissal from office would do for "the many injuries that Silas Dinsmore has heaped upon our honest and unofending citizens." Jackson himself was not beyond discharging an emotional barrage, which he heaped upon the congressman in every paragraph: "surprise and indignation," "wrath and indignation," "wanton insult," "petty tyrant," "lawless tyranny," "injuries heaped upon our Citizens." He ended his appeal by qualifying the use of strong language: "it is the language that freemen when they are only claiming a fulfilment of their rights ought to use—it is a language that the[y] ought to be taught to lisp from their cradles." Conflating his own emotions with the citizens at large, Jackson concluded that the "publick mind," for some time "iritated," was now "ready to burst forth in Vengeance."

Whether or not he truly believed the "publick" to be enraged with the Indian agent, it was Jackson, acting alone, who made the move. He took to the road with "a considerable number" of undocumented slaves, some of whom he armed, and burst into Dinsmore's camp. Much to Jackson's chagrin, the "petty tyrant" was absent. He did not get the showdown in person that he desired, but he went on to agitate in an effort to achieve a victory over Silas Dinsmore. And in a way he succeeded, because Dinsmore was never again in a position to challenge western travelers. He was called to Washington to clarify certain expenditures, then became patriotically involved in the unfolding War of 1812. Embroiled in the Lake Erie naval campaign, he eventually returned to Choctaw territory, only to find himself replaced. The story goes that this poor, forsaken "wanderer," who had overzealously approached his job as the Indians' protector, encountered Jackson some years later. No longer the man he was, Dinsmore expressed a desire to reconcile. Jackson, however, "glared upon him with the wrath of 1812 in his eyes." Whether or not the incident took place as described, it suggests in part, perhaps, what it was that Jackson meant by a redress of grievances.[6]

Burr

These incidents all point to the uncomplicated logic underlying Jackson's desire to enact moral order in the years before he finally went to battle on behalf of the United States. He wanted to serve as "rescuer," and only needed to be convinced that his advocacy or actions would contribute to securing justice for those he believed required protection. That is why the timing of Burr's appearance on the scene is important: no longer a judge,

4. *Aaron Burr, frontispiece to*
James Parton's early biography.

identifying with Thomas Butler in feeling abused and unfairly punished for having defended the principles of honor and justice, Jackson was ready for a new opportunity. He was always looking for his next chance.

When Aaron Burr—Colonel Burr, as he was ordinarily addressed— first visited Nashville in the spring of 1805, he drew admiring crowds. The ex–vice president exuded confidence. His reputation in the West had not been overturned by the slaying of Hamilton, an eastern elitist, who was seen as an arrogant power broker and was never popular in Tennessee. Burr had gumption. And in person, he could be an extremely charming individual. He was highly intelligent, spoke in solicitous tones, and entertained an audience with exceptional flair.

Ten years Jackson's senior, Aaron Burr had performed heroically in the Revolutionary War. He was not yet twenty when he volunteered and braved the hardships of the 1775 assault on Quebec. As the scion of early American spiritual leaders Jonathan Edwards and the Rev. Aaron Burr, the latter a president of the College of New Jersey (Princeton), he was as polished and conscientious about appearances as Jackson was brazen and uncultured. Like his father, whose name he shared, Burr was small in stature but possessed of a prodigious mind.

He had had a privileged childhood, but also a complicated one. His mother and father and grandfather Edwards all died when he was too young to appreciate their example, and he was raised by an apparently stern Calvinist relative. The youth was too lively for such a constricted environment, and found a means to advance independently when he was admitted to Princeton at the age of thirteen. One of his fellow Princetonians was the slightly older future president James Madison. Burr's pedigree pointed him toward the ministry, but after a brief flirtation, he turned to law.

Then the Revolution intervened, and the spare, spirited nineteen-year-old joined Col. Benedict Arnold's expedition to Canada. He endured the cold, wet wilderness, toting a heavy musket and knapsack as the deadly, abortive assault proceeded over several months. He saw cannons explode and comrades fall in great numbers. His commanding general, Richard Montgomery, was left dead in the snow. Arnold, too, was wounded. And Burr, a survivor, was untouched by any bullet. He arrived back from Canada, and proceeded to New York City in time for the British rout of Washington's forces in the late summer of 1776. Though witness to another American debacle, Burr performed ably, guiding a retreating brigade away from their British pursuers. One of the companies he led to safety was that of an artillery captain, a brash, young officer like himself—Alexander Hamilton.

A lieutenant-colonel by mid-1777, Burr enjoyed all but the idleness of the soldier's life. He proposed to General Washington a plan by which he himself would lead an assault against entrenched British forces on Staten Island. The plan was rejected, but the young officer was able to prove his toughness in another way, when his insistence on harsh discipline resulted in a mutinous attempt against him: he ended it instantly by slashing the ringleader's arm with his sword, as the man aimed a musket at him. If Jackson was ever made aware of the incident, he would surely have approved Burr's method.

Burr had the guts to express his diminished regard for Washington, whose lack of military genius concerned him. Young as he was, Burr displayed an outspokenness that would long distinguish him. He took chances. During the war, he kept company with the wife of a British officer posted to the West Indies, though her position made her suspect as a probable Tory. Her New Jersey home, coincidentally called the Hermitage, housed her and her five children, two of whom were in the British service. Theodosia Prevost was ten years older than Aaron Burr, and a close friend of soon-to-be traitor Benedict Arnold's wife. After her husband's death became known and after the fighting ended, Theodosia would become Burr's wife, in 1782.

Burr's budding career remained on track. He set up home in New York City, and began to practice law along with other young men who rose to prominence during the Revolution. For the next twenty years, his legal as well as political career paralleled that of Hamilton. They sometimes faced each other in court, other times allied as cocounsel, but in politics these equally agile and ambitious men drifted in opposite directions. Hamilton made his way under the aegis of Washington, while Burr advanced more or less on his own. Though aided at different times by the powerful Clinton or Livingston families, he was permanently associated with no one faction. He made headway as New York State attorney general in 1789, rising to the U.S. Senate in 1791, where he served through 1797. He became Jefferson's ostensible running mate in the presidential election of 1800, after delivering New York out of Federalist hands.

It was that election which marked a shift in Burr's fortunes. In an accident of voting procedure later remedied by a constitutional amendment, Burr tied with Jefferson in the electoral vote count. His questionable loyalty to the intended president (in the minds of some) arrested Burr's course; during the three-month interlude before the electoral deadlock was broken, a number of his fellow Republicans ceased to trust Burr's motives. On assuming office, President Jefferson marginalized Vice President Burr, depriving him of patronage power in the determination of federal appointments in his home state of New York. He would be dropped from the ticket in 1804, and replaced with another New Yorker, former governor George Clinton. The combination of Burr's estrangement from Jefferson, and Hamilton's vicious (and open) efforts to deny him political leverage of any kind, led inexorably to their infamous duel—and, no doubt, to the fugitive's subsequent hunger for adventure.[7]

There is no way to know whether the Jeffersonians' suspicions about Burr were well founded. Jefferson himself declined to make any public comment on the occasion of Hamilton's death. Even his curiously worded letter to Virginia ally William Branch Giles smacks of posturing: "Against Burr, personally, I never had one hostile sentiment," he wrote. Yet this is followed directly by a hostile implication: "I never indeed thought him an honest, frank-dealing man, but considered him as a crooked gun, or other perverted machine, whose aim or shot you could never be sure of." Jackson and Burr had gotten on exceedingly well during Jackson's term in Congress; they resumed communication around the time of Burr's first visit to Nashville, in the spring of 1805, when the New Yorker stayed with the Jacksons. Burr's need to recover lost status would have made sense to Jackson. Also, Burr understood the western mentality, that fierce spirit so well embodied in Jackson's competitive, open-book strategy for development. Jackson's 1805 Fourth of July volunteer toast went, "The rising greatness of the West—may it never be impeded by the jealousy of the East."[8]

That summer, amid travels, the unemployed former vice president wrote his daughter Theodosia back east, expressing sympathetic feelings toward the people of Nashville, whom he termed "sensible, well-informed, and well behaved." Enjoying domestic life at the Hermitage in the intervening year between his sensational duel with Hamilton and Jackson's with Dickinson, Burr commended his host for being "a man of intelligence, and one of those prompt, frank, ardent souls whom I love to meet."[9] "Prompt" meant unhesitating, ready for action. "Frank" again spoke to Jackson's openness and sincere conviction (it also had the connotation of lacking deliberative restraint). "Ardent," in Jackson's and Burr's lexicon, meant passionate and fierce.[10]

As Burr prodded Jackson on the Spanish issue, he figured he had found a military man with personal pride and a heart set on adventure, just as he was. To such men, strong measures required risk. As Jackson was probably aware, the former (and future) New York attorney handled the divorce cases of women who, like Rachel in 1789, were willing to go to lengths in order to be free of the past. One such woman, Maria Reynolds, had been a mistress of Alexander Hamilton; it seemed that, in more ways than one, Burr had made a habit of seeking out those with hearts set on adventure.

In June 1805, on the eve of his departure for New Orleans, Burr wrote Jackson a hasty note: "If I can be of any use to you in Orleans, pray command me."[11] Two months later, when Burr returned to the Hermitage from his travels south, he and Jackson appeared to share the view that the U.S. government was insufficiently attentive to the possibility of a conspiracy: Spain, and possibly France, they thought, might act to put an end to America's authority in the territories and undo the Louisiana Purchase of 1803, taking back New Orleans. Fears of dismemberment of the Union were palpable in letters of this time among leading citizens and in the press. Burr was tapping into a ready market for action.[12]

Jackson's impression about foreign threats hardened over the next year, as Burr wrote to him from Washington that there was "great reason to expect hostility" from the Spanish, involving the seizure of American vessels "and measures taken for the reduction of Orleans." The necessary force to repel such an assault would have to come, Burr kindled, "from your side of the mountains." His letter highlighted President Jefferson's unmartial qualities and ended, "All these things, my dear sir, begin to make reflecting men to think—make many good patriots doubt and some to despond." It was a striking appeal that played into Jackson's apprehensions and sense of prospect all at once. Jefferson had proudly written Jackson in 1803 words that Jackson must have greatly appreciated at the time: "The acquisition of Louisiana is of immense importance to our future tranquility, inasmuch as it removes the intrigues of foreign nations to a distance from which they can no longer produce disturbance between the Indians & us." Burr may have been baiting Jackson, in one sense, but Jackson was not easily duped. He had had his own suspicions about the Spanish ever since William Blount developed designs to acquire land from the French and Spanish long before the gallant Burr came to town.[13]

When Burr returned to Nashville once again in late September 1806, the controversy over Jackson's duel with Charles Dickinson and his quarrel with Thomas Watkins were still fresh. Enjoying Burr's company as he had the year before, Jackson was assisted by Thomas Overton, who enlisted the good name of the creditable Gen. James Robertson, in arranging a public dinner for Nashville's guest—the man Jackson now extravagantly referred to as "a true and trusty friend to Tennessee." To Brig. Gen. James Winchester, he wrote: "Should there be a war this will be a handsome theatre for our enterprising young men."[14]

Whatever his ultimate plan was, Burr expected to collect an expeditionary force in Kentucky and Tennessee and float down the Mississippi. One whom Burr had charmed, Senator John Smith of Ohio, said that Burr intended to foment revolution in Mexico, possibly with both British and American naval support. Jackson was in charge of building boats for which Burr had paid in advance, at his Clover Bottom boatyard. Believing that Burr was not doing anything that Jefferson was unaware of—or else to cover himself—Jackson wrote the president, "In the event of insult or aggression made on our Government and country from any quarter . . . , I take the liberty of tendering [Tennessee's volunteers'] services, that is, under my command."[15]

The tide turned. In November 1806, Burr was brought before a grand jury in Frankfort, Kentucky, and charged with making military preparations. He was defended by the rising young Lexington attorney Henry Clay, soon to be a U.S. senator. Jackson grew suspicious when word of the Kentucky charges reached Nashville, although Burr was not found to have broken any law. Burr had told Clay, as he subsequently told Jackson, that the Jefferson administration was not unaware of his activities. But this time, when he showed up at Jackson's doorstep, Burr was greeted indifferently and obliged to lodge at the Clover Bottom tavern. A few days later, in his role as major general of the 2nd Division of the Tennessee militia, Jackson issued an order alerting all to the "hostile appearance and menacing attitude" of the Spanish government, instructing his men to be "ready to march."[16]

Something was up. What it was remained unclear, though Jackson's altered impression of Burr's enterprise apparently had something to do with information linking Colonel Burr to the hated General Wilkinson.

Treason? Jackson's Ambiguous Position

Jackson characterized the prevailing uncertainty when he wrote the governor of Louisiana Territory, William C. C. Claiborne: "I fear there is something rotten in the State of Denmark . . . , the Ides of March remember." His paired allusions to *Hamlet* and *Julius Caesar,* both conspiracies of tragic proportions, were unusual references for one who ignored most literature. An attack might occur, Jackson warned Claiborne, from "your own Country" just as likely as from Spain.[17] Either Jackson smelled treason or he knew enough to anticipate the federal government's reaction. Had he turned against Burr? It would seem so. But at Burr's later trial, the ambiguity of Jackson's performance would temper that conclusion.[18]

To express distrust of Burr's activities was now the order of the day. The *Impartial Review* reprinted stories from eastern papers, which further served to set Tennesseans against their erstwhile friend. "Col. Burr, for some cause or other, has, during the last 18 months, been traversing 'to and fro' in the western country," the *Charleston* [South Carolina] *Courier* reported. Implying that a man needed a wife to succor him when he was no longer publicly employed, the columnist suggested that Burr had nothing left to do in life but resort to the cultivation of an unhealthy ambition. "The affair of killing Hamilton has driven him from his former residence at New-York. He has no wife—no rising family to induce him to forget his chagrin of disappointed ambition in the solace of domestic comforts." Intimations that Burr had somehow been driven over the edge resulted in a night of angry demonstrations in Nashville. On December 30, 1806, Burr was publicly burned in effigy by a group of men termed "patriotic." The *Impartial Review* assured its skeptical "Atlantic brethren" that the people of Nashville were staunchly loyal to the president, and that if Burr had been "conspiring to dismember our government," they had no part in it.[19]

Jackson had a unique perspective. More than Burr, the villain in his mind was Burr's chief contact in the area of New Orleans, Gen. James Wilkinson.[20] Their disagreement over Thomas Butler and the military's hair code had occurred two years earlier, and it still rankled. In this instance, Jackson's was by no means a lone voice: a Richmond, Virginia, newspaper editor had recently identified Wilkinson as a schemer by nature, a man without convictions who had devoted himself to "frivolous pomp; his obsequious court to every administration and to every party."[21]

After encountering the oily Wilkinson up close, in Richmond, at the time of Burr's eventual trial, Washington Irving would lambaste him in his 1809 political satire, *A History of New-York*. Here Wilkinson was thinly disguised as the fictional Gen. Van Poffenburgh: "His dress comported with his character, for he had almost as much brass and copper without as nature had stored away within. . . . His head and whiskers were profusely powdered, from the midst of which his full-blooded face glowed like a fiery furnace." The pompous Van Poffenburgh possessed the "ambition . . . to be thought a strict disciplinarian," and so he obliged each soldier "to turn out his toes and hold up his head on parade"; and then, "in an evil hour, issued orders for cropping the hair of both officers and men." There was a Butler figure in Irving's mock drama named Kildermeester. He was "a sturdy veteran, who had cherished, through the course of a long life, a rugged mop of hair . . . , terminating with an immoderate queue like the handle of a frying pan." Kildermeester not only resisted the general's order to cut his "eel-skin queue," he swore liberally—"discharged a tempest of veteran, soldier-like oaths"—and arranged his queue "stiffer than ever," vowing "that he should be carried to his grave with his eel-skin queue sticking out of a hole in his coffin." In this wonderfully absurd morality tale, the Wilkinson character was plagued by "bad dreams and fearful visitations" after Butler/Kildermeester's death from fever.[22]

At no point in his public career did Jackson display an appreciation for parody, at least not in existing records. Rather, as it pertained to Wilkinson, the utterly implacable Tennessean was attuned to new dangers. He sternly reminded Governor Claiborne of Louisiana Territory: "keep, a watchful eye on our General." To Tennessee senator Daniel Smith, at the same time, he painted a fearful scenario for a disintegration of the Union, in which he imagined General Wilkinson lurking in the wings, waiting for his chance to become a dictator: "the precedent set, in the case of Colo. B[utler]" had convinced him of this. A tyrant did not change. That, simply put, was how Jackson regarded Wilkinson's plot. "I as much believe that such a plan is in operation," he wrote Smith ominously, "as I believe there is a god." While there was not proof at hand, Jackson had already indicted the detestable climber who, in his mind, was intriguing with Spain as certainly as he had intentionally set out to destroy Thomas Butler before this. Burr, by comparison, was harmless.[23]

The letter to Smith is long, and it is filled with the familiar Jacksonian vocabulary. Jackson rhetorically searches out "deep designs . . . ripe for execution"; he is reminded of "rapacious hands"; he notes that "some such plan is on foot," that "a designing man forms an intrigue," and that what is made to appear one thing is "only a cover to the true object." Nothing is so reprehensible to him as men who pretend to be loyal and prove otherwise. A sense of pride bursts from the knowledge that he himself is incapable of betrayal.

Jackson, it would seem, held grudges better than most. He was capable of histrionic outbursts, but in this instance he was joined by others. Wilkinson was a notoriously suspicious character. His relations with the Spanish over the years were secretive and possibly subversive, and certainly designed to enrich himself. He had met up with Burr in Philadelphia not long after the Hamilton duel, and again later on the Ohio River west of Nashville. He had been integrally a part of Burr's plan from then until October 1806, when he smelled failure and alerted Jefferson by letter. From that point, he became the instrument of Burr's destruction.

But if Wilkinson's treachery was apparent to Jackson and others,[24] it was not to the president of the United States. Jefferson was convinced that the greatest threat came from his former vice president. Wilkinson may have been tempted, but to Jefferson, the nervy general had finally cast his lot with the administration. Claiming to know better than anyone else what to expect of Burr, Wilkinson would next try to recover glory for himself by stopping Burr's army in its tracks.

Jefferson seemingly wanted to be taken in by Wilkinson's selective use of evidence. The general supplied him with a damning letter he had earlier received from Burr, which gave the conspirator's exaggerated expectations from the armed force he was in the process of forming. Doctoring the letter, Wilkinson removed a reference to "*Our* object . . . so long desired" [italics supplied] and replaced it with the more neutral phrase, "The project . . . so long desired," so as to make the object/project singularly Burr's. With this clumsy effort to protect himself, Wilkinson professed his own astonishment at the "magnitude of the enterprise, the desperation of the plan." The affectation of shock and bewilderment bore out Jackson's low opinion of Wilkinson, but Jefferson continued to find the general useful, if not credible.[25]

Foreseeing none of this, Burr sailed from Nashville to the mouth of the Cumberland, on the Ohio River, where word filtered back to Jackson that the suspect was in the company of "arm'd men with Boats loaded with arms and ammunition . . . with intentions hostile to the peace and interests of the United States." Burr's expectations at this point are unknown, though his demeanor did not change. He proceeded down the Mississippi and arrived at Bayou Pierre, above Natchez, where years before Andrew Jackson had tarried with the estranged wife of Lewis Robards. Here Aaron Burr finally learned that President Jefferson, on the basis of Wilkinson's information, had issued a proclamation disavowing him and warning the nation of his plot.

Overwhelmed by the knowledge that he was being hunted, Burr decided to surrender to civil authorities in Mississippi Territory. He feared what would happen if the unpredictable Wilkinson were to capture him, and he was right. Wilkinson had already offered $5,000 to Silas Dinsmore, the Indian agent later to torment Jackson, if Dinsmore would seize Burr. Incredibly, while Burr awaited trial, balls were given in his honor in Natchez—he was working his magic on its people as he once had the people of Nashville. His target, he assured them, was the mischievous forces hovering about Spanish territory; he entertained no prospect of dividing the Union.[26]

Burr had tried the same tactic with Jackson on his last visit to Nashville, vowing that he would produce orders from the secretary of war. How did Jackson feel now? His words read self-servingly, making it hard to determine with any certainty. In a letter to Representative George W. Campbell, he wrote of the "general indignation" felt toward Burr, affirming that "if he is a traitor, he is the basest that ever did commit treason—and being tore to pieces and scattered with the four winds of heaven [traditionally a punishment for traitors] would be too good for him."

Jackson is calculating here. He does not toss words out with the raw anger and spontaneity that characterize his charges in the Sevier, Butler, or Dinsmore episodes. He knew quite well what he was doing in the letter to Campbell, as he had in the letter he had written two months earlier to Tennessee senator Daniel Smith. Wrote Campbell of Jackson's epistolary effort: "Its contents have been perused and particularly attended to." Jackson's subdued tone provoked the Scottish-born Campbell, in his reply, to become the more animated of the two of them: "Many persons [in Washington] . . . believed B. capable of committing any crime, however *base & detestable,* that can be conceived of by human nature. . . ." Having protected himself at the federal level by producing a paper trail, Jackson now learned that Burr's former colleagues on Capitol Hill had come to feel that Burr was making himself "the *scoff and ridicule* of mankind, by attempting a *mad, extravagant project,* without the probable means of carrying it into effect." Because of Campbell, Jackson knew where things stood, and where he should stand.[27]

Meanwhile, Burr was released from Mississippi's jurisdiction because he had done nothing illegal there. Rather than wait to be moved to a different jurisdiction to be picked up by agents of the U.S. army, he decided to flee the scene: this is when the real drama began. The once sartorial vice president put on a humble disguise and headed east, perhaps to friends in Georgia and South Carolina, or possibly to seek temporary refuge in Spanish Pensacola—he might have supposed he had friends there as well. But he was spotted one night in southern Alabama, his face partly hidden under a floppy hat. An observant small-town land office official identified Burr and notified the nearest fort. The commander took Burr prisoner, and assumed responsibility for his transfer to the seat of federal authority, where he would stand trial for treason. There was, en route, one more adventure, when in South Carolina the prisoner vaulted from his horse and called out for a "magistrate," in a bid to escape. Undeterred by this event, the vigilant officer who held Burr delivered his prisoner to Richmond, Virginia. There, Burr's trial would unfold, presided over by John Marshall, chief justice of the Supreme Court, in his role as judge of the U.S. Circuit Court of Virginia. Andrew Jackson would be called to testify.[28]

One communication from Jackson in advance of the trial is of particular interest. In mid-March 1807, he composed a letter to Secretary of War Henry Dearborn, which the editors of the *Papers of Andrew Jackson* assert he most likely did not send. Sent or unsent, it speaks volumes as to Jackson's long memory and uncensored expression of moral indignation when he felt himself injured. The secretary had written to him the prior December, disrespectfully hinting that he believed rumors of Jackson's collusion with Burr: "it is industrially reported" among Burr's cronies, wrote Dearborn, that "they are to be joined, at the mouth of the Cumberland, by two Regiments under the Command of Genl Jackson."[29]

Jackson conceived his answer without regard to protocol. He accused Dearborn of retaining an unjust prejudice against him emanating from Dearborn's unseemly alliance with his "intimate friend" Wilkinson, in the Butler controversy. Once again, Jackson made Butler a paragon of virtue, comparing him this time with George Washington; and he asserted that all who had taken part in Butler's dismissal were villains. In Jackson's words: "The late Colo. Thos. Butler of the U. States army, who had spent more years in the service of his Country, than did the ever memorable Washington, under the Combined influence and villanous treatment of yrself and yr. much loved Genl. Wilkinson, died the death of persicution. . . . He was a man of Worth, of honest principle & incorruptibe hart." When Jackson was not relying on his pen to beget justice, it was to reveal that he could not easily remain silent.[30]

Summoned to testify at Burr's treason trial, Jackson was keenly aware of the division of opinion in Washington. He was inclined to be heard in the interest of justice—on a grand scale. There is scant evidence of what he said in Richmond, but there are enough revealing references to piece together his sentiments. Two prominent observers left records: Virginia congressman John Randolph, who informed James Monroe that Jackson "does not scruple to say that W[ilkinson] is a pensioner of Spain"; and prosecutor George Hay, who stated to President Jefferson that "Gen: Jackson of Tennessee has been . . . denouncing Wilkinson in the coarsest terms in every company." Parton recorded perhaps the most colorful image of this historic moment, but unfortunately he did not name his source(s): "there are those living," he put it nebulously, who heard Jackson on the steps of the state capitol, as he "harangued the crowd . . . , defending Burr, and angrily denouncing Jefferson as a persecutor." Parton's source may not be exaggerating: "persecutor" certainly sounds like Jacksonian invective.[31]

The man who was put on trial for treason along with Aaron Burr was Harman Blennerhassett, one who responded as Jackson did to the former vice president's patriotic adventure seeking. Blennerhassett conveys just how close Jackson came to being implicated in Burr's scheme. Born in Great Britain in 1764 and educated among the Irish gentry, Blennerhassett was married to his own niece and had been living on an island in the Ohio River for eight years when Burr paid a surprise (and welcome) visit in 1805. Like Jackson, Blennerhassett at first responded favorably to Colonel Burr's craft, humbly asking to be a part of any prospective action he might lead in a "Spanish War" launched in response to "acts of aggression and injustice" against Americans.

Burr had advanced his cause with Blennerhassett by invoking the name of General Jackson, and the thousands of troops he was to raise. Tennessee militia was to be called into the field in support of General Wilkinson, who was expected to take the first Spanish fire in Louisiana. Or so it all seemed. Later, as everything began to unravel, Blennerhassett, like Jackson, felt a kind of contempt for Burr's wily and secretive (and dangerous) notions. But in Richmond, the disillusionment eased somewhat, and the Irishman again sensed what had first drawn him to the agile New Yorker. Indeed, his emotional shift away from and then back toward support of Burr mirrored Jackson's position.

According to Blennerhasset's private journal, on one evening in September 1807, he dined with Burr and counsel, and listened to Burr spin a self-deprecating yarn, the gist of which was that the smooth-talking politician had exhibited the character of a "snake" in a sensual encounter with a woman. The topic of conversation somehow shifted to "our late *adventures* on the Mississippi—on which Burr said little," Blennerhassett recorded, "but declared that he did not know of any reason to blame Jackson of Tennessee for any thing he had done or omitted." By this time it had been more than two months since Jackson had testified.[32]

In Richmond, Burr once again managed to live a life of relative ease and unconcern, considering the gravity of the charges against him. "I have three rooms in the third story of the penitentiary," he wrote his daughter. "My jailer is quite a polite and civil man." The door to his comfortable cell was kept unlocked each day until after dark. His admirers brought a variety of fresh fruit, and it may be that other appetites were satisfied as well. "My friends and acquaintance of both sexes are permitted to visit me without interruption, without inquiring their business, and without the *presence of a spy*," he proclaimed. The accused continued to charm.[33]

Burr had evidently lied to Jackson in assuring him that the federal authorities knew about—indeed had approved—his plans. Jackson hated liars, of course. His letters are replete with self-satisfied proclamations of his own honesty and consistency. But something, it appears, caused Burr's lie to pale in comparison to a greater injustice. On the basis of what he saw and heard in Richmond, Jackson was surer than ever that, while Burr may have been politically ambitious, his plot was being exaggerated; it was Jefferson's fear and dislike of Burr that had led to the trial.

Jackson came to see through the defendant's eyes. A defense witness openly testified to the machinations Jackson already suspected, and that Burr was now able to perceive himself: previously, Secretary of War Henry Dearborn had verbally accused Wilkinson of "several crimes," but, like the president, he came to support the unsavory general in the interest of convicting Burr. Burr complained in a letter to his daughter about what Jackson was inclined to suspect as well, that when those in authority were complicit in spreading slanderous rumors, the public was prone to take them at their word. "The most indefatigable industry is used by the agents of government," wrote Burr, "and they have money at command without stint. If I were possessed of the same means, I could not only foil the prosecutors, but render them ridiculous and infamous. . . . Nothing is left undone or unsaid which can tend to prejudice the public mind, and produce a conviction without evidence." It was precisely the kind of abuse of power Jackson might rail against in earnest.[34]

So for Jackson, who knew that politics was personal, the facts did not warrant conviction. What caused him to speak up at the courthouse, with that bravado western settlers were known for, was a combination of his disappointment in the president (and secretary of war) and his impulse to protect the spirit of enterprise, the passion to possess land. The Spanish were, to the westerners' way of thinking, a threat to American expansion. Burr was preaching to the converted, so long as Washington did not disavow him. But, of course, it did.

The long trial ended, and Burr was found not guilty of the charges. But he was branded a conspirator and outcast by most of his contemporaries and by history alike. For Jackson, he was destroyed by a bumbling and mischievous administration as much as by his own presumption. For Chief Justice Marshall, whose demanding definition of treason all but insured the outcome, the verdict meant something else. Treason, by law, could not occur except as a crime involving the actual levying of war, not mere intent.

When, in Richmond, he carved out a position on Burr's activities, Jackson must have thought about William Blount's censure for his overactive imagination. Back in 1797, Blount had sought to prod a reluctant federal government to move against the unpopular Spanish authorities on the new nation's southern boundary. Yet few of those who supported Burr in Richmond shared Jackson's and Blount's western biases, nor did they adore the imaginative, reputedly catlike Burr, so much as they saw Jefferson as "bloodthirsty," to repeat the characterization made by Maryland's Luther Martin, Burr's attorney and a virulent Jefferson hater.[35]

The thin-skinned Jefferson was enough incensed at an attempted theft of his duly constituted power to conduct foreign policy that he fed the public's fear of Burr. The president had worked closely with the prosecutorial team to overcome the power of his one legitimate political rival, Chief Justice Marshall, whose assertion of judicial omnipotence vexed Jefferson nearly as much, it appears, as Burr's conspiracy did. Jefferson's actions were almost unethical, were he not legitimately afraid of forces of disunion. In his Special Message to Congress, he had charged Burr with having sought out "ardent, restless, desperate, and disaffected persons" and having "seduced good and well-meaning citizens."[36]

Jackson's animus was rather differently centered. A good part of his opposition to Jefferson—what bothered him more than the question of Burr's guilt or innocence—was how that grotesque and faithless power-monger, the unprincipled Wilkinson, remained in the president's good graces. In another letter to Senator Daniel Smith after the trial, Jackson frankly wrestled with the implications of Wilkinson's escape from justice. Writing about this was "a duty I owe my own feelings," he spelled out, ever proclaiming his feelings. There remained "heavy clouds of guilt" hanging over Wilkinson, while he, Jackson, had suffered for being wrongly suspected by members of the administration. He could nonetheless take pride in the knowledge that "I am still pure," while Wilkinson was, transparently, "raising suspicions against others—to hide his own guilt."[37]

Jackson seemed to write without first drafts, or at least he did not evidence concern that his letter-writing style would suffer if he repeated himself whenever feelings were engaged. This was apparently his way of demonstrating disbelief at a perversion of justice: Amplifying the earlier mishandling of the Butler matter, Wilkinson's misdeeds in the Burr conspiracy now extended to "an *attack* on the *integrity* of the *union*." The trio of italicizations serves to dramatize the artlessness, if not monotony, of Jacksonian political thought: *he* knew what patriotism was, plain and simple. Refusing to let matters rest, Jackson urged the senator to let the president know that he needed to "shake off this viper."

To Jackson's amazement, Jefferson was showing no signs of abandoning his poisonous ally. Why would the president "shelter" Wilkinson from "an indignant publick?" Jackson was encouraged by pamphlets being produced, which put before the nation the man's betrayals, "both as a pensioner of Spain and a colleague of Burr's." The starkness of the facts led Jackson, finally, to the crux of his appeal: "I name this to you," he bade the senator,

> knowing you to be the real friend of Mr Jefferson and the republican cause and let me once more and for the last time repeat that, if Mr Jefferson hugs this man to his boosoom they will both fail—this has been long my oppinion I am now certain of it—the Publick mind now plainly evinces it—and notwithstanding I have loved Mr Jefferson as a man, and adored him as a president, could I see him to attempt to support such a base man with his present knowledge of his corruption and infamy, I would withdraw that confidence I once reposed in him and regret that I had been deceived in his virtue—[38]

This is the most relentless of Jackson's criticisms of Jefferson, whose populism he would later be said to have inherited.

To the zealot from Tennessee, there was no excuse for misjudgment of a man's character. Given Jackson's unmistakable aversion to anyone who would ally with his enemy, he could not even imagine the *mariage de convenance*—far less warm than a real embrace—to Wilkinson by the president. But Jefferson, too, had a strong need to see justice occur on his terms. He felt antipathy for Burr comparable to Jackson's for Wilkinson. He was as unsatisfied by the result of the Burr prosecution as Jackson was by Wilkinson's retention of authority on the frontier. Politics was inevitably dangerous ground for one who, like Jackson, proclaimed, "I am still pure," or who, like Jefferson, dreamed and wrote so much about happiness and cast his philosophy of government in terms of "harmony and affection."[39]

Jackson had been designated, in some circles, a friend to Burr, despite his dramatic displays of patriotism and adherence to the administration's course at key moments. At this time, as he did so often, Jackson felt underappreciated, even undermined. His inclination was to react forcefully. The energetic letter to Senator Smith revealed an intensifying desire to restore his name in the West, "to shew my [friends] that the confidence once reposed in my patriotism and republican principles, have never been violated on my part." He still felt that he had much to prove.

An Explanation

What, then, had taken place that so rocked Jefferson's second term? What should we call it? A conspiracy? A mercenary scheme? An unorthodox means of prompting government action? All of the above? It is less a matter of "what" than a matter of degree as to how Burr's thoughts (and Jackson's) are best construed. Just as the frontier condition made law and society relatively fluid in the early Cumberland, the entire Southwest was full of suspicion, investment schemes, and possible plots long before Aaron Burr entered the picture. The Mississippi River was of immense strategic value; that was why Jefferson had jumped at the chance to acquire Louisiana from France in 1803. He acted with dispatch, bypassing Congress. The oft-juggled territory (recently ceded back to France by Spain) involved the interests of the United States, France, Spain, and England—not to mention, of course, the Indians of the Southwest. Ambitious men, from George Rogers Clark at the end of the Revolutionary War to William Blount in the mid-1790s to James Wilkinson and Aaron Burr, all ruminated about prospects they saw here. Each man aimed to capitalize on political disorganization and the hardiness of Anglo-American settlers.

All the expansionists—including Andrew Jackson—felt that the U.S. government was behaving in too cautious and restrained a manner in confronting the Spanish, with so much land at stake. All espoused the western frontiersmen's desire for an empty horizon. Except for the puffed-up Wilkinson, who seemed to have only self-serving plans, the others believed in the Union and were convinced they had their government's true interests at heart. Western land was regarded as a zero-sum game: the most timely, the most adventuresome, the most expeditionary would win it. The way to avoid trouble, the expansionists understood, was to put as little incriminating information on paper as was possible while attracting powerful political cronies and raising a committed force. Eventually the government would acquiesce—as in the later case of Texas. The expansionists all saw the weakening of New Spain. What made Jackson different from the others was his refusal to stick his neck out unless he felt the War Department would back him up. This is absolutely key to understanding Jackson's future actions on the ground, actions that made him "heroic" in the minds of a majority of the people and made it difficult for the U.S. government to disown him.

Jackson's early patron, William Blount, was ready in 1797 to undertake an expedition against the same forces Burr wished to engage in 1805–6. Indeed, Blount and Burr were friendly; Blount's New York agent had conversations with then-Senator Burr.[40] These men perceived that destiny lay at New Orleans: why else was Wilkinson still there? Back in 1787, when U.S. authority was most tentative, Wilkinson had approached the Spanish governor with a plan to join the unattached territory of Kentucky to the Spanish regime. More than anyone else, perhaps, Wilkinson understood how power was configured in this hodgepodge region, which was precisely why Burr was drawn to his eventual betrayer.

Explaining strange bedfellows is not easy, but the entanglements we see here among the expansionists were in a certain sense unavoidable. These men were all part of a political genealogy and well known to one another: shortly before his plot to undermine the Spanish came to light, Senator Blount met for an intimate dinner in Philadelphia with then–Vice President Jefferson and the ever-intriguing General Wilkinson. It should hardly seem a coincidence that Jackson, who was beholden to Blount, was later responsive to Burr, who shared Jefferson's nationalist goals even if he could no longer run for office on Jefferson's ticket. The common denominator was New Orleans, where Jackson's future fame resided.

Why did Jackson not immediately perceive the danger of supporting Burr? Neither he nor any adventure-bound westerner wanted to suspect

Burr, hoping, as their predecessors had, that the central government was along for the ride—or soon would be. Burr was a gathering storm when he arrived in Nashville. He knew whom it was that he needed to rely on in order to be the catalyst, to fulfill the expansionists' common dream. He name-dropped, charmed, and held out promises. It was more than a con game—far more. Some inspired and inspiring American was destined to triumph here.

These tenacious men, the players in a western drama that already went back twenty years, wanted land for Americans and for themselves. The military might of the western states' militia was there to assist them, until the armed forces of the United States were called in. The trick that one of them had to pull off was to avoid jeopardy under the Constitution without abandoning what could only be called an extralegal enterprise. Among them, none but Jackson would succeed. And why did he? Because he was probably the least greedy, and he would be able to manipulate the politics of character so much better than Blount, Wilkinson, or even Burr could. That was Jackson's recipe for national renown: proclaiming his purity, as a mirror of the American heart. Even so, he just barely got away with his law-breaking, as we will see over the next two chapters.

Coda: Another Violent Scuffle

It has already been abundantly proven that Andrew Jackson never let up. Nor did controversy cease to follow him. As he was leaving Nashville to attend Burr's trial, a Davidson County grand jury had issued an indictment against him for "assault with intent to kill." On his return from Richmond, the case was at last heard. The man he was alleged to have intended to kill was Samuel Jackson.

This Jackson (no known relation) had been a party to conversations during the controversy over the forfeit notes offered in payment of the abortive Truxton-Ploughboy race. As a witness to the spiraling argument that ended in the death of Charles Dickinson, he had made his position known by giving his "oath" as to the correctness of Thomas Swann's understanding of who said what—by imputation, he questioned Andrew Jackson's interpretation of events. Complicating matters, Samuel Jackson had alienated himself from the Swann-Dickinson faction as well, over money matters, and was deemed a "rascal" (the opposite of "gentleman") by both of the feuding sides.[41]

The constant resort to litigation, publication, and violence in Andrew

Jackson's ultramasculine sphere is a phenomenon: every dispute seemed to result in a vigorous challenge and a lengthy argument. Women were not generally mentioned in these affairs, nor were they meant to be made privy to them (though it can be assumed they were within earshot or within sight of many manly confrontations). Yet it was on behalf of vulnerable womanhood that the gentleman's code was meant to be upheld. Men as protectors were supposed to prove their masculine "virtue" by qualifying as "gentlemen" in the eyes of other "gentlemen."

Andrew Jackson and Samuel Jackson had conducted business in land and slaves, and seem to have been on rather friendly terms from the late 1790s. Each would have recognized the other as a gentleman. Samuel was a dozen years Andrew's elder, a horse-racing enthusiast, with extensive commercial interests in Philadelphia. The two Jackson families socialized.[42] Yet on March 6, 1807, the temperamental general, unprovoked (according to testimony given in the indictment), "did Strike & thrust" Samuel "above the Short ribs" with his cane-sword, in an attempt at murder. John Overton, in defending presidential candidate Jackson in 1828, was obliged to explain away this incident, just as he had tried to iron out the irregularities of Andrew and Rachel Jackson's frontier marriage. According to Overton, Samuel Jackson had been the provocateur, throwing a "large rock" at the general's head, then stooping to grab another when the general, taken by surprise, removed his cane-sword and thrust it through "a loose coat that Sam Jackson had on, but not his flesh." A "violent scuffle" then ensued, which was broken up by bystanders.[43]

Whether or not the bystanders saw any blood—whether or not Samuel Jackson suffered any wound—is difficult to determine. The issue was more one of character and reputation, and whether Andrew Jackson had had his taste for blood satisfied when the obnoxious Dickinson fell. Samuel Jackson was a scrappy, enterprising frontiersman like Andrew Jackson himself. He chose not to prompt a fatal confrontation, but to seek to recover his honor in court. Whatever their falling-out was, it had not produced in Andrew Jackson the same kind of disgust that he felt toward the upstart Dickinson.

The jury heard the case in November 1807, upon Jackson's return from the Burr trial, and acquitted him of all charges. A few weeks later the two Jacksons were communicating civilly in an effort to resolve an outstanding business matter.[44] It was all part of the way of life in Jackson's Tennessee.

CHAPTER FOUR

Engaging the Enemy:
New Orleans

My mind for the want of provision is harassed—My feelings excoriated with the complaints of the men—I enjoy health—& may god bless you farewell.
—Jackson to Rachel Donelson Jackson, November 12, 1813

In his eulogy of Andrew Jackson, Levi Woodbury left posterity with a characterization to heighten the already palpable paradox: the Tennessee general, he said, was as personally tender and generous as he was publicly unyielding. Time eventually healed the impetuosity of the man, Woodbury explained, but nothing ever disturbed his fundamental sense of honor and decency. Political opponents had charged Jackson with "want of proper sympathies for the rest of mankind. But," said Woodbury, "in truth few men possessed more humane feelings."

Rather than offer vague generalities, the eulogist gave several examples. Jackson had shared his bread with the hungry soldier, gave alms to beggars, cared for his servants when they were sick, identified with the oppressed in society. Curiously, none of these examples manifest egalitarian principles. They constitute philanthropy, descending from a superior to a social inferior. Jackson was not a man who felt himself superior to others, Woodbury declared. But he was certain that he was meant to lead. The cabinet secretary continued to dodge the paradox:

> His iron will was mere firmness or inflexibility in the cause he deemed right. It was an indomitable resolution to carry out what conscience dictated. Judgment and the fruits of it, opinion and corresponding conduct, it seemed to him, ought to be inseparable. He knew of no compromise or tampering, or half-way measures. . . .[1]

Perhaps military values explained a certain inflexibility. What to Woodbury, and presumably his audience, appeared as acceptable allowances in the defense of moral right, to others might as easily translate into a repugnant insistence on the ability to define what is right for everyone.

Until 1813, when Jackson led troops into battle, his name may have been known outside Tennessee, but his political capital, it must be said, was modest. That year he began to make a difference militarily, and his restless, confrontational voice could not so easily be dismissed in official Washington. As he steered an army across the South and carved his road to the pinnacle of power, Jackson demonstrated that he was not above getting his hands dirty. His raw "humanness"—unmediated even by a proper education—was his political calling card. It followed him everywhere, even beyond the grave.

"I cannot disguise my feelings"

Jackson's protector, William Blount, may have died in 1800, but his half brother Willie came to assume the governorship of Tennessee in 1809, after Sevier had served out his second series of three successive two-year terms. The younger Blount was virtually the same age as Jackson. To come into the state's highest office, he had had to defeat former U.S. senator William Cocke, the same man Jackson had replaced in the Senate in 1798 as a result of the elder Blount's deft maneuvering.

The new Governor Blount continued to stand by Andrew Jackson. They had a history of friendship and cooperation. When a Knoxville business associate of Jackson named James Grant was engaged in the process of electing Tennessee's first member of the House of Representatives in 1795, he was open with Jackson about his personal preference, pronouncing Willie Blount to be his first choice for the congressional seat. He hoped Jackson would understand. At the same time, Grant confessed, he did not know whether Willie really wished to be in Congress: "Tho' I have not his sentiments on the subject yet—I think I am warra[nted] to say that if he would offer [himself for office] at all—he would not run against yourself."[2] When Willie Blount yielded and Jackson was elected to the House of Representatives, the Blount-Jackson accord was extended, as the Sevier faction, in this instance, was denied a patronage position. More than a decade later, Tennessee politics remained a perpetually strained popularity contest among "old hands."

It is hard to know just how close Jackson and Governor Willie Blount were, or whether their comfort with each other was a matter of compatible ambitions more than personal chemistry. At any rate, their many letters, while primarily conveying political news and frontier logistics, demonstrate how Jackson could act in concert with another man of influence. The chief subject of their preserved correspondence was military affairs or Indian policy.

An early letter from Jackson to Willie Blount, in 1798, is chatty and sarcastic, revealing a whimsical side. Apparently Blount had heard a rumor that then-Congressman Jackson was shot in the leg by a Northern antagonist. Remarking at once on the weather in Philadelphia and the reception he could generally expect owing to his exotic Southern manner in pursuing honor, Jackson reported: "I am in greater danger from the Ice, than from the Ball of a Northern Pistol." As to his legs, he made an intentionally ludicrous boast: "I do believe myself they are Pistol proof." Then he described congressional antics, in a frontiersman's vocabulary: "Sticks and Spittle, are substituted by the Eastern representatives, in Place of Pistols"; and he detailed the contests he had witnessed between "Spittle or tobaccho Juice" and "Tongues." He could joke about partisanship with Willie Blount, conveying "respects to your brother." And to Willie, he signed himself, "sincerely your Friend." Blount, for his part, remained solicitous and casual. He concluded an 1801 letter which asked for help in a land transaction, "I am with unfeigned esteem, Your friend." In that letter, too, he demonstrated a proper intimacy with "your good Lady," Rachel Jackson, conveying his own wife's "respectful compliments."[3]

As Blount assumed the governorship in 1809, state business dominated, but the tone of the correspondence remained robust and mutually supportive. Tennessee's new executive turned his attention to the frontier condition, and coordinated a policy aimed at once to defend against foreign encroachment and to deftly manage friendly and unfriendly Indian tribes. This was the moment when Maj. Gen. Andrew Jackson really began to consolidate his position.

Blount and Jackson saw eye to eye: the governor and the general despised inaction, and both perceived in Congress a dangerous timidity when it came to military readiness. Tennessee would have to set an example. "I believe," wrote Blount to Jackson, "if the people at home do not start some plan by which the militia of the Union can be well ordered &c. that we shall never have a respectable force in readiness to take the field." Americans had much at stake, he said, because "we boast the enjoyment of freedom." Jackson to Blount: "the Temporising spirit that appears to pre-vade in Congress under passing and degrading scenes, convince me, that let the pulse of the nation be what it may congress will try to paralise it."[4]

The difference in style is that Blount's letters are generally graceful, reaching evenly for oratorical persuasion, while the rougher Jackson con-tinues to exhibit his ready anger and frustration. Jackson takes everything personally, and his words retain a sense of outrage. He identifies offenses committed against the people, acts requiring an aggressive response. "Temporising" delay and "degrading" paralysis vex his wary judgment. "Dicipline" and "arms" are how he lists his priorities, noticeably putting discipline first.

Jackson's vision was of a citizenry up in arms, literally and figuratively. His syntax is strained, but his message undisguised: "Diciplined and anured [*sic* for inured, meaning habituated] to the duties of the field—when they are dismissed and intermix with their fellow citizens again the[y] will carry with them the knowledge of Tactics that they can difuse throughout our fellow citizens, will raise a military ardor, throughout the country." He was afraid, he said, that "military ardor" was on the wane and needed to be reignited before it was too late. Writing to William Eustis, President Madison's first secretary of war, he warned of "the hour of dan-ger," "the clouds of war," and prescribed, again, "military ardor."[5]

Jackson was closely attuned to military developments in the West at this time. It followed that he would eagerly take it upon himself to write William Henry Harrison in November 1811, after the portentous Battle of Tippecanoe, that "*the blood of our murdered Countrymen must be revenged—*That banditti must be swept from the face of the earth." Never disguising his intentions behind the gloss of fancy prose, refusing to wait for the exec-utive branch of the national government to make its case, he offered Har-rison the services of the Tennessee militia.[6]

The Indian peril that Harrison perceived as governor of Indiana Terri-tory since 1801 was brought on by his own empire-building designs. His scheme for the half-settled territories east of the Mississippi was not inconsistent with President Jefferson's policy of isolating and coercively relocating all Indians who refused to give up tribal culture and become domesticated on small, dependent farms. It was a policy that incoming President James Madison did little to alter after 1809.

The Shawnee leader Tecumseh and his brother Tenskwatawa, better known as "the Prophet," spoke for pan-Indian resistance to the encroach-ments of land-hungry American settlers. The widely traveled, oratorically impressive Tecumseh conceived a broad political strategy, while the Prophet projected a more frenzied, less studied reaction, emboldened by spiritual energy. The Battle of Tippecanoe was the result of the Prophet's impulsive bid to preempt Harrison's advance while Tecumseh was away, and Harrison's ruthless reply.[7]

From his first year as governor of Tennessee, Willie Blount discussed options with Jackson concerning the management of Indian affairs. He regarded Tennessee's remaining Indians as "tenants," whose relocation west of the Mississippi made sense in order to counter the European nations that were poised to stop America's expansion. "The time seems to be fast approaching," Blount wrote from Knoxville, "when it will be indispensably necessary for the general government to have Nations of friends settled on that their frontier [the trans-Mississippi West] . . . to gain strength in that quarter of our territory." The governor favored cultivating the already pacified Cherokees and Chickasaws, gently easing them across the Mississippi—acting to "secure the attachment of those nations for the United States for ever."[8]

In June 1812, Congress declared war on Great Britain, which nation had been to a certain extent orchestrating Tecumseh's activities. Now, under more pressing conditions, Blount and Jackson concurred that, as Jackson put it, "little confidence . . . ought to be placed in the aid or friendship of Indians." Yet at the same time, he wanted practical control over the tribes: "if they will go to war, those that are not for us must be against us." Jackson aimed to be just diplomatic enough to co-opt Indians by a combined show of strength and amity: "they will be obliged to be friendly with us to preserve themselfs—I believe self interest and self preservation the most predominant passion—fear is better than love with an indian." This was quintessentially Jackson's perspective on Indian relations, conveying his equally anxious speculation and unqualified combativeness.[9]

Jackson had long awaited the call of his country. Yet now, "when the din of war reverbrates from shore to shore," as he put it, when he was ordered into the field by the secretary of war, conditions remained, for him, far from perfect. He was to march his volunteer army to New Orleans and accept subordination to a man he utterly despised, Gen. James Wilkinson. "I cannot disguise my feelings," Jackson wrote Willie Blount. He would rather fight as a simple enlisted man, he said, than to accept the anonymity and disrespect he felt inherent in the orders from Washington. "There appears something in this thing that carries with it a sting to my feelings that I will for the present suppress," because, he said, his "beloved country" had to come before personal pride. "I will sacrafice my own feelings, and lead my brave Volunteers to any point your excellency may please. . . . all I ask is that we may be ordered to a stage where we may pertake of active service, share the dangers and laurels of the field."¹⁰

Jackson wrote as well to George Washington Campbell, now a U.S. senator, concerning the problem of Wilkinson's command: "Should we be ordered to join Genl. Wilkeson, he is so universally disliked by our citizens, that something unpleasant may arise." With obvious irritation, Jackson explained that his men were incensed when they heard about Wilkinson's authority over them, and were only mollified when they were told that Jackson himself would lead them. "Why then not let us have an officer," he pleaded, "in whom we have confidence, why corrode the feelings of an extensive & rising country in these trying times." His letters abound in references to "feelings"—his own and those he projects onto his men.¹¹

He had turned to his Tennessee Volunteers and pronounced the general order to defend the lower Mississippi. Showing characteristic zeal, he urged them, "with the feelings of a soldier," to warrant his faith in their ability, to honor their Revolutionary fathers, and "not prove themselves a degenerate race." The Jacksonian call to arms presumed that "Every Man of the western Country turns his eyes intuitively upon the mouth of the Mississippi." The destiny of Tennessee and the remainder of the West— especially bustling New Orleans—could not be separated.¹²

Jackson saw his chance. His feelings were strong, by his own avowal. He was unquestionably committed to achieving fame in war, and was only delayed by the time it took the government to pay the troops. Their pockets a little less empty, they were finally able to march south in early January 1813.

Men in dark clothes and hunting shirts, packing both winter and spring outfits (which they themselves supplied), made out their wills and left the Cumberland Valley. They sailed down the Mississippi River to Natchez, while the cavalry, under massively built Col. John Coffee, Jackson's trusted if yet militarily untested business partner, went overland, and arrived first. The Indians en route, Coffee wrote home, were "remarkably friendly and accommodating"—this could never be taken for granted—and food was plentiful. However, once in Mississippi Territory, the men received orders from Wilkinson to wait for further instructions. And there they waited, Jackson and Coffee admittedly eager for action, until word finally arrived from the War Department that their services were no longer needed; they were to deliver all public property (wagons and provisions) to Wilkinson in New Orleans, and return home without assistance from the army. It was a great disappointment, after all the excitement that had been generated and all the preparations that were made.

Jackson resolved to bear personal financial responsibility for bringing his young volunteers home, rather than leave them to their own devices hundreds of miles from Nashville. (Before the steamboat, the current of the Mississippi made return by water impossible.) Some 150 volunteers had fallen sick, and many of these men were immobile. And so it was, according to Parton, that Jackson acquired his reputation among the troops as a man "tough as hickory," who was considerate of his men's feelings so long as they accepted his sense of duty and discipline. "Old Hickory" was not only tough; he was generous. And while Wilkinson sternly warned Jackson not to disobey orders, the headstrong popular leader felt a higher authority demanding that he put his travel experience to good use, and guide thousands of youths past deep swamps and along the arduous roads that separated them from Nashville.[13]

He was still not an accomplished warrior, and the War of 1812 was not going particularly well for the United States either. But Jackson had proven himself a leader, and now he held a generalship over U.S. forces, not just Tennessee militia. His gamble paid off, too, because Washington eventually agreed to reimburse him for expenses incurred on the return of his army to Tennessee.

The Benton Interlude

Col. Thomas Hart Benton (1782–1858) had commanded an infantry regiment under Jackson on the indecisive march. Years later, after Jackson's death, and at the end of his own long career in the U.S. Senate, Benton recounted the manner by which his on-again, off-again political mentor got his first chance to lead troops. Jackson was distrusted by Madison's advisers, in part because of his habit of making enemies, in part because of his former association with Burr. But one winter day early in 1812, Benton rode out to the Hermitage, battling mud and ice and wind. He proposed a plan for raising volunteer companies, twice the number of men as were in the draft militia—men who were singularly attracted to the prospect of Jackson's generalship. Given this gift, Washington could not deny Andrew Jackson his command.[14]

Thus Benton rose in his general's esteem. They remained close throughout the Natchez episode. When the troops received the order to disband, Jackson asked Benton to travel to Washington to present his claims to the government and win compensation. Benton stayed in the capital nearly a month, and while he complained to Jackson by letter that "things go on but slowly here," he was also able to report his ultimate success.[15]

Upon his return to Nashville in July 1813, Benton had to confront an abominable situation. The man he so admired, and on whose behalf he had labored so faithfully, appeared to have betrayed their friendship. While the young aide was gone, General Jackson had involved himself in a duel between another of his young officers, William Carroll, and Benton's brother Jesse. Jackson had taken the side of Carroll.

There is a single hint of a Benton-Jackson misunderstanding apart from the duel. It begins with shared hostility toward Wilkinson, and how that sentiment may have turned to distrust. When Jackson wrote his November 1812 letter to George W. Campbell, airing his true feelings while resolving to swallow his pride for the sake of his country, Benton had (as Jackson noted to himself) "approbated" the contents of the letter before it was sent to Washington. On his return to Nashville, Benton felt it necessary to remind Jackson that John Coffee had met with the field officers, while they were all still in Mississippi, to discuss whether to complain to the president about Wilkinson's command. In that instance Benton had demurred, pointing to the "unhappy effect" that such a complaint would have on the officers' future political prospects. What political prospects did Benton see for himself? Some question now lingered in Jackson's suspicious mind as to whether the politicking Benton had enlarged upon Jackson's sentiments in Washington—to Jackson's detriment—and whether Benton was somehow protecting himself by distinguishing his sentiments from Jackson's.[16]

As to the Carroll–Jesse Benton duel, none of the participants emerges with his dignity intact. Carroll had come to Nashville from Pittsburgh only in 1810, and his closeness with Jackson apparently irked some of the frontier boys. After his return from the Mississippi march, Carroll had had a dispute with another soldier, a friend of Benton, whom Carroll decreed was not gentleman enough to warrant his agreement to duel. The "gentleman" Benton stepped in and issued the secondhand challenge, which Carroll was obliged to accept. Thus two "gentlemen" met, with their seconds. Jackson stood witness as Carroll sustained a bullet wound in the hand, while Benton bent down, turned aside, and in his crouched position, took a bullet in his rear end.[17]

Learning of his brother's humiliation, Thomas Benton demanded an explanation from Jackson. But Jackson, in this instance, decided to show no compassion. He took offense at Benton's "reproach," and "conduct . . . of the basest kind," accusing *him* of being the one to have betrayed a friendship. Putting the onus on Benton, he self-righteously posed: "Has any act of my life towards you since I took you by the hand of Friendship and appointed you my aid de Camp been inconsistent with the strictest principles of Friendship?" He mentioned nothing of the duel.[18]

Benton's reply was lengthy, lawyerly, and indignant, spelling out point by point why Jackson's "agency" in the preventable duel made him accountable. Jackson's behavior had been "savage, unequal, unfair, and base." Savage, because the duelists were set only ten feet apart; unequal, because "the parties were made to wheel," an unfamiliar protocol to brother Jesse; unfair, because Jackson had "secretly" coached Carroll in the wheeling maneuver; base, because "you avowed yourself the friend of my brother while giving to his adversary all these advantages over him." Benton presumed he could predict Jackson's rationale, and that it would be to deny that in approving the wheeling maneuver he had done anything more than to state *Carroll's* preferences. So Benton deftly, preemptively denied Jackson the opportunity to offer any extenuating circumstance: "From your known influence over Mr. C," he insisted, "you might have managed the affair as you pleased; if not, you were at least a free man, and might have quit him if you did not approve of his course."[19]

This assessment of Jackson's impulses and state of mind may or may not be accurate, but Benton assuredly knew Jackson intimately. What is especially interesting here is that Benton regarded his mentor and military superior as one who was known for contriving to escape accountability, no less than he was known for seeking the limelight. Nor is it easy to determine how much weight to give the Wilkinson complaint in the Jackson-Benton dispute: it surely played a role in souring the atmosphere, but not the central role. "I shall neither seek, nor decline, a duel with you," Benton concluded his letter.

Jackson, though at least as hardheaded as his former aide, wished for no duel either. Yet he apparently went further than Benton when he boasted that he would horsewhip the younger man for his disrespectful language. He tried, on the other hand, to explain that he knew Carroll even better than he knew Benton—for Carroll had lived for some time under Jackson's roof: "I hope it will not be imputed as a fault, much less a crime that I have formed a good oppinion of another besides yourself."[20]

Jackson's brusqueness and sarcasm did little to defuse the situation. It was a little over a month after Benton's communication that Jackson and the Benton brothers came face-to-face at the City Hotel in Nashville. Tempers flared. There are conflicting reports about who fired first, but what is certain is that Jackson received a bullet in his shoulder and bled profusely. Brawny John Coffee and the equally massive Stockley Hays, son of Robert and Jane Donelson Hays, drew weapons as well, and it remained for several bystanders to step in and bring the nearly fatal fight to an end.

Thomas Hart Benton published his version of events a week later, while Jackson slowly recuperated. Jackson, he claimed, had "commenced the attack by levelling a pistol at me, *when I had no weapon drawn.*" Jesse, in turn, had recognized that if he did not shoot, Jackson would kill his brother; as Jesse fired, so did four other pistols, "in quick succession," and Jackson fell. To substantiate the lethal nature of the circumstances, Benton added, "The pistols fired at me were so near that the blaze of the muzzle of one of them burnt the sleeve of my coat, and the other aimed at my head, at little more than arms length from it." Stockley Hays, taking advantage of Jesse Benton's weakened condition (ostensibly the body part that had ached since the Carroll duel), wrestled him to the ground and "attempted to stab him." Carroll was not excused, though he was not present. According to Benton, "Capt. Carroll was to have taken part in the affray, but was absent by permission of General Jackson . . . which reflects I know not whether less honor upon the General or upon the Captain." Affecting embarrassment because of his participation in these uncivil acts, Benton decried the practice of dueling, though it be conducted under pretense of gladiatorial manhood.[21]

As Jackson divided his world into friends and enemies, Thomas Benton surely reckoned that his Washington journey, undertaken to fulfill a perceived debt of friendship, had backfired. He evidently caused his sponsor, who demanded utter loyalty, to doubt his trustworthiness. The talented Benton exhibited obvious ambition, and perhaps that ambition refused to wait for Jackson's anointing. Benton sounded not unlike Jackson at a comparable age, when he had struck Governor Sevier as an overreaching opportunist. Dangerous consequences frequently accompany private ambition—it is almost a truism to say so.

Perhaps the realization that he had crossed a line prompted Benton to allow his brother's juvenile quarrel to derail a promising Tennessee political career. Unlike his response to the Dickinson debacle, though, this time the orthographically inventive James Robertson, a barometer of sorts, found himself empathizing with the wounded general. He had heard Jesse Benton, "while lying wounded [after the Carroll duel], make maney unjest and imprudant expressions." But he did not expect the less precipitate Thomas Benton to "have gon on as I understood he did. . . . I under[stand] Jessee attemted to assasinate you, he sartainly has forfited all clame to that of a gentleman."[22]

Jackson was badly hurt. The timing was particularly unfortunate, because his greatest opportunity for battlefield distinction was suddenly upon him. Word reached Nashville that a party of Creek Indians, influenced by Tecumseh's message, had attacked Fort Mims, on the Alabama River, on August 30, 1813. As John Eaton tells the story, these Creeks were incensed by the application of American laws in executing murderous Indians and, "infatuated to the highest degree by the predictions of their prophets," took up their war clubs, red sticks with sharp iron secured at the end, and went in pursuit. At Fort Mims, a thousand of the Red Sticks attacked and killed nearly 300 people, including many women and children. As Nashville reacted, Jackson shared with John Coffee his concern that the Spanish and British would become involved on the side of the turbulent Creeks.[23]

The order went out for the volunteers to march again. "Brave Tennesseans! Your frontier is threatened by invasion by the savage foe!" It was not a time for hesitation, with "scalping knifes unsheathed" and innocents endangered. "The health of your General is restored," Jackson nobly announced in the newspapers in late September. "He will command in person."[24]

Creek War

What was it like to engage in Indian warfare at this time? Descriptions vary only in considerations of the Indians' humanity, not in the imagery drawn from these encounters. Particulars included the dress and decorum of the advancing enemy; the mutilation of the fallen; the charred, desolate ground; and the desperate moans of the wounded, who in all likelihood were bound to suffer and die. Participants recalled the shrieks of charging warriors, the shock of surprise, the moment of panic, the blood that ran in creeks, stupefied looks on the faces of the uninitiated, bodies discovered later that were blackened by frost and exposure or, if not, mangled and eaten by animals. It was not just battlefield scavengers who validated these images, but ordinary travelers, passing between isolated forts, who routinely came upon the bones and artifacts of these engagements—sometimes decades after the event took place.

The prevalence of disease and scarcity of food was terrible enough for Jackson's army. But as death was intensely felt in the frontier culture, death at the hands of "savages" was all the more dramatically depicted. For such reasons, victories were greatly romanticized: the national popularity of William Henry Harrison, whose presidential nickname was associated with a single battle, "Tippecanoe," is a case in point. He needed no other qualification than the one engagement to be considered "great." Likewise, "Old Hickory," who would shortly be dubbed the "Hero of New Orleans," enjoyed an accelerated national reputation as he acquired his nicknames. The enduring political value of frontier fighting is attested by the mass of nineteenth-century memoirs and the legends persisting in twentieth-century textbooks. In accepting the public usefulness of building an Indian-fighting reputation, Jackson was aware of what it had previously done for Jack Sevier. He accepted the less humane designations he would have to bear as a necessary, perhaps even desirable, part of representing his western world.

White Americans demanded safety. Indians who resisted their intrusion were said to be frustrating the "simple" desire for "peace" that small-scale, settled agriculture presented. Even Parton, writing on the eve of the Civil War, shared the dominant view: "The Indian is a creature who does not improve upon acquaintance. Living near a tribe dispels so much of the romance. . . ."[25] These words sound obnoxious to modern ears. But on the frontier, beyond places like Nashville (by this time more secure in the belief that most Indians could be intimidated when necessary), distressed living conditions prompted emotional responses that only much later became unacceptable.

As Indian lands were carved up, the facts of topography began to produce a new psychology. Roads and settlements that had come to separate traditional Indian territories from each other caused Indians and whites alike to see a landscape to which both were unaccustomed: the Indians concentrated attention on the increasing numbers of settlers and squatters who foraged in their dwindling lands. Whites who designated certain Indian towns as "friendly" probably did not consider that the neighboring Indians were sizing up white towns in a comparable way. Mutuality demanded essential equality, but a federal government that mouthed a patronizing rhetoric expected its own definition of "reasonable" behavior to be understood by its subject peoples.

From the Indians' point of view, it was important to tread quietly but also to remain assertive in the midst of the aggressors who by now greatly outnumbered them. They clearly did not wish to permit ranging whites to march through their country, killing their game and fouling their water. It was difficult enough to restrain reckless young Indians from attacking vulnerable parties of these intruders. The wise understood that every perceived act of aggression would result in the U.S. government's seizure of more land.[26]

The ethnic mixture that Jackson's army faced in Mississippi Territory presented a complex picture. As one scholar has pointed out, the Creek War was as much an internal upheaval as a desperate reaction against white encroachment. Mixed bloods were prominent on both sides of the conflict. Elite mixed bloods (slaveholders interested in replicating the pattern of white social mobility) provoked Indian traditionalists to act to revitalize the thriving culture that had preceded massive white settlement. Opposing visions of Indian life turned violent. And what of the slaves themselves, caught in the middle? The well-to-do Creeks had been practicing a milder form of slavery than their white counterparts; thus there were black slaves along with their mixed-blood owners seeking safety inside Fort Mims. There were also black slaves who eagerly defected to the Red Sticks, wishing to kill whites and achieve freedom for themselves. Beyond Creek culture, the ill-defined Southwest, from New Orleans to Natchez and beyond, contained a variety of residents who exhibited fears and resentments, who lived heterogeneously, and remained uncertain about Spanish, French, British, and American intentions. Displacement, more than permanence, was the rule, both in Indian-occupied areas and in white towns.[27]

The experience of the Mississippi Choctaws offers a slightly different rationale for spiraling conflict on the southwestern frontier. In the past, Spanish governors had offered free land to American settlers, hoping that these people would transfer their allegiance to Spain. Over generations, as the settlers' numbers increased, an imbalance in trade between white Americans and their Indian neighbors led the Choctaws to "hunt for alcohol," that is, they were paid in rum when they delivered furs. Drunken Indians raided white settlements, a hopeless means, as one scholar explains, of mitigating the internal strife of a sad and slowly disintegrating culture. The Choctaws, "most powerful" of the Indian nations according to Secretary of War Henry Dearborn in 1801, quickly succumbed before an official policy intended at once to "civilize" Indians and acquire their land.

Each administration opened more land to white settlement. As impractical traders, the Indians participated in their own demise. Whites, meanwhile, looked for every opportunity to deny sympathy to Indians and to objectify a "wild" people—this justified their own expansion. A mutual lack of introspection explains why the two sides ultimately resorted to an emotion-filled vocabulary of power just as soon as cross-cultural communications stumbled.[28]

The immediate cause of Andrew Jackson's triumphant march against the Indians of the territories in 1813–14 was the Red Sticks' action against Fort Mims. With his arm still in a sling, Jackson pushed south into Alabama, slowed by an inconstant food supply. Galvanizing his forces, he adopted familiar language, emphasizing the need for "redress" of wrongs inflicted: "We are about to furnish these savages a lesson of admonition;— we are about to teach them, that our long forbearance has not proceeded from an insensibility to wrongs, or an inability to redress them."[29]

"I am anxious to reach the center of creek country," he wrote Col. Leroy Pope in Huntsville, "and give them a final blow." His realism was expressed to John Coffee, now a general: "I wish you to receive, & to treat with great kindness all such spies from the Creek nation [many Creeks disapproved strongly of the Red Sticks] as may offer you any communication. . . . We must have the truth; & whilst *that* shall be duly rewarded, false information must be severely punished." Friendly Indians, who included Cherokees, were to wear "white plumes in their hair, or Deer's tails."[30]

The first action took place at Tallushatchee, some forty miles south of Huntsville, in early November 1813, when Coffee's mounted riflemen, under orders from Jackson, encircled the Red Stick village and wrought devastation. "We shot them like dogs," related Davy Crockett, who was there. Not a single male was left alive. Fort Mims avenged, Jackson proudly reported the body count in a letter to his wife. More sensitively, he told the childless Rachel, "I send on a little Indian boy," orphaned in the bloodbath. Little Lyncoya would grow up at the Hermitage, along with Andrew Jackson, Jr., the son the Jacksons adopted in 1809, who was in fact the child of Rachel's younger brother Severn and his wife, Elizabeth. (Andrew Junior was one of a pair; the other twin, brought up by his natural parents, was named Thomas Jefferson Donelson.)[31]

After Tallushatchee, Jackson sought to establish a permanent depot in the area, and to pursue deeper into Creek territory. The next victory belonged to Col. William Carroll, who engaged the "concealed" enemy and beat back their frenzied charge, killing some 300 of the 1,000 or more who attacked. Jackson praised his colonel lavishly. To the general's consternation, however, limited rations prevented further movement. "The Creek war could now have been terminated in a few weeks," he wrote the commander of Georgia's army, were it not for this "want of supplies."[32]

No leader was ever permitted indecision, and Jackson was meant to be tested. His next major difficulty shook him to the core. To put it in the starkest terms, his army was without food, and he had on his hands what he called a "mutiny." It was December, and many of the men from poor families claimed that they "had not time to . . . provide themselves cloathing necessary for a Winter Campaign." They had enlisted for one year in December 1812, made the earlier abortive journey with Jackson, and had been mustered again into service after Fort Mims. They were under the impression that the inactive time between the first march to Mississippi and their current assignment counted as part of the agreed-upon twelve months. They understood that they could not be legally bound beyond December 10, 1813, just days away.

Jackson, hungry for military glory, was unimpressed with legal niceties. He read a first petition, which gave notice. It was the position of the majority of recruits as well as their officers: "They [the troops] say, and with truth, that with [their general] they have suffered—have fought & have conquered, they feel a pride of having fought under his Command. They have received him as an affectionate father, while they have honored revered & obeyed him." Jackson treated this language as a ruse, a cowardly deceit.

He replied at length that he could not predict what would occur on December 10, but that the result would not be "chargeable to any conduct of mine." Nothing would deter him, he wrote ominously, from carrying out "my duty." He referred to the soldiers' service as a "sacred pledge," minimizing the importance of the calendar. He promised that he would "pronounce their discharge" when it was given by the government, which he expected to occur soon. But, until that moment arrived, he sternly exhorted his men, they must undertake "the exercise of reflection," to demonstrate that the " 'Volunteers of Tennessee'—a name ever dear to fame," would never become "mutineers & deserters."[33]

Jackson himself was physically ill, and mentally distraught. He took out some of his hostility on Maj. Gen. John Cocke, whose army was positioned well east, but whom Jackson suspected of withholding supplies and undermining his campaign out of envy and spite.[34] After he learned that food was finally on the way, Jackson, joined by Coffee, rode out and met one company of his deserting troops head-on. He bellowed out that Coffee's men were to fire on any who should attempt to move past. None did. For the moment, a darker crisis was averted. In Parton's colorful account of the standoff, Jackson had fire in his eyes and invective on his tongue. "Few common men could stand before the ferocity of his aspect and the violence of his words. His ability at swearing amounted to a talent." Certain that he was morally right, the combustible general brooked no opposition.[35]

In a speech written with the aid of, and spoken by, Maj. John Reid, Jackson tried to rally the troops, reminding them of their recent successes: "The thunder of your arms was the signal to your enemy, that the slaughter of your countrymen would certainly be avenged." He sounded incredulous that these same fighters would so abruptly exchange "cheerfulness" for "complaints." "The heart of your General has been pierced," he lamented, with maudlin excess. Accepting his position as their "father," he found himself obliged to "suppress" his paternal feelings, he said, by resorting to the military code, and by threatening those who would desert camp. He had seen to it—he alone had seen to it—that they not disgrace themselves in the nation's eyes.[36]

To his wife, who appeared always to resign herself to the self-imposed demands of his career, he spared no information about his predicament: "I am sorry to say that my Volunteer infantry, in whom I had so much confidence . . . are about to disgrace themselves by a mutinous disposition in the face of an enemy, but the officers are more to blame than they men." After the intervention, he wrote to her again, hardly more optimistic: "we now have a prospect of ample supplies of provision, and no troops to eat it." And once more, two weeks later: "This was a grating moment of my life—I felt the pangs of an affectionate parent, compelled from duty, to chastise his child."[37]

Paternalistic language came easily to Jackson when he was invoking principles of honor, respect, and approval. He rationalized himself a natural superior within the military's caste-conscious surrogate family. Having risen to respectability over time as a property owner and state judge, he sought to enlarge further his authority. Within the military command structure the distinct masculine values of individual performance and personal loyalty merged: the soldier was meant to be an individual hero and a loyal follower at once. The military was, for Jackson, an idealized chivalrous fraternity (Masonic values in a warring situation) that supported a larger social harmony. That is why the prospect of mutiny threatened to overturn not just the general's personal authority but his faith in the social-izing effect that the military code was meant to have. Jackson idealized his role as the father figure in a brotherhood. His need to be appreciated in such circumstances was immense, but even more important, he refused to watch the destiny he imagined for himself slip away as it had before.[38]

One young officer, unswayed by the mutineers' interpretation of the terms of their enlistment, would profit from his loyal service by earning Andrew Jackson's solid friendship. Twenty-one-year-old Lt. Richard Keith Call, who had left school to fight under Jackson, approached the commander and asked to be transferred out of his "infected" unit—one of those that had forced Jackson's hand. Jackson refused, according to Call's later journal, at the same time crediting him: "if I had 500 such men I would put an end to the mutiny before the sun sets." As Cocke arrived with 2,000 men, Jackson's disaffected legitimately returned to Tennessee, though Jackson persisted in seeing all as malcontents. Lieutenant Call remained on hand to welcome the additional reinforcements who arrived in mid-January 1814.[39]

Jackson was in the process of collecting young men: Carroll was one, Benton—until he overreached—another, and Call a third. The impor-tance of the mentoring connection, especially in war, cannot be overesti-mated: friendship on Jackson's terms had very public consequences. It required a winning style of commitment, no better proven than on the bat-tlefield. It required one who understood authority and followed orders unquestioningly, who risked his life for the general, who stood his ground under constant fire. This meant everything to Jackson, and he was sure to reward those who gave him what *he* considered was his due.

With his new army forming, Jackson simply refused to be contained any longer. In December 1813, Willie Blount was prepared to accept limitations on his power as governor to order troops into the field. But Jackson, admittedly "wearied," wrote demonstratively to the state's executive, urg-ing him to rise to the occasion, to "cure the evil," and order a new draft. "I believe you have the power," Jackson prompted. "I believe every patriot, will Justify your exercising of it." Immediately, Blount acted to give Jack-son what he wanted—more men.[40]

Though confounded by logistical weaknesses, Jackson was adept at anticipating his enemy's moves. Capitalizing on the arrival of raw recruits, he marched to east-central Alabama in pursuit of the Red Sticks. On Jan-uary 22, 1814, forewarned of an attack by the several spies he had sent out, he stood his ground. The battle engaged; Red Sticks fired from behind logs and brush at irregular intervals. At one point, Coffee charged the concealed enemy and was repulsed. At another point, while the Red Sticks paused to reload, Jackson ordered brave Billy Carroll to charge, and it was Carroll who turned the tide of Emuckfaw Creek, as the battle became known. Coffee was seriously wounded in the fight (though he fought on), and Maj. Alexander Donelson, Jackson's aide and Rachel's nephew, was killed by a shot to the head. Coffee was married to Alexander Donelson's younger sister.[41]

It was at this moment that Jackson fully experienced the trials of war. He was in the middle of it now, close to the hottest action. He gave his wife details, holding back little while announcing his intention to see the war through to its end. She cried, "Oh my unfortunate Nephew he is gon," and uselessly begged her husband: "You have served your Country Long Enough you have gained maney Larells [laurels] you have Ernd them." As hard as the months of separation were for her, he was only beginning to realize his dream of battlefield honor. He replied to her mournful note the moment he received it eleven days later: "The brave must die, in a state of war the brave must face the enemy, or the rights of our country, could never be maintained—it was the fate of our brave Nephew Alexander Donelson to *fall*, but he fell like a hero. . . . we know we have to die." At least her nephew had died "roman like," and gloriously. As long as one's virtue survived, said Jackson, the living were meant to endure and accept the pain of loss. Thus he himself would be with her "on the wings of love & affection . . . the moment—I can with honor and safety to my country." Any sooner would be less than virtuous. He bade her, "my dearest heart," bear up "with fortitude."[42]

In Alabama, a war of nerves proceeded, and Jackson matched his determination to destroy the Indian enemy with a renewed insistence on military discipline. There were once again murmurs of resistance and threats of mass desertion. As a result, in March 1814, an enlistee named John Woods, not quite eighteen, became a martyr, and the enduring symbol of Jacksonian ruthlessness.

Woods happened to belong to a volunteer company of farmers whose supportive commander had made it clear from the outset that he was unwilling to commit his men to a length of service that would interfere with their growing season back home. Jackson, of course, would not be bound by conditions—subordination was a principle he did not negotiate. In this atmosphere of uncertainty and mistrust, John Woods stood guard duty one morning, in his first month of service. Cold and hungry, he sought permission to leave his post, and went to his tent to retrieve a blanket and have a bite to eat. An officer saw some discarded bones in the dirt and ordered Woods to pick them up, but he went on eating. There were words exchanged, and Woods refused to return to guard duty.

Jackson was shortly told of the incident, and construed it as mutinous. The offense should not have been a capital one, and had Jackson been told that Woods was not yet a part of the company when the earlier threats of desertion were made, the result might have been different. Troops along the frontier were almost always insubordinate and eager to go home. Congressman Burwell Bassett of Virginia had stated just a year earlier: "Our greatest difficulty results from what is our greatest boast, that our citizens are happy, and so independent, that they are unwilling to become soldiers until they feel the necessity." Owing more to existing circumstances than to subversive actions, Woods was convicted of mutiny, and Jackson saw to it that he was shot. The trial was held on March 12, "between two tents, the prisoner sitting upon a log." The sentence was carried out two days later and witnessed by the whole army. Jackson's position was that mutiny had to be stopped at all costs, the execution "essential to the preservation of good order."[43]

More Tennessee fighters arrived, thanks to the efforts of Judge Hugh Lawson White, who journeyed to Jackson's camp for a firsthand look, and helped raise a new army. That army included a twenty-one-year-old Virginia-born private named Sam Houston, who had come with his widowed mother to east Tennessee seven years earlier. As a teenager, Houston had left home, in an extraordinary resolve, to live with the Cherokees; he moved in and out of the white world at will, reading Homer's *Iliad* while chasing wild game and sleeping on the ground. This unusual, ardent young man, with his singular brand of loyalty, independence, and heroic display, would ultimately become the most "Jacksonian" of Jackson's acolytes.[44]

On March 27, Jackson led his revitalized force (which included friendly Cherokees and Creeks) against the persistent Red Sticks at Tohopeka, or Horseshoe Bend, a turn in the Tallapoosa River, not far from Emuckfaw. With support from Coffee's mounted infantry, he ordered his men over the high, compact Indian fortification and, to use Eaton's words, an "obstinate and destructive conflict ensued." Uniformed men and boys with fixed bayonets besieged the earth and log rampart toward the whooping, taunting sounds of a determined enemy. Billy Carroll again took part, and was wounded slightly. A private reported crossing the Tallapoosa just afterward to find his horse stained blood-red.[45]

One of the heroes that day was young Sam Houston, who vaulted the Red Sticks' fortification and was shot deep in the thigh with an arrow.

Jackson saw him at the field hospital and ordered him to remain on his back, but Houston disobeyed and returned to the action, this time receiving two rifle balls in the shoulder. The surgeon who examined him told Houston that he was likely to be dead by morning. Needless to say, he willed survival, and while slowly recuperating, the trooper wrote a Virginia friend that he did not mind a return to peace, though "the officers of the army would as soon war had continued."[46]

In the end, Jackson's men, with a three-to-one numerical advantage, exacted a great toll at Horseshoe Bend. "This battle gave a death blow to [the enemy's] hopes," wrote Eaton; "nor did they venture, afterwards, to make a stand. . . . In this action, the best and bravest of their warriors were destroyed"—557 left dead on the ground. Of Jackson's army, one-tenth of that number were lost. To make the body count accurate, the Tennesseans sliced off the tips of the dead Creeks' noses one by one. Some soldiers mutilated for other purposes, cutting long strips of skin from Indian corpses to make bridle reins.[47]

The Battle of Horseshoe Bend was certainly one of the most destructive encounters between whites and Indians in North American history. As a result, the Red Sticks were no longer a force of significance. Surviving warriors fled east to join the Florida tribes. The remaining Creeks submitted to harsh terms laid down by the victorious general that summer, ceding the greater part of their territory to the United States. Whether allied with or opposed to Jackson and the United States, the Creek nation was lumped together as one and left helpless and dependent. Jackson surveyed their wretchedness and deemed it unavoidable. To him, this was how all Indians, left to their own devices, would end up.[48] One Cherokee who fought with Jackson at Horseshoe Bend said much later that if he had been able to foresee the Trail of Tears, and Jackson's role in the ultimate removal order, he would have killed Old Hickory when he had the chance.[49]

Now a national military figure, the Tennessee militia's major general received appointment as a brigadier general in the U.S. Army. When William Henry Harrison resigned shortly thereafter, Jackson was elevated to major general in the U.S. Army. There was no higher rank.

The Presumptuous Edward Livingston

Jackson went on to distinguish himself at Pensacola in November 1814, attacking without orders from Washington and dislodging the preying

British who were being harbored by the ostensibly neutral Spanish. He arrived in New Orleans on December 1, to prepare the vulnerable city for the major assault that was bound to come.

The region extending from Spanish West Florida to New Orleans was an ethnic hodgepodge with uncertain loyalties. First settled by the French, the Spanish lands were by this time greatly populated by Scotch-Irish, and included former Tories who had fled the American Revolution. Land-hungry people of all types, as well as bandits, slaves, and mixed bloods, had little to fear from Spanish authorities, who were very much in the minority and poorly provisioned. The atmosphere prior to Jackson's arrival has been referred to as a "ponderous gothic drama": when the British sailed in, vague talk of insurrection and annexation was in the air, vigilante justice was considered, and American anxiety rose steadily. This was to be *somebody's* empire before too long.[50]

Jackson's sudden action at Pensacola gave a boost to Americans of the region who had seen too little of their country's might. A British force, only a fraction of the size of that which was already en route to the Gulf, had set fire to the U.S. Capitol and sent President Madison packing in late August. Jackson, ever impatient for confrontation, refused to become demoralized. He was all patriotic proclamations, rallying cries, and inspiration. He undertook vigorous measures. On the other hand, in New Orleans, Louisiana governor Claiborne (formerly a Tennessee congressman) had been fretting for months over the doubtfulness of citizens' loyalty: there were those, he said, "much devoted to the Interest of Spain, and whose partiality for the English, is not less observable than their dislike to the American Government." Connections between disaffected elements in New Orleans and their friends in Pensacola were known. Before he marched in, all Jackson could do was to exhort: "Whoever is not for us, is against us. . . . Summon all your energy, and guard every avenue with confidential patroles, for spies and traitors are swarming around."[51]

The general could count on few resources beyond those he could muster. He approached New Orleans worn down by dysentery. He also understood that he could afford no delay. One of the acts he took after his own appointment as U.S. Army major general was to promote William Carroll to major general of the Tennessee militia. He dispatched his trusted protégé to Nashville to form a new division of Kentucky and Tennessee volunteers, who were then to hasten down to New Orleans.[52]

In spite of his irritability, Jackson was aware of his intellectual limitations and knew how to attract capable thinkers to his causes. Among a handful of scholarly collaborators who saw in him a natural leader, the first was Edward Livingston, a key figure in the politics of early America. His friends were perpetually mystified by the depth of his intellect, the range of his wit, and yet the striking informality of his personal bearing.[53] Colleagues in Congress a long time before, Jackson and Livingston had once stood together, and stood apart, from the majority who had lavishly praised George Washington's administration. The two former congressmen met up once again on December 1, 1814, in what should have been an unlikely place: New Orleans. It was Livingston who would craft the richest historical documents to emerge from Jackson's anxious and decisive months in the besieged port as the War of 1812 headed toward its improbable conclusion. Livingston would be there as Jackson captured the national spotlight from which he would never again recede.

Edward Livingston is rarely given his due as a man of influence. Three years older than Jackson, he was born into what was arguably the most prominent family of New York State. The Livingstons, originally from Scotland, had established their dynasty over four generations by the time of the Revolution, active in law and jurisprudence as well as diplomacy. Of the eleven children of Judge Robert R. Livingston and Margaret Beekman Livingston, the second, Robert, and the last, Edward, would go on to achieve political renown.

In 1776, twelve-year-old Edward's thirty-year-old brother was a member, with Benjamin Franklin, Thomas Jefferson, John Adams, and Connecticut's Roger Sherman, of the select committee in the Continental Congress overseeing the draft of the Declaration of Independence. Their father having died the year before independence, Robert became, at a key moment, his brother's guardian and political mentor. Edward attended Princeton, then studied law with New York's most learned and powerful. He was given many opportunities, and he grew, not surprisingly, into an opportunistic political advocate.

Though his childhood was as privileged as Jackson's was obscure, Edward Livingston had much in common with his future friend and political companion. Early on, like the Southern lad who was slashed by an imperious redcoat officer, he had learned to hate the British war machine and its contemptuous power. Forced to flee the 13,000-acre family estate of Clermont during the Revolution, he had watched helplessly as the great house was set ablaze. The young, heroic Marquis de Lafayette and other French volunteers to the American cause had been entertained at Clermont, where Edward formed an enduring attachment to them. Just as his elder brother Robert would serve President Jefferson as minister to France,

Edward would one day serve President Jackson in the same capacity, and be publicly supported by an elderly Lafayette. But before life would acquire that kind of symmetry, Edward Livingston would have much hell to pay for his ambition.

Spurred by his influential older brother, Livingston earned election to the House of Representatives in 1795, and only after a belligerent contest. He allied with the antiadministration faction, just as Jackson would upon election to the House the following year. It was Livingston who rose amid debate over the "Address to the President" to argue the precise language that the opposition was prepared to accept in praising the retiring Washington. Edward Livingston's vocal opposition to the Jay Treaty meant something special because Jay was married to Livingston's first cousin. While it is uncertain how intimate Jackson and Livingston were in Philadelphia in 1797, it is fair to conclude that their political views were as close as those of any two national representatives could be at this time. They were Jefferson partisans; at the end of 1793, Jefferson had resigned as secretary of state, had broken with the administration, and now exhibited a fixation with the Federalists' betrayal of Revolutionary populism and purity.

Like Jackson, too, everywhere he turned, Livingston seemed to find himself amid controversy and forced to fight for his political life. The relationship each had with Aaron Burr exemplifies the problem: Both men had gravitated to Burr's spirited style of politics in the 1790s, renewing contacts with the tainted vice president in the murky period after Burr's fatal duel with Hamilton. In Livingston's case, the alliance had even stronger roots; during the long election season of 1800–01, when Jefferson and Burr stood tied in electoral votes, he remained solicitous of his fellow New Yorker. While it is still not clear to what extent Burr entertained the unnerving prospect of catapulting past Jefferson into the presidency, it is clear that the Livingstons were courted by both Republican candidates. When the Livingston clan ultimately gave their support to Jefferson, Robert was named minister to France, and his younger brother became district attorney for New York, and soon after, mayor of what was already the nation's largest city. While the Jefferson administration took care to isolate the mercurial Burr, whom Jefferson later termed "a crooked gun," Treasury Secretary Albert Gallatin expressed uncertainty about Edward Livingston's loyalty.

In 1803, New York mayor Livingston played into Gallatin's hands when he became embroiled in financial difficulties. He had left tax collection matters in the hands of an unscrupulous clerk who apparently thought he could elude agents of the Treasury Department in Washington. Innocent

5. *Edward Livingston, a Burrite in New York and a Jacksonian in Louisiana, whose wavering reputation among fellow politicians resembled that of his friend Jackson. Shown here as mayor of New York, a few years after he first met Jackson in Congress. Courtesy Clermont State Historic Site, New York State Office of Parks, Recreation and Historic Preservation.*

or guilty, the mayor was held responsible for the fraud that was uncovered. In spite of his difficulties, Livingston (like Jackson) had a chivalric side: later that same year, during a yellow fever outbreak, the financially embarrassed mayor took his civic leadership role to heart and routinely risked his life by visiting infected houses. He finally contracted the generally fatal disease. Now, appreciative New Yorkers stood watch at *his* bedside.

Mayor Livingston recovered, but his problems lingered on. Subject to partisan whispers, press rumors, and potentially devastating criminal charges concerning the misuse of public money, he perceived that neither Jefferson nor Gallatin would support him, and assumed responsibility for his employee's actions. Timing is everything: as his diplomat-brother concluded the much-heralded Louisiana Purchase on behalf of the same administration that refused to believe in Edward's sense of propriety in financial matters, the younger Livingston decided to start life over in New Orleans. He uprooted himself at the beginning of 1804, set up a law practice, and instantly became a leading citizen in the Gulf port, by then a city of eight thousand. The learned metropolitan had been an active Freemason in New York, and before long was named Worshipful Master of his Louisiana lodge.

Livingston, in his own hand, like Jackson conveys a self-conscious desire to see the world in dramatic terms. Aboard the vessel that took him to New Orleans, he recorded in his journal: "I hear a cry aloft, *Land, ho!* . . . it appears like a dark waving line ranging a long the horizon to the south west, but the light clouds, hanging over it, reflect the verdure of its forests or fields and give a delightful [articulation?] of the pleasure . . . of a new climate."[54] Just as he was putting his life back together, his old ally Aaron Burr arrived.

In the spring of 1805, not long after his first call at the Hermitage, Burr entered New Orleans. He took an interest in Ned Livingston's recent marriage to the nineteen-year-old widow Louise Moreau de Lassy, a refugee from anticolonial uprisings in the Caribbean. The ex–vice president termed her "charming," with "sparkling black eyes."[55] Her cultured new husband spoke both French and Spanish; as Mrs. Livingston, the widow would shine as a hostess.

Married as well to the science of government, Livingston gained a following in New Orleans by pronouncing his opinions on the prospects for legal and political reform in the newest U.S. dominion. He drafted a memorial to Congress, explaining the special needs of the multicultural population of Orleans Territory, and he laid out the differences among French, Spanish, and American jurisprudence, all of which were practiced in some form in the vital port city where he now made his home. But Livingston's political erudition did not change the opinions of those in Washington who questioned his moral integrity. As the Burr conspiracy ran its course—and just as Jackson wavered between his attraction to Burr and devotion to the federal government—Livingston once again lost ground. He did not go as far as Jackson to distance himself from the suspect conspirator, which made the early Burrite Livingston a potential target of James Wilkinson.

Oddly, Livingston had received friendly, almost obsequious letters from Wilkinson during his first year in New Orleans. Upon hearing of the Burr-Hamilton duel, for example, Wilkinson seemed eager to share his thoughts: he affected a distaste for the killing, but said he was most perturbed by the "English Subjects & Servants, and the Old Tories & Traitors of the Revolution, who in their Hearts thank Burr for killing Hamilton, and by way of recompense wish now to murder him peace meal." Wilkinson sympathized with Burr as he confided in Livingston: "poor fellow he is now down—whether to rise again or not, will depend on accident, as the combination against Him is all powerful." Of course, it was the erstwhile coconspirator Wilkinson who would eventually take center stage in that "combination" against Burr.[56]

This is one of the most remarkable (apparently unknown and heretofore ignored) documents among the shadowy mountain of evidence presented to history by the players in the Burr conspiracy. As shocked, perhaps, as Burr, when Wilkinson returned to New Orleans and inexplicably turned on him, Livingston not only denied having any role in Burr's alleged plot, but addressed his self-defense to the public in a precise and direct exposition of events. In the course of that urgent self-defense, he pinpointed Wilkinson's ignorance of facts and dramatically exposed the general's haughtiness as well as his deceptions. Wilkinson had leveled his groundless charges in the very courtroom where Livingston practiced—the defective general read out the charges with alarmist affectation. These constituted a "cruel insult," wrote Livingston, a "humiliation" that threatened the recovery of his good name.[57]

Livingston, like Jackson, was a longtime land speculator who understood the ambiguities involved in the acquisition of territory. He never quite knew what Burr was up to, nor whether Burr was conspiring to the extent that the government claimed. Like Jackson, too, Livingston found himself scrutinized in the national metropolis, looked upon as one who might have been seduced into endorsing the presumed traitor's activities. And like his Tennessee friend, Livingston was particularly incensed by the acts of Wilkinson, who to save his own skin had turned over evidence of the plot to President Jefferson, turning on Burr when hopes of success for their common enterprise had dimmed.

But Edward Livingston's trials go even deeper. In accepting land in payment for legal services, he found himself in possession of an area adjacent to the city of New Orleans known as the Batture, a new beach formed by deposits of the Mississippi River. Shortly before the end of his second term as president, Jefferson determined that the Batture was federal property, and sued Livingston. As it dragged on, the case turned rather personal. Livingston became as morose and irritated as Jackson had been in his own battles for vindication. In 1810, he countered Jefferson's ninety-one-page pamphlet on their controversy with a devastating response. Finally, in August 1813, a federal district court ruled in Livingston's favor. That should have restored his good name. Incredibly, despite the ruling, Livingston's financial arguments with the U.S. Treasury Department were not resolved in the courts until 1830.[58]

Meanwhile, Louisiana was admitted to the Union in 1812, as the eighteenth state. When a battle-hardened Jackson arrived in the slowly Americanizing city of New Orleans on December 1, 1814, Edward Livingston, its most outstanding legal mind, was there to greet him, and to render into French the general's opening address to the citizens. Livingston was promptly named a Jackson aide, serving at the rank of colonel.

They were men of similar temperaments, or at least informed by the same private sense of justice and humanity. Both felt the sting of having been prejudged and distrusted by high government officials. Both found themselves in trouble because of their connection to Burr—and their culti-vated distaste for Wilkinson. Livingston was a northerner who had adopted a southern sensibility, Jackson a southerner whose political chances would depend on finding northern support.

As a relative newcomer to New Orleans, Livingston continued to seek public support by acquiring distinction as a lawmaker. When he arrived on the scene, Major General Jackson craved distinction, too, but as a protec-tor. He needed a legal show of strength to go along with a military show of strength, if he was to convince a diverse citizenry—let alone endear him-self to them—in a time of war. Thus, when the impending British attack on New Orleans brought Jackson and Livingston together for the first time since 1798, these two self-styled republicans—close in age, self-conscious shapers of destiny, acutely aware of the cost of political enmity—pragmatically revived their former alliance. Indeed, from this moment on, the fortunes of these two ambitious men with a common pas-sion for fair play would remain intertwined.

On his first day in New Orleans, Jackson wore a small leather cap, a Spanish blue cloak, and tall, unpolished boots. The speech he gave to those assembled to greet him bears an ironic tone, given subsequent charges that Jackson went too far with martial law. After likening the Mis-sissippi River to "the pulsation of the heart," the general warned of ruin under the enemy's "military despotism" that would cruelly rob landowners of their slaves and compel men into military service "at the point of a bay-onet." Shortly, Jackson himself would feel obliged to employ veiled threats in order to bring into service every available man he could find, and he would welcome all free blacks who volunteered. He told people of color that they were America's "adopted children."

Livingston's French translation of Jackson's first speech to the people of New Orleans was said to have had "an electric effect" on the audience. It complemented a Jackson who knew no half measures. It described conflict in absolutes. With his Revolutionary consciousness, Livingston embraced Jackson's dauntless rhetoric under trying circumstances.[59]

Livingston, "a tall, high-shouldered man, of ungraceful figure and homely countenance,"[60] with a young, socially accomplished wife, embodied both high society and public commitment. He was appreciated for his learning and experience, yet followed by clouds of gossip. Therefore, his personal appeal is hard to calculate. Mature portraits of him show a high forehead, receding hairline, a diabolical pair of arched eyebrows, and a quite prominent nose. It was clearly Livingston's competence, as much as his family's eminence, that sustained him in the public eye. He was constantly by Jackson's side during the month preceding the final clash, and it is likely that most if not all of Jackson's important proclamations before and after the momentous battle were Livingston compositions.

"Where the Vaunting Invader in Agony Bleeds"

Loyalty remained of primary concern. On December 15, two weeks after his arrival, Jackson issued another address to the citizens of New Orleans, charging that "British emissaries have been permitted to propagate seditious reports amongst you." Then, on December 16, he declared martial law. Livingston gave his legal opinion that the general was proclaiming a suspension of civil authority "at his own risque and under his responsibility." To hazard personal fortune while acting in the public interest was nothing new to either Jackson or Livingston.[61]

Capt. Thomas Butler, nephew of the Butler who had refused to cut his hair, was in charge of upholding martial law (no doubt a Jacksonian measure for administering poetic justice). Anyone who wished to leave the city from this point on required a passport issued by the military authority. Street lamps were put out at nine at night, and those who challenged the curfew came under suspicion of spying. With the city on alert, slaves, horses, and carts were claimed by the army, and prisoners were released who would enter the militia. Once Jackson's eager correspondent, Gov. William C. C. Claiborne now resented the loss of his authority. He complained to Secretary of State James Monroe, and received, in the interim, no respect from General Jackson, who suddenly had little time for political etiquette.[62]

On December 18, Jackson reviewed the troops at the public square and read a Livingston speech before a large gathering of soldiers and citizens. Calling the British "men who dishonor the human race," Jackson addressed the mixed crowd: "Natives of the United States! They are the oppressors of your infant political existence. . . . Descendents of Frenchmen! natives of France! they are English, the hereditary, the eternal enemies of your ancient country." Jackson praised the uniformed companies and "the Men of Color" for their "ardor" and "noble enthusiasm," respectively. At this time, too, owing in part to the intercession of Edward Livingston, the notorious pirate Jean Lafitte was welcomed to the defense of New Orleans, along with the several companies of artillery he contributed.[63]

The British armada had sailed from Jamaica—approximately ten thousand sailors and ten thousand seasoned infantry. There were numerous possible routes to the Crescent City, 100 miles north of the Mississippi delta, and Livingston helped his general acquire topographical information. Still, the bayous and canals, lakes and swamps, proved confusing, and Jackson did not expect the British at their landing point on Lake Borgne, due east of his position, on December 23. The invaders came as close as six miles to Jackson's headquarters, marching through swamps to occupy a Creole plantation, before the American general was alerted.[64]

Without waiting for the British to coordinate their forces, Jackson attacked. A combined naval and ground assault that night resulted in dozens of casualties on both sides, and served, minimally, to announce Jackson's resolve. Some of the dead British were found to have been killed by Coffee's Tennesseans in the Indian manner, with tomahawk and hunting knife. By the time their decorated thirty-seven-year-old commander, Sir Edward Pakenham, arrived on Christmas Day, the British enjoyed clear numerical superiority. Pakenham was a man of daring who had distinguished himself against Napoleon and had every reason for confidence in opposing Jackson.[65]

The American line of defense slowly consolidated. In the damp, low-lying ground, embankments were hard to construct until one of the local French proposed stuffing cotton bales into the earthen fortifications. One defender, a merchant, saw his own valuable cargo moved from shipboard to the front lines, and asked Livingston for legal advice. The quick-witted New Yorker replied, "If this is your cotton, you, at least, will not think it any hardship to defend it." On New Year's Day, 1815, a British artillery barrage failed to create a breach in the lines. Jackson searched for reinforcements: first, 500 Baton Rouge militiamen appeared, and then, on January 4, a long-awaited Kentucky division, having descended the Mississippi, arrived, but less than a third had guns—and those their "fowling pieces and old muskets." The Kentuckians had expected to find weapons, supplies, and even clothing in New Orleans. They were no doubt as disappointed as Jackson's adjutant general Robert Butler, who had written home optimistically a few days before: "When *Kentuck* arrives we will laugh at them [the outnumbering enemy] I trust."[66]

Jackson remained physically weak from his long bout with dysentery. He looked "very badly," wrote one of the fighting Donelsons, "and has broken very much." While the troops celebrated New Year's Day with "half a gill of whiskey" each, as Jackson's gift, the ailing general sent a letter to Monroe on January 3, saying that it would be wise for Washington to appoint someone to succeed him, "when my want of health, which I find to be greatly impaired, shall oblige me to retire" from command. "I do not know what may be their future design," he added, of the lurking enemy.[67]

Two hours before daylight on January 8, the British attack forces were under arms. They crossed the open plain, bounded by a swamp on one side, the Mississippi on the other, to face the city's defenders. Jackson observed their movement through a telescope. His lines now extended a mile and a half, from river to woods. The courageous Carroll, described as stout, compact, and muscular, was to receive the main onslaught, and Coffee, beside him, was obliged to situate his men in swampy water. A total of 5,000 fighters awaited the advancing redcoats.[68]

Across that foggy field, Pakenham's orderly columns advanced. At the center of the American position, a Stars and Stripes flew from a high staff. The American batteries roared as Carroll's men trained their guns along the parapet. Jackson is said to have called out, "Give it to them boys; let us finish the business to-day." The Tennesseans fired at a distance of two hundred yards, on Carroll's command. In the recollections of those who were there, a thunderous fire poured forth for several minutes, along with cannon blasts and screaming rockets. Pakenham himself charged at the head of the mostly Irish 44th Regiment, riding through a storm of bullets, his horse shot out from under him. He mounted another, and a short time later one of the American artillery pieces showered its lead nearby, and the British commander fell mortally. Others of his field officers died as well in that charge; the lead column eventually crumbled, and turned in retreat. It took no more than twenty-five minutes for the main assault to be repelled.[69]

Less than half of Jackson's force actually took part in the battle. All the while, "Yankee Doodle" and other patriotic tunes played from behind the American lines. A significant portion of Coffee's men, from the swamp, never even had to discharge their guns, while some of their compatriots nimbly chased down stranded West Indian skirmishers who were unaccustomed to wilderness muck. The sole bright spot for the British was the rout of the Kentuckians on the other end of the line, along the banks of the Mississippi. But just when the attackers were about to turn the American heavy guns on Jackson's center, word arrived of the devastation elsewhere, and the momentarily successful British troops fatefully moved to rejoin what remained of their force. They would have no more opportunities. The entire battle was over in under two hours. New Orleans was saved, and in the process the proud British lost their best field officers: three major generals, eight colonels and lieutenant-colonels, six majors, and eighteen captains.[70]

In all, the British acknowledged the loss of 291 men, including their commanding general. There were 1,292 wounded, and nearly 500 captured and missing. The American side, incredibly, lost only 13, with 39 wounded, though some 500 of Jackson's men would die of fevers and dysentery in the weeks following the battle. The War of 1812 was over. It had actually ended, by treaty, right at Christmas, though this fact would not be conveyed to New Orleans, and into Jackson's hands, for weeks yet.[71]

The Battle of New Orleans served a purpose other than, and ultimately larger than, strategic. It gave Americans what the Treaty of Ghent did not: cause for cheer. No territory changed hands when that document was signed. Jackson bequeathed to future Americans the lone reason to retain nostalgia for a war that was decidedly unpopular.

From the start, history gave Andrew Jackson full credit for the exceptional triumph, though there are various interpretations of how the credit ought to have been apportioned. While Jackson was undisputedly the principal motivating force and wholly responsible for the city's readiness, the valor of General Carroll and his men on the line cannot be minimized. Equally, the arms, ammunition, powder, and intelligence supplied by the pirates under Jean Lafitte, who manned the deadly artillery that probably did more than the Tennessee and Kentucky rifles to rout the British, have not received anything close to the mythological status accorded to Jackson. Nor is it insignificant that, as they charged to within yards of the American position, the British 44th Regiment failed to bring their ladders to storm the ramparts. Jackson could hardly be credited for that piece of luck. And while he blamed poorly armed Kentuckians for not holding his right flank (owing, Jackson predictably accused, to their "want of discipline . . . , order . . . , obedience, and a spirit of insubordination"), the commander himself could as easily be faulted for neglecting to reinforce these raw troops.[72]

After the battle, Jackson maintained vigilance and martial law for longer than most thought necessary. The British did not immediately leave the area, and Jackson considered that "it behoved him not to relax in his system of defence."[73] On February 4, Edward Livingston led a team of Jackson aides to the British fleet, and arranged for a prisoner exchange and recovery of slaves who had joined the attackers. Livingston did not return for two weeks, and when he did it was bearing news of peace—but from a London newspaper obtained while he was in British hands. Jackson promulgated the news, but warned that it was unofficial, and that vigilance was still demanded. War fears past, the popularity of the imperious Jackson precipitously declined among Louisiana politicians.[74]

No one forgot the overcrowded guardhouse of late December, packed with the prisoners of martial law. Men had been arrested merely for lacking official passports, and only some of them gained their release by enlisting. But even after January 8, civilians were incarcerated simply for being resident aliens, and thirty were locked up without being charged at all. Though New Orleans wished to return to "normalcy," Jackson persisted, approving the arrests of dozens of militiamen for neglect of duty and mutiny. Amid preparations for battle, he had sanctioned the execution of six more militiamen for mutiny during the Creek campaign—an act that would later haunt him—and now he was preparing to do it again. A last-minute reprieve on March 1 saved the life of a man who had deserted only to succor his wife while they were being evicted from their home. The war had ended, but Jackson remained at the center of controversy. He further alienated Governor Claiborne by lecturing to him, "This Sir is not a time for Complaint, or equivocation."[75]

A courier from Washington reached Jackson on March 6 with news of the peace treaty. Yet on that day, he was still writing of the "conspiracy" in camp, the desertion of troops, "mutiny within the city," and the presence of the enemy's "Agents and spies." This behavior is hard to fathom. Jackson must have had more than an inkling, though not yet full evidence, of the lavish praise he was already receiving across America—that is, save for parts of Louisiana and Kentucky, where a less heroic and less sympathetic portrayal of his demeanor was being disseminated. Headlines expressed the general amazement. Religious jubilation followed, for when the relative casualties on the two sides were published, divine ordination seemed the only explanation. Congressman George Troup of Georgia declared that "the God of Battles and Righteousness took part with the defenders of their country and the foe was scattered as chaff before the wind."[76]

Monroe applauded Jackson directly, in tones that would be repeated most everywhere: "History records no example, of so glorious a victory, obtained, with so little bloodshed, on the part of the victorious." In Baltimore, on February 18, editor Hezekiah Niles conveyed the "Glorious News! Orleans saved and peace concluded," reprinting Jackson's mid-January letter to Monroe announcing that the disgraced British had set sail. Niles also reprinted praise of Jackson written by a friend who had volunteered for service on a gunboat, and saw considerable action: "Our beloved Jackson deserves immortality. He was always in the hottest and thickest of the fight; and although his health is much impaired he still sticks to his post." "Who would not be an American?" prodded Niles. "Long live the republic!"[77]

Patriotic mythmaking is always hard to temper. When the Fourth of July next came, a Virginian heralded in song the grand battle, the frontiersmen who fought it, and their indomitable commander:

> See the sons of the west, like a dark cloud of night,
> With eagerness forth from their deep forests throng;
> Their death-tubes of terror prepar'd for the fight,
> Like their own Mississippi, impetuous and strong;
> Tis Jackson who leads
> Them to glorious deeds,
> Where the vaunting invader in agony bleeds;
> Come, toast then our heroes, we swear this great day,
> We will hand down in glory till time pass away.[78]

The resiliency of tradition would effectively accomplish just that.

Returning to the epigraph from *Richard II*, we can discern what New Orleans meant, most tellingly. Jackson, at forty-eight, now possessed what had so long eluded him: a reputation for martial skill. He shed about him an air of good fortune. His "dancing soul" had feasted on battle, not so much in the sense of relishing bloodshed as in relishing victory. It was not death but *worth* that he had always craved. Causing death was a side effect of the struggle to leave obscurity behind. Worth was completeness, liberation, the possession of which alone gave him "a freer heart" and an "uncontrolled enfranchisement." Worth, manifest as public testimonial, was the prize that, in Jackson's mind, could come only from engagement.

CHAPTER FIVE

❧❧❧❧❧❧❧❧·❧❧❧❧❧❧❧❧

Political Instincts

When I review my whole public conduct I am content with it, my conscience are calm.

—Jackson to George Gibson, March 15, 1820

Everything Jackson did has been debated in terms of its propriety and civility. The question before biographers, likewise, has always been, Did he understand limits? When he implemented martial law, was he a republican general or a self-inflated dictator? In pursuing a policy that no Indian tribe ought to retain an independent existence east of the Mississippi, did he exceed the bounds of human decency any more than his predecessors? Another way of approaching the same question: Did he carry out policies consistent with the military leadership of his era, or did he overinterpret and overextend? In other words, is it a matter of degrees—that he was willing to *do* what others merely *talked* about? Or did Andrew Jackson, once a judge, now believe, consciously or subconsciously, that he could make the law?

Those aspects of his behavior that can be readily explained by environmental influences—the frontier that never quite left him, his intense pursuit of financial comfort—have remained of peripheral concern to most who have studied Jackson. It never seemed relevant, for example, that he gambled heavily on the horses he bred, or that as a merchant he sold whiskey and as a social being drank heartily (at least for a time). After all, so did most everyone in his world who could afford such luxuries. Rather, what caused others to question his trustworthiness was his ordinary state of mind, his everyday reactions: he seemed not to listen well or reason long, but to respond to provocation and act on impulse.

What of Jackson's sociability, more generally? We cannot fully understand the making of the president without knowing the habits that served him in politics: for example, how did he form and sustain friendships amid controversies he himself brought on? What were his methods of confronting his perceived enemies away from the dueling ground and the battlefield? These are the questions on which the balance of these pages turn.

On the other hand, descriptions of the domestic Jackson almost invariably fix on his mild, almost nonchalant manner. Neither the inventive farmer nor the studious gardener that Jefferson was, Jackson was rarely portrayed as a hands-on plantation owner who contemplated productivity figures, though in reality he must have been and done so. Instead, he was seen and imagined at home conversing vigorously with one or more guests, while Rachel saw to their other guests' personal needs. He was, visitors all reported, a busy entertainer. He was fond of relaxing with a pipe, described at different times as a corncob pipe or an Indian-style long, clay pipe—another indication of how the Jackson image at once borrowed from and resisted comparison to the frontier Indian.

In Jackson's day, there was some speculation about the propriety of pipe smoking. An almanac of the mid-1820s reflects on the question lightly:

"What harm is there in a pipe?" says young Puffwell.

"None that I know of," replies his companion, "except that smoking induces drinking—drinking induces intoxication—intoxication induces the bile—bile induces the jaundice—jaundice leads to dropsy—and dropsy terminates in death." Put that in your pipe and smoke it.[1]

In Jackson, the pipe was homely, part of his lack of ostentation when he was away from the action. The pipe was an accoutrement for the woodsman, a token of rugged authority just as it was for a later American warrior of a similarly controversial character, Douglas MacArthur, who directed the counterthrust that removed the Japanese from their island strongholds in World War II.

Perhaps the pipe contributed to Jackson's poor teeth and dreary cast. As a sickly, sallow-faced man, from his years in the army through his presidency, he gave his friends regular concern about his capacity to persevere, and he gave his enemies hope that something from his quarrelsome and questionable past might catch up with him. Of course, that was one of the remarkable paradoxes in Andrew Jackson's life: the sickly man was a mighty fighter, enduring the elements time and again during the trying years of middle age.

After New Orleans

Word of the incredible victory of January 8 reached Nashville sixteen days afterward. Immediately, Rachel Jackson left with their five-year-old nephew/son, Andrew Junior, to join her husband. She arrived in New Orleans on February 19, after a twenty-five-day journey. She was promptly adopted by the fashionable Livingstons, who escorted the plain frontier wife to the city's amusements. There was even a report of General and Mrs. Jackson dancing in their frontier style: "To see these two figures, the General, a long, haggard man, with limbs like a skeleton, and Madame la Generale, a short, fat dumpling, bobbing opposite each other like half-drunken Indians, to the wild melody of '*Possum up de Gum Tree*,' and endeavoring to make a spring into the air, was very remarkable."[2]

Rachel endeared herself to many. She received from the ladies of New Orleans a set of topaz jewelry. She attended the Washington's Birthday ball, writing her brother-in-law Robert Hays of a "cilleberation . . . beyond the power of my pen," though she seemed most impressed that she was seated at supper in view of a gold-lettered sign, lit up from behind by lanterns, that read: "Jackson and victory"; and she described a "most Elle-gent piremid," with "vive Jackson" on one side and "the Immortal Washington" on the other.[3]

On the same day that Rachel Jackson was writing so effusively to Hays (and just before official word of peace arrived from Washington), her husband authorized the arrest of the author of a newspaper essay he considered "inflammatory." Louis Louaillier, a representative in the state legislature and advocate for the French cultural community, had criticized the general's heavy-handed tactics toward "alien friends" in the city. When Federal District Judge Dominick Hall, responding to Louaillier's attorney, considered the legality of the arrest, Jackson exercised his power under martial law to arrest the judge for "aiding and abetting and exciting mutiny." Hall was promptly banished by Jackson "beyond the limits of my encampment," only to return when a copy of the Treaty of Ghent was received, and martial law ended. The judge responded by finding Jackson guilty of contempt, fining him $1,000. Edward Livingston served as Jackson's defense counsel, in a courtroom bristling with cheers and fears. To avoid further outbursts from both his defenders and detractors, Jackson paid the fine. He understood now that his services were no longer needed. But the Hall-Louaillier matter would come back to haunt him.[4]

The Jacksons left New Orleans for Nashville in April, presenting Livingston before their departure with the earliest known likeness of the hero general, an ivory miniature. It was inscribed in Jackson's hand: "Mr. E. Livingston is requested to accept this picture as a mark of the sense I entertain of his public services, and a token of my private friendship and Esteem."[5] Arriving at the Hermitage with a sprained foot and a "painfull arm," Jackson began a slow recuperation, writing Livingston in short order that President Madison had asked him to come to Washington "to aid in the organization of the army," if he felt up to it. Jackson said he preferred to submit a report, and to journey to Washington only when he could do so—and, he added, when Ned Livingston could accompany him.[6]

Despite his poor health, Jackson was giving real thought to a new project. He considered it important to gratify those who wished to study his personal history and reap lessons from it. Where did this American conqueror emerge from? a national audience wanted to know. And so he wrote to both Livingston and his wartime aide John Reid during the expectant summer of 1815, pondering the production of his authorized biography. It was understood that Reid (a Virginian who had written Jackson's speech before the would-be mutineers at the end of 1813) would commence it, sifting through papers at the Hermitage.

Even as Reid was taking the initiative, though, Jackson consulted with Livingston on the value of employing the recognized talents of some older patriots, too. Dr. David Ramsay of South Carolina, a noted intellect and author of the first history of the American Revolution (1789), undertook a Jackson biography, but died soon after he had begun. Calling it "the most unpleasant task" to compile one's own biography, Jackson foisted a compliment on Livingston: "I know of no pen that could do the subject more Justice than yours." Livingston replied that he had every confidence in Reid's ability to tell Jackson's life story: "He is eminently qualified to execute it."[7] Why Livingston did not comply with his friend's request is unclear. After Reid's sudden death from a fever in January 1816, the biography was carried forward by a twenty-five-year-old lawyer from Franklin, Tennessee, John Henry Eaton. Eaton completed Reid's work the next year.

Restive by nature, Jackson was able to spend just a few months at the Hermitage. It was a renewal for his wife as much as it was for his own battered body. Despite having many nearby friends, Rachel Jackson had endured a great emotional trial when forced to cope with his long absences. In April 1814, as war was intensifying, she had described her domestic routine to the general in the grimmest terms. She confessed that she grew agitated conjuring "the Daingers and perils you have to incounter"; she went long periods without word from the front, and easily fell ill, as did "four or five of the Negroes." Andrew Junior frequently cried out for his father. A late snow that spring seemed to make matters worse. It is one of the most touching of her surviving letters; Rachel felt she had to tell her absent husband how the snow was influencing her state of mind: "It was so Deep and heavy it broke large tops and lims of trees Every think appeared to Look mournfull of the vegitable kine but when the sun shone on them theay all were vivifyed. so will you have that Effect on my spirits when I see you returning to me againe nothing will animate or inliven me untill then." If in physical proportions oddly matched, the couple fulfilled one another emotionally. She, unlike him, was highly religious. But she was as tenacious about his uncorruptibility as he was. A direct, uncensored narration distinguishes their otherwise artless letters.[8]

Apparently the first person to write Jackson that America needed a president who hailed from the West was a Virginia state legislator named John Stokely, who penned his letter from the national metropolis in mid-February 1815: "on the News of your victory the Eyes of Every real ameri-can sparkled with emotions of Joy," he flattered. Congratulating Jackson on "the Immortal Honor which you have *Honistly* & *Gallantly* won," he suggested that the Battle of New Orleans provided a sufficient boost in popularity that "you ought to fill the Chair of the Chief magestrate of this Union in march 1817." (The next presidential election was to be held in the fall of 1816.)[9]

Stokely was by no means the only booster. Curiosity about the west-erner swirled in the East. Popular prints began to appear depicting Jackson at the site of his greatest battle; over the next several years more would emerge from presses in New York, Philadelphia, and Baltimore, and as far away as Paris.[10] In the autumn of 1815, as Jackson rode from Nashville to Washington, D.C., he had ready supporters eagerly awaiting his appear-ance. En route to the nation's capital, he paid a surprise visit to former president Jefferson at his second home, Poplar Forest, which lay west of Lynchburg, Virginia. Jefferson, at seventy-three, reciprocated by riding to Lynchburg three days later to attend a banquet, along with three hundred other prominent local citizens. There he toasted the victorious general in restrained style: "Honor and gratitude to those who have filled the mea-sure of their country's honor." Jackson lifted his own glass to the sympa-thetic Republican James Monroe, a Revolutionary War veteran and likely candidate for president in the upcoming election. Arriving in Washington itself, he met with the unmartial President Madison as well as Monroe. He was not entirely impressed by the former, if John Reid's characterization is indicative: "[Madison] was perplexed by the appearance of Genl. Jackson, who, whenever our conversation 'flaged' was looking, with a melancholy air [ou]t at the window, on the ruins of our publick buildings."[11]

Jackson's support came from some unusual places. For what it was worth—and there is no evidence that Jackson knew—the inexhaustible Aaron Burr, living now in relative obscurity in New York, wrote expansively at this time to his son-in-law, South Carolina governor Joseph Alston. After giving his firm opinion that Monroe was intellectually mediocre, and with a puffed-up war record, he added: "If, then, there be a man in the United States of firmness and decision, and having standing enough to afford even a hope of success, it is your duty to hold him up to public view: that man is *Andrew Jackson*. Nothing is wanting but a respectable nomination, made before the proclamation of the Virginia caucus, and *Jackson's* success is inevitable." It was too soon. Monroe was a man of manners and recognized judgment, a seasoned politician, a confirmed nationalist—and a seemingly "safe" selection.[12]

Jackson's sudden celebrity coincided with the reappearance of Napoleon in Paris, less than a year after his exile to the island of Elba. Both popular military figures were headliners in American newspapers throughout 1815, and the first series of Jackson portraits, done at this time, unmistakably modeled him on the French emperor. The Tennessean's hair, so distinctive in the way it shot out and stood up from his scalp, was rendered flat and wavy, like Napoleon's. As the Jackson scholar John William Ward has written, it was "Napoleon's energy and daring that captured the American imagination." Like Jackson, Napoleon was perceived as a self-made man, and Jackson was later dubbed by a French official *"Napoléon des bois,"* Napoleon of the woods.[13]

Jackson had followed Napoleon's career closely. Back in 1798, as a U.S. senator, he had closed a letter from Philadelphia to James Robertson by expressing the fantastic hope that if Bonaparte were to invade England, "Tyranny will be humbled" by the Frenchman's "conquering arm." In the spring of 1815, as he received news that the defeated conqueror had raised a new army, Jackson wrote to his confidant Livingston: "The *wonderfull revolution* in France fills every body and *nation* with astonishment. . . . Naepoleon reigns in the affections of the soldiers that were to oppose him." Nearly the same age as Jackson, the French adventurer was living to fight another day.[14]

But Jackson was destined to long outlive Napoleon, whose final defeat at Waterloo occurred in June of that year. He would succeed where Napoleon had failed. He would test the limits of his power as a general, and be exonerated after infringing on the authority of the executive branch. His righteous self-regard would earn him enemies, yet also earn him two terms as president. It was already apparent that this passionate power-seeker could not admit wrong: at New Orleans, the Kentuckians had let *him* down. It was they who had marred an otherwise perfect plan, not he who had failed to protect his flank. In Jackson's lexicon, "cowards" and "traitors" got in the way whenever failure loomed, that is, he invariably judged himself to possess the talent and nerve required to mastermind success. Accordingly, he had no patience for alternative explanations when he was settled in his own mind.

As the uncompromising victor journeyed east to Washington, his controversial decisions were known. Because he was not yet a realistic candidate for national office, though, his actions were not being scrutinized on moral grounds—not yet, anyway—so much as he was the subject of popular curiosity. As 1815 drew to a close, Americans were still finding ways to exhibit the burst of national pride occasioned by Jackson's marvelous victory in the opening days of that year.

The general soaked up praise. At the end of his Washington tour, when he was a week out of the capital on the road west, though still three weeks or more from Nashville, he was able to write with a long-deferred sense of contentment to Robert Butler, his adjutant general and the husband of Rachel Hays (one of Rachel Jackson's many nieces, the daughter of Col. Robert Hays). Jackson marked the letter "private" and confided it to the post rider, who outpaced him. The details would have to wait, he proffered, but "suffice it for the present to observe, that I had the pleasure of seeing all the great men of the city, was friendly greeted by all." It had taken an effort to escape the many well-wishers who would have waylaid him with banquets. Eager to return to his friends, Jackson appeared at this point already to have internalized the myth of his own omnipotence.[15]

Warring Again

The War of 1812 was a largely unnecessary conflict brought on by a young, assertive Congress. It was fought by the children of Revolutionaries to renew the earlier pledge of their aging parents. The country wanted nothing to do with Europe, while it insisted on confronting British harassment. From a military standpoint, the war did very little to boost American confidence. Indeed, up to the moment of Jackson's victory in New Orleans, it was draining and debilitating, without much prospect. Delegates to the Hartford Convention, at the end of 1814, earnestly planned New England's secession from the Union. "Another year of war might have brought the end of the federal Constitution," writes historian James E. Lewis.[16]

Though the Union was resecured in 1815, Jackson's generation remained concerned with the predicament of that Union. Argument centered on the question of state versus federal authority in the regulation of "internal improvements" such as turnpike and canal building,[17] and state versus federal authority in the regulation and limitation of slavery. These issues deepened in the national consciousness because of westward movement, calling attention to ongoing relations with the crumbling empire of Spain and the dwindling power of Indian peoples.

No one—least of all Andrew Jackson—doubted at war's end that territorial issues would continue to preoccupy the state and national legislatures. The instability of Spanish-held areas was of urgent interest. In the ports of Baltimore, Norfolk, and New Orleans, in 1815, U.S. privateers mounted campaigns to molest Spanish shipping as farmers, merchants, and restless army officers hungrily eyed the fertility of new soil. The lure of Texas lands loomed in the not too distant future. Jackson was not alone in his ambition to add territory, but it was he who was in the best position to act. As he solicited Edward Livingston, "Be good anough to give me the earliest inteligence of all these matters & things & your opinion as it respects a Spanish war. My eyes are open, my horses in keeping, the 8th. & 4th Regts in motion, & you have nothing to fear as I hope & trust from the result of war with Spain."[18]

In the spring of 1816, Jackson left home again and went on a long inspection tour of Gulf Coast defenses. After this, he personally oversaw new land cessions from the Cherokees below the Tennessee River and from the Chickasaws in southwestern Tennessee, Alabama, and Mississippi. He wrote John Coffee, who was negotiating with the Choctaws at the same time, that "an Indian is fickle, & you will have to take the same firm stand, & support it & you are sure of success." His tenacity was truly remarkable.[19]

Another noteworthy letter of 1816 is instructive. Jackson always felt comfortable addressing James Monroe with undisguised emotion. Here he discoursed on the need for unobstructed access to the Gulf. Leaving *any* southeastern territory in Indian hands, he said, threatened the security of military supply roads. He was resolute and absolute in tone as he projected the ill will of perceived enemies: the government needed to secure "roads unshakelled by Indian claims" (suggesting that Indians otherwise kept the United States metaphorically imprisoned). Frontiers were, by his definition, exposed to "savage murders & depredations" (the presumable natural inclination of all Indians); devious tribes displayed "Indian avarice" (for Jackson, the moral ambiguity of an entire race).

His rhetorical style was to pose a worthy objective—what might be gained—against a force that imperiled. Here it was that the United States required a steady flow of "scarce & precarious" military supplies in order that its "hardy soldiers [could] meet an invading enemy." Again, Jackson's method of persuasion was strongest when he took as his premise the actual presence or proximity of outside aggressors. He concluded this appeal, like most every appeal he made to a federal executive, by contriving their common sensitivity to the feelings of good and decent citizens: "and what is still worse," Jackson reminded Monroe, "the minds of your citizens irritated & disgusted, that so much blood has flown, & privations suffered. . . ." In the general's view, Americans were insufficiently protected; a paternalistic government bore a responsibility to exert itself to safeguard the vulnerable. Finally, the letter writer deposited a veiled threat, underscoring the conceit that he was singularly able to convey the impulses of ordinary westerners: not to do as Jackson proposed would have "a banefull effect upon their former spirit of patriotism—and I am fearfull that this thing in the end will involve our Government in much trouble & perplexity." Perplexity meant anxiety, distraction, preoccupation. He was projecting his own "perplexity" onto the people at large. In a profoundly emotional way, he was urging boldness on one with whom he felt he retained real influence.[20]

Jackson's generally cautious attitude toward outsiders is borne out in a letter he wrote to Rachel's nephew, seventeen-year-old Andrew Jackson Donelson, whom he had raised since the death of the boy's father in 1804. Donelson was traveling with John Eaton at this time, and seeking an appointment to West Point. "My dear Andrew," the uncle and adoptive father entreated, "you are now entered on the theatre of the world amongst stranger, where it behoves you to be guarded at all points. in your intercourse with the world you ought to be courteous to all, but make confidents of few." Jackson believed that deceivers were many, and that a "young mind," in particular, "is too apt" to be taken in by politeness before judging keenly. To avoid the "sorrow & regret" that come with the knowledge of having been deceived, one had to wait for proof of consistency before reposing confidence. There would be as well "many snares . . . laid for the inexperienced youth to draw him into disapation, vice & folly," and so young Donelson should seek out "the better class of society, whose charectors are well established for their virtue, & upright conduct." While a highly predictable discourse, this letter does demonstrate Jackson's certain preoccupation with deception: he repeats some form of the words *deceive* and *snare*, and warns of "specious [superficially pleasing, but insincere] display." The same kind of trickery he associated with Indians he seemed to attribute to more sophisticated cheats and panderers in the East.[21]

Though he was a notoriously dull and intellectually unimpressive man, Secretary of State Monroe became President Monroe, and took office in the spring of 1817. Jackson was glad of it, and wrote from Nashville to the new chief executive on the very day of his inauguration: "I have waited with anxious solicitude for the period to arrive, when I could congratulate my Country and myself on your being placed into the Presidential chair of this rising Republic." The letter went on for several pages, addressing issues of military preparedness, urging Monroe to demand "regular subordination and responsibility" from civil and military appointees alike, while warning against "caprice" in these same officeholders.[22]

During Monroe's first year in office, Jackson put himself in a position to lead the final assault against Spanish Florida, where the Indians who remained opposed to U.S. authority were now cornered. Jackson's orders from the president, via Secretary of War John C. Calhoun, stipulated that he should refrain from provoking a war with Spain. But Monroe knew what to expect of Jackson and could not have been entirely surprised by the aggressive posture the general assumed. When Jackson exercised judgment, it did not mean he exercised restraint.

Just as curious are suggestions in the correspondence of 1817, prior to Jackson's return to a combat command, of his desire to resign from the army and retire to the Hermitage. Leaving home to negotiate once more with the Cherokees, he wrote prayerfully to Rachel in solicitation of "that, all seeing being who has so often shielded me from the shafts of death. . . . I have long, very long, looked forward to that moment, when I could retire from the bustle, of Public life to private ease, & domestic happiness." To Louisiana planter Richard Butler, the cousin of his adjutant general, Jackson wrote similarly: "I have long wished for retirement, I had a hope after my many Privations, and watchfull nights that I would have been permitted." And to Monroe: "It is my wish to retire from publick life, for I am advancing to that age [he was fifty] which makes retirement desireable."²³

His undiminished pursuit of honor once again merged with self-serving statements of patriotic commitment, to forestall any such plan. At a distance from the national capital, Jackson was in a somewhat passive position, responding to events as they unfolded rather than dictating them. Washington politicians were already posturing competitively around regional favorites, future presidential hopefuls; their proximity to power gave them an advantage over Jackson, who could do nothing but rely on his influence with the president.

It was thus, without a wall of support, that the general found himself the object of William Crawford's persistent scorn. A man in his mid-forties, Crawford of Georgia was Monroe's secretary of the treasury. He was a popular man in Washington who might have successfully challenged Monroe in 1816 if he had made his ambition more plain. Tall, handsome, and a smooth, if sometimes tactless, conversationalist, he had been secretary of war at the end of the Madison administration, when he undercut Jackson's efforts to acquire Cherokee lands. That was enough to alarm Jackson. To his dismay, the Georgian had solidified his position in the new cabinet. When Jackson learned next that Maj. Gen. Winfield Scott had criticized him for disobeying an order from the War Department, he concluded (without, as yet, clear evidence) that "a *great* general in the East, has been acting the Pimp & spy of Mr. C[rawford] has been secretly araigning me . . . no doubt to make an unfavourable impression on the publick mind."²⁴

Writing to Scott, in fact, the confrontational Jackson went so far as to court a duel: "I think too highly of myself," he wrote, "to suppose that I stand in need of your admonitions." Branding the somewhat younger soldier "incompetent" as a source of truth, he defined himself in bold, chivalric—and unmistakably frontier—terms: "My notions Sir are not those now taught in modern Schools & in fashionable high life; they were imbibed in younger days." Then came the challenge: "I shall not stoop Sir, to a justification of my Order before you, or to notice the weakness & absurdity of your Tinsel Rhetoric. . . . your Ingenuity is not as profound as you have imagined it. . . . For what I have said I offer no apology—you have deserved it all & more." Thus he wrote with anxious anticipation to the Louisiana planter Butler, proud of having, in his own mind, "*unrobed*" his rival general: "I will never retire untill I can do it with honor." Jackson's metaphor—"I have *unrobed him*"—implies engagement in a manly confrontation; the uniform represents both power and masculine prowess, so that to unrobe another is to defeat him in a physical battle or even an epistolary battle of honor—in either case, it is to declare oneself the greater man.[25]

Jackson typically found friends in shared enmity. He was decidedly hopeful about his relationship with South Carolinian John C. Calhoun, who, like Jackson, was bound for conflict with the unpolished but politically astute secretary of the treasury—their fellow southerner William Crawford. A cool and self-possessed figure in his mid-thirties, Calhoun was a stern moralist and keen intellectual. At the end of 1817, in consultation with the president, Calhoun gave Jackson command of the campaign against the aggressive Seminole Indians of Florida. He was to "penetrate to the Seminole Towns," an order Jackson deliberated on and ultimately carried out as he saw fit. Before proceeding, he wrote firmly to Monroe on January 6, 1818: "the arms of the United States must be carried to any point within the limits of East Florida, where an Enemy is permitted & protected or disgrace attends."[26]

Controversy arose not because Jackson chased the Seminoles across the southern U.S. border, and only in part because he captured Spanish Pensacola (the first time he did so, in 1814, the British were occupying it amid war). What incensed his political detractors in Washington and marked Jackson as a wily despot was the summary execution of two British subjects at Fort St. Marks, farther east, for their collaboration with the Indians. One was an ex–British marine, Robert Ambrister, whose martial demeanor was readily apparent. The other, however, Alexander Arbuthnot, was a seventy-year-old Scottish trader who had exhibited a humane affinity with the Indians and in return was greatly honored by them. Arbuthnot was no warmonger. To Jackson, however, this unmartial man was as culpable as Armbrister, and the two were convicted in a hastily assembled military court: Armbrister was shot, Arbuthnot hanged from the yardarm of his own schooner. Jackson wrote Calhoun in his usual fashion: "I hope the execution of these Two unprincipled villains will prove an awfull example to the world, and convince [Britain] . . . that certain, if slow retribution awaits those uncristian wretches who by false promises delude & excite a Indian tribe to all the horrid deeds of savage war." To Rachel, he represented himself as an avenging angel: "I have destroyed the babylon of the South, the hot bed of Indian war & depradations of our frontier, by taking St Marks & pensacola."[27]

Caught in a diplomatic bind, the Monroe administration was forced to examine Jackson's decisions. Predictably, Crawford favored a reprimand—

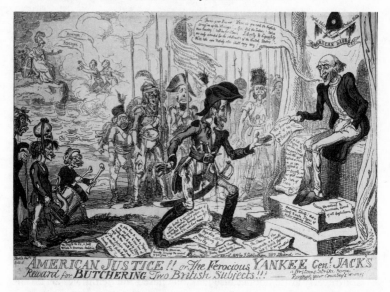

6. "The Ferocious Yankee." A piratical General Jackson is rewarded by President James Monroe for executing British subjects Robert Ambrister and Alexander Arbuthnot in this British cartoon of 1819. Courtesy Tennessee State Museum Collection, photography by June Dorman.

as well as the return of Florida to Spain. Unbeknownst to the touchy general, Secretary of War Calhoun, whom Jackson would long value as an ally, secretly urged his censure and roundly called for an investigation. With Attorney General William Wirt quietly concurring, the cabinet was nearing unanimous agreement but for the voice of Secretary of State John Quincy Adams. The supremely confident, independent-minded Adams took exception, and called Jackson's conduct "justifiable under his orders." He noted in his diary: "everything that [Jackson] did was *defensive,* that as such it was neither war against Spain nor violation of the Constitution." The two executions were legitimate acts, he said, acts of "retributive justice." Leader of the American team of negotiators at the Treaty of Ghent in 1814, Adams now proceeded to introduce relevant international law to the assembled cabinet, and in doing so single-handedly rescued Jackson from the principled solution—and possibly vengeful designs—of the others.[28]

Shortly thereafter, Adams went on to conclude a treaty with Spanish envoy Don Luis de Onís, acquiring the whole of Florida for the United

States and mapping the long border between Spanish and American possessions extending all the way to the Pacific. After three centuries, Spain no longer had a presence on the eastern coast of the continent. In Florida, Jackson merely accelerated what eventually would have come to pass, what Monroe himself wanted and perhaps invited when he approved Jackson's command. His commander's unruliness nonetheless remained of concern to Monroe, who took time—several months—before he communicated with Jackson on this thorny issue. Clumsily suggesting that Jackson allow him, or Calhoun, to (protectively) doctor his letters, Monroe acknowledged the general's patriotic intent without assenting to his actions. This left open the real possibility that the president was loath to own up to his share in Jackson's aggression.[29]

In Spanish Florida, Jackson had seemingly fulfilled the quest of William Blount, and Aaron Burr as well. He was, after all, much like his two predecessors, a man of ambition and enterprise who thought of land as the key to personal and national wealth alike. He proposed to give America what America wanted for itself, that which its highest officials, wrapped in the stiff half-measures of diplomatic doctrine, refused, in their "cowardice," to pursue. Their official pretense of shock, dismay, and consternation only served to lessen their moral authority in the eyes of Gen. Andrew Jackson, now poised—if his battered, rawboned frame could withstand further turmoil—to trade military for political authority.

James Parton characterized Jackson sharply in reflecting on the sum of his behavior at this time: "with all his virtues, his good intentions, his great services, Andrew Jackson could no longer bear opposition either to his will, his measures, or his opinions. His patriotism was real, but his personality was powerful, and the two were so intermingled with and lost in one another, that he honestly regarded the man who opposed him as an enemy to virtue and to his country."[30] Thanks to John Quincy Adams, there was now a clear line westward. Thanks to Andrew Jackson, there was little to prevent the final expropriation of all Indian lands east of the Mississippi.

Call, Eaton, Houston, and Carroll: Favorites

In the years between his triumph at New Orleans and his controversial actions in Spanish Florida, Jackson's personal mystique developed along with the romantic fancies of journalistic pens. One of the best of these belonged to the maverick Virginia freelancer Anne Royall, nearly the same age as Andrew Jackson. Touring the states, she spent some time in Nashville, and reported her first sight of the famed general:

> He was dressed in a blue frock coat with epaulettes, a common hat with a black cockade, and a sword by his side. He is very tall and slender. . . . His person is finely shaped, and his features not handsome, but strikingly bold and determined. He appears to be about fifty years of age. There is a great deal of dignity about him. He related many hardships endured by his men but never breathed a word of his own. His language is pure and fluent, and he has the appearance of having kept the best company.

As an apparent eavesdropper, Royall made the most of her brief glimpse of the man others wrote of as simply "the Hero," who typically rode the twelve miles from the Hermitage to Nashville in a carriage drawn by four horses, attended by servants in blue uniforms with brass buttons.[31]

Always in need of energetic friends to explain him to a critical world, the hero cultivated younger men on whom he came to rely. In the spring of 1818, Richard Keith Call, the young soldier who had resisted the temptation to desert with his fellows during the Creek War, and who had instead devoted himself to Jackson, became the general's aide in Florida. He returned to the Hermitage with Jackson after the campaign, and accompanied him to Washington in early 1819, where the general went to justify himself to his public critics. Congress had already begun to debate his behavior and would do so for an entire month—a spectacle some have described as the greatest tribunal since the Burr trial.

The key interrogator was Speaker of the House Henry Clay of Kentucky. "I love liberty and safety and fear military despotism," Clay railed while on the subject of war against Indians and believing, as Jackson did, in the need for retaliation. But the case of Ambrister and Arbuthnot was, he said, one for civil authority. Jackson had been too quick to brand aliens as outlaws and pirates, and Arbuthnot was most assuredly not a combatant: "It is not always right to do what may be advantageous." Second-guessing Jackson, he drove home his point that America was fighting "a great moral battle for the benefit . . . of all mankind," and so America must not be seen to exhibit "inhumanity, and cruelty, and ambition." Because the world was watching.

Clay was a great orator. He gave chase for hours, invoking distant times and imperial expectations: "Beware how you give a fatal sanction, in this infant period of our Republic, scarcely yet two score years old, to military insubordination. Remember that Greece had her Alexander, Rome had her Caesar, England her Cromwell, France her Bonaparte, and, that, if we would escape the rock on which they split, we must avoid their errors." The Senate had adjourned in order to hear Clay attack the absent Jackson, who was due in Washington that very week.[32]

Clay's fellow Kentuckian Richard Mentor Johnson, a colonel and noted Indian fighter, rose dramatically to challenge the Speaker of the House and to defend Jackson. But Clay was a hard act to follow. After such an impressive performance, Johnson was flustered by the sounds of walking, talking, and coughing that greeted his short speech, and so he put off his defense of Jackson until morning. Johnson had a pertinent point to make: the general was not "faultless," but in taking action had only "trodden in the footsteps of the immortal Washington," who had executed the spy John André, the genteel British courier sent to contact the traitor Benedict Arnold in 1780. Both generals were just in asserting the right of wartime retaliation. "Where pardon will have a pernicious effect on the interests of society," Johnson averred, "mercy becomes weakness and folly." Jackson would not pardon Henry Clay, who had the effrontery to pay a call on the visiting general, asking that Jackson overlook the speech, which he claimed was nothing personal.[33]

The most expansive defense of Jackson was compiled by his old Tennessee friend, the recently retired Judge John Overton, who published a long pamphlet featuring citations from widely recognized texts of international law. "When at war with a nation which observes no rules," he wrote, with reference to Indian warfare, "the attempt may be made of bringing them to a sense of the laws of humanity. . . . It is true, every associate of my enemy is my enemy. . . . We may refuse to spare the life of an enemy who has surrendered, when the enemy has been guilty of some enormous breach of the laws of nations." In drawing a distinction between lawful and unlawful war, Overton reached the conclusion that Ambrister and Arbuthnot "deserved to suffer death. . . . They were instigating this savage and motley horde to wage an *unjust* and *unlawful* war with the United States, without any authority." He noted the undeserved "asperity" and "want of charity" on the part of certain members of Congress, and credited Jackson for his moderation: "By acquiring the possession of the Spanish posts, he neither added to his power nor wealth. . . . All who are acquainted with General Jackson, and the weak and precarious state of his health, are perfectly satisfied, that nothing but an urgent sense of duty carried him to Florida."[34]

The intemperate Jackson and the unrelenting Clay would be at each other's throats, politically, for the rest of Jackson's life. It was, in a way, inevitable: politically speaking, they were mutually exclusive. Their very personae competed for anointing as the popular symbol of the West. Ten years younger, Clay had come to Lexington at the same age Jackson was when he arrived in Nashville. They invested in land and grew with their respective frontier towns. Both were longtime gamblers, Clay at the card table, Jackson at the racetrack. Outspoken and opinionated, they made friends and enemies easily. They understood gentlemanly honor in the same way, and Clay would fight a duel with Jackson partisan John Randolph, U.S. senator from Virginia, in 1826, at an older age than Jackson was when he retired his dueling pistols.

More significantly, Clay was a consummate legislator and public speaker, what Jackson could never be. Virginian Francis Walker Gilmer wrote that, relative to other congressional orators, he was "free and wild as the elk of the forest in his gestures. . . . Mr. Clay's voice has prodigious power, compass, and richness, and in some of its bass tones thrills through ones whole frame. He is aware of its seduction, and exerts it with great effect."[35] Margaret Bayard Smith, the friend of presidents, wrote about Clay what others were to say eulogistically of Jackson: "Whatever he is, is all his own, inherent power, bestowed by nature and not derivative from cultivation of fortune. He has an elasticity and buoyancy of spirit, that no pressure of external circumstances can confine or keep down."[36] If Jackson's pride rose with his military rank, Clay's derived from his performance in Congress; he would not allow a mere "military chieftain" to leapfrog him to national power without having ever studied the art of republican government.

Under these unpromising political conditions, Jackson and Call traveled together to Baltimore, Philadelphia, and New York, making valuable acquaintances and drumming up support. They took a return trip to Washington to see whether the Florida matter had blown over (it had not, and would not until Britain's mild reaction to the executions was comprehended). They dined with the president and then headed back to Nashville, where at a banquet presided over by Overton, the general was accorded community sympathy: "It was not to be expected," Overton enticed, "that you would wholly escape the censure of the envious and the malicious." But, never fear, "the voice of the nation," resilient as it was, could always be relied upon to override "insinuations . . . as ridiculous as they are unfounded." Those who knew Jackson best, Overton assured, always judged by motives and knew that "your military career has been as *satisfactory* as it has been brilliant." Unbeknownst to Jackson and his retinue, Monroe had just confided in his old mentor, Thomas Jefferson: "Had General Jackson been brought to trial for transcending his orders, I have no doubt that the interior of the country would have been much agitated, if not convulsed by appeals to sectional interests."[37]

Enduring political trials at his commander's side, Captain Call received an important education, and now made Nashville his home. As a member of the Jackson household, he mingled with the general's self-selected kin. John Eaton became his new best friend, while the up-and-coming lawyer/soldier Sam Houston and other firm allies of the eternally embattled Jackson, like Judge Overton, relaxed at the Hermitage. They were a brotherhood. Call served as Jackson's private secretary, writing letters to which Jackson put his signature. He also found himself penalized as a result of his Jackson affiliation when he fell in love with Mary Kirkman, whose parents detested Jackson and refused to let their daughter near him. It would be years before their Hermitage wedding was realized.[38]

As soon as he had arrived home from Washington, Jackson suffered a physical collapse. The personal attacks on him in Congress (in which he believed Treasury Secretary Crawford had a strong hand) were so destructive to his health that even Rachel Jackson adopted her husband's form of invective. It was "Green Eyed jealosey" that animated the attackers, she wrote: "What a Combination of villiney indeed . . . after all All the Fatigues and hard ships of so many companies after all araigned and Calld in question by a set of Reptiles." In May 1819, the old soldier wrote his ward and nephew, West Pointer Andrew Jackson Donelson, that his latest journey had "brought on one of the most violent attacks I ever experienced." He was thought to be in mortal danger, but his personal physician, army surgeon James Bronaugh (who had accompanied Call and him) "saved me." But Jackson could still only muster the strength to walk around the house: "I am very much debilatated." Four months later, he still had complaints: "Your letter . . . found me flat upon my back," he explained to another veteran of New Orleans, and for twelve days he was unable to sit up long enough to write. "My hand shakes from debility," he wrote Cadet Donelson again. "I cannot write with facility."[39]

In between, Jackson recovered enough to welcome President Monroe to the Hermitage in July 1819, staging a fine banquet. Monroe had just completed an extensive tour of the South, winding his way from Georgia to Huntsville, Alabama, to Nashville. Whatever mutual discomfort had strained the Monroe-Jackson relationship over the Seminole campaign was put in the past. Jackson traveled with the president as far as Lexington, Kentucky, where Henry Clay made it a point to snub him.

The year 1819 appears to have marked a turning point in Jackson's public life. The journey east and the controversy in Congress over his actions in Florida aroused much anxiety. Anxiety always bred in Jackson a renewed desire to assert his honor and guard his reputation, neither of which he could ever do quietly. Yet at the same time 1819 was a year in which Jackson seemed rather preoccupied with the deterioration of his physical health. He claimed to yearn for a tranquil, more domestic existence; he completely rebuilt the Hermitage—for Rachel, he said—and openly wondered whether he himself would long survive on the improved estate.[40]

Triumphant welcomes mixed with commotion and distraction in a year of nationwide financial panic. There were three significant portraits of Jackson painted in the early months of 1819: The first was done in Washington by seventy-eight-year-old Charles Willson Peale, by this time best known for his Philadelphia natural history museum. Once, Peale had been a Revolutionary radical, glorifying the war for independence in oils and capturing the manly spirit of George Washington on canvas, early and often. Later a Jeffersonian in both political and scientific disposition, Peale promoted patriotism to a new generation by hanging his Revolutionary portraits in the museum, exhibiting specimens brought back by Lewis and Clark, and keeping a live American eagle on hand. His Jackson portrait of 1819 is of no proud predator, rather a man of mildness and reserve. Coincidentally, Peale had just finished painting Henry Clay when he turned to Clay's antagonist. The dark-haired general's eyes are exceptionally soft, and he smiles faintly, like a healthy young father.

Peale's son, the distinctively named Rembrandt Peale, painted the second of the Jackson portraits of that year, a few weeks after the first. Jackson sat for the younger Peale in Baltimore, three times over three days. The result is a far more realistic, far less flattering image: the gaunt, silver-haired soldier's gaze reveals harsh, demanding eyes, crimped jaws, ample wrinkles. The overall cast is that of a fatigued, unpleasant-looking man. The third Jackson portrait of that season was done by the accomplished Thomas Sully. This is a romantic likeness of a magnificent fighting man standing before his horse, grasping the handle of his sword, and peering out. The image is conventional; it bespeaks martial excellence. There were, then, at least three possible Jacksons: Jackson as gentleman, Jackson as enigma, and, of course, Jackson as hero. Jackson's elusiveness to the modern mind is well symbolized in the confusion.[41]

Either because of his health,[42] or, very likely, his regard for the current president, Jackson declined his friends' offers to capitalize on his military achievements and run for Monroe's job in 1820. As he put it in the summer of 1819, after just having entertained Monroe at the Hermitage, he was more interested in supporting Monroe by putting the president "on his guard" that Treasury Secretary Crawford, aided by Henry Clay, was secretly working to unseat him. When Jackson first broached this subject with Monroe, the president said that he had received contrary indications of Crawford's intentions from the secretary himself. Jackson was not to be convinced and, by his own admission, grew hot: "I looked sternly at Mr Munroe, & replied, say to Mr Wm H Crawford from me that he is a Villain." Not satisfied after having alerted the unconcerned Monroe, Jackson repeated the same warning to Secretary of War Calhoun.[43]

The young men whom Jackson collected—whom he put to work promoting his and their careers at once—received a profound political education by feeling the cascading effect of Jackson's passions. Call, of course,

7. *Jackson sat for Charles Willson Peale in Washington in late January 1819. Courtesy Collections of the Grand Lodge of Pennsylvania on deposit with the Masonic Library and Museum of Pennsylvania.*

8. *Jackson sat for Rembrandt Peale in Baltimore only one month later. Yet the two likenesses suggest dramatically different men. Courtesy Maryland Historical Society.*

had the singular experience of accompanying the general in his travels at a critical time. But the life of John Henry Eaton was changed most by Jackson—at least with the most suddenness. Eaton's star first rose with the sales of his (and the late John Reid's) 1817 biography of Jackson.[44] He was appointed the next year to the U.S. Senate to fill the unexpired term of George Washington Campbell, whom Monroe had named minister to Russia. For Eaton, it was the beginning of a long Senate career that would not end until he accepted the cabinet position offered by President Jackson in 1829. For a solid decade he would be a most dutiful sentinel for Jackson on Capitol Hill. In 1819, however, Eaton was waylaid for a time on a delicate matter of business—the Jacksonian kind. He was assisted in this by his friend Captain Call.

The dispute with Andrew Erwin concerned the legality of land speculation involving Eaton and Jackson, which threatened a claim of Erwin's. To complicate matters, Erwin was Georgia-bred, a Crawford supporter, and seeking an appointment as district marshal for west Tennessee. After Erwin published an attack on Eaton and Jackson, the young senator resolved (or was prompted by Jackson) to seek satisfaction at the dueling ground. He invited Call to serve as his second, in charge of arrangements. Inexperienced in dueling procedure, Call required guidance from his mentor.

Were the subject less deadly, Jackson's letter would read like a cross-cultural handbook for one about to enter into a business negotiation. Honor was the frame of reference, but killing was the real object in this case. In the business of life and death, strategy was all that mattered now, and any tendency to trust had to be rejected.

> Captain Call,
> In prosecuting the business you have taken charge of, for your friend Major Eaton, you must steadily keep in mind that the *man* you have to deal with is unprincipled, you will be guarded in your acts, have every thing in writting, and hold no conversation with him unless in the presence of some confidential person of good character, he is mean and artful.

The general, as a severe judge of character, did not imagine he could be duped by anyone. He prided himself on knowing what to expect. He knew enough of Eaton's adversary to anticipate a choice between rifles or muskets, and he knew Eaton well enough to appreciate that the senator would be at a disadvantage in either case.

JOHN H. EATON.

9. *Richard Keith Call, Jackson's wartime aide who was later wed at the Hermitage, greatly profited from Jackson's military venture in Florida. Courtesy Florida State Archives.*

10. *John Henry Eaton, U.S. senator, campaign biographer, and noted beneficiary of Jackson's generosity.*

11. *The virile, assertive, yet unpredictable Sam Houston, dressed here in Cherokee attire and looking anything but soldierly. Courtesy Oklahoma Historical Society.*

12. *William Carroll, lesser-known hero of New Orleans, who offered Jackson friendship without surrendering his will. Courtesy the Tennessee Historical Society Collections, Tennessee State Library and Archives.*

These are not weapons of gentlemen—and cannot and ought not to be yielded to. Pistols are the universal weapons . . . of fire arms gentlemen use. . . . The next choice in the opponent is distance—ten paces is the longest—and *altho* the defendant may choose as far as ten paces, still if the offended is not as good a shot as the defendant, custom and justice will bring them to a distance that will put them on a perfect equality position—to prevent accident—let them keep their pistols suspended until after the word fire is given.

Jackson's cool conditioning is apparent here. He also seems to be equating Erwin with Charles Dickinson, the irritating dandy of thirteen years before, whose cockiness had infuriated him.

Charge your friend to preserve his fire, keeping his *teeth firmly* clenched, and *his fingers* in a position that if fired on and *hit,* his fire may not be extorted. . . . charge your friend to preserve his fire, until he shoots his antagonist through the *brain,* for if he fires and does not kill his antagonist, he leaves himself fully in his power.

This advice was almost a precise reflection on the 1806 Dickinson duel. "I have been always of the firm opinion," Jackson went on, "that a *base man* can never *act bravely.*" Erwin had already displayed "meanness and cowardice" in his published attack, convincing Jackson that the offender was not brave enough to go through with the duel. While of this opinion, Jackson preferred to fantasize a different alternative whereby the "cowardly" Erwin would shift his focus from Eaton to the general, assuming that Jackson was more likely to refuse to deign to acknowledge his challenge. In such a case, Jackson imagined, "I then have the right to choice of distance—take him at seven feet—placed *back to back*—pistols suspended—until after the word fire—and I will soon put an end to this troublesome scoundrel." He clearly needed to play out his fantasy for Call. "I pledge myself on the foregoing terms," he concluded his letter, "if my pistol fires—I kill him."[45]

At the age of fifty-two, Jackson had still not outgrown the advocacy of violence to settle personal quarrels. This was, at the very least, the eighth such episode in his life, since being slashed by a British officer as a teenager in Revolutionary South Carolina. There was his pro forma duel with Waitstill Avery in 1788; the rumble with Governor Sevier outside Knoxville in 1803; his caning of Thomas Swann, duel to the death with Charles Dickinson, and coming to blows with Samuel Jackson, all in 1806;

the shootout with the Benton brothers in 1813 (Jackson was by then forty-six); and his courting a duel, by letter, with Winfield Scott in 1817. As a combatant, Jackson is most clearly associated with personal antipathies and retribution (we can add the selected executions he ordered during the War of 1812 and the Florida incursion); there is no explicit account of his actually firing at an enemy in standard battle. Physically past his prime, the general was now reduced to fantasizing a scenario for killing political aspirant Andrew Erwin, if he did not first, vicariously, get the job done by the hand of his surrogate, John Eaton.

The duel was eventually averted through diplomacy. But Jackson was not satisfied. If he could not kill Erwin in the flesh, he would kill his chances for political advancement. He took his loathing straight to the president of the United States, charging that Erwin was a slave trader—it was the very same charge he had leveled against Charles Dickinson in 1806. (Recall that after the slain man was "resurrected" in the press, and mourned as a virtuous man who had been unjustly killed, Jackson countered that the "virtuous man" was a motivated slave trader.) The Dickinson shooting had done harm to Jackson's reputation. In the case of Erwin, however, the slave smuggling charge stuck. Attorney General William Wirt investigated and eventually found that the Erwin family's Savannah, Georgia, firm had smuggled forty-seven African slaves from Spanish-controlled Amelia Island, off the north coast of Florida, into the United States, and that Andrew Erwin himself had taken the slaves to Alabama. "I have used candeur in my former letters to you," Jackson wrote Monroe, recurring to his insistent cry that Erwin's appointment would play into Crawford's scheming hands: "Should you appoint Colo Andrew Erwin, a Bankrupt Merchant, a man without principle, and a tool to your enemies—believe me when I tell you, it will arouse the feelings of the people of the west part of Tennessee against you, lessen your popularity, and . . . strengthen your enemies." The Erwin episode drew Jackson, Call, and Eaton even closer.[46]

Sam Houston, like Call, had established a claim on Jackson's generosity through his devotion to the general's cause in the Creek War. Like Jackson himself, Houston started from nothing, grew up without a father, and, by pure force of personality, would go on to build an illustrious career on the strength of an extraordinary military victory: Jackson won at New Orleans when he was forty-seven; Houston would avenge the Alamo when he was forty-three, and would then be elected president of the Republic of Texas.

Houston was a scrambler. After recovery from the wounds he received in battle, he used his intimacy with the Cherokees to intercede in a quarrel that the Indians of eastern Tennessee had with Washington. Foreshadowing Jackson's ultimate project of removal of Indians to west of the Mississippi, Houston persuaded those Cherokees who had yet to be convinced that they ought to migrate. But unlike Jackson, Houston really did feel a strong attachment to the Indians' welfare; when government promises were not kept, he dressed himself in Cherokee garb and led a delegation to Washington. Received by Calhoun, Houston flaunted his unmilitary attire. A reputedly talkative, comical, theatrical fellow, and a rather amiable drinker, he proved he was not easily cowed by authority—much like his protector Jackson. After his audience with Calhoun, Houston returned to Tennessee and embarked on the study of law, setting up his practice thirty miles east of Nashville. In short order, he became a colonel in the Tennessee militia, was elected state prosecutor in Nashville, and in 1821—only eight years after he first enlisted—was a Tennessee major general. He was as Jacksonian in his ambition as one could be.[47]

Perhaps the most confusing relationship among the protégés was the one that subsisted between Jackson and the valiant William Carroll. In 1813, Jackson had taken Carroll's side in his quarrel with Jesse Benton. The following year, he entrusted the loyal Carroll, son of a Revolutionary War soldier, with responsibility for mustering critical troops into service. As a fighting general, Carroll could do no wrong. Yet something occurred just a year after New Orleans that would keep Jackson forever afterward suspicious of his proven student.

In a February 1816 letter from Jackson to John Coffee, who was at that time a commissioner running the line between Creek and U.S. lands, Jackson professed "astonishment" in having suddenly learned of a "secrete attempt of Doctor Bedford & Genl Carroll to injure you & my self." The language is the same as Jackson used in censuring his most relentless enemies, declaring: "such base ingratitude will meet its reward—It is evidence of such wanton wickedness & depravity of heart that I can scarcely believe it my self, that I have hug[g]ed such monsters to my boosom, called them friend, and risqued my life for the preservation of the charector & feelings of such a man as it appears Genl Carroll is."

The details are not given, though they appear to relate to a land purchase arrangement. Jackson was eager at this time to reward his Tennessee friends, as he was anticipating the development of new towns in northern Alabama. Carroll seems to have identified fraud, implicating Jackson and

Coffee. Dr. John Bedford, previously a Nashville physician, was integrally connected with the development of Florence, Alabama (until recently in Creek hands), where Coffee was to build a plantation and settle permanently. Disillusioned with Carroll, Jackson told Coffee that he was determined, on his next meeting with Carroll, not to "disguise . . . my feelings & contempt for such base conduct—under the auspices of undisguised friendship." And indeed, several days later he reported to Coffee that he had seen Carroll: "His looks denoted the sensations of his mind, he knew I was advised, of his conduct, and I thought I saw that a guilty conscience *needs* no accuser."[48]

If Jackson took no more dramatic action at the time, he stored his bile until 1820. That is when Carroll ran for the governorship of Tennessee, and Jackson threw his support to the opposition candidate. A mutual jealousy may also have driven a wedge between these two war heroes, but it is fair to say that Jackson's political opposition to Carroll was at least in part owing to their disagreement on the subject of relief for debtor farmers hurt by the nationwide Panic of 1819. Overborrowed Americans were ruined when credit suddenly tightened and banks demanded immediate repayments. Carroll, who had been in the hardware business, called for public relief of those, like himself, who had suffered financially. Jackson, like other large landholders and a good number of merchants, took the side of creditors and limited government, calling any other position "demagoguery." In other respects, Carroll and Jackson saw eye to eye on monetary policy and the defective character of a banking industry that seemed to have grown too large. Where they differed was in degrees, in remedying the immediate situation, and in deciding what constituted equality of economic opportunity. Importantly, Carroll overcame Jackson's opposition in 1820, and would go on to enjoy a remarkable six terms as governor of Tennessee.[49]

Carroll was every bit his own man. If Jackson resented this fact, the two ultimately found that they had much in common. Even after Carroll suggested a preference for the political views of Henry Clay in a suggestive letter of 1823 to the skillful Speaker of the House, it appears that the governor's personal relations with Jackson did not suffer greatly. He was occasionally a guest at the Hermitage during these years, and would comfort a bereaved Jackson on the eve of his presidency. All the same, the Jackson-Carroll relationship appears a peculiar one. Unlike Eaton and Call, who walked in the shadow of the hero, Carroll was hero enough that Tennesseans valued his commitment to them independent of his connection to Jackson. Like Hugh Lawson White, the Jackson adherent whose clear

13. Excerpt from Jackson's 1816 letter to John Coffee, wherein Jackson charges his erstwhile friend, Gen. William Carroll, with "wanton wickedness and depravity of heart." Courtesy the Tennessee Historical Society Collections, Tennessee State Library and Archives.

erudition prepared him for a judicial career that did not hinge on his friendship with the hero, the popular William Carroll proved that he did not need Andrew Jackson's patronage in order to advance.[50]

Election of 1824

Despite Jackson's fearful predictions concerning William Crawford's artifice, Monroe, as it turned out, was easily reelected in 1820, and Crawford continued in the cabinet for another four years. Jackson had to accept the limits to his influence with the president. Then in early 1821, after Spain ratified the Adams-Onís Treaty, Monroe appointed him the first U.S. governor of the Floridas. Before Jackson accepted the president's offer, Attorney General Wirt wrote privately to a friend that Jackson "considers Florida as being, in some sort his, by right of conquest[.] it is very probable that he would accept by pride of character—if it were only to keep alive the remembrance that we owe Florida to him." Justifying Wirt's conclusion that he did not want the post for reasons beyond the symbolic, Jackson made it clear that he did not intend to stay in Florida Territory longer than it took to organize the government.[51]

He traveled to Pensacola with his wife and Andrew Junior, accompanied by aide Richard Keith Call. As territorial governor, Jackson officially retired from the army, exhorting his "brother Officers" to treat their troops as "family," and to "Continue then as heretofore, when under my command, to watch over [each company] with a fathers tenderness & care; treat them like children, admonish them, and if unhappily, admonition will not have the desired effect—Coercion Must." It was the general's final word—urging toughness in order to avert "insubordination" and "cowardice," "disaster & disgrace"—words of warning he had issued many times before.[52]

When he lost interest in the executive's role after a few months, Jackson left Florida. He arrived back at the Hermitage in the fall of 1821.[53] Shortly thereafter, he sent an affectionate letter to Captain Call, who remained behind. In it he once again praised the young man for his courage, conviction, and talent, and offered paternal advice. But this was not a standard letter; it was in fact a rare testament from Jackson, imparting his outlook on life at age fifty-four. And it showed how much he identified with Call, fatherless from infancy and at twenty-nine the same age Jackson was when he was elected to Congress.[54]

Privy to the personal pain of a young man facing political adversity, he wrote, lamenting, "my Dear Call I have been Tossed upon the waves of fortunes from youthood, I have experienced prosperity & adversity—It was this that gave me a knowledge of human nature, it was this that forced into action, all the energies of my mind." For Jackson, then, it was circumstances more than nature that "forced" the will "into action," and experience that dictated his confrontational character.

Call had been denied promotion in Florida, and Jackson was perturbed. The problem lay in Washington, where Monroe had used his own prerogative to give away plum positions. Jackson saw in his aide the same deserving qualities he saw in his younger self, and empathized with Call's feelings of disappointment. Jackson's prejudices had hardened: government was fickle, and run by men with corrupt hearts who needed to be chased out. "I am Determined to try my influence in his [Call's] behalf," he wrote James Bronaugh, "and any thing I have in my power to give him, will be." It is interesting that Call's physical appearance and temperament have been described in terms very much like those used to characterize his patron. He was "tall and erect," "dynamic and ostentatious," intensely ambitious, and possessing "vanity beyond conception."[55]

Concerned with a worthy soldier's stunted career, Jackson did not simply berate Washington for overlooking Call. The letter to Call was about inner resolve: "Hence this neglect of the government may be of service to you. it has & will bring forth, from necessity, the best energies of your mind"—just as it had for Jackson—"& with your application and industry, you will, nay, you must succeed." But success, for Jackson, obliged one to size up people, with a suspicious eye: "as you progress through life—you will find many, professedly, friends. . . . in many Instances these professions are made with a view to obtain your confidence that it may be betrayed—To guard against such impositions there is but one safe rule—have apparent confidence in all, but never make a confident of any untill you have proven him worthy of it." Jackson had lately learned that even possessing heroic stature was no assurance of political advantage. Indeed, more than ever, he did not trust the chain of command.[56]

The vagaries of politics continued to swirl about Jackson's head as he read into the correspondence he was receiving from Washington. He accepted that his appointment to the Florida governorship was controversial—but had it been meant to reward or to isolate him? On Capitol Hill, there appeared to be new reason to regard Jackson as a loose cannon: although he had only been governor for a few months, he had impulsively tossed the last Spanish governor in jail for resisting his authority. Congress once again, though less dramatically, would debate his actions in Florida.

In Florida, too, he had been in "Delicate" health, according to his constant and dutiful wife, who sympathized with his every mood and action and complained only of the lack of Protestant community in the newly acquired territory. Her husband the governor was a better warrior than peacekeeper. The frontiersman who enjoyed cockfights and horse races had given his blessing to a deadly duel between two of his army officers, staged before the public in Pensacola. When the combatant to whom

Jackson had shown favor was gunned down, the ailing, gambling governor cursed his bad fortune and made clear to the unappreciated victor that he should leave town immediately. Jackson was not far behind.[57]

Florida held no allure for him. Though Call was eventually named a general of the militia by Monroe, and would forge a long and successful career in Florida business and politics, Jackson preferred the fertile scenes and relative calm of the Cumberland. Its frontier days were passing rapidly, and the improved Hermitage was at last a southern mansion. Its master tended to sleep later than the average farmer, and enjoyed retelling war stories—though without contemplating a return to war. This had become his base, where he digested news from the nation's capital.

Since Thomas Jefferson's victory over the incumbent John Adams in 1801, only Virginians—and only Jefferson's closest allies—had occupied the executive mansion. All America understood that a profound leadership change was to occur with the next election. By 1821, there were enough eager candidates—all Washington insiders—positioning themselves for the presidential election of 1824, that it was difficult to conceive a Jackson candidacy. Nationalists John Quincy Adams and John C. Calhoun were each engaged in soliciting support; Jackson's inveterate enemy William Crawford of Georgia was ostensibly the "Jeffersonian" candidate, by dint of his southern states'-rights stance. In the early stages, Crawford was the most active among those who aimed to succeed Monroe.

An anonymous letter sent to Jackson from Georgia, and signed "Friend," was received at the Hermitage early in 1822. The writer assured Jackson that Monroe was leaning more and more toward Crawford, that he had been made governor of Florida merely to force his resignation from the army, and that "Secretary [of State John Quincy] Adams is a poor timid Yankee, who can make no head against a Man of Crawford's energy. . . . so Crawford is the next Presidt. unless some other Man than Adams is taken up."[58]

Jackson had to speculate on whether the letter was genuine, or an attempt to further alienate him from Monroe and thus allow Crawford to improve his chances. "I hope in god for the sincere friendship I have had for, & the confidence I have had in Mr Monroe," he wrote four days after receiving the secret letter.[59] It would be much later that Monroe's private preference for Adams was finally revealed.[60] And Jackson, if he chose to run, would also have to contend with Clay—articulate, shrewd, and well-connected—who was bound to capture a portion of Jackson's natural constituency.

Jackson ruminated on the "Friend" letter. It only momentarily relieved him that his Washington correspondents were describing a "large majority" in Congress who were "virtuous," whose minds were happily "not poisoned" against him. He still believed that there existed a "*Secrete combination to destroy me.*" At this time, there was no indication that he was interested in joining the crowded field of presidential candidates. He had generous things to say about Adams and about Calhoun, who had begun to test the waters, and as to Crawford, "that arch fiend," he was entirely consistent. "I have always believed Mr Calhoun to be a highminded and honourable man, possessing Independence and virtue," wrote Jackson to George Gibson, one of the Washington-based watchdog-guardians of his reputation. "I have as far as I know Mr Adams, found him to be a candid independant man and should Mr Crawford be disappointed the nation will be well governed either by Mr Calhoun or Mr Adams."[61]

In 1823, one year closer to the election, Jackson's popularity was on the rise. "I have been so crowded with company," he wrote John Coffee from the Hermitage that summer, as he summoned energy.[62] He would need it, given the planning of his handpicked U.S. senator, John Eaton, instrumental in luring Jackson into becoming a U.S. senator (again—after a lapse of a quarter century). Jackson's physical presence in Washington was meant to coincide with his late but momentous entry into the race for the presidency.

The circumstances by which this all came to pass were, as usual, unusual. Tennessee senator John Williams, a Crawford supporter, was seeking reelection when Jackson's name was suddenly put forward by Williams's erstwhile colleague, John Eaton, and Jackson's wealthy neighbor William B. Lewis in the temporary state capital of Murfreesborough. Eaton and Lewis had married sisters, both of whom were orphaned young and taken in and raised by Andrew and Rachel Jackson; but both women also died young, not long after their respective marriages to Eaton and Lewis. Now, eager to promote their champion, Eaton and Lewis generated support by conflating Jackson's presidential and senatorial bids. The hagiographic Reid-Eaton biography of 1817 was reprinted at this time. Then, amid the politicking, Crawford suffered a debilitating stroke, rendering Jackson's greatest adversary speechless and nearly blind. The Georgian's strategists bided their time while their candidate made a partial, though not substantial, recovery during the election year. One curious footnote to all this: Governor Carroll's supporters voted for Williams over Jackson.[63]

Calhoun, just under forty, was far younger than any of the other prospective candidates when he entered the presidential competition in late 1821. He presented himself as the South's ethical answer to the sly and purportedly unprincipled Crawford. Concentrating on gaining a foothold in the North by mustering support in Pennsylvania, he opted out of the race in early 1824 when that state made its support for Jackson known, and nominated Calhoun for vice president. The South Carolinian acquiesced. Without opposition for the second slot, he figured he had time to reposition himself as a future presidential candidate.[64]

Jackson not only found wide support when he reached Washington, he had the comfort of traveling there in the company of two protégés, John H. Eaton and Richard K. Call. Eaton, though only thirty-three, was Tennessee's senior senator, and Call was a new Florida delegate. The three met up en route (Call coming from Pensacola via eastern Tennessee),[65] and they all lived under the same roof—the Washington inn operated by the O'Neale family, located between Georgetown and the White House. It was a choice of residence that would have dramatic consequences shortly after Andrew Jackson assumed the presidency in 1829.

This period of electioneering was a remarkable time in Jackson's career, one in which he mended fences. First, in 1822, he responded magnanimously to the entreaty of Thomas Watkins, whose "outward smiles and hidden enmity" Jackson had denounced in 1806, after Watkins's show of sympathy for Charles Dickinson's widow. Now removed to Virginia and serving as the personal physician of eighty-year-old Thomas Jefferson, the "much injured" Watkins wished to repair the old breach with Jackson. A mutual friend wrote that new enemies had uttered slanders about the doctor's "misconduct" in Tennessee, in part concerning his handling of a will, while citing "the unfortunate misunderstanding with you as proof of his Criminality." Asked to offer the "hand of friendship" to Watkins, Jackson did one better, and penned a note to Jefferson himself, attesting to his former enemy's honorable character.[66]

In September 1823, Jackson responded similarly to a letter from Judge John McNairy, another whose enmity had built during Jackson's dueling days. McNairy was important because he had been responsible for ushering in Jackson's Tennessee career in the first place. The judge made an effort to repair the breach by capitalizing on the recent death of a mutual friend, writing sensitively: "You and myself began life together, time rolls on apace, we shall soon cease to act." He expressed the desire both to restore cordial relations between Jackson and Senator Williams, and to mediate in the still pending legal case against Andrew Erwin, which had almost led to a duel between Erwin and Eaton four years earlier. Jackson replied: "Blessed is the peacemaker, *saith the Holy scripture*." He appreciated McNairy's desire "to produce harmony & peace to society." While he seemed incapable of forgetting that Williams had "endeavoured to secretly stab me" by spreading malicious rumors in Washington, Jackson did not fault McNairy for this, and indeed signed an agreement with Erwin two weeks later, ending (for the moment) their long dispute.[67]

In Congress, the mending of fences continued. Jackson was agreeable to Winfield Scott's solicitation that they meet on friendly terms. Even more remarkably, perhaps, Missouri senator Thomas Hart Benton, who had fled Tennessee after nearly causing Jackson's death in 1813, found the means to patch up differences with the new Tennessee senator. Eaton wrote to Rachel Jackson, "It will afford you great pleasure I know, to be informed that all of his old quarrels have been settled. The General is at peace & in friendship with Genl Scott, Gen Cocke [with whom he had also quarreled during the War of 1812]—Mr. Clay & what you would never had expected Col Benton: he is in harmony & good understanding with every body."[68] A dinner was held on Jackson's fifty-seventh birthday, March 15, 1824. Not only were staunch friends Eaton, Call, and Livingston there, but Henry Clay and John Quincy Adams as well.[69] The reconciliation with Benton would last, while that with Clay would dissolve permanently when the Kentuckian engineered Adams's election in the House of Representatives eleven months later. For the moment, at least, Jackson seemed to be learning the value of accommodating political differences.

Jackson saw his chances improving during 1823–24. To Edward Livingston of Louisiana, like himself bound for Congress for the first time since the 1790s, he had written in March 1823: "To render service to my country could alone constitute any motive for again acting in a public capacity." At that time, Jackson had just turned down an offer from Monroe to head a mission to Mexico, which would have taken him farther from the center of national power and debate. "Should I ever be again brought by the unsolicited call of my country on the public or political theatre, I shall calculate to have you near me," he vowed to Livingston. "My country has brought my name before the american nation and the people must decide—The Presidential chair is a situation which ought not to be sought for, nor ought to be declined when offered by the unsolicited voice of the people." He saw himself now as that candidate who alone might oppose "designing Demagogues"—the intriguing Crawford, most notably. Calhoun, though still in the race at this point, wrote Jackson one week

later: "I find few with whom, I accord so fully in relation to political subjects, as yourself. . . . The political gamblers will fail. The cause of the
Georgian [Crawford] is, if I mistake not, rapidly declining."[70]

Sam Houston had witnessed the first boost to Jackson's "unsolicited"
campaign when in the summer of 1822 the Tennessee legislature, by nearly
unanimous vote, recommended Jackson as "a person most worthy, & suitable to be the next President of our union." He wrote Jackson adoringly,
"You are now before the eyes of the nation; You have nothing to fear, but
every thing to expect. . . . You have friends throughout America: each has
his sphere, & each will feel & act, from the best motives." Houston himself
was elected, at the age of thirty, to the Eighteenth Congress; from his new
vantage point he would write a pseudonymous newspaper column in 1824,
signed "Virginian," in response to those who disparaged the "character and
qualifications" of his general. To the charge that Jackson was "deficient in
political experience," Houston countered, "Had Washington the political
experience of Jackson when he was elected President of the United States?
Had he not been accustomed to arms from his youth? Have we had a more
profound statesman in the Presidential chair since his day?" Jackson, he
attested, would be judged, like Washington, "through the tribunal of public opinion." And he would enter the presidency with "clean hands."
Eaton, too, put his pen to work, publishing *The Letters of Wyoming,* drawing a contrast between Jackson's way and the politics of intrigue, identifying Jackson with the simple virtues of the rural life and the noble values of
the Revolutionary age.[71]

As senator, Jackson introduced no legislation. He watched as others
acted on his behalf, writing Rachel in January of the mass of attention he
was receiving: "There is at present great feeling on the Presidential question throughout the United States, and great intrigue. I interfere not, but
it appears as you will see that my friends increase daily." Eaton occupied
himself compiling Jackson's letters for publication in the press, so as to cast
the candidate in a patriotic light and manifest his leadership qualities. "I
am without concealment of any kind," Jackson wrote to Pennsylvania congressman George Kremer. "In public or in private letters, I but breathe the
sentiments I feel, and which my judgment sanctions, and no disposition
will ever be entertained by me, either to disguise or to suppress them."
Letters, as Jackson would have it, established his utter lack of guile.[72]

As the election of 1824 approached, Jackson did not have—nor did he
apparently need to have—a specific political platform other than a disdain
for deception, the political disease. He claimed to represent the principles of

honor and forthrightness, "to do right and fear not," as Calhoun approvingly (and, as we shall later see, ironically) quoted back Jackson's own maxim to him.[73] The passive legislator wrote his friend William B. Lewis that "a man who is Governed by principle, in all his votes, is never in Danger."[74]

Though he was outshone on Capitol Hill, there were few in Washington with a comparable sense of mission. Jackson's impressions about government were formed by his frontiersman's understanding of social order and the processes of civilization. His politics were simple. They dealt in protecting "good" Americans from those in power whom he identified as corrupt and covetous. Obvious examples from his own experience were Gen. James Wilkinson and William Harris Crawford. He would, in turn, insist on elevating those he was able to identify as men of honor, who would be loyal to him and to the nation. What mattered to him was proper subordination. Loyalty meant knowing, implicitly, who commanded. He believed in the exercise of power by a strong, wary, resolute—and honorable—fraternity of soldierly men who had proven themselves unselfish, sober, and judicious. His enemies might characterize him as an inelegant, self-infatuated, and politically inexperienced militarist. But Jackson could counter (and his own mind, no doubt, did) that they were smug in their own way, too accustomed to power to claim to represent the honest voice of an idealized "people."

If there was one policy Jackson stood for that could be articulated easily, and that symbolized his overall approach to leadership, it was his Indian policy. As he had done in the past, he could be expected to place the noncompetitive Indian beyond the grasping reach of enterprising whites. He would personally direct this presumptively benevolent, but utterly *deterministic*, eviction; it was the obverse of his *opportunistic* eviction of the supposedly despotic Spanish.

Yet in 1824, there was no meaningful controversy among the candidates with regard to the government's treatment of Indians, and details of the Spanish problem had become moot, for the moment, since the Adams-Onís Treaty. Nor was Jackson obliged to emphasize his concern with debt reduction or his view that the banking system threatened liberty. What mattered more than policy choices were the leadership styles and personal attainments of competing candidates. Indeed, the 1824 campaign did not focus on platforms, organizing instead around networks of political friends. Editors complained that popularity had replaced principle in the political process. The candidates and their spokesmen wrote letters to drum up support from key state leaders, indirectly holding out promises of appointments. Jackson participated in the letter-writing campaign, but strenuously sought to avoid impropriety. He needed to sustain his self-image as a firm and guiltless political being—he was ever convincing himself of his moral infallibility.[75]

In every respect, the election of 1824 proved to be one of the most convoluted in U.S. history. When Congress adjourned in May, Jackson headed home, and left again for Washington with Rachel in mid-autumn. In between, his name was dishonored in the press by his enemies, none of whom appeared quite so zealous as Crawford supporter Jesse Benton. His more distinguished brother might have made amends with Jackson, but not so Jesse, who issued a long statement that was published in the *Raleigh Register* and reprinted elsewhere. Charging Jackson with having previously exercised nepotism in military appointments, he claimed in colorful language that Jackson now had sold out southern interests for northern votes: "The object of his going to the Senate was to electioneer for President. We find him in Washington, bowing and cringing to all his former foes." That line was apparently meant to embarrass Senator Benton. "He is seen," the tirade continued, "with hosts of sycophants, dancing attendance on his person and flattering his vanity. . . . As a politician, General Jackson could never rise above mediocrity." John Eaton came under attack, as well, as the "dependant biographer, who who [sic] as a reward for his writing was placed in the Senate of the United States." But nothing in the piece was stronger than the attack on Jackson's personal bearing: "Boisterous in ordinary conversation, he makes up in oaths what he lacks in argument." And even if one overlooked his "restless temper" and credited his accomplishment in New Orleans, "he has received all the honor and all the profit" for the gallantry of those who deserved the greatest praise, who "fought and suffered under his command."[76]

It was so potent an attack that Jackson went to some lengths to see that Jesse Benton's disreputable conduct was as exposed as his backside had been in the comical duel he had fought with Billy Carroll in June 1813, in which Jackson had participated as Carroll's second. The candidate had his nephew, Capt. Andrew Jackson Donelson, solicit statements from those who could spell out what had prejudiced Jesse Benton against so reasonable and generous-minded a man as Andrew Jackson: There was Robert Purdy, to whom Jackson had directed Jesse Benton, in a friendly way, for advice in 1813; Purdy now reported that he had strongly recommended that Jesse "let the affair drop," but Jesse had rejected this advice and went on to provoke the duel with Carroll. Building on Purdy's recollection, the present governor of Tennessee—the man Jesse had shot in the hand, the man who had fired a bullet at his buttocks—wrote to Captain Donelson, asserting that Jesse's surprising "manoeuvre" of showing his backside was a "disgrace" to the code of honor. Carroll stated that he and Jackson had agreed at the time to withhold information from the public, so as to avoid dishonoring Jesse Benton any more than his own irregular behavior ought to have done upon introspection. "I will just add," concluded Carroll, "that throughout the whole affair, so far from General Jackson's attempting to excite a quarrel, his advise [sic] to me was of the most conciliating and for-bearing character." As the election drew near, the charismatic candidate was still trying to put out fires.[77]

Jackson remained visible. When he and his wife were en route from Nashville to Washington in late 1824, future Virginia congressman Henry A. Wise, then a college student, saw them up close and later recalled his observations. He chose to concentrate on Jackson's two most prominent features, his undisciplined shock of hair and the irregular jaw and teeth:

> His presence immediately struck us by its majestic, commanding mien. He was about six feet high, slender in form, long and straight in limb, a little rounded in the shoulders, but stood gracefully erect. His hair, not then white, but venerably gray, stood more erect than his person; not long, but evenly cut, and each hair stood forth for itself a radius from a high and full-orbed head, chiseled with every mark of massive strength. . . . His cheek-bones were strong, and his jaw was rather 'lantern' [thin, almost transparent]; the nose was straight, long, and Grecian; the upper lip the only heavy feature of his face. . . . His teeth were long, as if the alveolar process had been absorbed, and were loose, and gave an ugly, ghastly expression to his nasal muscle. His chest was flat and broad. He was very unreserved in conversation, talked volubly and with animation, somewhat vehement and declam-atory, though with perfect dignity and self-possession.[78]

The Jacksons arrived in Washington at the end of the year, when the offi-cial electoral vote tally was already known: Jackson led the pack with ninety-nine votes, followed by Adams with eighty-four, Crawford with forty-one, and Clay with thirty-seven. Because no candidate held the majority, the House of Representatives, as provided by the Constitution, would elect the next president from among the top three electoral vote-getters.

Receiving daily encouragement (and social invitations) from well-wishers, Jackson wrote Coffee in early January 1825: "How the presidential question may be decided I know not. information of today, gives some reasons to believe that a coalition is about to be formed, which may be called a trio, the interest of Crawford, Clay and Adams combined, for the purpose of defeating my election."[79] On February 9, in the midst of a giant snowstorm, the votes were read out. Clay had succeeded in convincing the delegation of his home state to cast its lot with Adams, although the Kentucky legislature had instructed all to vote for Jackson. Clay had also orchestrated a behind-the-scenes campaign among several other key state delegations. The majority vote of each state's congressional delegation constituted a single vote; a simple majority of the states determined the winner. The final count, then, after Clay's manipulations, was thirteen of the twenty-four states for Adams and seven for Jackson, four for Crawford. It may not have been quite a "coalition," but Jackson had predicted the outcome accurately.

Rumor was that Clay and Adams had reached agreement beforehand, and that Clay was to receive the coveted cabinet post of secretary of state in return for his skillful maneuvering. The State Department was the surest stepping-stone to the presidency in those days: Adams had been Monroe's secretary of state for eight years, and Monroe, Madison, and Jefferson before him had all held that same office. To satiric commentators the short, rapidly balding Adams, attempting to stand tall on anything but solid ground, became "our Clay president," while in Jacksonian parlance, Clay had become a villain.

To William B. Lewis, Jackson wrote first on February 7, two days before the decisive House vote: "How the Election of President may result is impossible to tell. The rumor of Barter of office, intrigue and corruption still afloat, which I hope for the honor of the country there is no truth in." Five days after Adams's election, when the incoming president offered Clay the post of secretary of state, Jackson addressed the same correspondent: "So you see the *Judas* of the West has closed the contract and will receive the thirty pieces of silver. his end will be the same. Was there ever witnessed such a bare faced corruption in any country before?"[80] The arrangement became forever known as the "corrupt bargain."

Jackson, in fact, made out well, though he lost an extremely close election. His popularity soared, as Washingtonians noted his composure—or so the popular wisdom maintained over the next months and years. Disgusted as he was privately, the notoriously hot-tempered warrior was externally pleasant to all. He apparently gave President-elect Adams his hand (if anecdotal accounts are accurate) when they met at a large reception organized by outgoing President Monroe. The victor Adams, the same age as Jackson, was said to have appeared rigid and uncomfortable throughout, while Jackson stood gracious, contented, and quite nearly relieved.[81]

The old rules had worn out. Electoral politics was shifting with the disappearance of the Virginia dynasty and the seemingly nonsectional presidency, just as Adams became the first president inaugurated in pantaloons instead of Revolution-era knee breeches. North, South, and now West had distinct political personalities, and democratization of the citizenry was being revealed, and urged, in the pages of a more widely disseminating, highly politicized press.[82] The nation was turning away from the notion of gentlemen legislators agreeing on a quietly deserving republican for the chief executive position.

From here on, a more combative and better-managed presidential campaign would be the norm, predicated on the broad acceptance of democratic agitation. More visible candidates and more obstructive tactics would comport with a more widely held franchise. As he left for Tennessee, Jackson knew that he could rely on his embittered supporters, nationwide, to wreak vengeance on Adams and Clay.

CHAPTER SIX

The Avenging President

*I sincerely regret that your views are so different from mine. What-
ever you may think, one thing I know, I have never degraded myself
by keeping bad company, nor have I ever been degraded in the opinion of the virtuous and good. I have never deserted a friend without
cause, nor never will, as long as his acts were pure and upright.*
　　　　　—Jackson to Andrew Jackson Donelson, May 5, 1831

William R. Galt of Norfolk, Virginia, was ten years old in 1828 when
he accompanied his father on a visit to Andrew Jackson at the Hermitage. Years later, as vividly as he recalled his famous host, he remembered the dark presence of a renowned Mississippi duelist who was able
to take advantage of Jackson's hospitality coincident with their visit.
Except for the image of this frightening man in his broad-brimmed hat,
everyone who flitted about the busy plantation house was cheerful and
informal. The plain-speaking general smoked his corncob pipe and relished company.

It was during Galt's visit that Jackson's election first appeared secure,
when news arrived that the votes of one of the large states had been captured. The guests drank to Jackson's success, though the honoree reportedly shunned the intoxicating spirits. As the story proceeds, Galt recalls
warm moments with Rachel Jackson, whom he describes conventionally as
a "plain matron, whose whole existence was wrapped up in that of her husband." The slaves' cottages that he visited were "as neat and comfortable as
any houses I ever saw," where fibers were spun and "ordinary" clothing was
woven—both for the use of the slaves and for their presumably "ordinary"
master.

The reminiscence concludes with the boy and his father being escorted
to the gate by the general and his wife. "Now my little man, don't forget

14. Rachel Jackson, by Ralph E. W. Earl, 1827. Earl was a favorite of both Jacksons. He lived with them at the Hermitage during the 1820s and was later given a studio at the White House. Courtesy The Hermitage: Home of President Andrew Jackson, Nashville, Tennessee.

that General Jackson put you on your horse!" says the president-to-be. Rachel gives Galt a hickory switch to hold. The party then rides off from the happy Hermitage, lost in silence and profoundly grateful.[1]

Twenty-one-year-old Henry A. Wise, also a Virginian, was able to study Andrew Jackson "in his slipshod ways at home" at nearly the same time, perhaps a month or so before Galt. While he anticipated his accession to the highest national office, the general "showed no signs of impatience," in this account. As Wise explained: "He affected no style, and put on no airs of greatness, but was plainly and simply, though impulsively, polite to all." Jackson made it clear that he "took no trouble to look after any but his lady guests." With a "hidden vein of humor," he was, for the most part, "gravely respectful." His ear was alert, and he exhibited the power of concentration. If he noticeably misused words and pronounced them incorrectly, he was also a man of easy repartee who had comfortably adapted to the constant stream of visitors.

In his later memoir, Wise depicts one of the gatherings that took place during his visit. Jackson, whom he had earlier described as "long and straight in limb," "rounded in the shoulders," with "a high and full-orbed head," "deep-set, clear, small, blue eyes," and a nose "long and Grecian," he refers to this time only from the top: "His hair always standing straight up and out." The general's dear old friend, "queer-looking" John Overton, who had "lost his teeth and swallowed his lips," sat beside Jackson munching on toothless gums. Rachel Jackson, "plethoric and obese," spoke with some difficulty, in short, wheezing spurts, though she remained no less the lady of the house.

Wise goes on: Jackson, as host, engaged in a discussion about the "topics of the day," unremarkable until the conversation drifted to the life of the soul. That was when Jackson proved that he could be both argumentative and tactful, a broad-minded man—at least when it came to religion; he questioned the fixed doctrines of the Presbyterian (Wise's companion) who gamely disputed. Jackson screwed on a face that Wise characterized as "pious pugnacity," and carried on with fervor.[2]

If Galt's Hermitage was dreamlike, Wise experienced a rare, homespun vitality. The first memoirist abstractedly adored Jackson by way of nostalgia; the second had, by the time of his writing, completed a long public career. Wise had come to Nashville to practice law in 1828, and was elected to Congress from his native Virginia as a Jacksonian Democrat in 1833. While in his retrospective he calls Jackson "the greatest man, take him all in all, we have ever known," he ended up stridently opposing Jackson in the last year of his presidency. As we shall see, this was the course that many ardent Jacksonians of 1828 ultimately took.

Wise offers a fascinating portrait, feigning objectivity. It is Galt, however, whose child's imagination provides the more interesting contrast: his vulgar Mississippian with a desperate past, a recognizable "scoundrel," replays Jackson's brutal years as a man who could almost kill with his looks, and who appeared to thrive on the prospect of doling out death. By 1828, we are to understand, the stately president-elect had turned his back on that past, having been fashioned into a mature man of established principles. He had received by this time sufficient testimonials so that honor and integrity adhered to him. In the collective imagination, if not in his own, he had nothing to prove and everything to give.

Another accepted fact about the domestic Jackson was his hospitable nature. He made room for the many guests who happened by. James Alexander Hamilton, third son of the distinguished Federalist who fell victim to Burr's pistol, was a Jackson aide. He visited the Hermitage at Christmastime 1827. "I observed during all my visit," he later wrote, "that the table was loaded with food, and in all the spare rooms there was two beds." Jackson had so much company that at one point, when he wanted to inquire about New York politics, he addressed Hamilton: "we must take our horses; we have no opportunity to be alone here." On the evening of his arrival, the invited guest recalled, "there drove up a farmer with wife, children, and servants, to stay the night; and such was the usual course of things." The demands on Jackson's hospitality were great. In essence, Hamilton explained, "He kept a tavern, without the privilege of making a bill."[3]

The 1828 Campaign

In the years that separated his narrow defeat and his easy victory four years later, Andrew Jackson wrote warm and zealous letters to his backers, awaiting justice in state legislatures, where some presidential electors were still determined, and at the polls. Other than one business trip to Alabama and attendance at the anniversary celebration of the Battle of New Orleans on January 8, 1828 (accompanied by his wife, Generals Coffee and Carroll, and John Overton), he did not leave Tennessee. He tried to conceal his resentment, even in letters to first-term Tennessee congressman James K. Polk, who was full of nerve and endeavoring to serve the interests of his state's favorite son. Polk wrote with affectation on the "sharp shooting" on Capitol Hill; he called politics "the game." But Jackson, measuring his words, refused to march anymore at the head of his supporters' cheering section. No longer adopting a battle-hungry pose, he advanced instead his simple republican ideals, revealing less emotion and more calm and prudence. He separated himself from the "Visionary politicians" and their "disagreeable colision & dispute." Others wrote to give evidence of their devotion, and Jackson, quite self-consciously, responded in language that could sound even stately.[4]

Nashville was not the remote settlement it was when Jackson had arrived there four decades earlier. Its population neared 4,000, while in Davidson County there were 16,000 whites and 11,600 slaves. The surrounding lands were well occupied and much in use. Steamboats linked the Cumberland with the Mississippi, bringing to wider markets Tennessee cotton, tobacco, and, of course, whiskey. Nashville was conspicuously commercial, its groceries selling Holland gin, Jamaica rum, "Cicily Madeira," kegs of almonds, allspice, nutmeg, raisins, rice, and the "best Spanish segars." Booksellers prospered, presenting works of classical antiquity along with modern fiction like that of Washington Irving and James Fenimore Cooper. Theater was very popular, too.[5]

But the frontier mentality remained: general stores advertised "dipt candles," "sweet flour," coffee and sugar, "coarse shoes," and buffalo robes. Newcomer to Nashville Philip Lindsley, president of Cumberland College from 1824 to 1850, remarked about the poor quality of fruits and garden vegetables, and about the restlessness of the local population. "The characteristic vice of the present age," he said, "is *impatience of control.*" Itinerant entertainers—jugglers, fiddlers, animal trainers, fire-eaters—found Nashville fertile ground for charlatan games, and beggars with forged papers and war stories told exaggerated tales of shipwrecks and regularly knocked on doors with their palms outstretched. There was nothing resembling a public school system, but plenty of cockfights and horse races. Because Lindsley wished to reform the Tennesseans, no person who had taken part in a duel was admitted to Cumberland College during the tenure of the New Jersey–bred college president.

He would have had to exclude Congressman Sam Houston, who in 1826 fought a duel, similar to Jackson's with Charles Dickinson, across the Kentucky line. The quarrel between Houston and Gen. William White, a Jackson detractor, arose over the appointment of a postmaster in Nashville but grew in such a way that personal honor and political ambition became indistinguishable. Notes met acknowledgments, a challenge was answered, and the eccentric Houston practiced his aim in a meadow at the Hermitage. "On the first fire White fell badly wounded, Houston untouched, to the great gratification of all the good & moral part of society," Jackson gloated in a letter to Richard Keith Call. "I suppose Houston will have peace—White I think will not die." In his January 1825 inaugural address as the president of Cumberland College, Lindsley defined "manly vigour and maturity" as judgment, refined taste, "accuracy of thought, and clearness of reasoning"—intellectual faculties rather than brute physicality. He planned to tame the children of frontiersmen, if he could not tame the older generation.[6]

Jacksonians made constant reference to the Adams-*Clay* administration, for so it appeared to most. Vice President Calhoun remained politically exiled, and Secretary of State Clay seemed omnipresent. The administration needed to instill a monstrous fear of an out-of-control Jackson if it had any chance of overcoming the angry opposition that had coalesced around former Crawford and even Clay supporters, driven into the Jackson camp after the "corrupt bargain."[7] President Adams himself exhibited great restraint, even fatalism, as he contemplated being a one-term president like his father.[8]

But his supporters, afraid of a Jackson victory, turned up the heat nonetheless. The anti-Jackson forces impugned the general's credibility, and resorted to personal affronts on a grand scale. They supplied five explanations pointing to Jackson's unsuitability for the presidency: (1) he had stolen another man's wife; (2) he had unapologetically engaged in dueling; (3) he had ordered the deaths of American militiamen during the War of 1812; (4) he had overextended martial law and denied civil liberty in New Orleans; (5) he had taken the Florida invasion of 1818 too far, hanging two British subjects.

No one was more direct than the accomplished politician Henry Clay. Jackson's once and future nemesis spoke before his Kentucky constituents just after the "corrupt bargain" of 1825 had put him in the cabinet. Hard-pressed by negative publicity, Clay felt it incumbent upon him to explain why he had helped give Adams the presidency. So he went after Jackson's qualifications: "If General Jackson has exhibited, either in the councils of the Union, or in those of his own state, or in those of any other state or territory, the qualities of a statesman, the evidence of the fact has escaped my attention." His "competency" for the presidency was, Clay added, "highly questionable"; his attainments were merely military. As for the Kentuckian's efforts on behalf of one so unexciting as Adams, the explanation came easily: he had supported the more statesmanlike man. No matter how the public might laud the general for his gallantry, "the impulses of public gratitude should be controled, it appeared to me, by reason and discretion, and I was not prepared blindly to surrender myself to the hazardous indulgence of a feeling"—it simply was not "prudent," to Henry Clay, to elect a mere "military chieftain" as the nation's chief magistrate. After all, how could a "military chieftain" fully comprehend national purposes in a republic, or intellectualize progress? The Jacksonians might counter by comparing their candidate to "military chieftain" George Washington, but Clay's answer to that was: Washington had exercised "a perfect command of the passions," while Jackson only knew how to kill on a large scale.[9]

That was how things stood in the Clay camp in 1825. Over the next two years, every legislative initiative put forward by the Adams-Clay administration was stymied by the Jackson forces in Congress. Nothing of any significance was accomplished by the time the extraordinarily dirty campaign of 1828 got into high gear—though in a way, the campaign of 1824 never ceased. Clay's friend, Cincinnati newspaper editor Charles Hammond, led the attack by broadcasting his disgust with the "clumsy and fulsome flattery" shown toward Jackson. In his 1828 pamphlet, *View of General Jackson's Domestic Relations,* he assailed Rachel unjustifiably for her part in bigamy. Hammond did this by feigning an understanding of Jackson's plight: having responded to a sexually aggressive married woman, he did the proper thing by restoring her to decent stature in making her his wife. Having "fallen from the virtue of chastity," she was "a bruised and broken flower, which he alone can properly appreciate, and cherish." It was a monstrous publication, reducing its argument to the clear implication that, as first lady, Rachel Jackson would, simply by her presence, "offend" society, and sanction "a relaxation of the public morals."[10]

Hammond's attack reflected other, more general concerns. It was as much a jab at Rachel Jackson's lack of class refinement as her past promiscuity. Washington society had developed pretensions: Louisa Catherine Adams, the present first lady, was an accomplished hostess, musical, internationally traveled, and long accustomed to being in the public eye. In contrast, the wife of William H. Crawford was criticized in 1822 as "plain, almost to coarseness and is without any of the airs and graces, which seem appropriate to the wife of a president." How much less social skill would the Washington community discern in the frontier wife who managed affairs at the Hermitage for Andrew Jackson?[11]

Edward Livingston was among those urging Jackson not to give way to righteous indignation that the Adams camp could exploit. "Treat it with contempt," Livingston counseled, with regard to the attack on Rachel's virtue. Jackson's old ally had remained in New Orleans all these years, carefully orchestrating a political rejuvenation in his adopted state to coincide with Jackson's surge. In September 1828, Livingston was in Harrisburg, Pennsylvania, campaigning actively on Jackson's behalf in a key state. "I first knew him when we were members of the House of Representatives, more than thirty years ago," he said in his speech, reminding audiences that he was one of the general's oldest friends. "From that time we never met until he was called to conduct the defence of the city in which I lived. In his conduct of that defence, he developed the resources of mind that proclaimed him equal to any task." Livingston underscored that he knew Jackson to possess a strong sense of personal responsibility, an "energy combined with prudence," and the courage of his convictions in all areas of public life, not just on the battlefield. Jackson, he said, to counter the frontier candidate's detractors, combined "stern integrity" with "courtesy of manner." And, to show his own sense of propriety and obligation (as well as the ambition to join Jackson's cabinet), Livingston journeyed to Nashville in November. At a public banquet arranged by William Carroll and others, he was heralded as "the able and eloquent defender of our much slandered fellow citizen." Livingston was proving again that he was a "steady, unwavering friend."[12]

On the other hand, Louis Louaillier, the Louisiana legislator whom Jackson had summarily arrested and suspected of treason in 1815, spoke out in Clay-like terms against the presidential contender who disrespected the Constitution: the "military chieftain," while "skilful and brave," had committed "arbitrary" and "unjustified" acts. A pro-Jackson orator in Concord, New Hampshire, turned the tables on Louaillier: "As well might the character of Washington be impeached by the testimony of [Benedict] Arnold." Jackson's defense, prepared and launched by growing numbers of friends, was as forceful as the clamorous voices of his detractors. Epithets were slung back and forth; his military record remained front and center. As commander in chief of all the armed forces, he might, the *New York Advertiser* anticipated, do on a vast scale what he had done at the head of a smaller body of men: "What might be expected from his irascible temper, his lawless ambition, his fierce and vindictive spirit, when clothed with the immense power which the constitution reposes in the chief magistrate of the nation?"[13]

Senator Robert Hayne of South Carolina was one of the many who reassured Jackson that he need not step into the fray. He depicted Adams as weak, persuaded by Clay to "yield the reins of government." But to combat the unprincipled Clay was akin to "*savage warfare*," by which Hayne meant a species of war in which no act of restraint was ever reciprocated. Jackson's supporters would fight fire with fire. Though it was the kind of war Jackson understood, this time there were plentiful numbers of younger men to draft and carry out the battle plan.

Manliness was a potent theme in Jackson's 1828 campaign. The cerebral Adams was easy to caricature as unmanly, as much as the valorous Jackson was credited with "stern virtues" and passionate patriotism. Sam Houston vowed that Adams and Clay would "meet retributive justice . . . from the hands of an indignant and *manly* community." In Hayne's letter to Jackson, the same end was projected, but with cautionary advice attached: "There is still another motive that lurks behind the unmanly and ungenerous course of the Administration," the senator disclosed. "It is the desire to betray you into some indiscretion. They have taken pains to impress the public mind with the belief that your *temper* unfits you for civil government, they know that a noble nature is always liable to excitement, and they *have put*, and will continue to put into operation, a hundred schemes to betray you into some act, or expression, which may be turned to their own advantage." Jackson, he said, should guard against renewed attempts to spark an outburst from him; he should take care to retain "the high

15. Jackson as Shakespeare's callous Richard III, his face crawling with corpses. The caricature was printed during the 1828 election campaign. Courtesy the Tennessee Historical Society Collections, Tennessee State Library and Archives.

RICHARD III.

ground of leaving your cause in the hands of the people." The spite-filled campaign was even more relentless and retaliatory than that of 1824.[14]

The most renowned of the anti-Jackson propaganda was the so-called "coffin handbill," revisiting the general's unsympathetic decisions to mete out the ultimate punishment to those he regarded as mutineers in 1814–15. The accusative poster, topped with solid black coffins, isolated Jackson's "bloody deeds" while portraying the condemned militiamen as good sons and husbands. After standing before the firing squad, one of Jackson's bullet-ridden victims did not immediately die from his wounds; the youngster pathetically called out to the colonel in charge: "have I not atoned for this offense? *Shall I not live?*" The surgeon tried his best to preserve the doomed soldier through four days of "inconceivable agony." Likewise, young John Woods, the insubordinate enlistee who had become Jackson's scapegoat, was now glorified as "a generous hearted, noble fellow"; he never had a chance against the cruel commander who, "without knowing any thing of the merits of the case, repeatedly vociferated—'Shoot the damn'd rascal!' " As "appalling" as these incidents were, the handbill maintained that they provided only an "inadequate" picture of the career of sins that the indifferent and indiscriminate tyrant Jackson had cold-bloodedly committed.[15]

The most gruesome of anti-Jackson propaganda was David Claypoole Johnston's engraving of the general as an updated Richard III. Here was the most unmerciful villain in all of Shakespeare, who rose to power by ordering the deaths of his brother, his own wife, two nephews, and others whose loyalty came into question. In the engraving, Jackson's face is composed entirely of twisted corpses, and from his epaulettes dangle more naked dead. His collar is a cannon; a prison cell forms the center of his hollow chest. The tales of the six militiamen, Louaillier, and Ambrister and Arbuthnot are all suggested here. The engraver Johnston had been a stage performer and was well acquainted with the English bard. His Jackson, eyes cold and bloodless, wears an army tent for a hat. The Shakespearean caption below reads: "Methought the souls of all that I had murder'd, came to my tent."[16]

Until this haunting, near the play's end, the always-scheming Richard III seems unmindful of the pain he has inflicted. It is a play about pride and ambition. Any biographer would be hard-pressed to deny that Jackson was proud and ambitious. But Shakespeare's villain knows what he is, and cynically laughs at his own endless capacity to deceive and destroy others. Jackson, on the other hand, was a true believer: he saw virtue in his ambition to augment the power of his country. He believed that the many would share in and gain by his personal success.

If he was scarcely Shakespeare's brute, Jackson did refuse, like Richard III, to retreat in the face of common "logic," remaining instead committed in full to his fixed plans and irreversible decisions. Once engaged, he would not yield. He put his strong sense of propriety—his need for praise, his ambition—to the test. And then he charged ahead. Before entering into the final battle of his misbegotten career, King Richard says to an aide: "I have set my life upon a cast, / And I will stand the hazard of the die." Setting aside his complete moral bankruptcy, Richard III is, in political terms, a Jacksonian gambler.

Andrew Jackson was, in fact, a figure worthy of Shakespeare's art. He took to the national stage representing—be they right or wrong—deeply held principles. He declaimed and harangued and gambled on the results. But he was not Richard III. Nor the improvident Richard II. Nor the introspective Hamlet. He exhibited some of the capriciousness of King Lear, whose passions rise as his judgment weakens, and whose judgments further weaken as his passions rise. But Lear lost his senses, and Andrew Jackson was anything but mad.

In looking for historical comparisons, some have seen Jackson as Napoleonic. Johnston's 1828 engraving of Jackson as Richard III was probably influenced by an 1813 caricature of Napoleon surrounded by corpses. A man particularly suited to times of war, Jackson saw himself, above all else, as an inheritor of the struggle he had seen firsthand as a boy. He considered himself bound by the moral promise spoken and enacted by Revolutionaries. Their vision, that the new nation provided a haven for lovers of liberty, resonated with him. And as for the Napoleon comparison, Jackson was too responsive to the American frontier condition to be reliably compared to a European psychology of appetite and ambition, or universalized.

In a June 1828 letter to Senator John Branch of North Carolina, whom he would appoint secretary of the navy, Jackson espoused his creed and explained why he wanted to be the president. The federal Constitution, he said, was being subverted by the rampant misuse of power in the Adams administration. A strong hand, combined with an activist Congress, was needed to restore the "rightful sovereignty" of the people. Jackson charged that, without popular support, Adams's cabinet was seeking to impose its will "by intrigue, slander & management," as the heads of departments toured the country "circulating forgeries & calumnies." Jackson saw himself as a white knight waiting to march triumphantly into the capital city, refusing, meanwhile, to give in to political attack. "I do not yet dispair of the republic," he vowed. "I shall live to see the day, when virtue shall resume its former empire in the cou[ns]els of the nation; when the public good will be the sole end & aim of the Legislatures of the Union; when our national character will no longer be stained. . . . Virtue, I trust, will once more arise from her lethargy & dispel those corruptions." He was convinced of his own reasonableness, as much as he was convinced that the people wanted a leader who would insure the overthrow of the "monied aristocracy." The candidate had come to feel that his personal authority derived equally from the attractiveness of his noble bearing and his identification with popular causes.[17]

If he was a subject worthy of Shakespeare's imagination, Jackson's political stature in 1828 proved that he understood what King Richard III did not: the power of mutuality, the power of reciprocal loyalty. This was his political calling card. At the same time, Jackson gave little sign of valuing Shakespeare's art. Sketches from Shakespeare were performed in Nashville theaters in the mid-1820s, but there is little in Jackson's writings to indicate that he ever read a Shakespearean play all the way through. He owned an 1823 edition of Shakespeare's works (very possibly a gift) and an 1830 copy of *The Beauties of Shakespeare*, a collection of extended quotations from the various plays.[18] But if he had no literary pretensions, Jackson seemed to appreciate the drama of life quite enough to translate his own self-fashioned public persona into a dazzling symbol of possibility. In 1828, he was thoroughly convinced that America needed him in order to fulfill itself.

Aaron Burr, another adventuresome spirit, misunderstood and coldly fatalistic, wanted to see Andrew Jackson in the presidency. Here is one more tempting vignette to add to our examination of the anomalous election of 1828: "Mysterious messengers came and went," reports the historian Parton, who picked up the gossip of "law-clerks and office-boys." The shadowy Burr was back in New York, practicing law and living a more tranquil life than he had before his showy treason trial; but rumor had it he was pressing quietly for a Jackson victory, engaged in behind-the-scenes electioneering among the friends he had retained in Virginia. Whether Jackson knew of this (he did continue to correspond with several of Burr's old cronies) must remain pure conjecture.[19]

The election of 1828 was mired in hatred. In the end, Jackson defeated the incumbent Adams by 178 electoral votes to 83. The outgoing president made no audible protest while Jackson remained in Tennessee. President-elect Jackson wrote his loyal friend John Coffee from the Hermitage on December 11 that while their names were being dragged through journalistic mud, he and his wife had been preserved "from the wicked slanders of the combined and corrupt minions of a profligate administration . . . , the most bitter and wicked persecution, recorded in history."[20]

On December 22, 1828, Rachel Jackson suddenly died. She had been "Aunt Rachel" to many who came to call on the Jacksons, and she had effectively carried out the management of her husband's plantation business during his long absences. Other than her recourse to religious homilies, Rachel's most frequently remarked-upon quality was her total devotion to the general. She concurred with his view of humanity and often praised him, as during the Creek campaign: "You justly obsurve a virtuous man will meet The rewards Due to that high merit and Let me assure you no man is or Can be more praised and applauded then you are."[21] He, in turn, cherished his "ever faithfull and affectionate wife" (as she sometimes signed her letters), almost as if she were a doll—yet a doll whom he entrusted with financial affairs, and one to whom he spared no detail of the soldier's life. James A. Hamilton, meeting her barely a year before she died, noted that she was "correct and easy in her manners, playful in conversation, and fond of a joke." He also observed that she was, in

16. "Mrs J was a few days past, suddenly & violently attacked with pains in her left shoulder & breast." President-elect Jackson to Richard Keith Call, December 22, 1828, the day Rachel Jackson died. Courtesy The Hermitage: Home of President Andrew Jackson, Nashville, Tennessee.

outward appearance only, "an uncommonly ugly woman," and the first he had ever seen smoke a cigar.[22]

The last letter Jackson wrote before his wife died—just hours before—was to Richard Call, in Florida. Call and his wife, Mary, were particularly close to Rachel Jackson; she had felt for the young couple in their struggle against prejudice to unite. Her own romance with Andrew Jackson had succeeded, of course, only after she had endured a slow disconnection from her vindictive first husband. Wrote Jackson, revealing all:

> Mrs J. was a few days past, suddenly & violently attacked, with pains in her left shoulder & breast, & such the contraction of the breast, that suffocation was apprehended before the necessary aid could be afforded. Doctor Hogg has relieved her, & altho worse today, than yesterday, I trust in kind providence, that he will restore her to her usual health in due time to set out for Washington.

Jackson expressed his hope that Call would meet them at the Hermitage, so that they could all travel together to his inauguration. "I cannot leave her, believing as I do, that my seperating from her would destroy her & the persecution she has suffered, has endeared her more if possible than ever to me."[23]

At the funeral, beside the large garden adjacent to the Hermitage mansion, William Carroll propped up the bereaved husband, who by now walked with a cane. A weeping black servant, a "favorite" of Rachel, attempted to throw herself in the grave as the coffin was put in place. Jackson remained steady, instructing those who interceded to allow the old slave a final moment beside her mistress. He himself was accepting of fate. Dr. Felix Robertson, at this time Nashville's mayor, suspended business as a sign of respect. The town's church bells tolled throughout the hour of the funeral, which was being held some twelve miles away. "The road to the Hermitage was almost impassable," a Philadelphian who was there recorded.[24]

Without his wife, the sixty-two-year-old incoming president left Nashville and moved to Washington. John Overton had occasion to visit the empty Hermitage, and wrote to Jackson's other best friend, John Coffee, who now resided on a plantation in northern Alabama. "Mrs. J bedroom was closed," he reported of the ghostly encounter. "The overseer lives in the dining room—the parlour and drawing room were locked." The visitor was permitted in, the rooms unlocked, then locked again as he exited. "This was genteel," Overton continues in the letter.

"In fact the whole appearance of house, yard & garden, were neat and decorous—tho every thing looked lonesome, but this might have been owing to former recollections." His wistful tones made clear that for Overton, at least, the Hermitage had lost its charm. Meanwhile, in Washington, Jackson spoke with deep feeling of the loss of Rachel. When James A. Hamilton, acting secretary of state (until the arrival of Martin Van Buren) commiserated with him, Jackson said, more needful than commanding in tone: "I am glad you are here; you must give me all your time; you have all my confidence."[25]

In Washington, on March 4, 1829, as the oath of office was administered by Chief Justice John Marshall, Andrew Jackson, dressed in "a suit of plain black cloth," took the Bible and pressed it to his lips, then bowed to the crowd in attendance. In his inaugural address, he promised a mild administration: "I shall keep steadily in view the limitations as well as the extent of the executive power." The adoring crowd slowed his progress down Pennsylvania Avenue on this warm, bright day. Francis Scott Key, watching the spectacle, cried out repeatedly, "It is beautiful, it is sublime!" People of all social classes, whites and blacks, excitedly stalked the president's party. "The living mass was impenetrable," wrote one who was there. Arriving at the White House just behind the president, they acted out one of the most notorious scenes in American history, indiscriminately rushing through the front door and nearly crushing the president himself in their efforts to shake his hand. The celebrants' rowdiness ultimately compelled Jackson to seek shelter at his late lodgings. When the free-for-all died down, glass and chinaware had been shattered, some people had fainted, others left with bloody noses, and many had escaped through windows because the doors were blocked. Democracy had arrived.[26]

The Eaton Affair

Jackson's problems as president began, and in a sense detonated, with the selection of his cabinet. He had appointed his dependable protégé John Eaton as his secretary of war, for he had had so many run-ins with the War Department during his years in the military that he would brook no interference from an independent-minded secretary—the dutiful Eaton was perfect in this regard.[27] Eaton's wife was deceased, and a passionate attachment had at some point developed with Margaret O'Neale Timberlake, young wife of a navy purser who died while overseas in 1828—by his own hand, it was rumored. John Eaton married the widow, with little delay and amid rumors of impropriety, on January 1, 1829.[28]

The new president's cabinet was widely regarded as an awkward collection of unstatesmanlike political cronies. Jackson was early on made aware that his cabinet members' wives—and most prominently the wife of Vice President Calhoun—had chosen to snub Mrs. Eaton. Even at the inaugural ball, they had refused to be introduced to her.[29] One Washington socialite, who steered clear of the controversy, retrospectively termed Margaret "one of the most ambitious, violent, malignant, yet silly women you ever heard of."[30] Jackson was incensed, no doubt because he saw parallels to his own struggle with social status. His humble roots, his backwoods education, had been held against him in Washington. And he could hardly forget the obligation he had been under during the campaign just past to respond to moral questions concerning his marital history.

Eaton, like Andrew Jackson, was protective of his spouse. Both men had met their future wives as newcomers to a place and while boarding with the future wife's mother; both men were obliged to defend their behavior in light of the fact of the first husbands' long absences. The devastating loss of Rachel, fresh memories of the slanders leveled at her during the presidential contest, plus Jackson's constant perception that enemies swarmed about him, stimulated his martial inclination to seek justice and personal vindication for his choices.

According to Margaret Eaton's later autobiography, she had had many suitors, but was nonetheless chaste when she met John Timberlake at her father's tavern. First Lady Dolley Madison and other Washington notables had attended the Timberlakes' 1816 wedding. Margaret attests that as a temperamental sixteen-year-old, she was a "foolish young girl-bride," also "hasty," insofar as a son was born to her five months after the wedding. "Not a breath of disparagement was breathed against me then."[31]

Acknowledging her "giddiness," even as a mature woman, with a frivolous "unguardedness" of manner and "freaks of temper," she insisted that she had been a faithful wife up to the time her husband died at sea. "I have been the victim of political rancor," she insisted, adding that John Eaton "became very much attached to my husband, Mr. Timberlake; and the affection was reciprocated." Hastiness in remarrying? Margaret pointed out that by the time of her marriage to the Tennessee senator, the couple had known each other for ten years. "It began to be whispered that he loved me when my first husband was living," a rumor, she maintained, that was "the product of jealousy," because handsome Eaton was a widower who sought no more socially distinguished a bride than this tavern keeper's daughter. It was Jackson, she said, who had told his friend Eaton, "Go and marry her at once, and shut their mouths." What Margaret admired about Jackson was his simple consistency: "He did not like or dislike people: he loved them or hated them."[32]

Her own relationship to Jackson was one in which Margaret, by her own admission, played the role of child. She said whatever she chose: "My vivacity was an amusement to him. . . . He was to me like a second father." Her retrospective opinion of Rachel Jackson seems to point to what would have been, for Jackson, a common thread linking the two injured women: Mrs. Eaton denotes Mrs. Jackson as "a woman of uncultivated manners, but of unsullied heart . . . [who] had a sensitiveness that made these persecutions particularly intolerable to her." Jackson, she added meaningfully, "seemed to feel this, that every woman needed a defender." Once at a dinner at the Hermitage during Jackson's presidency, Mrs. Eaton found the host "stretched across" Rachel's grave. "This great old hater was a grand old lover," she concluded. His defense of female purity fortified his own overwhelming sense that virtue must be rewarded—or, in other words, that decency needed to be asserted, and he was the one to assert it.[33]

Jackson liked women who were personable, just so long as they were faithful. In this, he was embracing an eighteenth-century sensibility that had carried over into the nineteenth century. As novel after novel instructed, the reward of virtue was meant to be a life well lived, a life of quiet composure and domestic harmony. That is what Andrew and Rachel Jackson had professedly enjoyed, certainly to their neighbors looking in on them. They raised dutiful nephews as their own children, while offering their home to the children of neighboring planters who had died prematurely; they gave love and social advantages to the Indian orphan, Lyncoya, plucked from the field of battle in Alabama, when no one else would take him in. In the emblematic novel of sentiment, Henry Mackenzie's *The Man of Feeling*, the protagonist Harley rescues a desperate prostitute and reunites her with her utterly decent, despairing father. Harley roams a brutal world looking for opportunities to do good for those most in need.

In an odd way, it was the same for Jackson, who perceived a troubled world and remained upright. Harley is a pacifist; Jackson, of course, was anything but. Others may have perceived him as a callous warrior, though that is not what Jackson saw in the mirror. He imagined himself an unselfish man of feeling, with a fatherly concern for his flock, and whose mission it was to restore equilibrium where he encountered moral imbalance and discord. Margaret Eaton was not "lost," in the idiom of the sentimental novel; she was being slandered. "Would you abandon her to the insults of an unfeeling world?" the Man of Feeling asks the father of the prostitute. Jackson, the protagonist in a morality tale of his own authorship, was asking the same question. He empathized with the Eatons and contemplated what their fate would be if they did not have an avenging president to intercede in this latest case of threatened virtue.[34]

In a certain sense, the instigator of Margaret Eaton's problem—the president's problem by proxy—was a man whom Andrew Jackson and Rachel Jackson had professed to love quite nearly as much as they loved John Eaton. That man was Richard Keith Call. There was a stubborn streak in Call that would ultimately lead to Jackson's branding him a betrayer.

A militia general, Florida's voice in Congress in the mid-1820s, Call had lived with both Jackson and Eaton at the O'Neales' inn. A moralist like Jackson, he openly expressed his concern for Eaton's well-being. Eaton had been the first to take up residence at the O'Neales', in 1818, as a senator; it was he who arranged for Jackson and Call to board with him. Forebodingly, during his extended stay, Call heard numerous tales about Mrs. Timberlake's moral abandon, and he seemed to know enough not to dismiss the stories as mere gossip. He quarreled with her often, and after cautioning the unbelieving Eaton about her easy virtue, decided to take up Eaton's impulsive challenge that he "try her" himself. The incident that followed brought Margaret to tears and caused Jackson to lecture Call, who stubbornly insisted that her affectation of hurt was nothing but mock modesty.[35]

Around the same time as this was happening, Call himself concluded a long siege. He had endured years of emotional turmoil over his match with Mary Kirkman of Nashville. The couple, in love since 1819, was kept apart because Mary's parents detested Jackson and would not see their daughter fall in with a Jackson aide. In 1821, Jackson had written Call (then in Florida), advising him that he had seen Mary, and that she had had a revealing conversation with Eaton as well, confirming her strong feelings for Call, regardless of her parents' wishes. "You & Miss Mary ought to forget each other, forever," Jackson wrote then, "or at once marry. . . . you have friends who will aid you, in this number include me." The wedding ceremony in the summer of 1824 was held at the Hermitage. Afterward, when Jackson paid a peacemaking visit to the Kirkmans, Call's new mother-in-law allegedly ordered the general from her home at pistol point. She went so far as to mail to the editor of the Philadelphia *National Gazette* a ten-dollar bill along with a series of conciliatory private letters Jackson had sent her. She somehow thought that their publication would harm Jackson. It was not until a year or more later, when Call was apologizing to Jackson from Florida for his wife's delivery of a daughter—"we had flattered ourselves with the hope of giving our first borne the name of our best and dearest friend Andrew Jackson"—that Mrs. Kirkman's hostility diminished, though it never entirely receded.[36]

Eaton had continued on at the O'Neales' after Jackson and Call left Washington. Years later, when Call returned to the capital to attend Jackson's inauguration, Eaton had just married the widow Timberlake. As the Eaton affair exploded in Washington, Call found common ground with the Rev. Ezra Stiles Ely of Philadelphia, a respected acquaintance of Jackson since the 1790s, whose honesty and solid religious convictions led Call to believe that this was just the man to convince Jackson of Margaret Eaton's lack of virtuous character. Jackson's response was instantaneous and unequivocal: he dispatched William B. Lewis to collect testimonials attesting to Mrs. Eaton's purity, while discrediting Ely's information (and, by imputation, Call's). "You were badly advised," he wrote Reverend Ely just three weeks after his inaugural. Men "base enough" to have assailed the president's late, lamented wife were certainly "not too good *secretly* to slander the living." Because defending female virtue meant as much to him as defending his appointment of Eaton to the cabinet, Jackson would stay on the case for well over a year.[37]

It is also noteworthy that in writing to Ely, Jackson invoked the Masonic creed. In 1829, Edward Livingston, now U.S. senator from Louisiana, was offered the highest office in American Masonry, and would be installed in Washington the following year as "General Grand High Priest of the General Royal Arch Chapter of the United States." Eaton was a Freemason, too, and the president was convinced that his Masonic brother "could not have had criminal intercourse with another mason's wife, without being one of the most abandoned of men," and making a mockery of the brotherhood—which he and Eaton both took seriously. (Back in 1818, the year he was first elected to the Senate, Eaton had the honor of giving the oration at the Cumberland Lodge of Masons on the day the cornerstone of Nashville's Masonic Hall was laid.) Besides, Jackson advised Ely, "there could not have been any illicit intercourse between Mr. Eaton and Mrs. Timberlake without my having some knowledge of it; and I assure you, sir, that I saw nothing." And that "nothing" was absolute when the president's conviction was expressed: he trusted equally in the sanctity of the Masonic creed and in his own acute capacity to sniff out corruption.[38]

Call wrote the president in April proclaiming that he had no low motive, no desire to "prejudice" Jackson against either of the Eatons. Yet he was insisting, "I fear you are still deceived" concerning the history of their "domestic relations." Call claimed he possessed the "*most conclusive reason*" to believe that the couple had formed a pact in 1824 to marry in the event of Timberlake's death. He did not explain how this morbid hope was revealed to him, but stuck fast to his position. In reply, the president wrote fixedly: "I have ever believed her a virtuous and much injureed Lady—it appears you have thought differently, but as you have given me no evidence, entitled to any weight, in support of your opinion, I must be excused for adhering to my own opinion." In their standoff, Jackson was attempting to sound reasonable, as Call's animus was never made clear.[39]

Yet it was not only Call among those close to Jackson who felt this way. Andrew Jackson Donelson, the nephew he raised, now the president's personal secretary, thought ill of Margaret Eaton, and made his feelings known. Taking up his own defense, John Eaton warned Donelson's wife (and first cousin), Emily, who served unofficially as White House hostess, not to listen to any of the "meddling gossips" just then in the air of Washington. Eaton pointedly repeated to her what Rachel Jackson had told him about her first visit to Washington in 1815: many of the women she met had attempted to poison her ear with "little slanderous tales," but she had known better than to let others decide a person's character for her. Emily was "young and uninformed," Eaton reminded her, and rather than succumb, she should profit from the late Mrs. Jackson's infallible advice. But Emily and her husband demurred, associating themselves with publicly outspoken detractors of the Eatons in Tennessee. The two Donelsons became, in Jackson's words, willing "tools of . . . wickedness." Unfazed, Andrew J. Donelson protested to his uncle that it was his right to associate (or not associate) with whomever he and his wife chose, and that in complaining to Jackson merely to "excite his sympathies," the "childish" Margaret Eaton had given "abundant evidence of the indelicacy which distinguishes her character."[40]

The ghost of Rachel Jackson hovered over the Eaton affair. Citing rumors about the former Mrs. Timberlake that were current in 1824, Jackson revealed that his late wife had heard them, and he used this fact to further evince his disgust with Washington's treatment of women from modest backgrounds: "Female virtue is like a tender and delicate flower," he justified. "Let but the breath of suspicion rest upon it, and it withers & perhaps perishes forever. When it shall be assailed by envy & malice, the good & the pious will maintain its purity & innocence, until guilt is made manifest — not by *rumors* & *suspicions,* but by facts & proofs brought forth & sustained by respectable & fearless witnesses in the face of day." It is also worth noting that in writing his first letter to Ely on this subject, Jackson remarked that "the licentious and depraved state of society" needed "purifying." In relations between men and women, the Man of Feeling was unfailingly chivalrous; he always came down hard on those whom he felt threatened the cause of purity.[41]

The president's sensitivity to the insidious ways of Washington politics cut deep. Seeing his wife hurt incensed him, perhaps like nothing else. Rachel Jackson had revealed her feelings about newspaper attacks, in private letters, with her well-known piety: "I C[an do all] things in Christ who strengtheneth me," she wrote a close female friend. "the enemys of the Gen[era]ls have dipt their arrows in wormwood and gall and sped them at me Almighty God was there ever aney thing to equal it."[42]

The Eaton controversy reminded Jackson of what he needed no reminder. He had even alerted the long-trusted Call about it, first in the spring of 1827: "Dear Call, I have no doubt thro the newspapers, you have seen the base attempt, by Clay and his panders, to harrow up the feelings of Mrs J and myself." And in the summer of 1828: "The whole object of the coalition is to calumniate me . . . , even Mrs J is not spared, and my pious Mother, nearly fifty years in the tomb, and who, from her cradle to her death, had not a speck upon her character, has been dragged forth by Hammond and held to public scorn as a prostitute who intermarried with a Negro." The Eaton affair would cause the president to repeat his long deceased mother's "Christian" exhortation to him in youth: "Never to sue a man or indict him for slander."[43]

Having risked his relationship with Jackson, the embattled Call answered the president's letters on the subject in 1829 stubbornly, allowing that the president was more charitable than *he* could be, and predicting (accurately) that no matter what Jackson tried, the innkeeper's daughter would never be welcomed in the society of his other cabinet members. (When the visiting Eatons were later snubbed by what Jackson called a "coalition" in Nashville, Call's mother-in-law, the ever-vindictive Mrs. Kirkman, headed the group.) Meaningfully, Jackson scrawled on the back of one of Call's letters: "evidence of the falibility of the man and how far he will be carried by his prejudices."[44]

To save the friend at hand, Jackson was ready to write off another trusted friend in what was once a kind of triumvirate. He would get back at Call for breaking faith by naming John Eaton, rather than him, governor of Florida in 1834. To add insult to injury, in 1836, his last year as president, Jackson unceremoniously dismissed Call from his Florida military command. Thus let go, the once devoted Call turned his back on Jackson's party and joined William Henry Harrison and the opposition Whigs.[45]

Jackson had liked Margaret and family from the start. Right after moving in with the O'Neales at the end of 1823, the momentary senator had written his wife that Margaret's mother was an "amiable pious wife," and "Mrs Timberlake the maryed daughter whose husband belongs to our navy, plays on the piano delightfully." A sprightly Margaret had politely asked the general to "present" Mrs. Jackson "with her respects," and Jackson expressed unfeigned delight in the domestic scene: "When you come here," he assured Rachel, "I am convinced you will be much pleased with this family."[46] *He* certainly was, and he maintained his loyalty in 1829. "I would sink with honor to my grave, before I would abandon my friend Eaton," he wrote. "I will support him, he is a well tried friend."[47]

At the heart of it all, Jackson believed that the treatment of both Eatons was a masked attack on him, a political strategy motivated, as one historian writes, "by masculine malice, not feminine morality." Much as he blamed "satellites of Clay, who has duped some of our Tenneseens," there was also the vice president's ambition to contend with—and that would prove a significant, if not the underlying, element, as the Eaton affair unraveled during the next year. Jackson was slow to fault Calhoun for his wife's role in the early rumblings of domestic discontent within the administration; this was no doubt because Jackson did not believe that political wives were important enough to upset the political order. He was decidedly of the conviction that women did not belong in political life. As he wrote explicitly to Richard Call, he was never surprised by slanders initiated by his political enemies. It was the moral weakness he perceived in those he counted on as "personal and confidential friends"—such as Call and Calhoun—that "astonished and mortified" him. Indeed, the twists and turns of the Eaton affair never ceased to confound him.[48]

Amid the emotional trials of his early months in office, Jackson was alerted to the reversal of fortune of another of his friends, Sam Houston. After serving two terms in the House of Representatives, and then being elected governor of Tennessee, Houston married a woman who had apparently been convinced to marry him for the accompanying social advantages, though she was all the while in love with another man. One of the pallbearers at Rachel Jackson's funeral, the sensitive Houston had dissolved the marriage after only three months, writing a letter to his erstwhile father-in-law attesting to his wife's virtue. He resigned the governorship in April 1829 to relocate to Cherokee country, where he had found friendship and solace in the past—he had raised eyebrows in Washington on more than one occasion when he dressed in Indian clothing. Tennessee, for the moment, turned its back on him. The move to Arkansas Territory (eastern Oklahoma), where a portion of the Indians had resettled, was his first step on the road to Texas and greater renown.[49]

"I am rejoiced that you have cleaned the stalls of Washington," Houston wrote from Indian country to President Jackson in September of that year, while bemoaning his own inability to forget politics. "When I left the world I had persuaded myself that I would lose all care, about the passing of political events. . . . It is hard for an old Trooper, to forget the *note* of the *Bugle*."[50] Jackson thought at first that Houston had gone "mad," but he did not abandon him—not by any means.

As the impulsive advocate of the resettled Indian, frontier attorney Houston purveyed legal advice among the Cherokees. He did not stop looking after his own interests, however. While speculating for himself in Osage land, he built relationships with a variety of Indian merchants from his well-situated "Wigwam Neosho" along the Texas or Military Road. The president entertained granting the self-exiled Houston a lucrative government contract for supplying rations to the Indians, though he was outbid by another. Jackson was obliged in the end to deny Houston the contract, but his dilatory posture made it clear that his fondness for Houston was unabated.[51]

Houston, in true Jacksonian fashion, came under press attack for his expectation of presidential favor. He fired back with a proclamation that amounted to political satire. He promised to give a reward to "the author of the most elegant, refined, and ingenious lie or calumny." Less good-naturedly, when he came back to Washington in 1832, he physically assaulted loose-lipped Ohio congressman William Stanbery, striking blow after blow with a stick. The startled representative looked up at his antagonist, who stood over him with a pistol; it was a scene reminiscent of something the rambunctious Andrew Jackson might have done at an earlier age.[52]

The president openly sympathized with Houston, reportedly saying that a few more such beatings would satisfy his desire for congressmen to "learn to keep civil tongues in their head." When the Rev. Joshua Danforth pressed Jackson to disavow his "favorite," the president replied that he fully understood Houston's ire. The principle was simple: to suffer slander was, in Jackson's view, worse than to be murdered, for death preserved "good character," and a "good heritage" descended to one's children; slander left one alive, but "a living monument to disgrace," and only conveyed "infamy" to one's children. Meanwhile, one of the Jackson faithful, Rep. James K. Polk, saw to it that Houston was not subject to retaliatory action by the Congress.[53]

The American Temperament

Alexis de Tocqueville spent 1831–32 touring America from New York to New Orleans, encompassing seven thousand miles in less than nine months. He wrote of a country in which manners held power over politics, and where legislators were subject to the "daily passions" of their constituents. He was cautious in projecting the future of a people so prone, as he saw them, to jealousy and mistrust. Along these lines, he perceived Jackson in superficial terms, as "the slave of the majority" who "tramples on his personal enemies, whenever they cross his path."

The Union, Tocqueville said, had occurred by "accident." America's future was assured, with or without that union, by the natural endowments that still lay before an impatient, energetic, acquisitive citizenry. Tocqueville regarded democracy as a mixed blessing, and found it paradoxical: "It is possible to conceive of men arrived at a degree of freedom that should completely content them; they would then enjoy their independence without anxiety and without impatience. But men will never establish any equality with which they can be contented." Andrew Jackson would not have accepted the notion that a passionate regard for equality under freedom could lead to a lifetime of discontent—but this was what Tocqueville came away with, when he generalized that there was little suicide in America, but much insanity.[54]

Michel Chevalier came from France to Jacksonian America shortly after Tocqueville, in 1833, but stayed longer—two full years. His observations were in many ways similar to those of his countryman, and perhaps presented with greater flair. He found in Americans' lives "the appearance of general ease," and reported "the material work of settlement . . . well advanced." He summed up the people's potential by investing their collective mind with the signifying marks of "a mission to perform, nothing less than to redeem a world from savage forests, panthers, and bears." The democracy he uncovered expressed itself vocally: "Democracy everywhere has no soft words, no suppleness of forms; it has little address, little of management; it confuses moderation with weakness, violence with heroism. Little used to self-control, it gives itself unreservedly to its friends and sets them up as idols to whom it burns incense." Chevalier could have been speaking of the frontier-bred Andrew Jackson himself.[55]

What, then, did the Jackson phenomenon do for American manners, or to put it another way, how do the expressions of others provide insights into Jackson's mind? These are pertinent questions to pose at this moment in the story. Jackson had immersed himself in a series of self-justifying actions which would shape the mood of his presidency. He enlarged the Eaton affair into a test of personal loyalty, and was about to wrap himself in the flag and tangle with the vice president over states' rights. Then, with Calhoun chastised, he would turn his full attention to the mission of destroying the Bank of the United States on behalf of "the people," taking on a majority in Congress. He aimed to do the political equivalent of redeeming America from "savage forests, panthers, and bears."

None of this happened suddenly, because "the people" did not yet have their voice. Ever since the "corrupt" election of 1824, Jackson had strongly supported the direct election of the president. This way, he contended, the people would be heard. He was confident that a war on the bank would do as much, empowering citizens to overturn the operation of "privilege" in American politics—what has ostensibly made Jackson a "democrat" in the historical imagination.

The limitations of this term should be obvious by now: As a man of his time, with static social views, Jackson did not possess the acuteness to identify the potential of Indians or African-Americans or even white women to contribute substantively to America's future. He did not believe in complete equality of opportunity. "Humanity," for him, consisted of patronizing acts toward any group deemed inferior to white men. His democracy mirrored his own life: he meant to let loose those forces that had allowed *him* to pursue *his* ambition on the frontier. He welcomed social ferment in which ordinary, young, unprivileged white men, like the Overtons, Coffees, Bentons, Carrolls, Eatons, and Calls, whom he had taken to his breast, would seize control over their futures and make their fortunes in land. He embraced the ideal of the self-made man.

The democratic people, in Jacksonian relief, increasingly appeared to outside observers to be consumed by money rather than by political power.

This was not just how Tocqueville, but also how the English traveler Frances Trollope found Americans. Having plied the Mississippi by steamboat and spent many months in Cincinnati as Jackson assumed the presidency, she formed quite settled opinions about westerners. They gave constant evidence of a "spirit of enterprise," she said, but they could not "resist the smothering effect of a demand for dollars." Disappointed by their coarseness, she nonetheless marveled, "Any man's son may become the equal of any other man's son; and the consciousness of this is certainly a spur to exertion." This was Jackson's catechism, of course, and it persisted, feeding a widespread self-satisfaction with which proud Jackson himself can be easily identified. Mrs. Trollope was criticized by Ohioans for refusing to believe that "all American citizens were equally eligible" to become president of the United States. Jackson confirmed—rather than was responsible for—that notion.[56]

Individuals' preoccupation with the improvement of their personal circumstances led foreigners to conclude that Americans had become "all business," their souls absorbed in the pursuit of a visibly better life. Their pursuit made the pace of life fast (compared to the American past, compared to Europe). The people of the 1820s and 1830s were a restless, fortune-seeking people. Measuring their worth according to their industry and exertions did not dampen their enthusiasm for the value of honesty, as Jackson's own rhetoric epitomizes; but as Mrs. Trollope put it, no two Americans ever carried on a conversation "without the word DOLLAR being pronounced between them. Such unity of purpose, such sympathy of feeling, can, I believe, be found nowhere else, except, perhaps, in an ants' nest." Americans' peculiarity was seen, both by others and by themselves, in their common manner of honest, earnest dealing; their goal was simply to live well, and this was the way to do it. Their enemy was whatever stood in the way of their living well—or, whatever they were *convinced* preyed on them, tyrantlike. This was the tone Jackson adopted, too, when he articulated his political agenda, especially when he was poised to attack the banking system.[57]

Before we turn to the dual threats of Calhoun and the banking power, we need to consider Jackson's final decree on Indian affairs. If his presidency was metaphorically devoted to America's redemption from "savage forests, panthers, and bears," in Chevalier's phrase, then Indian removal is key. It was the Indians' vision of America—unbounded and unregulated—that Jackson had to strike at first, realizing politically what he had fought to achieve militarily.

One cannot appreciate the American temperament during Jackson's presidency without reflecting on dramatic events that accelerated the course of Indian removal. After retiring from the U.S. Army, Jackson had continued to believe that the aboriginals stood in the way of the justifiable expansion of his country. He had a conception of civilization that placed the idealized "American people" at a deliberately chosen place on nature's spectrum between "opulent" city dwellers (divorced from, and thus unproven in, the natural realm) and the uncivilized, morally unfit Indian "barbarian." Back when he had personally overseen the destruction of the Red Sticks in the Creek War of 1814, Jackson addressed his victorious troops, explaining that, while brave, the backward Indians possessed a fatal ignorance of the valuable energy generated by brave men who were also civilized: "They knew not what brave men could effect.... Barbarians they were ignorant of the influence of civilization and government over the human powers." It was inevitable, in Jackson's mind, then and as president fifteen years later, that the North American Indian was to disappear from the white man's America.[58]

This "ill-fated race," as Jackson termed them, would be in a state of "degradation" for as long as they lived side by side with whites. In the developmental model of American nationhood, they were children who could not mature, a dying breed unequal to the task of taming and improving the land. The premature death of sixteen-year-old Lyncoya in 1828, the Creek orphan the Jacksons adopted, confirmed, in a way, the notion that Indians could not "grow up" as white America sprang ahead. Lyncoya, as Jackson had once noted, could not break free of the Indian in him. The fact that they were America's children could not save the Indians. Jackson rationalized, as he superintended the final amputation, that tearing eastern Indians from their traditional lands was an act of paternal concern. He knew what was best for his children and was only trying to save them, or forestall their sad destiny.[59]

Prior to his presidency, Jackson's executive decision making was most often tested in Indian policy. He used only decisive words, ignoring the niceties of legal argument: "There can be no question but congress has the right to Legislate on this Subject," he recorded in the years between the Seminole War and the election of 1824. The United States, self-constituted and self-governing, did not need to step lightly, or consult solicitously, with lesser peoples. Where the federal government was strong enough, he would direct it to pass laws (unilaterally) for the "welfare & happiness of the Indian and for the convenience and benefit of the

u. states." Why negotiate as putative equals? "It appears to me," he had written quintessentially to then–Secretary of War Calhoun, "that it is high time to do away with the farce of treating with Indian tribes."[60] As always with Jackson, when power was put in his hands, he rejected compromise. On the ground, as the general, he had acted firm and guiltless in the presence of Cherokees, Choctaws, Chickasaws, and Creeks.

In his first annual message to Congress, in December 1829, Jackson acknowledged that certain of the eastern Indians had "made some progress in the arts of civilized life," but he still claimed that their independence was best preserved west of the Mississippi. He further insisted that no state government should be obliged to contend with Indian sovereignty issues. His highly political move here was to court former Crawford supporters in Georgia, where gold had been found on Cherokee land, land that whites were eager to exploit. Secretary of War Eaton had no qualms about carrying out the president's wishes with regard to the forcefully negotiated removal of Indians. Eaton's successor, Lewis Cass of Michigan (like Eaton, a prominent Mason), would be even more outspoken and equally as convinced as Jackson that Indians were a degenerating race.[61]

Congress approved the Indian Removal bill in the spring of 1830, authorizing Jackson to commence negotiations with those who spoke for the tens of thousands of Indians who still lived east of the Mississippi. Cold-bloodedly, he proposed to finance removal by selling Indian lands to whites, who would pay considerably more than the government doled out to the politically and legally disadvantaged Indians. He called the Indians who resisted him "poor and deluded," and he charged that lawyers like the former attorney general, William Wirt, who defended the Georgia land claims of the Cherokees, were interested only in money. The president told one Cherokee delegation a revealing parable: the Catawbas he knew as a boy in the Waxhaws were once a powerful, violent tribe, he said, who roasted their Cherokee prisoners and ate their intestines. But the fierce Catawbas had at length become a poor and miserable group, surrounded by whites. Only in a new environment might Indians have a future, and reach upward toward civilization. Meanwhile, the president made it clear that he was helpless against whatever form of intimidation the Georgians were going to apply to appropriate Cherokee land.[62]

The condescension Jackson showed was not his invention. Government officials had for decades expressed exasperation with the "stubbornness" of Indian leaders who were unable or unwilling to comprehend the "humanitarian" character of directives emanating from the nation's capital.[63] For

Jackson, however, removal may have represented something more than the accomplishment of a political goal. So often likened by his more sophisticated eastern opponents to the "barbaric" sons of nature he disparaged, the president was engaging in an act of exorcism as well as national self-definition, applying raw power and his unyielding will to the removal of a shadow that seemed to follow him. In early 1829, when he arrived in Washington to assemble his cabinet and prepare for inauguration, his lodgings were popularly called "the Wigwam."[64]

In every letter to an Indian, in every treaty negotiation, he was obliged to employ the standard address of "Brother." Others who had never lived within a day's ride of Indians might feel a distant empathy and conjure nostalgia for the romantically "vanishing" Indian. Not so Jackson. He had struggled often with what he imagined were intractable Indians, while being himself dismissed as one who did not belong in polite society. "Great pains have been taken to represent me as a savage disposition," he wrote John Coffee in 1824, "who allways carried a scalping knife in one hand, and a tomahawk in the other, allways ready to knock down, and scalp any and every person who differed with me in opinion." He was seen on his "good behavior," wrote a proper Bostonian in 1833, after Harvard honored the president with a doctor of laws degree; "the charm of his personal presence" surprised those who had been taught to expect a man without manners. Margaret Bayard Smith of Washington, D.C., a Crawford supporter in 1824, mourned the death of Rachel Jackson only insofar as Mrs. Jackson possessed the ability to "control the violence of his temper, sooth the exacerbations of feelings always keenly sensitive and excessively irritable, who heal'd by her kindness wounds inflicted by his violence." But on meeting him not long after, Smith wrote, "I shall like him if ever I know him, I am sure,—so simple, frank, friendly. He looks bowed down with grief as well as age and that idea excited my sympathy." Images of the savage president abound, though they cannot possibly capture the whole Jackson. Hardened partisan editors and frustrated eastern politicians were the ones responsible for constructing such prejudicial images. They confined Jackson to a cultural prison from which he could hardly have escaped, even if he wanted.[65]

The response of Massachusetts congressman John Davis to his first private meeting with Jackson in December 1829 is as revealing as Margaret Smith's: "I have been to see all the lions and bears," Davis wrote his wife colloquially, "and no one surely makes a more comical appearance than the head of the nation." The trappings of Jackson's storied past seemed to define him. As Davis looked around the president's office, "the first object of interest which struck my eye was the three honest old fashioned pipes laying side by side like three quiet neighbors upon the stove." The congressman chuckled at the kinds of souvenirs with which Jackson chose to surround himself: an "old fashioned mug" made of hickory, "with a limb singularly formed for a handle," and varnished; another cup, this one hickory bark with a band of silver shaped around it, of which Jackson willingly spoke at length, praising the patriotic citizens who had given it to him. To Davis, the cup he took such pride in resembled "half of a cocoa nut shell." He described the owner of these rustic memorabilia: "The hero looks old and his hair which is grey and stiff stands up all over his head as if it were electrified and strugling [sic] to disengage itself from its parent." Without overturning the savage image, Davis affected surprise at how well the president handled his removal from the wild, where he ostensibly felt most at home: "There was no want of civility or decorum and I asked for no office nor sought any favor. The visit I doubt not was quite agreeable."[66]

Of course, the image of the Indian as "lordly savage," the unrestrained, amoral son of the forest who was not rule-bound, repelled Andrew Jackson. This was the image he found hardest to shake when it was being applied to him, as the untutored child of the frontier West. But his own aggressiveness belied his effort to rise above the cartoon image. Before he became president, Jackson was consistently dismissive of the federal government for its weak-willed accommodations with Indians. He preferred dictating terms or carrying out what can only be called primitive aggression in asserting whites' power over the Indian nations.[67]

Calhoun and Nullification

John Caldwell Calhoun of South Carolina served as vice president for four years under John Quincy Adams, all the while associating himself with the Jacksonian opposition; and then, in an unprecedented and never repeated event, he retained his office under the new administration. Calhoun possessed unmistakable ambition: he wanted to be president, and he presumed that the thin, aging Jackson would not run again in 1832.[68] His plan was hindered by two related factors: the rise of Martin Van Buren and the progress of the Eaton affair.

Van Buren was a scrappy, often ingratiating political operator from New York State who had created a strong statewide patronage system by the early 1820s. In the presidential campaigns of 1824 and 1828, he had traveled extensively outside New York, looking to revive a Jeffersonian North-South coalition and avert a permanent sectional divide. While initially a strong Crawford supporter, he ultimately found in Andrew Jackson a perfect standard-bearer for his brand of political democracy. John Quincy Adams regarded Van Buren as the second coming of Aaron Burr, and even saw similarities in the manners of the two men. Whereas Burr had electioneered to unseat the elder Adams in 1800, advancing himself to the vice presidency, Van Buren skillfully sewed up a similar coalition in 1827–28, though it was not until Jackson's second term that he occupied the vice president's chair.[69]

Jackson and Van Buren both wanted to reform Washington, though Van Buren was a political wheeler-dealer and party organizer, and Jackson an uncompromising commander who concentrated on building a team based on personal loyalty. In rewarding Van Buren with the office of secretary of state in 1829, Jackson got what he asked for: a responsive aide who was rich in opinions but willing to yield to his president. In the Eaton affair, Van Buren, a widower, endeared himself by demonstrating a conciliatory spirit toward the controversial couple.[70]

Calhoun, on the other hand, found it increasingly hard to maintain his loyal pose. But his ignoring the Eatons was not enough to cause Jackson to lose confidence in him, because as Monroe's secretary of war, the determined South Carolinian had consistently stood by him — or so he believed. The Calhoun-Jackson correspondence, from 1818 until 1828, certainly conveyed that impression. During the Adams years, Calhoun became something of a sycophant, once writing the general that "there can be no triumph over you that will not be a triumph over liberty." Contemporaries remarked upon the physical similarity between the two men, southern-born, of Scotch-Irish origins, with long faces and hollow jaws, and hair that stood up. On the surface, they seemed well matched.[71]

Everything changed in 1830. Jackson was growing more and more comfortable with Van Buren as chief adviser, much to the detriment of the expectant Calhoun. Then the president was afforded a fresh glance at the past, an adjusted perspective on the politics surrounding his Florida incursion, and the gloves, so to speak, came off. He learned that he had been wrong to believe that Calhoun was his foremost friend in Monroe's cabinet. William H. Crawford, an old enemy but no longer the force he once was, approached the president with documentary evidence that Calhoun had urged Jackson's arrest in 1818, along with some form of punishment. Crawford hated Calhoun worse than he ever hated Jackson — Calhoun was his competition for southern support on a national slate. Now, he wished to reconcile with Jackson, set the record straight, and cure the president of his singular belief that it was Crawford who had led the effort to censure him for his invasion of Florida.[72]

In May 1830, Jackson confronted his vice president from an incontestable position. Calhoun's betrayal was not a case of conspiratorial fantasy. Everything at once came together in Jackson's mind: at the start of the administration, the vice president had opposed the selection of Eaton to the cabinet, hoping instead that a South Carolinian like Senator Robert Hayne would succeed him in the War Department; Calhoun's wife had been instrumental in the Eatons' social ostracism; Calhoun was plainly disappointed that Van Buren held a dominant position in the administration; Calhoun had grossly misrepresented his position in Monroe's cabinet. But the final proof of Calhoun's defection and disloyalty was emerging in 1830: for so long a nationalist, he was linked suspiciously to those South Carolina partisans who were noisily protesting a tariff law. Their cry was for "nullification," a controversial doctrine asserting a state's right to nullify any act of Congress it considered injurious to its interests.

Hayne had risen from his seat in the Senate in January 1830 to protest the tariff and to challenge the extent of the federal government's power. He was a small man of graceful southern manners. Hayne's charges were answered by his more renowned Massachusetts colleague, the orator Daniel Webster. The dark-complexioned intellectual, nicknamed "Black Dan," provided sound evidence of prosperity in the western states, for which he credited the strength of the federal union. Striking at the alliance of South and West, he put supporters of the "Carolina doctrine" very much on the defensive. The debate was bitter at times as Webster enhanced his national reputation by denying the right of any individual state to resolve constitutional issues by itself. He heralded the Union with almost religious ecstasy: "When my eyes shall be turned to behold for the last time the sun in heaven, may I not see him shining on the broken and dishonored fragments of a once glorious Union. . . ."

Vice President Calhoun had openly differed with Jackson on the tariff in 1828, when Jackson was clearly articulating his preference for calm dialogue and mutual concession on this issue. Now, though, both sides were growing more impassioned. During the Webster-Hayne debate, Calhoun presided awkwardly in the Senate, gavel in hand, as yet unwilling to take any more public position. For a time, he resisted association with the militants of his state. Later it was said that as Webster spoke, Calhoun occasionally passed notes to his friend Hayne.[73]

Nullification, as put forth by the Carolina faction, was subversive. It diminished the power of the national union, a union "more perfect" (to borrow from the Constitution's preamble) than a mere alliance of individual states. To apply the doctrine of nullification to an act of Congress that regulated trade but posed no appreciable threat to life or liberty defied the founders' logic. Whatever else might be said of his desire to expand the power of the presidency, Jackson considered the United States to be a metaphorical fortress of popular government. As a machine, its practical operation functioned to his satisfaction. Responding to the Carolina challenge, and acting out of devotion to a principle that was larger than any one man, he waited until it was time to take careful aim at a mutinous minority.

As the historian Merrill D. Peterson has written, "Most Jacksonians were intellectually and emotionally predisposed to view their world through the Jeffersonian categories of government and society." Thomas Jefferson was nearly four years in his grave, but the popular founder's birthday was routinely and prominently celebrated. President Jackson was given to understand that the Jefferson's birthday banquet of April 13, 1830, designed by Senators Benton, Hayne, and others as a symbol of intersectional alliance (in the political spirit of Jefferson), was this year to be turned into a coming-out party of sorts for the nullifiers. Or perhaps Jackson backers, especially Van Buren, were baiting the nullifiers, and working on the president so as to force a confrontation with Calhoun. It is not entirely clear, even now, which faction was the more devious.[74]

Nevertheless, the birthday celebration did go forward. And, as was customary at public dinners, a lineup of toasts was scheduled, many of which were to be delivered by states'-rights politicians who claimed Jefferson as the earliest advocate of their position. (The sharp-witted, seventy-nine-year-old James Madison, Jefferson's closest associate, was quick to brand such a notion "heresy.") Jackson was game. When the president was called on to volunteer a toast, he rang out, "Our Federal Union—it must be preserved." It was a sublime moment, by all accounts. Calhoun followed directly: "The Union—*next to our liberty the most dear.*" In asserting his respect for states' rights over the cause of union, Calhoun at last threw down the gauntlet and expelled himself from the administration. For his part, Secretary of State Van Buren, most disingenuously, made an effort to sound accommodating in his toast: "Mutual forbearance and reciprocal concession."[75]

Jackson's two letters to Calhoun in May 1830, though no doubt written in conjunction with one or more of his advisers, stand as illustrations of the president's steadfast posture in any issue conflating the personal with the political. The first, which contained a key communication from Crawford concerning the Florida invasion, stealthily presented to Calhoun his options. It hardly mattered how Calhoun replied—Jackson had a villain in his grasp. The vice president's reply, at any rate, was a bombastic effort to depersonalize nullification—which he proposed was in the best interests of the country.

Jackson's follow-up letter to Calhoun had a tone of finality to it. It was not conduct, Jackson wrote, or even motive that Calhoun was meant to explain. It was, in effect, character. He allowed that he had always consid-ered Calhoun a virtuous man, and had given him the benefit of every doubt. But now it was clear that Calhoun had been living a lie after "endeavouring to distroy" Jackson's reputation. "I had too exalted an opin-ion of your honor and frankness," the president penned in a careful hand, his script just as wide as it was ordinarily, but more uniform, more bal-anced and legible than most of his familiar correspondence. "I had a right to believe that you were my sincere friend," he went on, with devastating directness, "and until now, never expected to have occasion to say to you, in the language of Caesar, *Et tu Brute.*" No further communication was nec-essary, he made sure to append to the letter, before his broad signature.[76]

Andrew Jackson Donelson preferred Calhoun to the interloper Van Buren. This, combined with his and his wife's treatment of the Eatons, led to the Donelsons' banishment from the White House in June 1830. It would require a series of impassioned letters from his uncle before Donel-son made the effort to patch up their differences. He returned as the presi-dent's private secretary in September 1831, as the Eatons, not coincidentally, left Washington for Tennessee.[77]

In the course of their correspondence during that particularly tense political year, the president poured out his heart to his estranged nephew and aide. One long, rambling sentence tells most of the story:

> I wish you were here but my dear Andrew from what I have suffered
> by my family being arrayed against my best friend, by the contrivance
> of those, whose object is no longer doubtful (as I always knew myself)
> to crush me; as much as I desire you, and your dear little family with
> me, unless you and yours can harmonise with major Eaton and his
> family, I do not wish you here because I have experienced so much
> pain, and my enemies have profitted so much by the division, that I

cannot think of encountering such scenes again, but with harmony between my family, and Cabinet, I put my enemies at defiance.[78]

Jackson had the need to align with his true friends against Calhoun's once secret, now (to Jackson's mind) open and undeniable atrocities. In the same letter to his nephew, he explained his rambling: "I have been prolix, that you might have some idea of the treachery of this world." It was essential to convince; Jackson could not rest until he had. And so he never rested.

The cabinet had thus split into Van Buren and Calhoun factions, leading Jackson in the spring of 1831 to take dramatic, unprecedented action. With Van Buren's concurrence, the president decided to dissolve the cabinet entirely, and to start all over with different and, he anticipated, unquestionably loyal players. The Eaton affair officially ended when John Eaton resigned in April. Soon after, Jackson would appoint him governor of Florida.

What to do next? What arrangement would restore peace to the political household? The president thought he could convince the circumspect Hugh Lawson White of Tennessee to succeed the unpopular Eaton, but White did not want to be a party to contention, and so New Hampshire–born Lewis Cass, longtime governor of Michigan Territory, became the secretary of war. Van Buren was appointed U.S. minister to England, succeeded at the State Department by the trusted Edward Livingston. In the summer of 1832, murmuring, "The hope of the country rests on our gallant little state," Calhoun went home to South Carolina, the state where Jackson (ironically, it now seemed) was born. As the leader of the nullifiers, Calhoun resigned the vice presidency to enter the U.S. Senate, where he no longer had to pretend.[79]

Having put his house in order, Jackson overpowered the Carolina opposition with his grand Nullification Proclamation, issued in early December 1832. It was authored by his favorite speechwriter, Livingston, over the course of just a few days. One congressman, on reading the text, referred to the philosophical new secretary of state, somewhat uncomfortably, as "the Montesquieu of the Cabinet." It was an apt association, as the influential eighteenth-century French political analyst made his mark just as Livingston hoped to, by codifying just forms of national management. As to the doctrine of nullification, Jackson wrote to John Coffee, in his inimitable manner: "Can any one of common sense believe the absurdity, that a faction of any state, or a state, has a right to secede and destroy this union, and the liberty of our country with it, or nullify the laws of the union; then indeed is our constitution a rope of sand; under which I would not live." Livingston put the issue in more exalted language, though it was framed in the first person—"I, ANDREW JACKSON, *President of the United States*, have thought proper to issue this my PROCLAMATION, stating my views of the constitution and laws. . . ."[80]

Livingston's prose abounds in discovery, with historical allusions and phrases like "the dignity of the nation," or "perpetual bond of our Union," versus the "ruinous and unconstitutional," "reckless, destructive course." If the federal Union had been constituted in vain, and a small majority within a single state could repudiate the work of the founders, then "state pride" was capable of undoing the principle that Americans were "one people." If the Union was formed by compact, and that compact could be dissolved when a certain element merely felt "aggrieved," then a compact does not mean what it is supposed to mean: "an agreement or binding obligation." States' rights were not trampled by such a compact, Livingston contested: "The Union was formed for the benefit of all." Altering this common understanding could be a ploy only designed to conceal "the hideous features of disunion." And so, before they took the "perilous path," Carolinians needed to detect that "exaggerated language" which pretended to speak of liberty, but which really served to deface an already "happy Union." The address ended with an appeal to all citizens to cast aside "the madness of party or personal ambition," and venerate their republican institutions with renewed confidence.[81]

The proclamation masked the extent to which many in the Northeast and West commiserated with sensitive South Carolinians, and it failed to note that there was no clear-cut distinction among nullifier, nationalist, and classical states'-rights positions. Still, Calhoun looked irresolute and Jackson sounded statesmanlike. His handling of the nullification crisis was arguably the noblest action Jackson took over the course of his two terms. The nullification ploy marked the end of Calhoun's chances to be a national candidate, and consigned him to the isolated position of an embittered sectional advocate. During the last months of his life, when Jackson was reviewing the course of his presidency, he was said to have remarked that his main regret was in not having ordered the execution of John C. Calhoun for treason.[82]

As a direct result of Jackson's nullification message, Congressman James Blair of South Carolina, a Union man born, like Jackson, in the Waxhaws, physically attacked Duff Green, editor of the pro-Calhoun *United States Telegraph*. "What changes in the affairs and passions of men!" exclaimed

Representative John Quincy Adams in his diary. Green had set up his newspaper in 1826 for the sole purpose of defaming then-President Adams and electing Jackson. Entering office, Jackson had rewarded Green with a lucrative business as official printer to the Senate. Over time, though, Green became a Calhounite. In Adams's bitter words, Green was merely the latest victim of Jacksonian violence, who reaped what he had sown: "Men baser than himself have supplanted him in the favor of Jackson." As one who knew defeat, Adams could only shake his head without pity at the editor who lay in a heap on Christmas Eve, 1832, politically exiled and "nearly killed." The following week, Calhoun took his seat in the Senate.[83]

The Second Term

Newspapers were the common denominator in the vulgar commonness and increasing vituperation of Jackson-era politics. One of the weapons Andrew Jackson deployed in his 1832 campaign against Henry Clay was a curious man named Amos Kendall. This Dartmouth-educated native of rural Massachusetts was born in 1789 to a modest family, the son of a Congregationalist deacon. Intellectually gifted but financially hard-pressed, he arrived penniless in Lexington, Kentucky, in 1814, and prophetically, it would seem, landed a job as tutor to the Clay children. Awkward and intense, Kendall adapted emotionally to southern culture, including slave ownership, like another Jacksonian northerner, Edward Livingston (to whom Jackson had once sold forty slaves). In his autobiography, Kendall noted caustically that he had learned the popular art of southern politics: to "drink whiskey and talk loud, with the fullest confidence."

The reformed puritan ultimately bought his way onto a small newspaper, and later advanced to editorship of one of Kentucky's most prominent papers, *Argus of Western America*. Yet his politics gravitated away from Clay and toward Jackson, and in 1827 Kendall announced by confidential letter to Jackson that although he had been "one of Mr. Clay's family," he was now appalled by Clay's depravity. Jackson's appetite was whetted by Kendall's defection, and in 1828 he went on to win the electoral votes of Clay's Kentucky. The grateful victor made the diligent Kendall his White House political manager, an adviser every bit as trusted as Martin Van Buren.

The fiercely loyal Kendall, a gnarled little man whose hair had gone white by the time he turned forty, wrote some of the president's key position papers. He also founded a pro-administration newspaper, the *Washington Globe*. His young, apolitical second wife, daughter of a poor papermaker, readily socialized with Margaret Eaton, which obviously redounded to Kendall's credit. Whereas Livingston's pen produced the constitutional theory that Jackson could not articulate himself, the newspaperman Kendall was a master of vitriol, whose pen could fume the way Jackson's mouth did.

When Jackson's first cabinet was dissolved, the public perception of Kendall's importance increased, and the term *Kitchen Cabinet* came to describe the influential, unseen presidential advisers. These included Kendall, fellow Kentucky editor (and another former Clay supporter) Francis Preston Blair, and Jackson's wealthy Tennessee neighbor William B. Lewis. The eavesdropping Congressman Henry Wise wrote that Kendall's function was to give an everyday elegance to the languid intellect of the president, insofar as Jackson "could think, but could not write; he knew what nerve to touch, but he was no surgeon skilled in the instrument of dissection." Wise found Kendall "unscrupulous" but "indefatigable" and "able," having delivered up the secrets of Clay's former strength.[84]

The incumbent president won reelection over Clay by a substantial margin, 219 electoral votes to 49.[85] When he began his second term, Andrew Jackson was in his sixty-seventh year, the oldest man to serve as president up to that time. He would be the first president to enter his seventieth year while in office. His predecessors had all ended their presidencies while in their mid-sixties: Washington left office at sixty-five and was dead two years later; Adams and Jefferson were each sixty-five when their terms came to an end; Madison, aptly called "the last of the fathers," left office at sixty-six and survived nearly until the election of 1836, when he was a mentally sound eighty-five; Monroe, retiring a month shy of his sixty-seventh birthday, died on the Fourth of July, just as Adams and Jefferson had— they in 1826 and he in 1831; John Quincy Adams, who was born the same year as Jackson, returned to the House of Representatives and served Massachusetts beyond Jackson's two terms, expiring at his desk on Capitol Hill in 1848. He survived Jackson by three years. Of Jackson's six predecessors, all of whom he interacted with, only Madison and the second Adams were alive when Jackson was reelected in 1832.

The gaunt, irritated, yet unassailable figure who kept succeeding at fighting off natural as well as human adversaries now braced for further battles. He continued to assemble (and reshuffle) a team of associates who would carry out his vision of eradicating all forms of "corruption" from public life. His crafty, completely trusted, second-term vice president and preferred successor, Martin Van Buren, understood precisely what Jackson wanted in a political friend: uncritical displays of devotion. Van Buren no doubt had to swallow a certain amount of pride to conform to Jackson's wishes; he did so and reaped rewards. His flexibility was especially appreciated during the early part of the second term, when Jackson's oldest confidants, John Overton and John Coffee, both died. While suffering from rheumatism, Overton last visited his "near neighbour and old friend the President" in Washington in 1831, telling one correspondent, "Having commenced my career with him at the bar, I am now resting myself at his house." Their forty-four-year bond was so strong that as he was dying in 1833, Overton appealed to Dr. Samuel Hogg—the same doctor who had tended to Rachel at the end of her life—to tell Jackson "that he saw him die, and that he died a man."[86]

Coffee, too, had responded faithfully to every one of Jackson's entreaties over the years. When the Eaton affair divided the president's White House family, it was Coffee who spoke most freely with the affronted Andrew Jackson Donelson. Coffee knew precisely what the president's personal shortcomings were, especially the "unfounded jealousies" Jackson felt toward any he suspected of inconstancy or betrayal. And so Coffee admonished Donelson to avoid the people Jackson suspected, to make both Donelson's and Jackson's lives go more smoothly.[87]

Overton sometimes strayed into politics in order to apply his argumentative style to the defense of his famous friend. Coffee recognized himself as one who was ill suited for acrimonious debate. During a rare visit to Washington in 1833, a short time before his death, he wrote a letter to his wife, a Donelson, sighing: "The more I see of public men, the more I am disgusted with public life." Coffee, an old business partner of the president, preferred business to politics. While assisting prominent people like Madison and George Washington Campbell in the settlement of their western land claims, he contented himself as surveyor general of federal lands, marking ceded Indian territories and laying out new towns. He successfully raised cotton, corn, and wheat on his Hickory Hill plantation in northern Alabama. He rejected every prospect of elective office. He was a hearty soldier like Jackson, but Coffee left his military career behind him after New Orleans, and took the road to personal comfort and financial success that Jackson might have realized except for a pronounced inability to resist the lure of fame.[88]

One of Jackson's consistent cheerleaders during his bid for a second term, and a Van Buren backer to boot, was William Carroll, still in the Tennessee governor's chair eleven years after having first arrived there without Jackson's help. "You must permit me to congratulate you on the glorious result of the recent election," Carroll wrote at the end of 1832, emphasizing that it was the popular vote that had made the difference this time. Modern Americans take for granted what was in fact first ushered in that year: democracy took hold at polling places. For the first time since independence, more electoral votes were popularly cast than decided by politicking within state legislatures. This presumptively made Jackson the people's choice, and not merely the preference of those whom Carroll dismissively called "time serving politicians." There was no more Jacksonian sentiment than that which Governor Carroll was expressing.

Voters drawn from the "honest yeomanry" had no interest or ambition to gratify when they reelected Jackson, according to Carroll, who was proudest of the victory over nullification. In defying the laws of the Union, South Carolina had "played the part of a bragedocio." Calhoun's state still needed to make its surrender total: "she should be coersed into her duty if milder measures will not answer." Like those who opposed Jackson's will in wartime, Carroll saw South Carolina as a selfish, disobedient entity wishing to "indulge" its "whim" while complaining about "imaginary wrongs." Jackson's courageous onetime second in command was willing to take up arms again, even now: "You may rely upon my hearty co-operation in every thing that has for its object the preservation of the Union, and when all peacable measures have failed . . . , a resort must be had to arms if necessary."[89]

As in the past, Carroll sounded rather like Jackson, frightened of no adversary, eager to act. But Jackson persisted in keeping him at arm's length. Why? Carroll applauded his chief magistrate—his general—at every turn. He differed with Jackson on the banking issue, but so did Edward Livingston. It is clear that Jackson never sought to bring Carroll to Washington. There was the moment of Carroll's "ingratitude" that Jackson and Coffee detected back in 1816—but Jackson had had a far worse experience with Thomas Hart Benton, and recovered from it. For another brief moment in the early 1820s, Carroll may have flirted with Henry Clay[90] as his economic policies and Jackson's diverged. Was their break irreparable because Carroll favored a progressive-minded banking system, and Jackson had old-fashioned, small-scale notions about merchants extending credit on the basis of a man's honor? No, there was probably something else, something deeper.

Carroll seems by far the more generous-spirited in this relationship. Jackson had hogged all credit for victory at New Orleans, even though Carroll had withstood the primary British charge. Carroll appears accepting. On a personal level, it seems to be Carroll who made sure that they got along. Jackson's motive is all the more suspect when one considers that the only time he was prepared to offer Carroll a job it was to get rid of him: in 1829, the new president planned to nominate Carroll for a diplomatic assignment in South America, coinciding with Sam Houston's contemplation of a second run for the Tennessee governorship—against Carroll. Houston was "Jackson's man," and Carroll was his own man. Suggestive as Jackson's behavior is, the inner workings of the Jackson-Carroll relationship ultimately remain a mystery.[91]

Whatever their hidden differences, the Tennessee governor's economic views did not begin to trouble Jackson the way the national banking establishment did. The president stubbornly refused to believe that the Bank of the United States, under private management, could contribute to the democratization of American society by extending credit to the yeomanry of the country. He insisted that banks, as monopolies, only served to undermine republicanism.

The Bank of the United States was perfectly well managed. It regulated the availability of credit through its practical control over the loan activities of state banks. But to Jackson, the national bank was a morally suspect institution, a symbol of secret manipulation. His combined ignorance and excitement led to a personal war against the bank's recharter and the removal of federal deposits: "Divorce the government from the banks," as Jackson put it often.

Jackson hated the "corrupt" Henry Clay, of course, which was how the Bank War was sparked. When he ran against the incumbent in 1832, Clay had unwisely calculated that making an issue of the bank would injure Jackson's reputation and doom him to defeat. By provoking Jackson, Clay only energized him, and brought Amos Kendall's passion-tipped pen into action. The president's election-year veto of the bank recharter bill succeeded; he arranged for public funds to be placed in certain state banks, Jackson's "pet banks," as they were dubbed. A chaos of speculation ensued in the states, to which Jackson responded with the 1836 "Specie Circular," directing that only gold and silver—no paper currency—would be accepted in payment for public lands. This led to the Panic of 1837 and a four-year-long depression. How all this happened makes sense only in light of our prior understanding of Jackson's impulses.

During Clay's challenge in election year 1832, the opposition to Jackson was not yet a distinct political party. But as Jackson's adherents eagerly embraced the name Democrats, his various detractors would translate their frustration with his authoritarian manner by dubbing themselves Whigs, replicating the name and self-image of the Revolutionaries of 1776. As the bank recharter controversy enlarged, voters tended to characterize Jackson's leadership qualities and personal disposition according to their interpretation of this one dominant issue. Either he had imperial pretensions, or he was a most amiable and well-mannered republican with a deep concern for the freedom of the nation's children. Meanwhile, as government deposits were withdrawn from the Bank of the United States, the bank acted to limit its loans; predicting financial ruin, the Senate, led by Clay, formally censured the president for exceeding his executive authority. Jackson responded by claiming a special responsibility as "the direct representative of the American people," an assertion mocked by the great orator Daniel Webster, Whig senator from Massachusetts, who perceived in the president's words a desire to supplant the Constitution by becoming the American people's "sole representative."

Jackson was not grasping; though misguided, he was pure of heart. He had to have believed his populist rhetoric, just as he continued to see himself as a conquering knight. He imagined that he was rescuing "the people's" money, as he had sought to rescue John Eaton's honor and Margaret Eaton's threatened virtue. In his mind, the bank was an institution that operated against independent manhood. The practical-minded French intellectual Michel Chevalier was in New York on New Year's Day, 1834, when the banking crisis was in high gear. He characterized Jackson this way: "President Jackson, a brave man, zealous for the good of the country, but too hasty towards those who contradict him, declared a war to the death against the Bank and pushed it with all his energy and fury, in the same cut-and-thrust style that he had the war against the Indians and English twenty years before." The president had shut his eyes to any advantages the Bank of the United States might deliver and, with what Chevalier called "empty prejudices," he pounced.

Jackson's exclamation to Van Buren is oft quoted: "The Bank is trying to kill me, but I will kill it!" These words suggest that Jackson could not separate an attack on himself from an attack on "the people." Nicholas Biddle, the bank's president, wrote Henry Clay, calling the veto message "a manifesto of anarchy." But as the election itself proved, Jackson was able to convince a vast majority that his understanding of finance was as good as his declared purposes.

17. *"Go home, and leave the government to me."* Whig
Almanac *of 1835 denounces "King Andrew I," whose
democratic pretensions are ridiculed. Courtesy
American Antiquarian Society.*

When Jackson resolved to deal the "monster" bank its death blow, his
champion on Capitol Hill was his reformed assailant, Thomas Hart Benton. A short time before, the president had finally had the "Benton bullet"
of 1813 surgically removed from his arm after it had slowly slid down from
his shoulder, causing months of additional pain. To Jackson, the bank was
just another foreign body (indeed, he disapproved of its foreign investors),
only this time he was his own surgeon, sending Kendall on a mission to
northern cities to choose those banks which were better suited—"in hands
politically friendly," wrote Kendall—to receive the government's funds.
Jackson was always trying to find out who his true friends were; when he

found them, he found "the people's" friends. This simple formula was how he justified his hatreds.[92]

Another threat appeared before the president in January 1835, perhaps the only one that his undeniable self-righteousness had not caused. As he emerged from the Capitol after attending funeral ceremonies for a congressman, a man came within ten feet of him and fired straight at Jackson with two separate pistols. In both instances, the flash was seen, the explosion heard, but neither weapon discharged. "The powder of the best quality, & the balls rammed in tight," wrote Meriwether Lewis Randolph, a grandson of Thomas Jefferson. "The percussion caps exploded, but without igniting the powder. Were I inclined to superstition, the conviction that the President's life was protected by the hand of a special providence would be irresistible." Though frail, Jackson rushed at his assailant with his uplifted cane as a navy lieutenant knocked the man down. The assailant turned out to be an unemployed housepainter named Richard Lawrence who had previously done some work at the White House, and who held the president responsible for his situation. Judged mentally incompetent, the would-be assassin was never brought to trial. By all accounts, Jackson was unfazed. "I went over to the old man," wrote Randolph, "about an hour after the occurrence of the affair, and found him as cool, calm and collected, as though nothing had happened." Those who already marveled at the president's capacity to endure were no less astonished that two well-aimed pistols, both in working order, had somehow failed to take his life.[93]

The anti-Jackson press supposed the incident to have been set up as a ploy to evoke sympathy, while pro-Jackson newspapers questioned whether the president's political enemies had instigated Lawrence. Jackson (presumably influenced by others) personally pointed the finger at Senator George Poindexter of Mississippi. Poindexter was a Natchez lawyer, the general's staunch defender in the Seminole War debate on Capitol Hill in 1819, and an equally firm supporter in 1828, who had since become alienated. He was a friend of Henry Clay (and, it was often remarked, physically resembled Clay); as a tariff opponent, Poindexter threw his support to Calhoun in 1831. To make matters worse, he was the recipient of two personal loans from bank president Nicholas Biddle in 1832 and 1833. Jackson was said to have snidely remarked that Poindexter had "induced" his third wife to marry him with a promise of $20,000. Hearing the report, the senator wrote to the Baltimore *Patriot,* asking for clarification from the president: "I have at least the consolation to know that I did not steal her from her lawful owner!"

So crude and knowingly provocative a challenge caused many to suspect that a duel was brewing. But that was not at all Poindexter's plan. Rather, once Jackson's publicly voiced his suspicion (the president told lawmakers that "approximately fifty people had seen Lawrence enter Poindexter's home"), the senator desperately sought official exoneration. He knew the impact of gossip. Jackson was extremely popular in Mississippi, and Poindexter, having lost reelection, did not wish to return home under a cloud. So he begged Congress to investigate formally. It did, and the altogether specious allegations were disproved. Poindexter moved to Lexington, Kentucky, Clay's hometown, for a while, but lived his last years, no doubt with some discomfort, in a Mississippi town named after his nemesis: Jackson. Meanwhile, the aggravated charges of 1835, growing out of the action of a lone gunman, were explained by the New York *Evening Post* as "a sign of the times."[94]

Jackson not only survived two terms, he made the presidency more powerful than any of his predecessors had. As a man of extraordinary will, he eclipsed even Jefferson, single-minded architect of the Louisiana Purchase. Jefferson had acted with questionable constitutional authority so as to complete the timely acquisition of the new West and double the size of U.S. territory in one stroke. Jackson oversaw Indian removal, but unlike Jefferson he paid relatively little attention to the conduct of foreign relations until near the end of his second term, entrusting Secretaries of State Van Buren (1829–31) and Livingston (1831–33) with the details.[95] The one exception was Mexico, as it concerned the southern U.S. border.

Projecting his vision for the acquisition of Texas to his envoy to Mexico in 1830, Jackson discerned America's destiny as he had in overpowering the Spanish in Florida: "Our future peace with Mexico depends upon extending our boundary farther west. . . . But candour dictates that the fact should be disclosed that the Government possessing the Mississippi must at some day possess all its *tributary streams*. . . . Our right by the Louisiana treaty, being once complete to all this boundary and more." Jackson sought, without appearing aggressive, what he eventually obtained.[96]

Sam Houston understood his desire. At Jackson's request, Houston conferred at the end of 1832 with a group of Comanche Indians whose open hostility prevented the emigration of defeated eastern tribes—Choctaws, Chickasaws, and Creeks—to the Southwest. It was after this mission that Houston spelled out his larger plan to the receptive president: Texas should be wrested from war-torn Mexico ("The Government is essentially despotic, and must be so for years to come"), and eventually become part of the United States. The Americans in Texas, he wrote, were overwhelmingly in favor of forming an independent government, separating from Mexico. The land, he went on to assure, was "richer and more healthy than West Tennessee." Houston himself, after having traveled "nearly five hundred miles across Texas," was preparing to make it "my abiding-place. In adopting this course *I will never forget* the country of my birth."[97] And so it was, in 1836, not very long before he left office, that Jackson received a gift from his rough-and-ready ally—the capture of the president of Mexico, Santa Anna, and the prospect of an Americanized Texas.

Houston had followed closely in Jackson's footsteps. In the early 1820s, he was a prosecuting attorney in Nashville and major general of the Tennessee militia—as well as a frequent guest at the Hermitage. He was the heir to Jackson in other important ways, as a man whose frontier experience allowed him to move—even more literally—in and out of the unrestrained Indian style of an out-of-doors existence. He was, like Jackson, a political soldier who crossed boundaries to get what he wanted. It was thanks, then, to the spiritual inheritor of Jacksonian boldness, Sam Houston, that the retiring president, like Jefferson before him, was able to envision a western future for the deserving yeomanry of his country.

Also in 1836, two controversial men, both integral to Jackson's career, died. The first was Livingston, in the spring, and then the political pariah Aaron Burr, in the fall. Livingston was one of the great public intellectuals of his day, who stood toe-to-toe in legal sagacity with Jefferson. Indeed, one prominent eulogist insisted that Livingston could be ranked alongside Jefferson and Madison in "talents, integrity or patriotic spirit," and that the French placed him second only to Benjamin Franklin as a philosopher.[98] As a national leader in 1833 of the Freemasons, he embodied Jackson's commitment to community and fraternity, inviting the fury of the anti-Mason John Quincy Adams, and suffering insults, along with Jackson, for his Masonic affiliation. He was, in Adams's open letter, part of a "vicious, immoral, and unlawful world." But accusations such as this only drew him closer to his president.[99]

His only deficiency, albeit a critical one, was his inability to relate to "the people" of nineteenth-century America, those whom his rhetoric was meant to serve. Livingston was an Enlightenment democrat who did not adapt comfortably to the social changes of the early republic; he was more comfortable with liberal language than with "real folks." It was his constitutional genius and scholarly conceptions that translated the militancy Jackson felt into elegant words. His well-crafted Nullification Proclamation stands as a testament to the unobstructed nationalism of Andrew Jackson. In Overton County, Tennessee, a town named Livingston was incorporated just before he died.[100]

And then there was Burr, whom both Livingston and Jackson, as young radicals, looked up to as a talented political organizer and man of action. If Livingston symbolizes the constitutional democrat in Jackson, Burr represents Jackson the restless adventurer. At the peak of his popularity, Burr compounded friends as Jackson went on to do. While he failed to expand the Union, he was spectacularly fulfilled, in his eightieth year, through the machinations of Sam Houston.

Texas had been Burr's dream first. The unfortunate dreamer endured his exile and bore his untouchable status well. He had sat, serene and self-possessed, through his trials in 1806–7. After acquittal he promptly lost everything that his political skill had once brought him: high office, powerful friends. It was as if he had agreed to be hated, patiently awaiting the day when his persecutors' hypocrisy would be discovered and the amorality of politics understood.

Recognizing the elusiveness of the "real" Burr, a shadowy figure constructed mostly from anecdotal evidence, the historian James Parton observed rightly: "With all his faults, he was never given to self-vindication." In his twilight years, as an ingenious, good-humored New York attorney, Burr continued to surround himself with young men who found something irresistible in him. He was hale and hearty, remaining the subject of rumors about sexual intrigues. Unlike the thin-skinned Jackson, Burr apparently felt little need to speak out against his enemies or secure his posthumous reputation. "His conversation upon the past was remarkable for its candor, humor, and charity," wrote Parton. "He denounced no one—not even General Wilkinson, of whom he spoke more severely than of anyone else." History would not acknowledge him as one of the founders, when he was, in fact, the covetous side of Jeffersonian democracy, which Jefferson smoothly denied. And he was one of the first, if not the first, to see presidential possibilities for the decisive Gen. Andrew Jackson.[101]

Toward the end of 1836, the sickly president had another bout with the poisons in his body. His life was despaired of when he started coughing up blood, but then he revived. He always seemed most alive when his will was challenged and he was forced to confront either physical or political mortality. The "old iron-gray knight," as an English visitor described the bony, erect chief executive around this time, still retained his "warlikeness" and "energy" despite everything that came at him. What was it that kept him going? He knew that the Indians he removed from the Southeast were not about to recross the Mississippi and undo his legacy. No, he hung on mostly to make sure that the bank he had killed did not rise from the ashes.[102]

He was present in Washington for the inauguration of his successor, standing at Martin Van Buren's side under what Senator Benton described as a "balmy vernal sun." As the ceremonies ended, and he descended the Capitol steps toward his carriage one last time, cheering sounds went out to him from the assembled crowd. "It was the acclaim of posterity, breaking from the bosoms of contemporaries," Benton devotedly proclaimed. "Uncovered, and bowing, with a look of unaffected humility and thankfulness, he acknowledged in mute signs his deep sensibility to this affecting overflow of popular feeling. I was looking down from a side window, and felt an emotion which had never passed through me before."[103]

His presidency was finished, but as one might imagine, haggard old Andrew Jackson would not relinquish the political stage easily. He was torn between a desire to escape and a compulsion to control the future.

CHAPTER SEVEN

❯❯❯❯❯❯❯❯❯❯❯ ❮❮❮❮❮❮❮❮❮❮❮

Courting Posterity

I have no doubt but you have seen the attack made upon my fame in the Senate of the United States by Mr. Conrad of Louisiana. . . . You being a participater in that defence . . . , therefore it is that I should address you, requesting that you will have the goodness to give me your recollection of the conduct and impressions of Judge Hall . . . and Luweller.

—Jackson to Richard Keith Call, Aug. 20, 1842

Jackson often expressed solemn, even religious awe in ruminating on the fact of mortality. In the midst of the Eaton affair in 1829, he responded to a letter from one of his Donelson kin who had just made a pilgrimage to Rachel's tomb at the Hermitage. The president wrote then of his yearning, in his "enfeebled health and constitution," to "place my earthly house in order and prepare for another, and I hope a better world." He wished to be "in the solitary shades of my garden, at the tomb of my wife, there to spend my days in silent sorrow and in peace from the toils and strife of this world." Similarly, to the Rev. Hardy Cryer in 1832, he wrote wistfully, "My only ambition is to get to the Hermitage so soon as the interest of my country and the will of the people will permit me, and there to set my house in order and go to sleep along side of my dear departed wife."[1]

These were fairly common sentiments, but that does not mean that they did not disclose Jackson's real feelings. It is difficult to characterize his ambition at such times, when he professed that all he felt was a sense of duty to country. To enact his vision of the popular will and defend his honor against his all too evident enemies made it impossible, at any rate, for him to rest.

A man named Cunningham, in Louisville, Kentucky, encountered the retiring president en route home to Tennessee, in the spring of 1837. "The

General is very much debilitated," he wrote his friend Reuben Lewis, the brother of explorer Meriwether Lewis. "Indeed he was so feeble in appearance that his friends urged him strongly not to expose himself to the fatigue of shaking hands with the crowds that pressed to see him, but he withstood every solicitude utterly regardless of his own comfort."

What explains Jackson's fortitude, even at the end of his public career? He cared deeply about how "the people" perceived him, for he had always believed that popular judgment would prevail over politicians' manipulations in the life of his legacy. Louisville had been a hotbed of anti-Jackson agitation not many years before; but that did not dissuade him. Cunningham described a "toilworn face and shrunken cheek" as he stood beside Jackson, witnessing the beaming faces of "ladies and small children" who took the old soldier by the hand, in what the charmed observer called "one of the most sublime moral spectacles I ever beheld."[2]

Just as soon as he arrived at the Hermitage, which had been undergoing refurbishing in anticipation of his retirement, Jackson dashed off a letter to his successor. Complaining of a bad cough, he said he was anxious to get well so that he might "amuse" himself by riding about his farm and visiting his old neighbors. He expressed gratification at the reception along his journey home, "every where cheered by my numerous democratic republican friends," and termed this the true "patriot's reward," and "my solace to the grave." But how much solace he enjoyed is questionable, to judge by the sentiments which followed. Be on your guard, he instructed Van Buren, against *"apostates, ambitious, and designing men—demagogues."* Still fearful of the banks, he exhorted the new president to see that Secretary of the Treasury Levi Woodbury, a Jackson holdover, "have the Banks *well examined.*" Jackson's italics throughout the letter reveal the persistence of the democratic catechism: be true to *"the people, the working classes,"* and then *"the people will sustain you."* Check the corrupting influence of banking interests, *"and the republic is safe, and your administration must end in triumph."*[3]

"I will make him feel upon this subject"

In a perfect Jacksonian world, friendship endured beyond the grave. He had never forgotten the injustice done by Gen. James Wilkinson to Col. Thomas Butler, who "died under that persecution," as he wrote to the new secretary of war, Joel R. Poinsett of South Carolina, in the autumn of 1837. Recalling for Poinsett the "famed *order for croppen the hair,*" Jackson recommended the grandson of Butler for appointment to the United States Military Academy. Because the sixteen-year-old's widowed mother could not provide for his education, Jackson stepped in on behalf of "a youth who has, from the military services of his family, great claims upon his country." He did not spell out that the boy was also the grandson of his old friend Robert Hays, Rachel Jackson's brother-in-law, the justice of the peace who had performed the Jacksons' 1794 marriage ceremony. Richard J. Hays did indeed go to West Point the following year, thanks to Jackson, but he proved "deficient" and withdrew after one year.[4]

For many years and with utter consistency, Jackson had boasted his principle of friendship, regarding himself as one who never deserted a friend. When Henry Clay had the gall to campaign for William Henry Harrison right in the center of Nashville, he made it a point during his speech to allude to the financial improprieties of Jackson appointees— making particular mention of Edward Livingston. Jackson then published a blistering response in the press and wrote to Livingston's widow, whom he had known since 1814: "I never forget a friend or abandon one." He considered it his duty to answer every "lying demagogue," as he glibly termed Clay. With accustomed spite, he assured Louise Livingston that the attack on her late husband "has recoiled upon him with great force and like the shirt of Nessus it will stick to him as long as he lives and live after him." In Greek legend, Nessus was a centaur struck by the poisoned arrow of Hercules, for trying to abduct his wife; in Jackson's mind, the two incidents, fictional and actual, both concerned acts of chivalry. Jackson would have his literary arrow bearing poison, that it might kill Clay politically.[5]

While claiming that he never deserted a friend, Jackson found in his late years that he could not always count on reciprocity. The friend on whose behalf he had expended the greatest energy came to disappoint him the most. After the purge of the first cabinet in 1831, he had continued to take special care over John Eaton's career. First he planned for his secretary of war to get his old Senate job back—literally to trade positions with Hugh Lawson White. But White spoiled Jackson's plans when he refused the cabinet post, professedly on moral grounds, not wanting to be perceived as the recipient of patronage. Henry Wise later wrote of White that he believed Jackson "misled by mercenaries and aspirants," and ultimately willing to "prostitute his power to his passions to defeat his political opponents."[6] Jackson did not appreciate White's stand—it seemed to him both ungrateful and disloyal. Soon after this, White went over to the opposition party, bemoaning Jackson's "excesses." In 1836, he was one of three Whigs to run for president, winning 10 percent of the popular vote and the electoral votes of Tennessee and Georgia. His candidacy helped to divide the Whigs and pave the way for Van Buren's victory.[7]

Eaton, meanwhile, accepted the governorship of Florida Territory in 1834, a position Jackson had briefly held in 1821. When its appeal ceased, as it had for Jackson, Eaton was named minister to Spain. In 1840, after four years abroad, Eaton no longer felt beholden to his longtime patron, and made the same party switch. "Never," wrote the furious Jackson to the tried and true Amos Kendall, "did I so much regret the ingratitude and depravity of man, more than I have the course of Major Eaton. . . . *He is a lost man.*" In becoming a Whig, Eaton—who as far as Jackson could see had no reason not to support Van Buren—had suddenly turned into "one of the basest apostates that ever lived."[8]

Jackson endured these unpalatable defections as if they were oppressive, unwarranted coincidences, rather than something he had had a hand in bringing on. He was reading the newspapers regularly, but without adequate reward. His iron will had not been bequeathed to Van Buren, who was a gifted but politically wounded president. There were no more Jacksons in the Democratic Party. Jackson's strong words to Van Buren as he took office in 1837 had been meant to prepare his successor for the kinds of dogfights he himself had weathered, but Van Buren was perhaps less inspired—for it could not be said that he understood the vagaries of politics any less than his predecessor. He lacked Jackson's sense of a right to command, and he could not make Jackson's bank policy stick. Too many Americans were coming to consider it publicly irresponsible for the federal government to hang the banks out to dry. Van Buren, able but not endearing, was blamed for the depression that Jackson's policy had helped bring on.

Jackson was determined to be proven right. That was his way about everything. He counted on the younger men for vindication, but they could or would not comply. Van Buren was turned out of office in 1840. Eaton and Richard Call recognized the leadership of a rival hero of the War of 1812, William Henry Harrison. Jackson could only assume they had done this for money and for office. "What apostacy! and how degraded a situation," he wrote to the loyal editor Francis P. Blair in the fall of 1840. He soothed himself by imagining the "scowls" of Eaton's and Call's former Democratic friends, and predicted that their new political allies "will laugh them to scorn." He was most of all irked that Eaton had not even paid him a visit since his return from Spain, and, as he put it to Kendall, had turned on those who "risqued much, in time of his need, to save him and his family from *degradation* and *infamy*." Jackson acknowledged a "heart felt contempt" for men like Eaton who, he calculated, put office ahead of friendship: "If ever I have the opportunity *personally*, I will make him feel upon this subject."[9]

So that was Jackson's explanation: they had all been corrupted. Only his Kitchen Cabinet, in the end, had remained pure. Hugh Lawson White attempted to explain for history the rationale behind the defections. Jackson, he suggests, had become less magnanimous and less republican as he aged. His ambition to personify America, to be remembered forever for masterful achievements, had clouded his view of what was right for the country:

> As I believe, he has come home determined to destroy every man who dared to differ with him in opinion as to his successor. . . . If it be his will, let him proceed. Angry discussion can never add to my comfort, it may to his. Our temperament and aim are, I believe, a little different. . . . In the temper he now is, and with enfeebled faculties, he views everything as an *enemy* that stands in the road of his ambition. He *personifies* truth, justice and everything else which obstructs his course, and attacks them with all that gallantry, with which he assails political or personal opponents. He has determined he will die *having* the character of a *great* man. While my highest ambition is to die conscious that I *deserve* the reputation of an *honest* one.

White had concluded that the personal and the political were one in Jackson's mind: no one but he embodied the popular will, and no one but his stand-in, Martin Van Buren, embodied the Jacksonian political program. White had known Jackson since the mid-1790s, when at twenty he had fought under John Sevier against the Cherokees. John Adams was the president when Representative Andrew Jackson had lauded White before the U.S. Congress. Now, as a mature statesman, the same Hugh Lawson White delivered a stinging rebuke of everything Jackson stood for.[10]

A Slow Drift toward Death

Nevertheless, Jackson did not want to die without giving the country what he imagined it wanted from him. Accustomed to crowds and adulation, he welcomed the decade of the 1840s in grand style, risking life and limb in

18. Trevor Thomas Fowler's portrait of the seventy-three-year-old ex-president, 1840. Courtesy National Portrait Gallery, Smithsonian Institution.

the process. He did this because his legacy seemed in jeopardy. January 8, 1840, was the twenty-fifth anniversary of the Battle of New Orleans. The old hero traveled one last time to the scene of his triumph, accompanied by Andrew Jackson Donelson. They moved over rough, snow-clogged roads for the first leg of the journey, then climbed aboard a steamboat only to be slowed by a blizzard on the Mississippi. Jackson was intent, but he was suffering.

Their party arrived just in time, on the very morning of January 8, to the sound of celebratory cannon fire. Exhausted and still feeling ill, Jackson gave the people—reportedly thirty thousand—what they came to see. He sat in an open carriage and waved. Spectators stood on balconies and rooftops. He received the salutes of volunteer troops. He met with veterans of the great battle. The only stop on the tour that he was unable to accomplish that day was a scheduled march to the battlefield itself.[11] While physically frail, Jackson proved that his spirit refused to be crushed. He survived the fêtes and the demanding crowds, probably unaware that he had become a relic, a masterpiece of ancient chivalry for those who wished to glimpse a hero from the fading past. The Irish portrait artist Trevor Thomas Fowler painted Jackson while he sat aboard the vessel *Vicksburg* on his river voyage back to Tennessee.

When his successor lost to Harrison that fall, Jackson could hardly expect to exercise any more political influence. He consoled Van Buren the only way he knew how—by raging at the political world: "The democracy of the United States have been shamefully beaten, *but I trust, not conquered.*" He hoped that the "hydra of corruption" would not crush the honest citizens who were left to endure administration by the moneyed power, without his protection.[12]

Jackson could take solace in the fawning correspondence he routinely received at the Hermitage. Looking at the autumn of 1841, for instance, he kept a letter from a man in Connecticut who merely requested an autograph. "If at some leisure moment, you will write a line or two—or simply your name + direct it to me, you will confer a favor I shall never forget. I wish to see and transmit to my children the hand writing of *Andrew Jackson,* a man whom I venerate more than any other now living." A New Hampshire man wrote just to tell him that, in the same way that he did not know how to exalt God, he could not think of a title by which to address Andrew Jackson: "No human title would add to the power or splendour, to the love or veneration, we *feel* to Our God, or the Benefactor of our Country." A rural Tennessean who at eighteen had seen Jackson presiding in a courtroom, and who had cast his eye on him once again four decades later during Jackson's most recent appearance in New Orleans, wrote to say how much he regretted having come so close to finally shaking Jackson's hand without succeeding. Wishing him serenity in his "latter days," this long-time supporter—a self-described democrat "since the struggle between the elder Adams & Mr. Jefferson"—informed the old soldier that he had "done more for his Counterey than any man now living or that ever did live Genl Washington Excepted."[13]

Of course, Jackson had also made enemies, not only among national politicians but in communities around the country. He received letters from these people as well—unsigned. One of June 1841, from New Orleans (that Jackson retained), was especially poisonous. The embittered writer said he had previously known Jackson personally, and criticized him as "arbitrary in temper and despotic in Conduct character and opinion." Jackson, he charged, was a hypocrite with respect to Thomas Jefferson, claiming an attachment to the Virginian that was false: friends of the letter writer "could recollect the deep denunciations and bitter curses they heard you pour out repeatedly on Jefferson, his policy and character from the year 1805 to 1811." Yet since Jefferson's death in 1826, Jackson had changed his tune. The anonymous critic accused, sarcastically, "Knowing you as I do, it must have cost you a great sacrafice of your fierce and dogmatic spirit to suffer uncontradicted this misrepresentation of your opinions and views, and shew you up as the servile follower of a man who you hated." He was not quite through berating Jackson, mocking him for pronouncing Kendall's name as "kindle," and reminding him again that his most outstanding attribute was an "overfed vanity." He signed off, "this is the whole catalogue of your merits—farewell."[14]

In the spring of 1842, Van Buren paid a visit to the Hermitage, and Jackson began to wish again for a Van Buren presidency. The only problem, in his mind, was that Van Buren did not support the annexation of Texas, now an independent republic presided over by Sam Houston. The alternative Jacksonian candidate, James K. Polk, was pressing for Texas statehood. Francis P. Blair wrote prophetically from Washington: "You will live to see those of your friends whom you put in, again restored with your principles, to power."[15] It was true that Jackson would live to read of Polk's victory over the notorious Clay, who had thus lost in all three of his bids for the presidency. Clay was still being penalized for his "corrupt bargain" with Adams twenty years before.

In 1843, Amos Kendall's biography of Jackson began to appear in installments. One would naturally expect Jackson to take a lively interest, but he did more than that: he expended a good deal of his dwindling energy making certain that Kendall got the details right, especially those that glorified his subject for posterity. Jackson made an effort (unsuccessful) to retrieve his 1813 correspondence with Wilkinson. The history of the Battle of New Orleans, in particular, required his maintenance, lest the grim facts of martial law plus the inconvenient executions that Jackson's opposition had used with effect in 1828 continue to haunt his legacy. So he collected "two bundles of papers" from the son of the late John Coffee, while commenting curiously that "it is doubtful whether Genl Carroll will give any thing." He exhorted Kendall to echo the standard interpretation of the Hall-Louaillier episode, insisting that his authorized biographer paint him as the injured party.[16]

The Hall-Louaillier episode remained of special concern, because it cast Jackson in the rather undemocratic role of tyrant. He could see how, retrospectively, it was possible to castigate him for having overreacted. The war was decidedly over in March 1815, and civil government ought to have been promptly restored. He needed history to appreciate that his actions were patriotic rather than self-promoting. In this cause, Jackson found himself obliged to ask a favor from a wartime aide who had "apostacized" and joined the Whig Party, Richard K. Call, who in 1842 was governor of Florida and who would back Clay in the next presidential election. Jackson wrote: "You being a participater in that defence"—New Orleans—"therefore it is that I should address you, requesting that you will have the good-ness to give me your recollection of the cond[uct and] impressions of Judge Hall . . . and Luweller." The letter was signed, "very respectfully your friend."[17]

He wanted Call to repeat what Judge Hall was meant to have said upon Jackson's declaring martial law: "Now the country may be saved." This would ostensibly cause the judge to look inconstant and make Jackson appear justified in his subsequent upholding of military discipline in the city he had saved. Call wrote back promptly, wholly confirming Jackson's interpretation of events. Call's letter was published in the *Washington Globe,* the principal Jacksonian newspaper, in 1843. By then a thankful Jackson had already written back to Call, revealing his larger purpose: "your communication just received, is the more highly appreciated, and will be important to the faithful historian." The septuagenarian was court-ing posterity.[18]

Jackson felt death approaching in the early months of 1845. He had just finished congratulating the soon to be inaugurated James Polk (with refer-ences, as always, to rumors, potential policy disasters, and "vile slanders"), when a sense of endings began creeping into the last lines of his letters. "P.S. I am greatly afflicted," he wrote to Polk at the end of February. "When I attempt to walk, I am at once suffocated for want of breath." To Francis P. Blair in March: "I have been seriously attacked a few night ago, with pain in my right side as well as heretofore in the left. I am allways ready to say the Lords will be done." To Jackson's cotton broker in New Orleans: "Under the present attack which I am labouring, this may be the last letter you may receive from me. If so I hope to meet you in a blissful immortality." In April, the tone became even more abrupt: "I am very sick, must close." But the dying man still found the energy to warn the new president outright on negotiations with London over Oregon Territory: "No temporising with Britain on this subject now, *temporising will not do.*"[19]

May brought worse tidings. He was anxious about Amos Kendall's future in the Polk administration. "I have been waiting to see what the President has done, or intends to do for you. . . . I would like to know what is to be yr. destination." This was followed by a hope "that we may at last meet in a blissful immortality." The same phrase repeated in a letter to Andrew Jackson Donelson, then in New Orleans, along with news of a further ailment: "it will be almost a miracle if I should survive my present attack. I [am] swollen from the toes to the crown of my head, and in band-ages to my hips. Have had a violent bowel complaint which avraged from six to eigh passages for 24 hours, with a constant nausea at my stomach. How far my god may think proper to bear me up under my weight of afflictions, he only knowns."[20]

Jackson had always accepted death as a part of his world, the ultimate human event—a function of life. It was not to be feared, nor welcomed, nor fought particularly, but expected and approved. Whether on the battlefield or in private life, he never railed against the ultimate doom, as did poets who scorned or despised or were awestruck by death's power; nor did he feel that degree of resignation, which certain sects of the Protestant faith taught. When Rachel died, he was said to have lashed out against the scurrilous editors whom he believed had hastened the event; but he did not protest beyond that.

Jackson bore death with a calm consciousness. As such he perceived a kind of purity in it. Death was an event that disclosed something further about the moral character of the deceased, that spoke to the quality of the life lived by the deceased. Others during the age of Jackson found great suspense and uplifted affection in the process of dying, much more than he did. When they communicated with friends and with the public, just as thousands of ordinary letter writers did, literary giants like Lord Byron and Washington Irving shared accounts that were alternately heart-rending and composed, passionate and inspiring, in recounting the experience of loss.[21] But there was no special aura about dying for Andrew Jackson. Rather it was a law of life. It may sound odd to characterize in this way a man whose entire adulthood was spent overcoming illness and pain, whose life was one of resistance. But while he himself forestalled death's beckoning for so long, he would have accepted it at almost any time; he saw it as he saw his other moral obligations—as something manifest, something entirely unambiguous.

The last letter Jackson wrote was to President Polk, on June 6. His adopted son, Andrew Jackson Jr., was in the room as he penned it, and attested that his father had announced that this might be his last letter. It contained cautions about potential frauds emanating from the Treasury Department that "would blow you and your administration Sky high." It ended, "I can write no more, friendship has aroused me to make this attempt. yr friend, Andrew Jackson."[22]

Jackson died on June 8, 1845, around six in the evening, after telling his slaves, "I want all to prepare to meet me in Heaven. . . . Christ has no respect for color." Sam Houston arrived shortly after his patron had expired. He wrote from the Hermitage to Polk, noting that Jackson's countenance appeared in death as it had in life, and that he had, according to his physician, "departed with perfect serenity of mind, and with full faith in the promises of salvation."[23]

A dozen years earlier, Jackson had commented on the death of his friend John Overton in a letter to William B. Lewis: "I regret he is gone, but when I reflect he is beyond, where the wicked cease to trouble, and where the weary are at rest, altho I could lament in the language and feelings of David for Absalom, I am constrained to say *peace to his manes,*" peace to his spirit.[24] A touching sentiment, but perhaps better applied *to* Jackson than *by* him. In the Old Testament, Absalom was slain in battle while opposing his father, King David, who yet went on to mourn him with a desperate grief that surprised all. It was the weary combatant Andrew Jackson, more than any other figure of his time, whom the "wicked" had never ceased to trouble, and whom America would grieve in heroic strains.

Only ten weeks before Jackson's death, Commodore J. D. Elliott of the U.S. Navy had written to the ex-president, offering him the sarcophagus of a Roman emperor, which Elliott had transported to Washington from Palestine aboard the U.S.S. *Constitution.* "I pray you, General, to live on," he wrote, while assuring that "an emperor's coffin awaits you." Jackson replied graciously that he was constrained from accepting the commodore's offer: "I cannot consent that my mortal body shall be laid in a repository prepared for an emperor or king. My republican feelings and principles forbid it." He added, "True virtue cannot exist where pomp and parade are the governing passions." And then he explained the arrangements he had already made: "I have prepared a humble depository for my mortal body beside that wherein lies my beloved wife."[25]

Jackson refused an imperial sarcophagus, but his coffin was preserved with unusual care: it was placed inside a leaden casing, which was in turn soldered shut and set inside a limestone- and brick-lined vault. Over his remains was laid a limestone slab with the words "GENERAL ANDREW JACKSON" inscribed into it.[26] This was what he had envisioned: a funeral at the Hermitage and to be buried in the garden, beside his wife. The immoderate general, the avenging president, was finally at peace.

Washington, Jefferson, and Jackson

Andrew Jackson was, in his own way, a Shakespearean tragic hero. In his impetuousness, his precipitate anger, his Lear-like howling, and his sensational inability to countenance any form of dissent, he imagined himself an infallible judge of others. Every tragic figure requires a flaw rooted in good intentions, and Jackson's was his incessant pursuit of virtue in the political realm, where virtue, so greatly desired, can scarcely exist.

What could have so muddled his judgment that he should expect wide concurrence with his views from men who strived for position and authority, who wished, like him, to be remembered? He held this expectation because he had, during his rise to respectability, acquired a dangerous kind of self-love. He saw hypocrisy in others, never in himself; he mistook his own ceremonial pronouncements of his love of virtue for genuine self-worth. "Virtue is a very vain and frivolous thing if it derives its recommendation from glory," wrote the French essayist Michel de Montaigne, a humanist who composed in the decades before Shakespeare.[27] Jackson proved himself virtuous *to himself,* and demanded concurrence. Vanity is a failing common to the overeducated as well as the ignorant, and people with suppler minds than Jackson's.

The human condition is shaped by variability, by inequality and competition. Jackson sought notice—he took the patriot field early—hoping that his deeds would not so quickly pass away. The orphaned child of the frontier Carolinas grew up with turmoil and desired to redress injustices. He saw war firsthand, at a young age. He knew sorrow. The discontent he experienced in an unstable world both led him to gamble and produced an incentive to climb the social ladder. Of course, this in itself is not startling. To be American was, and is, to be acquisitive.

To acquire land was not enough; he had to acquire honor as well. If he lacked in health, he possessed instead an abundance of fire. He had to show that he was not one of the multitudes, that he could rise above the ordinary meekness, gaiety, and sensuality. After his youthful wandering, he increasingly developed a Spartan consciousness, demanding and self-demanding, with a love of valor and a contempt for easy riches. Something inside cried out for a cause—this is the impulse common to all potential leaders of others. His cause was protection of the self-made common man, meaner versions of himself.

As he began to build, he wished not to be burdened by a sense of debt, both in practical and moral terms. He sought avenues of advancement based on intrinsic merit, so that he could go on to offer advantages to others, that they should owe their happiness to him. His sense of justice was biblical and absolute: an eye for an eye. To the pious Rachel, he wrote of his being an instrument for the "Just Vengeance of heaven—having vissitted and punished with death, the exciters of the Indian war, and horrid massacre of our innocent women & children on the Southern frontier. I have destroyed the babylon of the South."[28]

Restless as he was, over time his demands increased. Every act required some form of recompense. He did not accept that, once he gave blood and toil, rewards could be deferred. He was similarly slow to accept the corrupt nature of politics, though he ultimately realized that appointments to office were an implicit bargain for support and only in part a measure of a man's worth. Yet he never lost faith in his own ability as a moral guide. From his start in public life, he believed that anyone who failed to recognize his worth was wicked, and deserved to be stripped of power by moral means. He wanted the power to reward and punish, such as the army presented to its generals as a means to repel the forces of destabilization. In a half-settled, morally suspect world, he felt embattled, besieged.

What George Washington, Thomas Jefferson, and Andrew Jackson—the three traditionally "great" early presidents—had most in common was the perception that virulent enemies were plotting against them. This will doubtless seem perverse, even obnoxious, to modern patriots, who are taught to see the nation's founding in glorious terms, comfortably maintaining a clear conviction that the founders were noble and dignified leaders. These are merely the myths of history, old yet persistent, sustaining the nation's optimistic vision and serving a psychological function, generation by generation.

Historic memory and historical reality are not the same thing. The idealized memory needs to be adjusted. Washington's intellectual limitations, like Jackson's, caused many prominent men to scoff at his qualifications for national leadership, which wounded the general's pride (in both cases) and aggravated their potentially explosive temperaments. The founders often behaved irrationally.

The humane Jefferson, generally presumed Jackson's temperamental opposite, was merely quieter in his belligerence. He wrote a letter to his alter ego James Madison, for instance, wishing Patrick Henry dead for opposing their legislative agenda; it was not merely a rhetorical flourish. To Washington, he termed Alexander Hamilton a slanderer, "whose history, from the moment at which history can stoop to notice him, is a tissue of machinations against the liberty of the country." Early American politics was nasty, and classical notions of public virtue, though much touted, were almost never practiced. These leaders' common desire to see their will enacted in public measures was often frustrated, and none of them shrugged it off as simply the nature of republican politics.[29] Neither Washington nor Jefferson nor Jackson was accepting of the eventual routinization of opposition political parties. None of this in and of itself makes them unrepublican, though it does humanize their stature.

Washington and Jackson had a good deal in common. Throughout their lives, both men were sharp businessmen and hungry speculators in land. They thrived on taking risks. In politics, they required men of letters, men of superior intellect, to help them shape and present their ideas to the public: Washington had Hamilton, Jackson had Livingston. As wartime commanders, Washington and Jackson exhibited horrible fits of temper when their integrity was challenged. Their manner was different in that Washington was extremely sober and aloof, ill at ease with strangers and notably impersonal, while Jackson was more natural and more companionable; yet both were as headstrong as they were daring. They required constant attention from their young, respectful, loyal subordinates—best described as courtiers, in the old, chivalric sense. There were few people with whom they could speak candidly. (Washington and Jackson, incidentally, showed a playful side to women, toward whom they were otherwise courteous and amiable.) And both briskly took steps to counter the claim of any general who confronted a decision or suggested that their orders were imperfect.[30]

As the astute Washington biographer John Ferling puts it, the so-called First of Men was "unable to take responsibility for failure." (Jackson did not believe himself *capable* of failure.) Rival general Charles Lee referred to Washington as a "puffed up charlatan"; his last secretary of state, Timothy Pickering, termed him "vain and weak and ignorant"; Dr. Benjamin Rush, a sensitive judge of others, insisted that at no time after 1777 did he believe Washington "first in war." John Adams asserted that Washington would not seek a third term because he feared competition—it was not for noble purposes that he chose not to run. And yet in refusing a salary (or a crown) during his years of service, Washington made possible all the subsequent homage he received as a man of the strictest rectitude who performed selflessly. In death, he became the ultimate symbol of nostalgia for the Revolution; he was elevated to godlike status—"To draw his true portrait is more than mortal hands can do!"—that he might continue to shed blessings among his national posterity.[31]

Jackson attempted to convey a selfless quality, too, but convinced only writers of the most florid prose that he was Washingtonian in this way. An 1824 vindication of his execution of Ambrister and Arbuthnot in Florida opened: "General Jackson may with justice be styled the Cincinnatus of America; a man who has never solicited or refused an office, and who, after discharging the duties assigned him, has uniformly retired to private life to enjoy the sweets of tranquillity." This was the precise manner in which Washington was depicted by his contemporaries after the Revolution was won—"Unambitious of farther honors he had retired to his farm in Virginia"—and it explains why no one feared that the first president would abuse his executive power.[32]

Jackson was eulogized for his "immoveable nerve," "vigor and bold-ness," and "indomitable spirit"—his endurance. To those mythologizing Jackson who wanted to link him to the first president, the most ethereal image of their hero that they could construct was to declare that he had served as a "noviciate . . . in the school of virtue" under General Washing-ton. They invoked his childhood experience to suggest that a torch had been passed: During the Revolution, "it was necessary for the youthful aspirant after fame to inhale a pure spirit from his living predecessor; as if nature, fearful lest the race of such men might perish, had directed them to exist in continued and unbroken succession."[33]

In Jackson's day, Washington's foibles were forgotten. The national father was, as Henry Clay put in when he was looking to disparage Jackson in 1825, "Illustrious. . . . There was in that extraordinary person, united a serenity of mind, a cool and collected wisdom, a cautious and deliberate judgment." More important still, "No man was ever more deeply pene-trated than he was, with profound respect for the safe and necessary prin-ciple of the entire subordination of the military to the civil authority." At least in this last statement, Clay was able to draw a distinction between Washington and Jackson that in some way reflected historic reality.[34]

George Washington's early chroniclers invariably described their subject in terms of loftiness and solemnity—the quiet force of his personal bear-ing. Those of Jackson's contemporaries who wrote of him, whether famil-iarly as "Old Hickory," or adoringly as "the Hero," or disapprovingly as a limited and flawed "military chieftain," all placed their emphasis on a per-sonal forcefulness set less by virtuous example (the Washington image) than by unconquerability in action. Jackson's characteristic strength was anything but Washingtonian reserve.

Knowing that Washington was as erratic, as covetous of land, and at times as hot-tempered as Jackson, should give us pause. Washington came of age in an era when heroism was publicized in rarefied terms and news-papers generally preferred chaste classical allusions to earthy depictions.

For that reason, the backwoods Washington was essentially lost, and he became simply (and misleadingly) "the first of men" and "the best of men." Before we deride Jackson for his limitations, we ought to show sensitivity to the changing environment, and recognize that the language that was applied to him was the language of his time.

All who worked around Washington, and all who worked around Jackson, understood how important it was to give the commander what he wanted, to keep the general happy. Differences between the two men's leadership styles widen when they enter the presidency. Here Washington was more likely to yield to the argument put forward by a cabinet secretary than Jackson was. Washington appointed to his cabinet the greatest talent he could find; Jackson appointed men whom he expected to think like him and do what he said. Washington knew his intellectual limitations and took considerable time to reach decisions,[35] while the more impulsive Jackson made it appear, when the issue was close to his heart, that he was somehow the recipient of a pure light of inspiration. Though both were easily angered when criticized in the press, Washington grumbled in private, and Jackson made his consternation public.

Juvenile biographies written about the two presidents within a year after Jackson's death are illuminating. The preface to an 1845 *Life of Jackson* directs "young countrymen" to read about Jackson and then encounter Washington's life for another model worth imitating. The first general-turned-president was found upright by means of simple comparisons to Napoleon: "The ambition of Washington was a virtue, that of Napoleon a vice. The limits of one was the freedom and independence of his country; that of the other the subjugation of the world." And metaphorically: "Napoleon was a bright but scorching luminary, scourging the earth with consuming fires; Washington was a genial sun, mild yet radiant." Jackson, dead less than a month when the author completed his work, was adjudged "great and just in life, calm and resigned in death." His patient submission in the dying process was fresh in people's minds.

As a president, however, people knew better. In 1845, Jackson could not be convincingly described as anything but imperious, though the author of *Life of Jackson* hoped that the passage of time would soften memory, as it had with his giant predecessor: "The many and strong prejudices engendered by his bold and energetic administration of public affairs, will gradually become less as time erases from memories the influence of his policy upon individual interests and happiness." No one could doubt that he had had a "remarkable career," as the anecdotes related in the text suggested. This Jackson was Solomon-like, thoughtful, and ordinarily fair-minded;

his frontier encounter with Indian agent Silas Dinsmore, for instance, became the tale of a man who simply wanted to help decent folks who had been cruelly detained for lack of a passport. Never mind that Jackson was ready to become violent in defense of slave-owning, or that he ignored the conditions in which the nearby Indians were living. He was an angel of mercy, to Dinsmore's deviltry.[36]

Jackson's posthumous association with Washington aside, the election of 1824 made the link between them seem credible. With the idealized Battle of New Orleans alive in memory, campaign strategists like John Eaton had applied the "Washington treatment" when they set their candidate above politics. "He was above self-promotion," one modern commentator has written of Eaton's Jackson.[37] In a time when the heroes of the Revolution were either dead or about to disappear from view, books celebrating their exploits were emerging from presses across the nation. The construction of candidate Jackson as the second coming of Washington (in terms of his military prowess and discerning judgment), and as the second coming of Jefferson (in terms of his political spirit and popular identity), proved a highly effective tool. This shows how easy it was to manipulate the political record: in the mid-1790s, Jackson had protested Washington's acceptance of British power in the weak-willed Jay Treaty, and in the following decade he as strongly disapproved of Jefferson's peevish handling of the Burr affair.

The Jefferson-Jackson connection was the more palpable to nineteenth-century Americans. On January 8, 1829, at the first anniversary celebration of the Battle of New Orleans to be staged after Jackson was elected president, a supporter at a Boston banquet toasted his man and his inherited principles: "The *Democratic* Tree of Liberty," it went. "Under the culture of the PLANTER—JEFFERSON, its roots struck *deep* and *immovable;* under that of the FARMER OF TENNESSEE, it shall bloom and blossom like the Rose."[38] Jackson naturally adopted Jefferson's distinctive view of the arable West as a landscape suitable for republican manners and humane interactions among hardy yeoman farmers. Both men were highly suspicious of physically inactive, city-bound speculators in stock paper. Their agrarian ideal made Jefferson and Jackson closer than either was to Washington, a pro–urban growth, pro–commercial elite Federalist. When stymied by an organized opposition in the national metropolis, Jefferson and Jackson alike responded by saying that their true constituency was the largely agrarian citizenry, and that such people were more reliable barometers of political justice than the moneyed few.

Unlike Washington, both Jefferson and Jackson provoked political unrest while emphatically denying that they did so. Exploiting social tensions for political gain, they were moralists and ideologues who behaved as they did because they possessed a strong intuitive sense that they were needed to prevent corruption. Washington did not believe that so fluctuating a wind as popular opinion could ever be tamed, and he did not respect it; he had no difficulty reserving power for those already accustomed to exercising it. Yet Jefferson and Jackson saw popular opinion as a remedy and sought to actualize it in policy. They professed having assumed executive authority solely to bar powermongers from usurping the people's right, all the while protesting that they really preferred to retire from public cares.

It is interesting to compare their sense of who the enemy was: Jefferson termed the Federalists "the Monarchical party," and though the Federalists were long defunct, Jackson continued to call his opposition by that name, or simply "the aristocrats." Jefferson and Jackson each contrived a vocabulary that he expected would resonate beyond the political elite. That vocabulary included words that identified the core values of their common constituency—"harmony and affection," to Jefferson; "to do right and fear not," to Jackson. To their political enemies they applied ringing words expressing opposite values. In Jefferson's case, the opposition consisted of "engines of despotism" and "intriguers." For Jackson, "hidden intrigues," "vile calumniators," and "conspirators" denoted the political antagonist. Convinced and committed as they were, both Jefferson and Jackson may have perceived threats out of proportion to reality.

Jefferson, the most refined among the writers of his generation, estimated the sensibility of the recipient of each of his letters, and painstakingly sought to please. Jackson, like Jefferson, wrote with vigor, but without classical allusions or euphonic phrasing, and occasionally without tact. Jefferson sought to disguise his ambition and his intolerance in his prose; Jackson disguised little. While flattering the late president in his memoir, and seeking to prove "elevation of mind" along with the better-known irascibility of temper, Thomas Hart Benton described Jackson's literary scope: "He had vigorous thoughts, but not the faculty of arranging them in a regular composition; either written or spoken. . . . His conversation was like his writing; a vigorous flowing current, apparently without the trouble of thinking, and always impressive." That is, Jackson acted out his impulses in speech and on paper just as he did in his more visible command performances. His thoughts were like actions—generally unmediated.[39] This said, as a dramatic public actor he was more Jeffersonian than he knew: their pronouncements rang with a similar kind of heartfelt nationalism and bespoke universal principles, but each was unaware of the true insularity of his "Union" values.

As men who mistrusted those in power, Jefferson and Jackson imagined that their presidencies gave voice to ordinary Americans. Jefferson had even dubbed his election the "Revolution of 1800" for overturning snobbery, pomp, and bigotry. Jackson's inaugural free-for-all produced the same impression. In fact, though, all Jackson's election accomplished was to replace one ruling clique with another. What passed, in his mind, for democracy was a military chain of command; insubordinate officers—his first cabinet—were reassigned. Jefferson, at least, kept his cabinet intact. If democracy existed under Jackson, it was not issuing from a reconstituted Washington, as Jackson would have it; rather, democracy lay in the expressions of personal independence that Chevalier, Tocqueville, and Trollope identified when they traveled inland and mingled with unexceptional, entrepreneurial citizens.

As to the most obvious failure of democracy, all three "great" presidents—Washington, Jefferson, and Jackson—owned considerable numbers of slaves. Jefferson's position on slavery is best known, because he recognized the moral dilemma and addressed it in his book, *Notes on Virginia,* which has remained controversial among historians since the civil rights movement of the twentieth century. Jefferson (in print) tried to encounter race in scientific or philosophic terms, while endeavoring, at Monticello, to be a benevolent master. He rationalized that his slaves were better off under his management than they would be if freed, given the hostile social climate (which he had not invented). Washington, lauded for having emancipated his slaves in his will, is made to appear enlightened in this regard and too often overlooked for having, in fact, adopted a largely pragmatic view toward slavery, and by no means a humanistic one. He took no steps to emancipate slaves during his lifetime, nor did he enact legislation; he never did anything that would impinge upon his ability to live the patrician life to which he had grown accustomed. He expressed regret that slavery existed in America, but he considered even gradual emancipation an event that would produce "mischief."

Jackson, lacking any qualms about the ownership of human property, was honest in his concern for particular slaves, and paternalistic in a sense comparable to his starkly demanding, occasionally punitive, yet consistently fatherly approach to his white soldiers. Like his Virginia-reared predecessors, he bought and sold slaves through most of his adult life;

Washington, Jefferson, and Jackson all considered blacks largely ignorant and, stereotypically, irresponsible and untrustworthy. There is no rewriting of history that can explain away these unpleasant facts. Yet at the same time, we are instructed that these three men were, in many ways, more ordinary and typical of their place and time than generations of legend builders have since succeeded in portraying them.[40]

Like Washington, Jackson received a meager education. Eulogizing the first president, America's first historian of the Revolution, David Ramsay, noted: "His learning was of a singular kind; he overstepped the tedious forms of the schools, and by the force of a correct taste and sound judgment, seized on the great ends of learning, without the assistance of those means, which have been contrived to prepare less active minds for public business." Similarly, Jackson was "the unlettered man of the West, the nursling of the wilds, the farmer of the Hermitage, little versed in books, unconnected by science with the tradition of the past." Yet both leaders were lionized as the bravest of the brave, a quality that was meant ostensibly to rationalize how intellectual mediocrities could be worthy executives. In Jackson's case, it was a remarkable "unity of mind" that enabled him to develop "political doctrines that suited every emergency, with a precision and a harmony that no theorist could hope to equal." Both Washington and Jackson were meant to have possessed not only a rare, desirable, energetic nature, but also a kind of sublime, inner-directed magnanimity, for which no formal education could adequately prepare a man.[41]

While Washington was heavily invested in western lands, mainly acquired as payment for his early military service, he conceived of the West as a Federalist did: they were lands that would enjoy orderly growth as appendages of eastern power, accepting a subordinate position within the commercial orbit of the East, and governed by speculating men from the East. Jefferson and Jackson both welcomed the prospect of social diversity in the growth of western settlement; the prospect was too inviting— republican empire—not to take risks on behalf of it.

As to the process of populating the West with yeoman farmers, Jefferson was the more direct and the more exuberant. The West was Jefferson's "chosen country," as he anointed it in his first inaugural address in 1801. It was a prophetic speech, which historian Peter S. Onuf describes as "a paean to the immortal nation, an exultant leap into futurity." Precisely four years later, in his second inaugural address, Jefferson proclaimed: "The larger our association, the less it will be shaken by local passions; and in any view, is it not better that the opposite bank of the Mississippi should be settled by our own brethren and children, than by strangers of another family?" He recognized that his acquisition of Louisiana Territory without prior congressional authorization, in 1803, was an extralegal executive act, but he committed himself to it out of a sense of patriotic foresight. To a supportive senator he called his decision to treat with France independent of Congress, "seizing the fugitive [volatile, momentary] occurrence which so much advances the good of the country."[42]

Jackson, in Florida, showed comparable patriotic foresight. He prodded the Spanish in the direction they would eventually have moved, ending a diplomatic stalemate and making possible the Adams-Onís Treaty of 1819, which provided for a new burst of settlement and expansive sentiment. Hounded by accusations of unconstitutionality by his political opposition, Jackson proved himself a Jeffersonian first by carrying out his own "exultant leap into futurity" on the ground, in Florida, and then, as president, tacitly supporting Sam Houston's assault against Mexican forces.

Jefferson and Jackson alike endured the politicization of their sex lives. Jefferson ignored the scandal begun after he was in office, when a disappointed office seeker who had earlier exposed Alexander Hamilton as an adulterer suddenly turned on the president. Linking Jefferson with his biracial servant Sally Hemings was meant to embarrass a sitting president, not disqualify him for office holding. His attraction to a woman of low social standing, a woman he legally owned, was designed to shame him, to catch him at something that most already knew was common on southern plantations. The philosophic Jefferson was supposed to be dignified and morally above such scandalous private behavior.

When Cincinnati editor Charles Hammond promulgated his information about the suspect circumstances of Jackson's union with his wife of thirty-seven years, his intention was quite different: to wrest an election away from a candidate by portraying him as profligate and undeserving of the public trust, a reckless, volatile adventurer. Hammond's representation that in the Robards case, the notorious Jackson, who "spent the prime of his life in gambling, in cock fighting, in horse racing . . . tore from a husband the wife of his bosom," has caused the historian Norma Basch to conclude that Jackson's offense was being depicted "more as an abduction than as a seduction." If wife stealing was an affair between men, Jackson's taking of Rachel Robards "signified his inability to honor the most elemental of contracts, along with his readiness to employ force." Sexual fidelity was the foundation of social stability, and if Jackson was purporting to be "a man's man," then he ought to be trustworthy.[43]

Jefferson's behavior may have been unbecoming, but it took place on his own property. Jackson's unconventional romance covered several states, involved the law (Robards's suit), and implied a lack of respect for the rights of other men. The noble image cultivated by Jackson appeared to his enemies as an outstanding fraud on the (male) voting public. If there was one thing Jackson could not stand, it was to dishonor manhood; for he relished men's company and identified strongly with the cause of fraternity and good fellowship.

"The Medicine of Life"

The historian Bertram Wyatt-Brown has written, "Jackson drove away his own dread of anonymity and emptiness by embracing both a love of friends and undying vengeance against enemies."[44] He was referring in part to a survivor of early tragedies, a man without family, without any biological children, who sought to imbibe a sense of community with an urgency and compulsiveness that may have made him unusually "needy." Yet the flaw in his character that caused him to lose faith in or lose the friendship of the Bentons, Carrolls, Eatons, and Calls was something he never understood. Only Benton, the one dependent friend who dared to denounce him—who once took deadly aim at the haughty general and then fled from his presence—only Benton loved the hero at the end of his life. Carroll supported Jackson's administration, but seemed to subsist without the warmth he had once enjoyed; both Eaton and Call became children who divorced their all-consuming, out-of-control father. Andrew Jackson Donelson, too, felt smothered, at least for a time, though his practical interests lay in returning to the fold.

For one as "needy" and demanding as Jackson was, there was an added sense of purpose to be found in caring for the life of his community. Indeed, this was why Freemasonry existed at all; and Jackson was, throughout his rise, a solid member of the dynamic brotherhood. His protégés were active in the organization as well: in 1814, Junior Warden Sam Houston, of the Clarksville, Tennessee, lodge, certified the membership of Richard K. Call, who later established the Tallahassee, Florida, lodge;[45] Eaton and Livingston were, of course, prominent brothers as well.

A Masonic manual published in Nashville in 1824, at the conclusion of Jackson's term as Worshipful Grand Master of Tennessee, underscored "Jacksonian" as well as Masonic ideals concerning male friendship and community values: "All Masons are to be *good and true*—men of honor and honesty," it asserted, "by whatever religious names or persuasions distinguished." A Mason was to be "a lover of peace, and obedient to the civil powers," just as Jackson often, if defensively and unconvincingly, proclaimed. Masons were to "seek to acquire, as far as possible, the virtues of *patience, meekness, self-denial, and forbearance,* which give him command over himself." While Jackson privileged "honor and honesty" over "forbearance," he must still have believed himself true to the key criteria of the Masonic code.

At any rate, the domestic Jackson—the Jackson described by visitors to the Hermitage during Rachel's lifetime—was this kind of a man, quite different from the public battler. He welcomed strangers. A Mason learned to distinguish manipulative men from true friends, as the handbook explained, differentiating between "confederacies of bad men [that] ought to be called conspiracies" and "pure principles of friendship." This was the test Jackson took every day of his political life; he both thrived on and was undone by the need to make such distinctions. But he refused to give up trying: "A faithful friend is the medicine of life," assured the Masonic manual—and this was Jackson's aphoristic way of seeing the world, too. "The neutral disposition, frigid and reserved, neither speaks good or evil"—again, Jackson would have agreed, asserting the positive value of passion—"but the man who feels the emotions of brotherly love is warm to commend." By inculcating social duties, by remaining on the lookout for merit, the brotherhood of Freemasons gave Jackson precisely what he needed: fraternity on a large scale, and, like elective office, confirmation that he was important—and popular—even when he did not lead men into battle.[46]

Though Thomas Hart Benton may be considered, in terms of political performance, to have repaid Jackson for his early patronage, the one protégé who truly fulfilled both Jackson's emotional need for gratitude and his political expectations was the knight errant Sam Houston. The iconoclastic, seminomadic president of the Republic of Texas mirrored Jackson in the way his aggressive actions annoyed staid members of the Washington community whom Jackson had long faulted for what he regarded as their political myopia. They were supposed to be representatives of the people, but he saw in them only narrow self-interest. The gadfly Houston gave them the lesson they needed. Jackson hated Clay for his brashness, but he adored Houston for his. In either case, what Congress thought of as polite manners, Jackson saw as pretense. He himself tried it on for size while courting presidential electors during his otherwise unproductive Senate term in 1823–25, but it did not last. Neither Jackson nor Houston would be tamed by parliamentary procedure.

Jackson most resembled, of all Shakespeare's creations, the Roman consul Coriolanus, who resisted any law but his own and fought his enemies with moral fury. As a tragic hero, Coriolanus was so rigid that he would sooner die than compromise a principle. Fatherless, he was reborn in war. Though he had a faithful wife, he was married to action. Single-minded, he isolated himself from his devoted friends, and so doomed his chances for personal peace. His life was ruled by military discipline; his temperament was ill-suited for any but dictatorial government. A proud, anguished absolutist, Coriolanus could not comprehend the art of republican politics. Ironically, the consul's downfall was his pronounced disdain for the common people, which was precisely Andrew Jackson's strength: he may have alienated those closest to him, but he always retained a glowing reputation among "the people" as their truest champion.

There was in Jackson's personality a paradoxical combination: imperiousness (unassailable opinions) and identification with the democratic (folk) temper. Whatever made him ambitious and at times ruthless also made him desirous of giving generously. A powerful sense of personal honor and obligation carried him to life-endangering exertions that invariably, and remarkably, proved life preserving. The will he must have had, to have endured not just the bullets he carried inside his body, but the succession of diseases, the marches and overland travel, while administering lands under cultivation, pursuing political advantage, contesting lawsuits, adopting children, and opening his home to a constant stream of visitors, suggests strongly that Andrew Jackson never expected solitude and probably never craved it either.

He was not given to reflection, but he maintained sturdy principles of conduct that, in his mind, never steered him wrong. He stated often in letters, in nearly the same language every time, "I have never abandoned a friend, without being forced to do so, from his own course toward me, and I never break with one, without giving him a fair opportunity to explain."[47] He was explicit. He was blunt. He was opinionated. In the same way that he carried on in politics—when power was put in his hands, there were no half measures—he understood friendship on terms that he dictated, and that generally demanded subordination. He never realized this about himself, or so it would seem from a half-century's worth of letters and the stories that others (mainly friends) told of him.

But is it not a contradiction in terms to seek friendship without acknowledging the value of compromise? Jackson, in this sense, deep down, did not really understand the "common good" in the Jeffersonian sense of the term. He merely reinvented the enemy "aristocracy" in order to kill the Bank. He was not a liberal democrat. He did not allow for the free exchange of ideas. He did not learn from reading, or aim to improve himself through the acquisition of new knowledge. He did not respect the rule of law unless he made it. He did not, for that matter, have a concept of social justice, because his justice was static, constantly reaffirming his own impulses and justifying his own life experience. It was, as Marvin Meyers described Jackson's crusade against the Bank of the United States, "a way to damn the unfamiliar."[48]

Jackson was incapable of seeing the problems with Indian removal or African-American enslavement, because he liked what had existed before him. He wished to preserve an idealized world of white yeoman gentrification, replicating his own path to respectability. However, his failure as a democrat must be shared with other elected leaders of his time. They, as well as he, were relics, stuck in an unreal world of chivalry and affairs of honor, personalizing freedom as property ownership. They, as well as he, adhered to a bloated form of the American language, full of exaggerated charges and exaggerated pride, such that Tocqueville, Chevalier, and Trollope identified in their published critiques of democracy.

The Jacksonian language, like the Jacksonian landscape, suited America's state of defiance. In spite of all the lofty oratory in Congress, the politics of Jackson's time was vicious and often violent. Jackson did not invent either viciousness or violence, though there was no one more addicted to its political manifestation. He saw it everywhere, and he practiced it, self-protectively, all the time. His patriotism was comprised of unstable ingredients, one part expanding Union and two parts escalating bluster.

Seen in the context of his political generation, Jackson was not necessarily any more fierce, profane, or irrational than his competition. Calhoun, though he shared Jackson's ethnic identity, ultimately felt greater sympathy for the mind of John Quincy Adams; mentally and morally, the stiff, Yale-educated, southern fire-eater understood the stiff, tactless northern abolitionist. Jackson and Calhoun ought to have found common ground, as both opposed a national consolidationist trend that threatened the former strength of the South. Instead, they ended up as deadly foes. Clay, a hardy westerner and longtime gambler like Jackson, conceived himself a voice of reason and moderation, temperate and unprovocative;

yet he failed to see Jackson's success as the essential democratic upsurge it was. Though politically brilliant, Clay was incapable of moving past resentment of Jackson's popularity, which he described as a chimera. Crawford, unpolished and intriguing, enjoyed a devoted partisan appeal, just like Jackson; but they could not see the similarities between themselves. All the campaigners Jackson contested were, like him, political alchemists; at any given moment, they were not entirely sure of the implications of what they had concocted.

Students of political history too often refashion the republic in rational terms, giving undue weight to grand prescriptions. This is a highly ideological perspective and a gross misreading of the past that transforms someone like Jackson into an administrator seeking to "restore" something as intangible as "virtue" in government. The political pronouncements of this unlettered man were no more rooted in rational prescriptions for government than his adherence to the culture of the duel was a rational means to preserve "honor."

Indeed, all the talk of honor did little to channel passions. The pattern of vilification and vindication we have seen belongs to an irrational world, a cultural system in which an individual sense of justice (personal justification) held more power over the mind than the jurisprudence of constituted state authority. On the frontier, practical assertiveness took one far; gentility or refinement was mere public gesture, designed for the greater ceremony of a metropolitan forum. Both types of behavior, however, were forms of stagecraft. Jackson drifted between—or was caught between— two different places where masculine theater was demanded. Whether roles were decreed or he invented them hardly matters. He, like many others of his cohort, though none, perhaps, with quite so much at stake psychologically, remained stuck in an illusory world of chivalry and affairs of honor.

Sometimes satire is the most succinct form of historical depiction. An anonymous Jackson hater succeeded in capturing his subject's humanity when he parodied Jackson's newfound religiosity in 1828. It was a year of gross charges and countercharges, when slave-owning Democrats accused the devout President Adams of political immorality. A pious exclamation from Jackson was meant to come out like this: "By the immaculate God! Clay and all his friends are G—d d——d liars, by G—d!"[49]

That same year, Robert Walsh composed a popular biography called *The Jackson Wreath,* in which he set down the reasoning that Jackson's defenders, since 1814, had come to employ in explaining the general's raw nature to the public. Walsh covered every contingency in his career: "The impetuosity of his nature, his impatience of wrong and encroachment, his contempt for meanness, and his tenaciousness of just authority, have involved him in bitter altercations and sanguinary quarrels:—his resentments have been fiercely executed, and his censures harshly uttered: yet he cannot be accused of wanton or malicious violence."[50] The verdict on Jackson rests on one's interpretation of "just authority," that is, the extent to which Jackson accurately perceived "wrong and encroachment," or whether "impatience" and "tenaciousness" represented a refusal to respect an honest difference in opinion.

If Jackson appears now to have been less admirable than the historical imagination has contrived, and rather stormy and indiscreet and limited, we should not be at all surprised. Romanticized frontier figures of the eighteenth and nineteenth centuries, alike in their lack of education, enlarged in value as national icons when western legend came to symbolize the American spirit. To Jackson, we can add such storybook heroes as Daniel Boone and Davy Crockett. Given their humble roots and lack of social prospects, it is perfectly understandable that they should act, and have little to say that was not cliché. In his characterization of the first frontier-bred presidential candidate in 1824, the campaigning Sam Houston allowed that Jackson was all the more remarkable because he "literally fought himself into notice!" The federal government gave him no appointment "until he had gained at least five decisive victories over the Indians, and compelled them to sue for peace." No one could have predicted his success. No one should have been surprised by his roughness.[51]

In an 1823 letter one Tennessee judge, John Overton, wrote to another, Hugh Lawson White, presciently alluding to White's questions about Jackson's inflexible ways. "[I]n the moral, as in the natural world the God of nature designed great vicessitudes [sic] should occur," the philosophical Overton supposed. "I am almost constrained to believe that agitations and broil are as necessary to purify society, as high winds, thunder and storms, so purify the air." It was meant as a subtle defense of Jackson's passions, to say that Jacksons were as necessary to progress as enlightened thinkers. "In the moral world," Overton went on, "the violence of passion in civil society is checked and allayed by those sober, thinking and influential men in society—who can command themselves—keep down their own passions to the standard of reason and prudence. It was this virtue, *prudence,* that distinguished Washington." Overton, at least, would not have invested Jackson with Washingtonian excellence (in the way Washington was generally idealized). Knowing White to be a man of scruples, and Jackson to be a hotheaded warrior, Overton begged for the judge's understanding: "you know how difficult, nay impracticable, it would be for him [Jackson] or any other man to chasten the passions . . . even among his best friends. His friendship for you, I know, and I should be sorry that any thing should occur to produce any alienation on either side."[52]

Jackson may be considered a significant president if significance means changing the office. He headed a coalition of discontents, took on the Washington establishment, grabbed power, and crippled patrician politics. In the executive branch, he employed the muscle of scrappy journalists, after which other such men who had begun their careers as humble trades-men appealed successfully to an expanding electorate and ended up in the once noble Senate.[53] Jackson's idea was a simple (naïve?) one: remake Washington by remaking political man. As his aide James A. Hamilton wrote of Jackson in 1828, "His intercourse has been much greater with men than books. He therefore well knows how to adapt his deportment to the character and condition of the different classes with whom he meets. He possesses an independent spirit, and great confidence in his own powers."[54] Jackson indeed reinterpreted the presidency. At the same time, though, the anarchic condition of his cabinet suggests an inability to administer government other than to move from crisis to crisis—crises he either cre-ated or exacerbated. He used them as litmus tests, to demand loyalty. His vanity was corrosive. It is hard to avoid seeing Jackson as insatiable, always interfering in the lives of others.

To his enemies, he appeared as a trickster or cult leader who worked his magic on the lost and vulnerable. In this view, the election of the imagined democratic "Hero" might have given many ordinary people the sense that they partook in his power; but it was a false sense of power, because Jack-son was a tyrant and Jacksonian democracy a misnomer. The Whig Party came into existence as an alternative, offering Jackson-style populist rhet-oric combined with prudence in governmental affairs. The Whigs said that Jackson had perverted the republic when he seized onto a kind of mock-regal pretense—that which the original American Whigs had col-lectively fought in the 1770s.

Typical of the censure Jackson received from opposing politicians, Con-gressman John Davis discharged his vitriol in an 1834 letter to his former colleague George Briggs. Davis had recently resigned his seat in the House of Representatives to become governor of Massachusetts, and felt compelled to express his frustration both with Jackson's executive style and with the fawning, submissive men whom the president required around him: "I notice the more arbitrary the measures become the less the laws, the constitution and the principles of civil liberty are regarded, the louder the Kitchen Cabinet sings its hosannahs to their chief." Among the chorus, Davis was most disgusted with the fanatical Isaac Hill, senator from New Hampshire and longtime editor of the *New Hampshire Patriot*. Hill had done much to secure Jackson's reputation in New England, and went so far as to declare his man the greatest of all the presidents. "Hill advances him before [i.e., ahead of] the combined character of Washington & Jefferson and I dare say if he would utter all he wishes he would place him over the great ruler of the universe. As the progress of tyranny advances their courage seems to increase & their hopes to brighten. In truth it seems to me they shout with joy at the prospect of conquering the constitution." It appeared, at least to this one public servant, that Jackson considered himself God.[55]

If this were so, he would have been a wrathful God. For there was contained in Jackson an extraordinary rage, a taste for revenge, that burst easily when he felt possessed of the might he needed to see his will fulfilled. In such situations, the perception that he had dedicated friends and supporters was crucial, and he projected onto these people his greatest expectations: either they would follow his orders and become heroes (subordinate only to him), or they would fail to carry out their orders, and let him down in a most profound way. Once Jackson had resolved on an action, his expectations from handpicked subordinates ran perilously high. Generalship defined him. He was unalterable in purpose. He invested his all in the loyalty of his troops and thrashed about when defections occurred, just as he had roared at the mutineers who defied him during the War of 1812.

His union with Rachel Donelson Robards, amid unclear legal and legislative conditions, attests to his resort to self-sustaining moral solutions. His adherence to the code of masculine honor, involving himself repeatedly in extralegal duels, supplies further evidence that he believed that there were higher obligations than the law narrowly defined. His interpretation of the authority granted to him in fighting the Creeks and later the Seminoles in nominally Spanish territory taught him that the ends justified the means. As president, Jackson saw total solutions to the questions of Indian removal and banking power, and his disciple Sam Houston carried out his will by conquering Texas for America. Also, as president, Jackson did not easily accept power that was mediated through law, or where he was not the ultimate judge. It often appeared that the only way he understood the exercise of power was to adopt scare tactics. This made him notorious. In the minds of those who did not see democracy at risk, it made him decisive . . . and great.

He was the spirit behind what some would call western adventure and others would call colonial conquest. At the beginning of this book, the genial comic, political wit, and Cherokee-American Will Rogers was quoted, stepping out of his normally soft-spoken character, swearing up a storm in recalling the devastating impact that Andrew Jackson's Indian removal policy had on his country. For many decades now, most Americans have ceased feeling any sort of emotion with respect to the seventh president. Before that, he was known for the role he played in the evolution of concepts of white democracy and white expansion. As John William Ward wrote in the 1950s, "It was Jackson himself who pointed out to contemporaries how they could justify their acquisitiveness by subsuming it under the divine plan of providence."[56] The true Jacksonian faith was not bred in a surrender to God but in an intuitive confidence that the quintessentially American act, favored by God, was to chart new territory, to tame nature, to make precedents.

The declarative poet Walt Whitman once referred to America as the "athletic democracy." That was Jackson's idealization of the masses as well. They cut down trees and felled forests, carved out roads in order to secure their settlements to previously developed places, and fought (when necessary) with bravery and skill. They shot straight, both literally and figuratively, and they loved and protected their women. It sounds old-fashioned. But so was the self-made president from the frontier of middle Tennessee who thought in terms of the "heroic virtues," and who was entirely convinced that it was his destiny to save the purity and vigor of the American republic.

A Savior Who Blusters

Perhaps now, understanding his extraordinary appeal in the nineteenth century as a man who epitomized a nation's energy and drive, what Jackson represents in the historic memory can begin to mean more. Americans vote with their hearts, not their heads—that is what explains Jackson's political success. Otherwise, it would be nearly impossible to explain a savior who blusters.[57]

Surely his career tells us something about the nature of the electorate, and, more forebodingly, perhaps, what it means to the nation's integrity when a man of platitudes, a mediocre intellect with a glamorous surface appeal, is hailed strictly for his imagined sense of fairness and compassion. On the other hand, supporters were convinced he would use power wisely because he was attuned to the voice of the people. From the much-embellished Battle of New Orleans on, he became a symbol of national confidence, of peace through strength. His legacy, in that case, might be seen in modern strategists who put little trust in diplomacy, who adopt a pragmatic yet unabashedly aggressive posture toward foreign threats; or it may be embodied in the assumption that it is America's destiny to police the less powerful, less abundantly endowed nations of the world. He is, then, as European visitors to Jacksonian America invariably remarked, symbolic of American self-assurance and complacency.

There are others in America who identify with the world's oppressed and seek remedies for the sins of violence and covetousness. To them, Andrew Jackson must seem, even more conspicuously, to personify American hubris. He is a typology, a personality like World War II general Douglas MacArthur, another zealot who wanted to be president. Both generals believed that there was no value in limited war or limited political causes. While admired for wartime victories, both were castigated for having shown insufficient restraint. Jackson the "MacArthurite" was a soldier ill-suited for civil leadership when peace and prosperity were sought, a dangerously self-absorbed leader whose political nature was to divide.[58]

But can it be said that Andrew Jackson was necessary to his time? Was not his bold resolve what a majority of Americans demanded in order to fulfill the founders' dream of a manifest continental destiny? This is arguably the case. While the phrase "manifest destiny" itself was not coined until 1845, the year of Jackson's death, the generation of Washington and Jefferson had first established the notion that the moral consciousness of a liberty-loving people ought to sweep across space as well as time. The Revolutionary generation had neither the armed force nor the will to actualize the vision of its nationalistic poets and land-hungry syndicates. Jackson gave them what they wanted but did not dare to attempt.[59]

He strove to hold the expanding nation together. In his farewell address upon leaving office in March 1837, Jackson issued a plea: "At every hazard, and by every sacrifice, this Union must be preserved." He feared an end to national community through "division and dissension"—sectionalism. If the Union did not survive, he said, it would become "humbled and debased in spirit," and the way opened for America to be reunited under "the absolute dominion of any military adventurer."[60] These were the words of speechwriter Roger B. Taney of Maryland, a loyal ally in the Bank War, the man Jackson had appointed chief justice of the Supreme Court at the beginning of 1836. Though he did not write the address, it was Jackson at his most statesmanlike. One can only wonder whether the inclusion of the phrase "military adventurer" was Taney's or Jackson's idea.[61]

While in retirement Jackson firmly believed that his presidency and his life had been singularly devoted to the preservation of what he termed "our happy union," his ignorance of the powerful dynamics of the slavery issue contributed to, rather than counteracted, the forces of disunion. He simply did not feel that the morals of slavery were deserving of his careful consideration; it was just another issue manufactured by his enemies. The way he saw it, on his own plantation impertinent slaves might be justly whipped, and yet he saw no reason not to be kind toward this inferior species of humanity while they contributed to the farm's profit. He reserved an imperious disdain for the abolitionists who were increasingly identified, in his mind, with the presumed mental aberration of outspoken elder statesman John Quincy Adams.[62]

To Adams, Jackson increasingly represented some sinister quality in the American character. When, in his first term, Jackson finally learned of how strongly and consistently Adams supported him during the Florida controversy of 1818–19—while Calhoun was trying to ruin him—the sitting president sought a reconciliation with the man he had beaten. It was Adams who refused the invitation to dinner and a restoration of personal relations. Once when Jackson tried to shake his hand at the funeral of a mutual friend, Adams looked at him coldly. Adams's antagonism grew as Jackson's administration became, to his mind, more and more disorderly. Jackson was, he wrote in his memoirs, "a barbarian who could not write a sentence of grammar," a man whose character was "rancorous and vindictive." The slavery issue merely intensified a firm hatred of Jacksonianism. After Jackson died, Adams remembered him as a "hero," a "murderer," and, curiously, an "adulterer."[63]

When in 1835 a Charleston, South Carolina, mob burned unwanted abolitionist literature, Jackson backed the states'-rights southerners, whom he had opposed on nullification, by decrying this mischievous use of the national postal service. New England–born Amos Kendall, postmaster general at the end of Jackson's second term, insisted that the Post Office was meant "to serve the people" of the states, not to be manipulated by one section as the "instrument" of the other states' "destruction." Later, Kendall would go even further, taunting the abolitionists that he would subscribe to their project when they proved their commitment to amalgamation of the races by arranging interracial marriages for their own daughters. If Jackson preferred to disregard the explosive potential of the slavery issue, his aggressive aide embraced the controversy.[64]

Jackson arose because America was bursting at the seams. Though young as a nation, it had matured conspiratorial fears at every step of its partisan evolution. Jefferson had smelled conspiracy among British-leaning Federalists, and indeed a segment of New England aired secessionist views during the War of 1812. Westerners never stopped anticipating a Spanish conspiracy against their settlements. That is why Burr was eagerly supported in Nashville and elsewhere, when he showed up claiming that, in John Overton's words, he was "patronised by the Government" in planting a new, armed settlement in the area of New Orleans.[65] Nationalists wanted the frontier strengthened in expectation of an eventual war with Spain. Jackson emerged as the answer to every imagined threat: Spanish, British, and Indian.

Enemies were a necessary stimulus. To preserve a way of life, that it might grow and prosper, required total commitment and complete hegemony. The limits of his understanding did not limit his popular appeal. He was America's defender, and as a defender, he received wide publicity, from 1814 on, in the national press. His later political genius grew from the conviction, put forth by Jackson and planted in the electorate by his faithful aides, that one who could smash foreign enemies could smash domestic political conspiracies to subvert the popular will.

What Jackson most shared with George Washington was extrinsic to character and extrinsic to political thought. It was the majority's indefinite but powerful perception that because he had triumphed, they had triumphed. Symbolic qualities tend to mean more than native intelligence or even practical policies. Jackson's well-crafted persona was so credited that people believed it to be his essential character. Heroes remove uncertainty.

For that reason, too, the homes of presidents continue to attract visitors. In Jackson's time, Washington's Mount Vernon grave site was a shrine for pilgrims. After having just consecrated a new Methodist church in 1830, a cohort of more than five hundred Masonic brethren appeared there, standing in a "Cordon around the Grave," scattering sprigs of evergreen symbolic of the Resurrection, as a sign of their pure faith. Jackson himself attested that Washington's memory was no better maintained than by the honors which "Religion and Masonry" accorded it.[66] Similarly, future president John Tyler, in his eulogy of Jefferson in 1826, observed: "Like Mount Vernon, Monticello shall catch the eye of the way-farer and arrest his course.—There shall he draw the inspirations of liberty."[67]

It should be no surprise that Andrew Jackson's Hermitage was also consecrated by nineteenth-century patriots. In his eulogistic tribute read on July 4, 1845, in Wilkes-Barre, Pennsylvania, Hendrick B. Wright linked Jackson with his two renowned predecessors, projecting that his tomb would become a "modern Mecca," where westward-moving pioneers would pause to "drop a tear," and give thanks to an illustrious hero. "Virginia has her Mount Vernon, and her Monticello," Wright closed his speech. "New England is the repository of the remains of the compeers of Washington and Jefferson; Tennessee has her Hermitage!"[68]

Andrew Jackson's passion and Andrew Jackson's fame are one, the sum of a lifetime of vigilance and abandon. If these two seemingly contradictory qualities are able to coexist, they did so within the anguished frame of this driven man. Totally unrepentant, refusing to be turned away from any object in which he had invested his heart, the American conqueror coveted nothing more and nothing less than dominion over the national household. He wanted to be the unerring father who rewarded loyalty and love and punished all moral transgressions. To be so anointed, he was willing to take on the world.

❧❧❧❧❧❧❧❧❧·❧❧❧❧❧❧❧❧❧

The Union of Andrew
and Rachel Jackson

The circumstances surrounding the Jacksons' union have never been properly set forth. Most chroniclers have strenuously attempted to "clear" the Jacksons of the charge of bigamy, of having acted immorally or precipitously. While Andrew Jackson did indeed acknowledge marrying Rachel Donelson Robards before her divorce had been granted by legislative decree, the Jacksons and all who have cared to protect them insist that at worst they made an honest mistake in construing a *preliminary* legislative action as a *final* divorce ruling.

John Overton's retrospective explanation for these events was publicized in 1828. He gives the end of 1790 or early 1791 as the date when Andrew Jackson volunteered to accompany Rachel 400 miles southwest to the commercial hub of Natchez, where she sought to escape her abusive husband, Lewis Robards of Kentucky. Professing only chivalric intent after she indicated that no other friend or relative would escort her through Indian country, Jackson is supposed to have bid farewell to her in Natchez and journeyed home alone, without romantic prospects. He is further supposed to have learned while at court in Nashville, in May 1791—there "attending to his business"—what Overton learned at the same time: that Robards had won legislative authorization (in Kentucky's parent state, Virginia) to divorce his wife. Within a month or two, Jackson went back to Natchez. That autumn, he and Rachel married in Natchez, returning, once and for all, to Tennessee. For the next two years, all assumed that a divorce had taken place.[1]

John Overton's chronology

Dec. 1790/Jan. 1791   AJ and RJ travel with Stark party to Natchez
May 1791   AJ is in Nashville, hears that divorce was approved

Summer 1791	AJ travels to Natchez
Autumn 1791	AJ and RJ are wed in Natchez, return together to Nashville

This is an odd-sounding explanation for many reasons. First, Rachel had a large family and numerous protectors in Nashville. It is hard to conceive that she would have unilaterally chosen the Natchez area as a safe haven, or that her family would have recommended it without volunteering escorts. Overton states that it was Col. Robert Stark, the leader of a migrating party, who "with urgent entreaties" pressed Jackson to come along. But Stark did not plant the idea in Rachel's mind. So, either Rachel determined, independently of Jackson, to flee south, or Jackson was involved from the start. His known willfulness, and familiarity with both the Natchez Trace and the American community in Natchez (see below), makes for strong circumstantial evidence that Jackson influenced Rachel's decision. It seems a case of Overton protesting too much, in insisting that it was Stark who arm-twisted Jackson into accompanying the party south.

An enterprising graduate student of biographer Robert Remini pored through Spanish archives in the 1970s and found that Jackson was in the Spanish-controlled Mississippi River port of Natchez in the summer of 1789, a half-year after his arrival in Nashville. Other records indicate that he was there in March and again in July of 1790, returning to Tennessee with wine, rum, sugar, salt, knives, and iron pots to sell to his neighbors. For the rest of that year, he was actively practicing law in Tennessee, leaving for Natchez once more around February 1791.[2]

The trail to Natchez was long and hazardous. The frequency of his visits to Natchez after January 1790 no doubt had something to do with Jackson's interest in Rachel, and not simply a quest for new merchandise. Curiously, though, he was in Tennessee in April 1791, and appears not to have been in Natchez at all between April and October of that year, when Overton has him traveling there to marry Rachel. An October 1791 letter to Jackson from the merchant George Cochran of Natchez, terming Jackson "my best friend" and "saluting Mrs. Jackson," thanks Jackson for writing to him in April 1791. Cochran bemoans not having seen nor heard from his best friend since "your departure from this Country."[3]

Cochran's letter unmistakably puts Andrew and Rachel Jackson together, married, in the Cumberland settlement in the spring of 1791. Thus Overton's chronology is definitely flawed. Perhaps the most interesting piece of evidence, however, is an inventory relating to the estate of the late John Donelson, prepared even earlier, in January 1791. This document also refers to Rachel as "Mrs. Jackson." But it was in January 1791 that Overton says Jackson had *just left* Tennessee to accompany Rachel to Natchez to escape her husband. Furthermore, Overton was himself one of the signatories of the estate inventory.[4]

The web woven by the protective Overton becomes even more tangled. He states that Jackson, after depositing Rachel, had "descended the river, returned from Natchez to Nashville," arriving back at court by May 1791. Around then, he is meant to have heard that Robards had won legislative authorization to divorce his wife,[5] upon which he resolved to go back to Natchez, marrying Rachel there in the fall. Their union, we should note, is undocumented, and Jackson, a lawyer, never produced (nor is there mention of his having preserved) a marriage certificate. He did not name a witness to the ceremony, nor give the name of the officiator.

If Overton's calculations make no sense, Jackson did not set him straight. No doubt 1790–91 was hard to recall accurately after thirty-odd years. In Overton's flawed reconstruction, it was two or more years after their Natchez journey when the Jacksons finally received word that Robards had not really been granted a divorce but had merely received *permission to sue* for divorce. That divorce was made official in September 1793, on grounds of desertion and adultery.

Robards had sought and obtained permission to sue on December 20, 1790. The document reads: "A jury shall be summoned who shall be sworn well and truly to enquire into the allegations . . . that she hath lived in adultery with another man since such desertion. . . ."[6] *Lived in adultery.* Regardless of what Jackson is meant to have construed, Robards had to have learned of his wife's cohabitation with Jackson *prior to* December 20, 1790. Jackson was a keen enough student of the law of the frontier to know how unlikely it would have been for Robards's first petition to result in a legislative decree of divorce without a lengthy investigation of the charges. Kentucky was still part of Virginia, and approval would have to have come from Richmond. What other conclusion can be drawn, but that Andrew Jackson knew full well what he was doing when he took Rachel in his arms?[7]

In truth, Jackson accompanied Rachel and the Stark party to Natchez at the end of 1789 or the very beginning of 1790. Spanish records evidence Stark's presence in Natchez at that time. If Jackson returned to Nashville after two months (as records also indicate), and he returned alone, then he could not have married Rachel in Natchez until the following year, because he did not learn of Robards's divorce action until at least January

1791. Jackson appeared in court in Tennessee frequently between April and July 1791. The Cochran exchange implies that he was not in Natchez that summer and fall, indicating that Rachel and he were together in Tennessee by then.

Even if Overton was merely a year off in his chronology, as some have rationalized, it is still the case that nothing fits. Jackson allowed Overton to put the undocumented Natchez marriage ceremony in the wrong season, an anniversary he should not have forgotten. In autumn 1790, Robards had yet to sue for divorce; in autumn 1791, Rachel had already been known as Mrs. Jackson for at least nine months. If they had married in Natchez, when could the ceremony have taken place?

Most likely chronology of events

Dec. 1789/Jan. 1790	AJ and RJ travel with Stark party to Natchez
Apr. 1790	AJ returns to Tennessee; RJ remains in Natchez
July 1790	AJ travels to Natchez, stays through early autumn
Oct. 1790–Jan. 1791	AJ, as attorney, appears frequently in Tennessee courts
Dec. 1790	*Robards sues for divorce in Kentucky on grounds of AJ and RJ cohabiting*
Jan. 1791	AJ possibly learns of Robards's divorce action
Jan. 1791	*RJ listed in estate papers as "Rachel Jackson"*
ca. Feb. 1791	AJ travels to Natchez
ca. Mar. 1791	AJ and RJ return together to Nashville
Apr. 1791	Estate papers of Jan. 1791, listing "Rachel Jackson," are actually filed
Apr. 1791	AJ writes Cochran (of Natchez) from Nashville
Oct. 1791	Cochran, writing AJ, conveys regards to "Mrs. Jackson"

Parton makes vague reference to a log house in Bayou Pierre, on the Mississippi River above Natchez, where "the couple lived awhile after their marriage."[8] The part of George Cochran's letter directed to Rachel mentions wistfully "your friendly retreat at Bayou Pierre," where Cochran, a bachelor, had enjoyed "agreeable hours" in her company. By including the reference to "agreeable hours" in a letter to her husband, to whom he writes admiringly, it seems most likely that Jackson was living at Bayou Pierre at the time the merchant enjoyed Rachel's company. (Such an interpretation is consistent with epistolary protocol in this period.) If Andrew

Jackson was not in the Natchez area after March 1791, Cochran is referring to the couple's presence at their "retreat" in 1790 and/or early in 1791.

The telling reference to "Rachel *Jackson*" in the January 1791 estate inventory indicates that Cochran had to be aware of the Jacksons' unorthodox marriage no later than April 1791, when Jackson wrote him (a letter that has never been found). It makes sense that Cochran, who claimed that he thought of Rachel as a "sister," understood the nature of the relationship prior to that time, when Andrew Jackson and Rachel Donelson Robards were, knowingly, adulterers. The only remaining puzzle is how she could have been known as Mrs. Jackson in January 1791, when, seemingly, she had been living at Bayou Pierre for one year, and her new husband was at that moment in Nashville without her. The apparent answer is that a tradition existed for circumventing, or acting in place of, the busy legislature. The Donelson family was a part of this deception as much as Andrew Jackson was.

Along these lines, there is one rather engaging possibility: that Andrew and Rachel Jackson willfully let it be known that they were living as husband and wife at Bayou Pierre. They *wanted* Lewis Robards to sue for divorce on the grounds of adultery and desertion—cohabitation— because divorce was extremely rare; it was *only* obtainable through the state legislature, and *only* granted if the specific kind of evidence was submitted which the legislature accepted.[9]

Adultery was, in this sense, the result of careful planning. Jackson, as state prosecutor, knew the relevant laws. He knew that he and Rachel could not live as husband and wife in the Cumberland until after a decent interval; he understood that it would be a long while before Richmond acted. Natchez, or Bayou Pierre, was far enough away (and politically detached) to allow them the freedom to begin a life together, while Lewis Robards was convinced (or cajoled?) to take the self-respecting action of his divorce appeal. All the parties involved must have understood what was happening.[10]

The couple cohabited in Natchez with the Donelson family's blessing. The citizens of the Cumberland did not have to know too many of the details, and all was well. If Andrew and Rachel Jackson were wed in Natchez, it would have to have been in the spring of 1791. More likely, there was no Natchez wedding—an invention to placate interested voters in 1828. In any event, after the Robardses' divorce was certified by the Virginia legislature, Mr. and Mrs. Jackson were finally united by Robert Hays on January 17, 1794. They were then able to live as husband and wife in Tennessee without fear of recrimination. It was only the altered conditions of the mid-1820s—the nasty tone of presidential campaign polemics—that obliged John Overton to fix dates, eliciting an explanation that we can now see was as weak as it was unnecessarily complicated.

The interpretation presented here, once scandalous, is bearable now. It reflects a modern sensibility. By knowing the truth, few twenty-first-century Americans would any longer construe Andrew and Rachel Jackson as moral transgressors. But some of the same evidence (at least circumstantial) existed in 1828, when it was employed for the purpose of denying Jackson the presidency on moral grounds. In that year, the Cincinnati editor Charles Hammond widely disseminated an accusatory pamphlet in which he plausibly responded to John Overton's recollection in 1828 of having " 'anticipated' that Robards would apply for a divorce!!" Hammond's double exclamation is followed by the inference to be drawn from the highlighted word: "The Judge [Overton] knew that Robards had just grounds to apply for a divorce; hence he 'anticipated' both the application and success." Hammond also mocks Jackson's retrospective claim of innocence in deciding to accompany Rachel to Natchez; he meanly attributes the couple's actions to "the gratification of their own appetites."[11]

What about the legal environment in Kentucky and Tennessee when Hammond was contriving his attack? How much clearer were matters of morality and divorce law in 1827–28 than they were in 1790–91, when the Robards divorce case was adjudicated? For insight, let us turn to a Tennessee dower case on which Jackson's stalwart supporter Judge John Catron ruled in 1826.

One Mary Dickson was divorced in Kentucky in 1818, having by law "abandoned" her first husband—abandonment then defined as three years of living apart. In Kentucky, a divorced woman who abandoned her husband was proscribed from remarrying until after the death of the ex-husband. But Mary moved to Tennessee, where she was legally able to marry again, and she did so in 1821. The second husband died in 1822, and his children by his first marriage objected to Mary's claim on any portion of her second husband's property on the grounds that her first husband, in Kentucky, still lived. If Kentucky's marriage and divorce law applied, Mary's second marriage constituted bigamy.

In his opinion, Judge Catron observed that communities should not permit divorces to come about "upon every slight pretext . . . , to gratify the lust or interest of particular individuals." Also, he went on, society should see to it that a person could not simply flee across a state border in order to escape the first state's proscription against easy remarriage—for the second state "will run the hazard of becoming the receptacle of the refuse, pro-scribed, and prostituted vagabonds, outcasts from a population" within "sister states." Given these qualifications, the circumstances surrounding the Jacksons' union might still have appeared morally questionable.

In the end, however, Judge Catron dismissed all moral arguments, con-cluding that the Kentucky law was ill-conceived insofar as marriage only exists when a husband and wife are willing to share a life together: "It is impossible, in the nature of things, that all the relations of wife shall exist when she has no husband." He ruled that Mary Dickson was "lawfully mar-ried to John Dickson, and is entitled to dower." In this light, while Catron feared opening the possibility of unregulated divorce, he was fundamentally supporting the principles that lay behind the Jacksons' earlier actions. His 1826 decision leaves the impression that Rachel's marriage to Lewis Robards was no marriage at all, and that had the event taken place in 1826 and not 1790, she would not have been restricted from remarrying to Andrew Jackson and pursuing her just happiness as a free individual. But such subtle reason-ing, of course, would not have persuaded the polemical editor Hammond.[12]

On the subject of the Jacksons' union, Professor Remini has adopted an agnostic position, saying that no single scenario "can be proved absolutely," though his explanation suggesting cohabitation from the middle of 1790 is certainly the most credible that he offers in the first volume of his trilogy.[13] More important, the "official" White House explanation, according to its Web site, is the whitewashed version: "Andrew Jackson married [Rachel] in 1791; and after two happy years they learned to their dismay that Robards had not obtained a divorce, only permission to file for one. Now he brought suit on grounds of adultery. After the divorce was granted, the Jacksons quietly remarried in 1794. They had made an honest mistake."[14]

Among the various positions taken over the history of this scandal, no one has produced evidence to suggest that Lewis Robards was harmed. It is inter-esting to note that self-divorce announcements in early American newspa-pers were generally placed by husbands, informing the community that their wives had become "runaways" and had abandoned their duties as spouses. Many Americans used this customary practice in lieu of a legal divorce, and so Andrew and Rachel Jackson's decision to escape to Natchez merely fol-lowed the informal rules of separation acceptable at the time. The parties involved all understood that desertion was the first step to divorce; many Americans never even bothered to get an official one. Robards probably agreed to sue for divorce, in return for some financial settlement, because the Jacksons were planning to make their marriage legal, as they did in 1794.

The Jacksons did not make an "honest mistake." Rather, they did exactly what was needed to move from separation to divorce. Rachel's family, Jackson's friends, and the larger Nashville community no doubt accepted the informal practice as Andrew Jackson went about it. The couple's behavior only became an issue in 1828 because marriage practices (moral meanings) had changed. Marriage as a symbol of moral standing was enhanced, as evidenced by Hammond's harangue.

Thus, in 1790–91 the Jacksons did not feel they were doing anything wrong, even though, *in strictly legal terms*, Rachel did commit adultery and abandon her first husband. Her new husband was actively complicit in her actions. What the episode tells us has less to do with the couple's morals than with their class aspirations. Informal separations were more common among the lower class, whereas a formal divorce (especially one granted by a state legislature) was the resort of the middle and upper classes. In 1828, Jackson could no longer acknowledge the lower-class component of his frontier marriage. Middle-class norms now informed politics, and even Old Hickory, the self-made man of the West, felt obliged to conceal what, thirty-eight years later, appeared to be an immoral, irregular, and bigamous union.

NOTES

❯❯❯❯❯❯❯❯❯❯·❮❮❮❮❮❮❮❮❮❮

List of Abbreviations

Bassett   John Spencer Bassett, ed. *Correspondence of Andrew Jackson*, 6 vols. (Wash-
             ington, D.C., 1926–34)
Curtis   James C. Curtis. *Andrew Jackson and the Search for Vindication* (Boston, 1976)
Dusenbery   B. M. Dusenbery. *Monument to the Memory of General Andrew Jackson:
             Containing Twenty-Five Eulogies and Sermons Delivered on Occasion of His
             Death* (Philadelphia, 1846)
Eaton   John Henry Eaton, *The Life of Andrew Jackson* (Cincinnati, 1827)
James   Marquis James, *The Life of Andrew Jackson* (Indianapolis & New York, 1938)
LC   Library of Congress
PAJ   *The Papers of Andrew Jackson*, ed. Sam B. Smith et al., 5 vols. to date
             (Knoxville, Tenn., 1980–)
PUL   Princeton University Library
Parton   James Parton, *Life of Andrew Jackson*, 3 vols. (New York, 1861)
Remini   Robert V. Remini, *Andrew Jackson*, 3 vols. (Baltimore, 1998 [New York,
             1977–84])
THQ   *Tennessee Historical Quarterly*
TSLA   Tennessee State Library and Archives
Ward   John William Ward, *Andrew Jackson: Symbol for an Age* (Oxford & New
             York, 1955)

Introduction

1. Alexander Walker, *Jackson and New Orleans. An Authentic Narrative of the Memorable Achievements of the American Army, under Andrew Jackson, before New Orleans, in the Winter of 1814, '15* (New York, 1856), 321–48. This is the best account of the battle, based on interviews with the participants on both sides.

2. Adam Smith, *The Theory of Moral Sentiments* (New York, 2000), part 3, chap. 4, 222. Smith was speaking of the human tendency to retain a short memory and repeatedly reveal the limits of empathy. Emotions, in his words, "discolour our views of things" and, we might add, in a historical sense just as easily cause us to apply current rules of judgment to past historical actors.

3. Ben Yagoda, *Will Rogers: A Biography* (New York, 1993), 281. An Oklahoma high school teacher reports recently on a speaker from the Cherokee capital of Tahlequah who still refuses to carry a twenty-dollar bill on his person.

4. Dusenbery, 50, 99.

5. On the development of a sense of national moral superiority from 1750 to 1828, see Andrew Burstein, *Sentimental Democracy: The Evolution of America's Romantic Self-Image* (New York, 1999). In the view of John William Ward, Jackson produced a certain change in

temperament: "In 1825, Americans were to save the world by example; in 1845, Americans were to save the world by absorbing it" (Ward, 136). Americans' self-satisfaction is a frequent characterization of Jacksonians in Europeans' travelogues, such as Alexis de Tocqueville, *Democracy in America* (New York, 1945 [1835, 1840]); Michael [Michel] Chevalier, *Society, Manners, and Politics in the United States* (New York, 1961 [1836]); and Frances Milton Trollope, *Domestic Manners of the Americans* (New York, 1927 [1832]).

6. Parton, 1:vii.

7. See Scott E. Casper's treatment of Parton's career, in *Constructing American Lives: Biography and Culture in Nineteenth-Century America* (Chapel Hill, N.C., 1999). Parton's *The Life of Aaron Burr* was first published in 1857.

8. Schlesinger's own recent memoir offers an honest assessment of the controversy that still surrounds his *Age of Jackson*. See *A Life in the Twentieth Century* (New York, 2000), esp. chap. 18.

9. James C. Curtis, *Andrew Jackson and the Search for Vindication* (Boston, 1976), ix.

10. Remini has recently refashioned books on Jackson from his three-volume biography. *The Battle of New Orleans* (New York, 1999) and *Andrew Jackson and His Indian Wars* (New York, 2001) are both virtually identical to his previous books in tone and rendering; in the *New York Times Book Review* (July 15, 2001), historian Andrew R. L. Cayton observed that in the latter work, "biographer and subject almost completely converge." Schlesinger's remarks on Remini were made for the 1984 National Book Award jury.

11. Remini, 1:13, 198–99.

12. Donald B. Cole, "Honoring Andrew Jackson Before All Other Living Men," *Reviews in American History* 13 (Sept. 1985): 359–66; see also Douglas R. Egerton, "An Update on Jacksonian Historiography: The Biographies," THQ 46 (1987): 79–85; also its predecessor, Charles Grier Sellers, Jr., "Andrew Jackson versus the Historians," *Mississippi Valley Historical Review* 44 (Mar. 1958): 615–34.

13. The historiographical debate over Jackson's Indian policies can be seen on a spectrum of passions by comparing the indictment by Michael Paul Rogin, *Fathers and Children: Andrew Jackson and the Subjugation of the American Indian* (New York, 1975), against the defense provided by F. P. Prucha, who seeks to prove that "Jackson was genuinely concerned for the well-being of the Indians and their civilization," in "Andrew Jackson's Indian Policy: A Reassessment," *Journal of American History* 56 (Dec. 1969): 527–39, quote at 533.

14. The great question facing writers of history is: How do we avoid propagating myths about historical actors? Hannah Arendt has written unreservedly about the anthropocentric consciousness as it pushes outward. She outlines a human capacity that by its very nature is communicative: it "transcends and releases into the world a passionate intensity from its imprisonment within the self." We can apply this both to author and subject.

If Jackson represents, in Arendt's phraseology, a living spirit driven to survive and achieve, the next question must be: Who is most competent in interpreting his life? With passion ever intervening, is it possible now to evaluate his self-revelatory actions with greater truthfulness than Jackson's biased contemporaries exhibited? Historians like to think so, and Arendt seems to agree: "Action reveals itself fully only to the storyteller, that is, to the backward glance of the historian." See Hannah Arendt, *The Human Condition* (Chicago, 1958), quotes at 168, 192.

If it is not the actor so much as the storyteller who makes the story, then nothing is more important than humility and self-monitoring in the storyteller, insofar as we are all imprisoned by the time and culture from which we derive our "truths." Many successful biographers of our time, in pretending (or unconsciously seeking) intimacy with their subject, distort history with varying degrees of subtlety. I critique contemporary authors' refashioning of past "greatness," in a piece titled "The Politics of Memory," in the *Book World* section of the *Washington Post*, Oct. 14, 2001. Historian Michael Kammen has compellingly examined the illusion of retrieving or reliving the American past in *A Season of Youth: The American Revolution and the Historical Imagination* (Ithaca, N.Y., 1978) and *Mystic Chords of Memory: The Transformation of Tradition in American Culture* (New York, 1991).

15. These five key friendships relate to the process by which Jackson capitalized on his public actions during and after the War of 1812 and became a national figure and presidential candidate. When he is a much older man, his cultivation of men like Amos Kendall becomes utterly essential to the handling of his presidency. The point of concentrating on these five is to identify those relationships, formed at a critical moment in his rise, which tell us the most about how Jackson drew upon the talents of others to publicize his deeds and his virtues, enabling him to fulfill his political ambition. He had other confidants, such as John Overton and John Coffee, and the weaker-willed William B. Lewis, who also appear in these pages; but Jackson's particular interactions with Livingston, Eaton, Houston, Call, and Carroll are the most revealing of his conscious struggle to accomplish a legacy.

Chapter One. The Formative Frontier

1. AJ to Mills, July 8, 1824, facsimile at the Virginia Historical Society; further clarification by Jackson in AJ to Amos Kendall, Apr. 19, 1843, Bassett, 6:215–16; details on the border dispute in James, 791–97, and Elmer Don Herd, Jr., *Andrew Jackson, South Carolinian* (Columbia, S.C., 1963).

2. James H. Merrell, *The Indians' New World: Catawbas and Their Neighbors from European Contact through the Era of Removal* (Chapel Hill, N.C., 1989), 103–4, 171–209.

3. Fred Anderson, *Crucible of War: The Seven Years' War and the Fate of Empire in British North America, 1754–1766* (New York, 2000), 5–6, 12, 44–61.

4. Merrell, *The Indians' New World*, 195, 210, 214–21, 226.

5. Parton, 1:196.

6. Parton 1:254. At the same time, Philadelphia's most prominent male citizens, patriotic members of the Sons of St. Tammany organization, occasionally dressed up and took on the manner of Indians, and celebrated (in the company of real Iroquois) the enduring harmony among whites and Indians in Pennsylvania. For whites to symbolically, and amid revelry, exchange their own for traditional Indian character in the pacific East obviously stood in utter contrast to the actual, rather serious conditions in the West Jackson knew and experienced. See Roger D. Abrahams, "White Indians in Penn's City: The Loyal Sons of St. Tammany," in William Pencak et al., eds., *Riot and Revelry in Early America* (University Park, Pa., 2002), 179–204.

7. Tobias Smollett, *The Expedition of Humphrey Clinker* (New York, 1967 [1771]), 230. Eighteenth-century terms need to be clarified, because Andrew Jackson was both an eighteenth- and a nineteenth-century man. *Sensible* meant subject to the positive passion of generous commitment; *effeminate* meant both unmanly and too desirous of soft (often urbanized) pleasures. In his 1819 *Sketch Book,* Washington Irving wrote an essay, "Traits of Indian Character," that furthered this perception, accenting the Indian's "loftiness of spirit" and "chivalrous courage." Bemoaning the fate of those who still inhabited frontiers of white settlement, Irving wrote, "How truly are we the dupes of show and circumstance! How different is virtue, clothed in purple and enthroned in state, from virtue naked and destitute, and perishing obscurely in the wilderness!" See *The Works of Washington Irving* (New York,

1897), vol. 1. On the Anglo-American perception of Indian qualities over time, see esp. Richard Slotkin, *Regeneration Through Violence: The Mythology of the American Frontier, 1600–1860* (Middletown, Conn., 1973), and Robert F. Berkhofer, Jr., *The White Man's Indian: Images of the American Indian from Columbus to the Present* (New York, 1978).

8. James, 14; Parton, 1:46–48. Parton claims that the Jacksons came up from Charleston, but the research of James (p. 789) disputes him, focusing on the fact that the majority of Scotch-Irish in the Waxhaws came via Pennsylvania. On the Scotch-Irish, Germans, and Quakers who came to the Carolinas from Pennsylvania and Maryland, see Robert W. Ramsey, *Carolina Cradle* (Chapel Hill, N.C., 1964).

9. Eaton (p. 9) puts the death "shortly after," while Parton (1:50) states that the event occurred when Elizabeth was "far advanced in pregnancy." James (p. 9) indicates, colorfully, "February [1767] . . . While a heavy snow fell in the southerly Waxhaws," and Remini (1:427n9) accepts Parton.

10. Eaton, 9–10.

11. Parton, 1:62–67; Henry A. Wise, *Seven Decades of the Union* (Philadelphia, 1872), 102. A Kentucky pioneer of the same era, who became a doctor, wrote in his 1848 memoir that in the 1780s and 1790s western settlers spoke "a dialect of old English, in queer pronunciation and abominable grammar," which he described as "*rudely* vernacular." See Daniel Drake, *Pioneer Life in Kentucky, 1785–1800,* ed. Emmet Field Horine (New York, 1948), 126.

12. Davie himself was seriously wounded at Stono, in a cavalry charge. He had graduated Princeton as a member of the class of 1776. See Blackwell P. Robinson, *William R. Davie* (Chapel Hill, N.C., 1957), chaps. 2–3.

13. Andrew Jackson Papers, LC, microfilm reel #64. On Tarleton's activities in the Waxhaws, see esp. John Buchanan, *The Road to Guilford Courthouse: The American Revolution in the Carolinas* (New York, 1997), chaps. 6–7; also Robinson, *William R. Davie,* chap. 4.

14. AJ to Amos Kendall, May 10, 1843, Bassett, 6:217–18; Parton, 1:72–75; Remini, 1:14–17; James, 19–21; Dusenbery, 10–11.

15. Remini, 1:19; James, 22–24. On the general tenor of the war in the Carolinas, see David Ramsay, *The History of the American Revolution,* ed. Lester H. Cohen (Indianapolis, 1990 [1789]), chap. 19; and Buchanan, *The Road to Guilford Courthouse.*

16. Benjamin F. Butler, in Dusenbery, 60. This Benjamin Franklin Butler was Jackson's second-term attorney general, a New York associate of Martin Van Buren, and not the New Hampshire–born Union Army general of the same name.

17. Parton, 1:87–89; Eaton, 11–12; manuscript of Henry Lee's *Life of Jackson,* Andrew Jackson Papers, LC, microfilm reel #64, pp. 3–5. Lee lived with Jackson at the Hermitage during the 1820s.

18. Eaton, 12.

19. Dusenbery, 34.

20. Parton, 3:685. For a modern scholar's similar characterization of the Scotch-Irish of this time, see David Hackett Fischer, *Albion's Seed: Four British Folkways in America* (Oxford, 1989), 605ff.

21. Even his adoring eulogist, Virginian Hugh Garland, wrote of this period in Jackson's life: "Bereft of the guardianship of father or mother, or friends, with the idle and dissolute habits contracted in times of confusion and civil war, he soon squandered the little patrimony that was left him . . . , doomed to a life of profligacy." See Dusenbery, 187.

22. Robinson, *William R. Davie,* 28–29; Parton, 1:97–105.

23. Rachel Klein, *Unification of a Slave State: The Rise of the Planter Class in the South Carolina Backcountry, 1760–1808* (Chapel Hill, N.C., 1990), 104–7; Andrew Burstein, *Sentimental Democracy: The Evolution of America's Romantic Self-Image* (New York, 1999), chap. 5;

Jefferson to Martha Jefferson, Mar. 28, 1787, *The Family Letters of Thomas Jefferson*, ed. Edwin Morris Betts and James Adam Bear, Jr. (Columbia, Mo., 1966), 35.

24. Boone was first crafted into a hero in 1784, in John Filson, *The Discovery of Kentucke and the Adventures of Daniel Boon* (New York, 1978), a facsimile of the first edition.

25. Joel Barlow, *An Oration*, facsimile reprint in *The Works of Joel Barlow* (Gainsville, Fla., 1970), 20.

26. James, 38; Remini, 1:34; Parton, 1:110; James W. Ely, Jr., and Theodore Brown, Jr., eds., *Legal Papers of Andrew Jackson* (Knoxville, Tenn., 1987), 4.

27. The westward-moving state of mind at this time is examined in Burstein, *Sentimental Democracy*, 153–66, 203–7; Slotkin, *Regeneration through Violence*, esp. chap. 9; Peter S. Onuf, "Liberty, Development, and Union: Visions of the West in the 1780s," *William and Mary Quarterly* 43 (Apr. 1986): 179–213; Arthur K. Moore, *The Frontier Mind: A Cultural Analysis of the Kentucky Frontiersman* (Lexington, Ky., 1957); Henry Nash Smith, *Virgin Land: The American West as Symbol and Myth* (Cambridge, Mass., 1950); cynical citation is from Henry Toulmin's *The Western Country in 1793*, in John A. Jakle, *Images of the Ohio Valley* (New York, 1977), 102; Eaton, 14.

28. The extant journals of emigrants and foreign travelers provide a useful window through which to view shared experiences on the trans-Appalachian frontier of the late 1780s. Through their descriptions of a fledgling society and a rustic physical environment, we can know more about Jackson than what he himself communicated. For this, Harriet Simpson Arnow's *Seedtime on the Cumberland* (New York, 1960) is a superb resource.

29. Arnow, *Seedtime on the Cumberland*, 215–16, 235–37; James, 48–51; Parton, 1:126–27; description of Nashville in Eastin Morris, *The Tennessee Gazetteer* (Nashville, 1834), 108.

30. Arnow, *Seedtime on the Cumberland*, 196–99, 207, 220, 227–33; Thomas Perkins Abernethy, *From Frontier to Plantation in Tennessee* (Chapel Hill, N.C., 1932), chaps. 1–2; Morris, *The Tennessee Gazetteer*, xiv–xviii.

31. Arnow, *Seedtime on the Cumberland*, 198–99, 282–306, 334–35.

32. Parton, 1:155–57; John E. Ferling, *The First of Men: A Life of George Washington* (Knoxville, Tenn., 1988), 410–11; PAJ, 1:49n.

33. Nathaniel J. Sheidley, "Unruly Men: Indians, Settlers, and the Ethos of Frontier Patriarchy in the Upper Tennessee Watershed, 1763–1815," Ph.D. dissertation, Princeton University, 1999, 8–11, 62–78, 111–15, 139.

34. Dusenbery (p. 16) notes: "Jackson soon became known as one of the boldest of the brave spirits with which the country abounded," and vaguely suggests that the nicknames "Sharp Knife" and "Pointed Arrow" were given to him during the early period of his residence in Tennessee. This is the same language used in Alexander Walker's 1856 *Jackson and New Orleans* (p. 22), in which the author cites the two nicknames and states that Jackson was "not only a terror to the prowling aborigines, who hung around the settlements, but to the even more ferocious frontiersmen." A. W. Putnam places Jackson in battle with Indians, specifically in 1789, as "bold, dashing, fearless, and mad upon his enemies," but this is highly questionable. See Putnam, *History of Middle Tennessee* (Nashville, 1859), 316–18. Eaton (p. 15) writes: "Indian depredations being then frequent on the Cumberland, every man of necessity, became a soldier. . . . Although young, no person was more distinguished than Andrew Jackson, in defending the country against these predatory incursions. . . . He aided alike in garrisoning the forts, and in pursuing and chastising the enemy." While he no doubt contributed muscle to refortifying the settlement, Jackson is not held by any modern scholar to have taken part in "chastising" hostile Cherokees.

35. James A. McLaughlin to Amos Kendall, Mar. 13, 1843, Bassett, 6:213–14.

36. AJ to McKee, Jan. 30, 1793, PAJ 1:40.

37. AJ to McKee, May 16, 1794, PAJ 1:48–49; Rogin, *Fathers and Children*, 132–33.

38. William Graham Sumner, *Andrew Jackson* (Boston and New York, 1882), 6–8.

39. Elliott J. Gorn, " 'Gouge and Bite, Pull Hair and Scratch': The Social Significance of Fighting in the Southern Backcountry," *American Historical Review* 90 (Feb. 1985): 18–43. The memoir of Dr. Daniel Drake describes the social gatherings of this period: "[I] well recollect that profanity, vulgarity & drinking were their most eminent characteristics. . . . Some sort of physical amusements, including fights, in which biting & gouging were essential elements, with the beastly intoxication of several, would generally 'wind up' these meetings." See Drake, *Pioneer Life in Kentucky*, 183. The records of a slightly later period are hardly less remarkable for the lack of polish and courtesy. See James I. Robertson, Jr., "Frolics, Fights and Firewater in Frontier Tennessee," THQ 17 (Dec. 1958): 97–111. These kinds of behavior were yet to be linked to a southern military tradition, or a martial self-awareness, which southerners only began to take special pride in after 1830. See R. Don Higginbotham, "The Martial Spirit in the Antebellum South: Some Further Speculations in a National Context," *Journal of Southern History* 58 (Feb. 1992): 3–26.

40. Parton, 1:120.

41. AJ to Avery, Aug. 12, 1788, PAJ, 1:12.

42. Samuel Johnson, *A Dictionary of the English Language* (Philadelphia, 1813). Johnson associates his meanings with such classic thinkers and wordsmiths as John Dryden, John Locke, and Francis Bacon. Jackson owned the Philadelphia, 1818, edition of Johnson's *Dictionary*.

43. Jackson's handwritten notes on a conversation with Rev. Joshua Danforth, Apr. 30, 1832, Hurja Collection, TSLA.

44. Remini (1:39) fails to cite as his source Parton's correspondence with Avery's son. See Parton 1:160–62. Parton identifies inaccuracies in the son's letter, but accepts the general truth of his story, in which the "irritable" Jackson first issued a "peremptory challenge" by writing on "the blank leaf of a law book" as soon as the offensive remark was spoken. The duelists met after sundown at "a hollow north of Jonesboro." Both fired, though neither was hit, and they shook hands before parting. Remini states, "The two men fired simultaneously—both into the air!" James (p. 46) earlier wrote of the incident: "Both parties fired in the air." This appears to be the case, but Remini could not have known whether their fire was "simultaneous." His conjecture that the duel was "a tidy and sensible charade," designed to afford Jackson official satisfaction for a moment of public embarrassment, is quite plausible, and is precisely the conclusion Parton wants his reader to draw.

45. Sheidley, "Unruly Men," 89–91.

46. Arnow, *Seedtime on the Cumberland*, 344, 357–58; Putnam, *History of Middle Tennessee*, 248; Parton, 1:139.

47. Reuben Gold Thwaites, ed., *Early Western Travels, 1748–1846* (Cleveland, 1904), 3:82–87.

48. ibid., 276–79.

49. S[amuel] Putnam Waldo, *Memoirs of Andrew Jackson, Major-General in the Army of the United States and Commander in Chief of the Division of the South* (Hartford, Conn., 1819), 39.

50. Charles Royster, *A Revolutionary People at War: The Continental Army and American Character* (Chapel Hill, N.C., 1979), 235; Arnow, *Seedtime on the Cumberland*, 350; Walker, *Jackson and New Orleans*, 154–55.

51. AJ to Jefferson, Aug. 3, 1804, PAJ, 2:32–35. Queues, often braided, worn with a ribbon, were a regular feature of the eighteenth-century British and American soldier's appearance. The Cherokee creation legend contains a reference to the long, beautiful hair of a man selected to help populate the earth.

52. Joseph Earl Dabney, *Mountain Spirits: A Chronicle of Corn Whiskey from King James' Ulster Plantation to America's Appalachians and the Moonshine Life* (New York, 1974); Reginald Horsman, *The Frontier in the Formative Years, 1783–1815* (New York, 1970), chap. 6; Arnow, *Seedtime on the Cumberland*, 424–25; Lewis L. Laska, " 'The Dam'st Situation Ever Man Was Placed In,': Andrew Jackson, David Allison, and the Frontier Economy of 1795," THQ 54 (Winter 1995): 337.

53. Parton, 1:249; Dusenbery, 159, 209.

54. James, 349, citing Jackson's philosophy that "subordination must be obtained first, and then good treatment."

55. Power of Attorney, in PAJ, 1:23–24; advertisement in PAJ, 2:40–41; AJ to John Overton, Nov. 30, 1799, PAJ, 1:224–25; "List of Negroes for A. Jackson," Nov. 8, 1790, in AJ Papers, LC, microfilm reel #1. On Jackson's active involvement in the continental slave trade, see in particular the correspondence growing from his conflict with Silas Dinsmoor, in PAJ, 2:261–62, 286–89, and Parton, 1:349–59. In one instance, expressing awareness of the emotional consequences of trading in human beings, Jackson contemplated the sale of a slave named Sampson, and his family, declaring to Rachel a preference for selling at a distance from Nashville. AJ to Rachel, Sept. 18, 1816, PAJ, 4:62; Remini, 1:391.

56. Anita S. Goodstein, "Black History on the Nashville Frontier, 1780–1810," THQ 38 (Winter 1979): 401–20.

57. Parton, 1:133.

58. Frances Clifton, "John Overton as Andrew Jackson's Friend," THQ 11 (1952): 23–40.

59. Remini, 1:44–45; Parton, 1:135–36; Ely and Brown, eds., *Legal Papers of Andrew Jackson*, xxxvi. Jackson's "beat" was the Mero District, which included Sumner and Tennessee Counties in addition to Nashville's Davidson County.

60. Parton, 1:136, 241; James, 68; "List of Taxable Property," in PAJ, 1:34.

61. Ely and Brown, eds., *Legal Papers of Andrew Jackson*, 5–6; [Sir Geoffrey Gilbert], *The Law of Evidence* (London, 1760), 2, 4.

62. Thomas Sheridan, *A Complete Dictionary of the English Language* (Philadelphia, 1796); Fintan O'Toole, *A Traitor's Kiss: The Life of Richard Brinsley Sheridan, 1751–1816* (New York, 1997), 34–38.

63. Sheridan, *A Complete Dictionary of the English Language*. Sheridan's definition of "passion" matches that of the renowned Dr. Samuel Johnson, who expands the meaning of "passionate" to include: "causing or expressing great commotion of mind." See Johnson, *A Dictionary of the English Language*.

64. Parton, 1:148–51. Overton acknowledged his subjectivity, as he and Jackson shared not only Mrs. Donelson's cabin but its one bed. "As young men of the same pursuits and profession," he wrote, "with but few others in the country with whom to associate, besides sharing, as we frequently did, common dangers, such an intimacy ensued as might reasonably be expected." Parton seems convinced of Jackson's complete innocence of the adultery charge.

65. See especially Curtis, 26–27. In Jackson's first authenticated (though apparently no longer extant) letter to Rachel, he makes reference to "my good old Mother Mrs. Donelson." See PAJ, 1:92.

66. On marriage and divorce customs in Scotland, Ireland, and the American backcountry, see Fischer, *Albion's Seed*, 669–83. The author emphasizes sexual openness in these communities, as well as a warring mentality and distinct ideas about gender roles. See also Leah Leneman, *Alienated Affections: The Scottish Experience of Divorce and Separation, 1684–1830* (Edinburgh, 1998), detailing the custom of informal or self-divorce on the basis of adultery and desertion. For further discussion, see Appendix, note 10.

67. Parton, 1:151. Jackson's local defenders in the presidential campaign of 1828 quoted a Virginia legislator, still living, who had passed judgment on Robards' complaint (Kentucky then being part of Virginia) and who now reflected on Robards as a man of "wild habits and harsh temper," cruel to his "lovely and blameless" wife; by producing this picture of an injured Rachel, the Nashville pamphlet was meant to convince readers that Robards had deserted his wife, rather than the other way around. See discussion in Norma Basch, "Marriage, Morals, and Politics in the Election of 1828," *Journal of American History* 80 (Dec. 1993): 910–11.

68. It is pertinent to note that Maj. Henry Lee of Virginia, the controversial son of a Revolutionary War hero, found life in his native state intolerable after he had become sexually involved with his wife's sister. In the early 1820s, this "seducer," so-called, found peace — and acceptance — at the Hermitage. According to Parton, it was "the indignation of his neighbors" from which Lee had fled west. See Parton, 2:653–54.

69. AJ to Rachel, May 9, 1796, PAJ, 1:91–92.

70. Parton, 1:169–71.

71. Overton to AJ, Mar. 10, 1796, PAJ, 1:85.

Chapter Two. Fraternity and Defiant Honor

1. AJ to Hays, Jan. 8, 1797, PAJ, 1:112.

2. The cited language is as recorded in the third person and copied into the *Annals of Congress*. See PAJ, 1:106–7.

3. For an overview on White's relations with Jackson, see Lorman A. Ratner, *Andrew Jackson and His Tennessee Lieutenants: A Study in Political Culture* (Westport, Conn., 1997), 73–82.

4. Speech of Dec. 30, 1796, PAJ, 1:108; AJ to Sevier, Feb. 24, 1797, PAJ, 1:126–27. The point about Jackson's long adherence to the principle of chain of command is made by Remini, 1:95, though I do not see evidence, as Remini does, that the speech was "nearly outstanding," and "earned him the respect of his colleagues at the very outset of his brief career in Congress."

5. *General Advertiser (Aurora)*, Mar. 20, 1795; AJ to Macon, Oct. 4, 1795, PAJ, 1:74; Jefferson to John Adams, Dec. 28, 1796, a letter never sent, because James Madison, inspecting it, thought it too conciliatory and easily misused by the Republicans' antagonists. See James Morton Smith, ed., *The Republic of Letters: The Correspondence Between Thomas Jefferson and James Madison, 1776–1826* (New York, 1994), 954–58; AJ to Hays, Dec. 16, 1796, PAJ, 1:103.

6. Parton, 1:206–12.

7. AJ to Hays, Nov. 9, 1797, PAJ, 1:152.

8. William H. Masterson, *William Blount* (Baton Rouge, La., 1954); Arthur Preston Whitaker, *The Mississippi Question, 1795–1803* (New York, 1934), chap. 6; Buckner F. Melton, Jr., *The First Impeachment: The Constitutional Framers and the Case of Senator William Blount* (Macon, Ga., 1998); Remini, 1:102–7; biography of Cocke in *Biographical Directory of the American Congress* (Washington, D.C., 1950), 997.

9. Cocke to AJ, Apr. 18, 1797; AJ to Cocke, Nov. 9, 1797, PAJ, 1:130–31, 152–53. Cocke had signed the April letter, "your real friend."

10. AJ to Cocke, Nov. 9, 1797, PAJ, 1:152–53.

11. Cocke to AJ, June 25, 1798, PAJ, 1:203.

12. AJ to Cocke, June 25, 1798, PAJ, 1:204.

13. This procedure is confirmed in Jackson's exhortation to fellow Mason George W. Campbell in 1807, when the latter was embroiled in a land dispute with the universally esteemed James Robertson. "Will you permit me," writes Jackson, "to bring to your view a subject that has been made known to me as a brother—I mean the dispute that is likely to arise between you and Genl Robertson respecting a peace of land, This dispute I would advise to be left to two or three Brothers to decide—Should it get into court, it will be expensive, create passions that never ought to exist, between brothers." AJ to Campbell, Jan. 15, 1807, PAJ, 2:147–48.

14. W. G. Hunt to AJ, Oct. 9, 1824, a letter signed "Yours fraternally," and sent locally, addressed simply: "M. W. [Most Worshipful] Andrew Jackson, Late Grand Master of the Grand Lodge of Tennessee"; Jackson's gracious reply to the lodge is dated from the Hermitage the following day, both letters in Jackson Papers, LC, microfilm reel #33. On Apr. 29, 1828, presidential candidate Jackson wrote to James Alexander Hamilton, son of the late Alexander Hamilton: "I presided several years as Royal Arch Mason in the grand Lodge of Tennessee, but have not attended the sessions for two years or thereabouts." See Bassett 3:399. Wilkins Tannehill's *The Masonic Manual, Or Freemasonry Illustrated* (Nashville, 1824) was dedicated to "The Most Worshipful General Andrew Jackson, Grand Master of Masons, in the State of Tennessee." On Tannehill's career, see Anita Shafer Goodstein, *Nashville, 1780–1860* (Gainesville, Fla., 1989), 50–52.

15. Robinson, *William R. Davie,* chap. 8.

16. PAJ, 1:200, 253–54; Steven C. Bullock, *Revolutionary Brotherhood: Freemasonry and the Transformation of the American Social Order, 1730–1840* (Chapel Hill, N.C., 1996), 143, 228, and *passim.*

17. Parton, 1:227.

18. Ely and Brown, eds., *Legal Papers of Andrew Jackson,* 212–15.

19. ibid., xxxiv–xxxv.

20. AJ to Hays, Sept. 9 and 23, 1801, PAJ, 1:254–55.

21. Carl S. Driver, *John Sevier: Pioneer of the Old Southwest* (Chapel Hill, N.C., 1932); Arnow, *Seedtime on the Cumberland,* 194–95, Parton, 1:230.

22. From 1785 to 1788 Sevier actively encouraged North Carolinians to settle on east Tennessee Indian lands. As the fate of Franklin became clear, he spread word of a broad Cherokee threat in the region so as to shift North Carolinians' focus away from the abortive secession movement. In doing so, he won over backcountry settlers who had come to oppose separation from North Carolina. See Sheidley, "Unruly Men," 181–85. A clear explanation of events surrounding the Franklin episode is offered in Pat Alderman, *The Overmountain Men* (Johnson City, Tenn., 1970), 183–236; see also Driver, *John Sevier,* chaps. 4–5; Abernethy, *From Frontier to Plantation in Tennessee,* chap. 5. The best account of the jurisdictional issues of the 1780s is Peter S. Onuf, *Origins of the Federal Republic* (Philadelphia, 1983).

23. As Yale professor William Graham Sumner put it in the 1880s, "The two men were too much alike in temper to be pleased with each other." See Sumner, *Andrew Jackson,* 16–17.

24. AJ to Sevier, May 8, 1797, PAJ, 1:136; Johnson, *A Dictionary of the English Language* (1813).

25. McNairy to AJ, May 4, 1797, PAJ, 1:133–35.

26. Sevier to AJ, May 8, 1797, PAJ, 1:137–38.

27. AJ to McNairy, May 9, 1797; to Sevier, May 10, 1797, PAJ, 1:138–41.

28. Remini (1:100–1) uses even stronger language to describe the Jackson-Sevier dynamic in 1796–97, conceiving that Sevier might have been "jealous of Jackson's new popularity in the state and fearful of what he might accomplish as general." While such a correlation

between the exchange of letters and Sevier's support of Jackson's competition makes good sense, Sevier's jealousy seems hard to justify. Jackson seems rather more calculating than unbalanced at this juncture. Remini's idea may have derived from Parton's comment, conflating incidents of 1797–98 and 1801–03, after Jackson's years as a respected state judge, and after Jackson had successfully contested Sevier for the position of major general. Parton (1:231) states, "Perhaps the veteran Sevier did not relish the rapid rise to popularity and high office of so young a man as Jackson." In this instance, Marquis James more convincingly links Jackson's knowledge of Sevier's questionable land-sale practices from 1795–96 (which Jackson had yet to act upon) to the tension between them in 1797, when Jackson perceived that Sevier sought to slow his rise in Tennessee politics. See James, 89–91.

29. Parton, 1:232. In the earlier contest, Sevier had been the sitting governor and therefore ineligible to serve concurrently as major general of the militia, but he had still made clear his preference for someone other than Jackson.

30. PAJ, 1:337–45. The Jackson letter to the *Tennessee Gazette* was reprinted as a broadside. For a view sympathetic to Sevier, see Driver, *John Sevier,* chap. 8.

31. AJ to Sevier, Oct. 3, 1803, PAJ, 1:369; original in AJ Papers, TSLA. The source of the dialogue is Parton (1:164), who heard it stated more than a half century after the incident, yet its plausibility is supported by even earlier publications. Philadelphia wit and popular essayist Francis Hopkinson argued in favor of dueling culture in the mid-1780s: "He who has not spirit to defend his own honour, will make but a poor protector of the delicate sex." See "On Duelling," in *The Miscellaneous Essays and Occasional Writings of Francis Hopkinson* (Philadelphia, 1792), 2:33.

32. AJ to Sevier, Oct. 2, 1803, PAJ, 1:367.

33. Johnson, *A Dictionary of the English Language* (1813); *The Compact Edition of the Oxford English Dictionary* (Oxford, 1971), 1:1470.

34. Sevier to AJ, Oct. 3; AJ to Sevier, Oct. 3, 1803, PAJ, 1:368–69.

35. AJ to Sevier, Oct. 9, 1803, PAJ, 1:375–76, Sevier to AJ, Oct. 10, 1803, PAJ, 1:380; "Veritas," in PAJ, 1:498. There is sound speculation that "Veritas" was Jackson's close friend John Coffee.

36. Affidavit of Andrew Greer, PAJ, 1:489–90; letter of Thomas J. Vandyke, Oct. 16, 1803, published in the *Tennessee Gazette,* Dec. 21, 1803, PAJ, 1:505.

37. Sevier to Robertson, Nov. 8, 1803, PAJ, 1:490; AJ to Jefferson, Oct. 17, 1803, PAJ, 1:389.

38. The preceding discussion is significantly drawn from Kenneth S. Greenberg, *Honor and Slavery* (Princeton, 1996); Bertram Wyatt-Brown, *Southern Honor: Ethics and Behavior in the Old South* (New York, 1982); and Steven M. Stowe, *Intimacy and Power in the Old South: Ritual in the Lives of the Planters* (Baltimore, 1987), quote at 7. Two new and significant studies of this subject are Joanne B. Freeman, *Affairs of Honor: National Politics in the New Republic* (New Haven, Conn., 2001) and Dick Steward, *Duels and the Roots of Violence in Missouri* (Columbia, Mo., 2000). Freeman focuses on elite behavior, while Steward eyes frontier society. Note that there was not a uniform response to lies or insults at this time; some men sued in court, and many saw the culture of the duel as barbaric rather than noble behavior.

39. Remini, 1:87–90; Laska, " 'The Dam'st Situation Ever Man Was Placed In.' "; John Overton to James King, May 23, 1797, attesting that Overton had "particularly directed Mr Jackson to take security" against his failing financier, in Claybrooke Collection/Overton Papers, TSLA; "Statement Regarding the Allison Transaction," (circa 1801), PAJ, 1:251–52.

40. "Agreement with Thomas Watson and John Hutchings," Feb. 16, 1802, PAJ, 1:278–80.

41. Stanley F. Horn, *The Hermitage: Home of Old Hickory* (Richmond, Va., 1938), 18–21; Parton, 1:307–8. English philosopher Jeremy Bentham's estate was called "Hermitage." It

was also the name of the Paris cottage of Jean-Jacques Rousseau, built in the 1750s, and the palace in St. Petersburg, Russia, built by Catherine II around the same time. See the *New Century Cyclopedia of Names*, ed. Clarence L. Barnhart (New York, 1954), 2:1990. In addition to being Jefferson's early choice, "Hermitage" was the name of other Virginia residences of this period, notably the Richmond estate of the Mayo family.

42. Gordon T. Chappell, "The Life and Activities of General John Coffee," THQ 1 (1942): 125–46.

43. AJ to Coffee, Mar. 7, 1804, PAJ, 2:9.

44. AJ to Hutchings, Mar. 17, 1804; Jackson and Hutchings to Boggs and Davidson (Philadelphia), July 31, 1804; James Irwin to AJ, Jan. 25 and Feb. 9, 1805; AJ to Edward Ward, June 10, 1805; "Memorandum re Purchase of Slaves from Richard Apperson and Cotton and Tobacco from Bennett Smith," PAJ, 2:10, 30–32, 47–50, 59–60, 261–62; James, 99–101; Parton, 1:244–49.

45. Parton, 1:253; William P. Anderson to AJ, June 25, 1809, PAJ, 2:216–17.

46. Parton, 1:267–68; *Impartial Review*, Jan. 25, 1806, noting, in advance of the race, that Ploughboy was up for stud; "Announcement of Race between Truxton and Ploughboy," Mar. 1, 1806, PAJ, 2:90.

47. Parton, 1:268; Remini, 1:136–37; PAJ, 2:77. Remini takes dramatic license, dressing up the encounter by relating Jackson's posture: "Eyes aflame, voice rasping, he demanded an explanation and an apology."

48. Parton, 1:269; Swann to AJ, Jan. 3, 1806, PAJ, 2:78.

49. AJ to Swann, Jan. 7, 1806, PAJ, 2:79–80.

50. Dickinson to AJ, Jan. 10, 1806, PAJ, 2:81–82.

51. Swann to AJ, Jan. 12, 1806, PAJ, 2:82.

52. Parton, 1:278–79.

53. Robertson to AJ, Feb. 1, 1806, PAJ, 2:83–84.

54. AJ to Thomas Eastin, Feb. 10, 1806, PAJ, 2:87.

55. John Coffee statement, Feb. 5, 1806, AJ Papers, TSLA; Parton, 1:287–89.

56. See especially Freeman, *Affairs of Honor*, introduction and chap. 4. Few "murders" staged on the dueling ground between "gentlemen" were ever prosecuted.

57. *Impartial Review*, Mar. 1, 1806. An article in the same paper on March 22, titled "Assassination," reported on an attempt on the life of the famed pamphleteer Thomas Paine in New Rochelle, New York.

58. AJ to Hutchings, Apr. 7, 1806; Hutchings to AJ, Apr. 14, 1806, PAJ, 2:93–95.

59. Dickinson to Thomas Eastin, May 21, 1806, PAJ, 2:97–98.

60. AJ to Dickinson, May 23, 1806; "Arrangements of Thomas Overton and Hanson Catlet for Duel," PAJ, 2:98–99; Parton, 1:290–93. At his brother's suggestion, Thomas Overton had come over from North Carolina and settled in Nashville in 1802. The letters of Jackson and Dickinson that amounted to a challenge and its acceptance were subsequently published in the *Impartial Review*, on June 14, 1806. An illustration of the dueling ground appears in *Harpers Weekly*, Jan. 8, 1859, p. 21.

61. Parton, 1:295–301, as told to him by "an old friend of General Jackson, who heard them related, and saw them *acted*, by General [Thomas] Overton," who died in 1825; statement of John Hoggalt, June 24, 1806, Andrew Jackson Papers, TSLA; Remini, 1:141–43; James, 115–18, takes more liberties in his account, incorporating questionable dialogue.

62. Parton, 1:299, 304. A statement by both seconds present at the duel, issued on June 20, 1806, verified that Jackson's fire was not outside the understood procedure. See statements of Thomas Overton and Dr. Hanson Catlet, Figuers Collection, TSLA; statement of George Ridley, AJ Papers, TSLA; also PAJ, 2:104–5.

63. Parton, 1:305.

64. Robertson to AJ, Mar. 25, 1805, PAJ, 2:53.

65. Demonbrum, as his name was spelled in the newspaper, is referred to in other records as Timothe De Monbruen. Born in 1737, he was still alive and in Nashville to greet the visiting Marquis de Lafayette in 1825.

66. AJ to Watkins, June 15, 1806, PAJ, 2:102–4. According to the editors of the *Papers of Andrew Jackson,* Jackson was under great strain, and so John Overton authored (with Jackson's full concurrence) this letter for publication.

67. AJ to Eastin, circa June 1806, PAJ, 2:106–7.

68. Harrison to Jackson, June 30, 1806, AJ Papers, TSLA; also PAJ, 2:105.

69. Overton to AJ, Sept. 12, 1806, PAJ, 2:108–9.

70. Epigraph in Parton, *The Life and Times of Aaron Burr* (New York, 1858). The reader should note that everything in Hamilton's history identifies him, too, as a man of unusual, if not "irregular," ambition.

Chapter Three. Judging Character: Burr

1. The foregoing analysis is adapted from Andrew Burstein, *Sentimental Democracy: The Evolution of America's Romantic Self-Image* (New York, 1999), esp. chaps. 5 and 7; Richard Slotkin, *Regeneration through Violence: The Mythology of the American Frontier, 1600–1860* (Middletown, Conn., 1973); Henry Nash Smith, *Virgin Land: The American West as Symbol and Myth* (Cambridge, Mass., 1950), esp. chaps. 5–6; Albert Furtwangler, *Acts of Discovery: Visions of America in the Lewis and Clark Journals* (Urbana, Ill., 1993); Perry Miller, "The Romantic Dilemma in American Nationalism and the Concept of Nature," *Harvard Theological Review* 48 (1955): 239–53; John McWilliams, *The Last of the Mohicans: Civil Savagery and Savage Civility* (New York, 1993).

2. "Eulogy by Levi Woodbury," in Dusenbery, 70–75.

3. AJ to Jefferson, Aug. 3, 1804, PAJ, 2:33–35.

4. AJ to Butler, Aug. 25, 1804, PAJ, 2:36–37.

5. "Toasts for Independence Day Celebration," PAJ, 2:64–65. Jackson's Toast #11 repeated language contained in Jackson's letter to Jefferson: "The army of the united States—May the officer and Soldier that is willing to defend liberty ever enjoy freedom—may he never be doomed to persecution and Tyranny under a government of laws to satiate the private spleen of a would be Despot." An extended eulogy of Butler was printed in the *Impartial Review,* Dec. 13, 1805, describing the "virtue, honor, benevolence, honesty, a sound heart and a clear head, united with bravery," that constituted Butler's character. It referred to his long hair as "a gift of nature," that no one had the right to take away, asserting this as an opinion Butler held "till his death."

6. AJ to Campbell, Oct. 15, 1812, PAJ, 2:334–36; Parton, 1:349–59, 2:580–81; Curtis, 44–45.

7. Burr's early years and rise are still no better chronicled than in Nathan Schachner, *Aaron Burr* (New York, 1937); the first encounter with Hamilton is in Broadus Mitchell, *Alexander Hamilton: The Revolutionary Years* (New York, 1970), 19–20. I have relied, too, on the microfilmed *Papers of Aaron Burr;* the *Political Correspondence and Public Papers of Aaron Burr,* ed. Mary-Jo Kline (Princeton, N.J., 1983); and *The Papers of Alexander Hamilton,* ed. Harold C. Syrett et al. (New York, 1961–87). On Burr's electioneering in New York on behalf of Jefferson, see esp. *Political Correspondence and Public Papers of Aaron Burr,* 1:419–26; on the ambiguity of the Burr-Jefferson relationship in early 1801, see ibid., 530–45; also James Roger Sharp, *American Politics in the Early Republic* (New Haven, Conn., 1993), chap. 12.

8. Andrew Burstein, *The Inner Jefferson: Portrait of a Grieving Optimist* (Charlottesville, Va., 1995), 234; PAJ, 2:63. Burr's ability to influence rurally based politicians is recounted in Parton, *Life and Times of Aaron Burr*, chap. 14.

9. *Correspondence of Aaron Burr and His Daughter Theodosia* (New York, 1929), 210, 213. The long letter was begun in May and dispatched in August 1805, after considerable southwestern travel.

10. Johnson, *A Dictionary of the English Language* (1813).

11. Burr to AJ, June 2, 1805, PAJ, 2:59.

12. As the historian James E. Lewis, Jr., writes of the early years of the republic with respect to these perceptions, "The lines between domestic and foreign policy were blurred." See Lewis, *The American Union and the Problem of Neighborhood* (Chapel Hill, N.C., 1998), quote at 9.

13. Burr to AJ, March 24, 1806, PAJ, 2:91–92; Jefferson to AJ, Sept. 19, 1803, PAJ, 1:365.

14. AJ to William Preston Anderson, Sept. 25, 1806; AJ to Winchester, Oct. 4, 1806, PAJ, 2:110–11.

15. Thomas Perkins Abernethy, *The Burr Conspiracy* (New York, 1954), 69–70; "Account with Aaron Burr," Oct.–Dec. 1806, also Jackson's and Coffee's statements "To the Adams County Superior Court," Mar. 25, 1813; AJ to Jefferson, Nov. 4, 1806, PAJ, 2:113–15, 398–99.

16. Parton, 1:320–21; Abernethy, *The Burr Conspiracy*, 96–99; *Impartial Review*, Oct. 4, 1806.

17. AJ to Claiborne, Nov. 12, 1806, PAJ, 2:116–17.

18. Jackson was obliged, during his campaign for the presidency in 1828, to recall the chronology of his actions—when and how he came to be suspicious of Burr. In vehemently denying the claim of a man (serving, in 1828, as a judge) who said Jackson had promised him a captain's commission in Burr's army, Jackson cited the Nov. 12, 1806, warning letter to Claiborne as proof of his timely display of fidelity to the United States. See Bassett, 3:391–95.

19. *Impartial Review*, Dec. 27, 1806, and Jan. 3, 1807.

20. Jackson's suspicions, while they might seem on the surface the subjective outpouring of a man of passionate temperament and extreme sensitivity to alleged wrongs, are found in the perceptions of at least some milder minds of the day. In his serious early biography of Burr, legal scholar Samuel L. Knapp, a conservative New Englander, wrote: "General Wilkinson saw that the public were watching his movements, and that intimations of his being in the pay of Spain were often made in the newspapers, and that his situation was becoming critical, made a bold attempt to throw the whole odium on the shoulders of Colonel Burr, who had then lost much of his political popularity in the Atlantic states. . . . Wilkinson saw that he was only to attribute vast plans and treasonable purposes to Colonel Burr, and the world would in general believe him without proof. They thought, or were easily brought to believe, that nothing short of empire would satisfy his ambition. He knew, also, that Mr. Jefferson was naturally a timid man when arms or blood was mentioned, and that he could easily disturb his nerves by suggestions of a warlike conspiracy." See Knapp, *The Life of Aaron Burr* (New York, 1835), 108.

21. *Richmond Enquirer*, Sept. 5, 1806, cited in Abernethy, *Burr Conspiracy*, 94.

22. Washington Irving, *Knickerbocker's History of New York*, in *The Works of Washington Irving*, vol. 4 (New York, 1897), 234–39.

23. AJ to Claiborne, Nov. 12, 1806; AJ to Smith, Nov. 12, 1806, PAJ, 2:116–19.

24. Republican congressman John Randolph, a correspondent of Jackson, was perhaps the most outspoken in this regard. He sought to launch an official House investigation into Wilkinson's past, and was in turn called by Wilkinson a "base, calumniating scoundrel, poltroon and coward." The Randolph-Wilkinson quarrel was publicized in Nashville's

Impartial Review. See PAJ, 2:180–81; also Royal Ornan Shreve, *The Finished Scoundrel* (Indianapolis, 1933).

25. Walter Flavius McCaleb, *The Aaron Burr Conspiracy and a New Light on Aaron Burr* (New York, 1966 [1903]), chaps. 6 and 12; Dumas Malone, *Jefferson the President: Second Term, 1805–1809* (Boston, 1974), chap. 15. Wilkinson was later obliged to confess to his critical deletion of self-incriminating words from the letter to Jefferson, when he appeared before a closed session of the grand jury in June 1807. Jefferson testified with greatest candor in a letter to James Monroe in 1812 that dealt exclusively with Wilkinson's motives. Here the ex-president alluded to "his Spanish mysteries," termed Wilkinson "injudicious," and refused to credit him with a sense of honor except in the single instance of his "zealous" support of the government "in the case of Burr's conspiracy." Jefferson to Monroe, Jan. 12, 1812, Thomas Jefferson Papers, LC.

26. Abernethy, *Burr Conspiracy*, 175, 204–12.

27. AJ to Campbell, Jan. 15, 1807; Campbell to AJ, Feb. 6, 1807, PAJ, 2:149–51. In Congress, Campbell expressed reluctance to jump to conclusions about Burr's guilt, claiming that the nation's newspapers were doing just that. See Weymouth T. Jordan, *George Washington Campbell of Tennessee: Western Statesman* (Tallahassee, Fla., 1955), 46–47. The success of Jackson's strategy is proven by a letter the president sent to Wilkinson at this time: "Be assured that Tennessee & particularly Genl. Jackson are faithful." Jefferson to Wilkinson, Jan. 3, 1807, Thomas Jefferson Papers, LC.

28. Documents pertaining to the capture and delivery of the fugitive Burr are in the *Nicholas Perkins Papers,* Tennessee Historical Society Misc. MSS file, TSLA. Major Perkins took charge of the prisoner on Feb. 24, 1807, at Fort Stoddert, initially intending to deliver him "by the most eligible route, over land, to the Executive of the United States at Washington City." Also see Abernethy, *Burr Conspiracy,* 217–26.

29. Dearborn to AJ, Dec. 19, 1806, PAJ, 2:125.

30. AJ to Dearborn, March 17, 1807, PAJ, 2:155–57.

31. PAJ, 2:164–65; Parton, 1:333–34; Parton, *The Life and Times of Aaron Burr,* 458; Shreve, *The Finished Scoundrel,* chap. 15. Those predisposed to view Burr simply as a conspirator drew upon stories and a vocabulary that had arisen during the contested election of 1800. Knowing Burr in a different context, Jackson could well have dismissed this fixed view. For strong evidence that Burr's persona was manipulated by New York editor James Cheetham, in the *American Citizen,* from 1800, see Nancy Isenberg, "The Little Emperor: Aaron Burr, Dandyism, and the Treason Trial of 1807," in Jeffrey L. Pasley, Andrew Robertson, and David Waldstreicher, eds., *Beyond the Founders* (Chapel Hill, N.C., forthcoming).

32. Raymond E. Fitch, ed., *Breaking with Burr: Harman Blennerhassett's Journal, 1807* (Athens, Ohio, 1988), xi, 91, 188–202; Sumner, *Andrew Jackson,* 25–26.

33. *Correspondence of Aaron Burr and His Daughter Theodosia,* letters of July 3 and July 6, 1807, 222–23. As a widower, Burr was widely known as a ladies' man, and wrote unabashedly of his exploits in his correspondence with his daughter.

34. McCaleb, *The Aaron Burr Conspiracy,* 275–76; *Correspondence of Aaron Burr and His Daughter Theodosia,* letters of May 15 and Oct. 9, 1807, 217, 225. Again, for insight into the irrationality of anti-Burr propaganda, see Isenberg, "The Little Emperor."

35. Malone, *Jefferson the President: Second Term,* 330–31.

36. Special Message to the Senate and House of Representatives, Jan. 22, 1807, *The Works of Thomas Jefferson,* ed. Paul Leicester Ford (New York, 1892–99), 10:346–57.

37. AJ to Smith, Nov. 28, 1807, PAJ, 2:174–75.

38. AJ to Smith, Nov. 28, 1807, PAJ, 2:175–76.

39. In addition to the recurrence of these words in his correspondence over the years, Jefferson's first inaugural address, March 4, 1801, notably proclaimed: "Let us restore to social

intercourse that harmony and affection without which liberty and even life itself are but dreary things." See *The Portable Thomas Jefferson,* ed. Merrill D. Peterson (New York, 1975), 290–95. For Jefferson's sentimental assumptions, see Burstein, *The Inner Jefferson.*

40. Whitaker, *The Mississippi Question,* 109–10.

41. Parton, 1:270, 277, 281–82. A letter from Thomas Swann to the editor of the *Impartial Review,* May 24, 1806, referred to Samuel Jackson as one who bore a resemblance to Andrew Jackson not only in name but in "disposition" as well.

42. PAJ, 1:223, 298.

43. PAJ, 2:172–74.

44. PAJ, 2:178–79.

Chapter Four. Engaging the Enemy: New Orleans

1. Dusenbery, 75–77.

2. Grant to AJ, Aug. 13, 1795, PAJ, 1:66.

3. AJ to Blount, Feb. 21, 1798; Blount to AJ, Dec. 7, 1801, PAJ, 1:182–83, 259–60.

4. Blount to AJ, Mar. 15, 1810; AJ to Blount, Feb. 15, 1810, PAJ, 2:236–40.

5. AJ to Blount, Feb. 15, 1810; AJ to William Eustis, May 10, 1811, PAJ, 2:237–38, 260–61.

6. AJ to Harrison, Nov. 28, 1811, PAJ, 2:270.

7. R. David Edmunds, *Tecumseh and the Quest for Indian Leadership* (New York, 1984).

8. Blount to AJ, Dec. 28, 1809, PAJ, 2:226–27. Jackson's response to this letter is lost.

9. AJ to Blount, June 17, 1812, PAJ, 2:305.

10. AJ to Blount, Nov. 11, 1812, PAJ, 2:336–37.

11. AJ to Campbell, Nov. 29, 1812, PAJ, 2:343–44.

12. AJ to the Tennessee Volunteers, Nov. 14 and Nov. 24, 1812, PAJ, 2:340–43.

13. Eaton, 19–23; Parton, 1:381–82.

14. Parton, 1:361–64.

15. Benton to AJ, June 15, 1813, PAJ, 2:406.

16. Benton to AJ, July 9, 1813; AJ's Memorandum, July 13, 1813; AJ to Felix Grundy, July 15, 1813, PAJ, 2:409–11.

17. Parton, 1:386–87; James, 151–52; Charles Nisbet Chambers, *Old Bullion Benton: Senator from the New West* (Boston, 1956); PAJ, 2:408.

18. AJ to Benton, July 19, 1813, PAJ, 2:413.

19. Benton to AJ, July 25, 1813, PAJ, 2:413–15.

20. AJ to Benton, Aug. 4, 1813, PAJ, 2:418–19.

21. "Thomas Hart Benton to the Public," Sept. 10, 1813, PAJ, 2:425–27. Parton's telling of this episode (1:390–97) is replete with extensive unattributed quotations, which makes for interesting reading but ultimately sheds little light on Jackson's behavior.

22. Robertson to AJ, Sept. 16, 1813, PAJ, 2:427–28.

23. Eaton, 26–29; AJ to Coffee, Sept. 29, 1813, PAJ, 2:431. For a more detailed account of the Fort Mims attack, see Remini, 1:187–90.

24. "To the Tennessee Volunteers," Sept. 24, 1813, PAJ, 2:428–29.

25. Parton, 1:401. Other pertinent reflections on Indians' combined love of freedom and improvidence or lack of restraint are given in Rogin, *Fathers and Children: Andrew Jackson and the Subjugation of the American Indian* (New York, 1975), chap. 4.

26. The understandings conveyed in the above paragraphs are gleaned from the following classic treatments: Jakle, *Images of the Ohio Valley,* chap. 5; Michael D. Green, *The Politics of Indian Removal: Creek Government and Society in Crisis* (Lincoln, Neb., 1982); Bernard W. Sheehan, *Seeds of Extinction: Jeffersonian Philanthropy and the American Indian* (Chapel

Hill, N.C., 1973), esp. chap. 7; Francis Jennings, *The Invasion of America: Indians, Colonialism, and the Cant of Conquest* (Chapel Hill, N.C., 1975), esp. chap. 9; Edmunds, *Tecumseh*; Samuel Kercheval, *A History of the Valley of Virginia* (Winchester, Va., 1833), esp. 255–58.

27. Kathryn E. Holland Braund, "The Creek Indians, Blacks, and Slavery," *Journal of Southern History* 57 (Nov. 1991): 601–36; Thomas D. Clark and John D. W. Guice, *The Old Southwest, 1795–1830* (Albuquerque, N.M., 1989), chaps. 7–8.

28. James Taylor Carson, *Searching for the Bright Path: The Mississippi Choctaws from Prehistory to Removal* (Lincoln, Neb., 1999), esp. 60–69.

29. Eaton, 30.

30. AJ to Coffee, Oct. 7, 1813; AJ to Pope, Oct. 31, 1813, PAJ, 2:435–36, 443; Pathkiller (Cherokee) to AJ, Oct. 22, 1813, PAJ, 2:439–40.

31. Eaton, 42–44; Crockett, cited in Remini, 1:193; AJ to Rachel, Nov. 4, 1813, PAJ, 2:444; Parton, 1:339–40.

32. Eaton, 47–50; AJ to Maj. Gen. Thomas Pinckney, Dec. 3, 1813, PAJ, 2:465–67.

33. William Martin to AJ, Dec. 4 and 6, 1813, PAJ, 2:467–69, 474–77; AJ to Martin, Dec. 6, 1813, PAJ, 2:470–74.

34. Additionally, Cocke proved an embarrassment to Jackson by destroying a friendly Creek village that Jackson had promised to protect. Cocke was unaware of its friendly status. Parton rationalizes Jackson's enmity toward Cocke, and probably overstates Jackson's concern for the friendly Creeks. See Parton, 1:452–57.

35. Parton, 1:463. Remini's borrowing from Parton's telling is critiqued in the introduction to this book.

36. "To the First Brigade, Tennessee Volunteer Infantry," Dec. 13, 1813, PAJ, 2:482–84; Parton, 1:473.

37. AJ to Rachel, Dec. 9, Dec. 14, and Dec. 29, 1813, PAJ, 2:478, 486–87, 515.

38. For a theoretical basis to the foregoing, see David H. Morgan, "Theater of War: Combat, the Military, and Masculinities," in Harry Brod and Michael Kaufman, eds., *Theorizing Masculinities* (Thousand Oaks, Calif., 1994), 165–82. Group solidarity could bring cohesion to the entire army under Jackson's command, but it could just as easily produce a sense of "us" versus "them" among enlisted men who identify with their comrades but not their superiors. Morgan writes, "The traditional bracketing of the terms *officer and a gentleman* neatly encapsulates the interplay between class and military masculinities." (p. 175)

39. Herbert J. Doherty, Jr., *Richard Keith Call: Southern Unionist* (Gainesville, Fla., 1961), 1–7; Eaton, 80–81; Parton, 1:475.

40. Blount to AJ, Dec. 22, 1813, PAJ, 2:498–99; AJ to Blount, Dec. 26, 1813, PAJ, 2:504–6; Eaton, 85–90.

41. Eaton, 105–8.

42. Rachel to AJ, PAJ, Feb. 10, 1814, 3:28–29; AJ to Rachel, Feb. 21, 1814, PAJ, 3:34–35.

43. Parton, 1:504–12; Sumner, *Andrew Jackson*, 38–39; Bassett cited in Lewis, *The American Union and the Problem of Neighborhood*, 50; Eaton, 119.

44. Parton, 1:499–500; *The Autobiography of Sam Houston*, ed. Donald Day and Harry Herbert Ullom (Norman, Okla., 1954), 3–7; William Carey Crane, *Life and Select Literary Remains of Sam Houston, of Texas* (Philadelphia, 1885), chap. 3.

45. Thomas Kanon, "'A Slow, Laborious Slaughter': The Battle of Horseshoe Bend," THQ 58 (1999): 2–15; Parton, 1:512–20.

46. *Autobiography of Sam Houston*, 12–15; Parton, 1:521; Houston to Capt. Alexander Campbell, Apr. 25, 1815, *Sam Houston Papers*, Center for American History, University of Texas, Austin.

47. Eaton, 124–30; Kanon, "'A Slow, Laborious Slaughter."

48. Parton, 1:549–60; Remini, 1:222–32; Curtis, 55–56; Rogin, *Fathers and Children*, 156–59. The heavily psychological Rogin is most critical of Jackson's imposition of law upon the Creeks: "Jackson claimed power to destroy the Indians but not to protect them. . . . Jackson emphasized discipline and law. But his was not a law which limited and structured desire, providing ideals to hold the self responsible. Rather his ego merged with a primitive law, sanctifying primitive aggression."

49. Kanon, " 'A Slow, Laborious, Slaughter,' " 11–12.

50. Clark and Guice, *The Old Southwest, 1795–1830*, chap. 3.

51. Claiborne to AJ, Aug. 12, 1814, PAJ, 3:115–16; Eaton, 215–17.

52. Eaton, 219–20. From Nashville, on October 14, 1814, Carroll wrote Jackson with pride that the appointment was official: "I have the honor to inform you that I have been elected your successor as Major General of the second division of the militia of Tennessee." (PAJ, 3:161) The easily threatened Jackson must have felt particular confidence in the loyalty of Carroll to allow him to march in his own ambitious footsteps.

53. See, for example, William Drayton to Congressman Churchill C. Cambreleng, Apr. 6, 1838, letter in the *Papers of Edward Livingston*, PUL. "I could, with great pleasure," writes Drayton, "bear testimony to the vigor of Mr. Livingston's intellect, to the depth & variety of his researches, the extent of his acquirements, the exuberance of his benevolence, the unaffectedness of his manners . . . and the charm of his conversation, alternatively instructive with information, brilliant with wit, & sparkling with repartee."

54. Fragment of a journal, dated Sunday, Jan. 8, 1804, in *Edward Livingston Papers*, PUL.

55. *Correspondence between Aaron Burr and His Daughter Theodosia*, 211.

56. Wilkinson to Livingston, July 23, 1804, marked "Confidential," in *Edward Livingston Papers*, PUL.

57. Draft of Edward Livingston's Address to the Public, Dec. 26, 1806, in *Edward Livingston Papers*, PUL.

58. The only substantial biography of Livingston is the uncritical, but thoroughly researched, William B. Hatcher, *Edward Livingston: Jeffersonian Republican and Jacksonian Democrat* (University, La., 1940); see also, Parton 1:222–24, 2:18–21, 28–32. Livingston and Jefferson reconciled in 1824. See Livingston to Jefferson, Mar. 25, 1824; James Monroe to Jefferson, Mar. 27, 1824; Jefferson to Livingston, Apr. 4, 1824, all in Thomas Jefferson Papers, LC.

59. Parton, 1:614–15, 2:21–22; Alexander Walker, *Jackson and New Orleans* (New York, 1856), 13, 17–18. The ultimate effect on the larger public of Livingston's embellishment of Jackson's words remains uncertain. Walker is a credible historical investigator, excellent on details, yet his idolization of Jackson is unabashed. Remini (1:249) somewhat loosely and too effusively relates the people's reception of Jackson's first address in New Orleans and Livingston's French translation: "They were impressed by the heroic stance of his commanding presence; they felt new confidence that this man would indeed save the city. . . . A sigh of gratification seemed to pour out of the crowd and wrap Jackson in a brief embrace." Parton also draws liberally on Walker's text.

60. Walker, *Jackson and New Orleans*, 17.

61. Thomas L. Butler to New Orleans Citizens and Soldiers, Dec. 15, 1814, PAJ, 3:204; Matthew Warshauer, "The Battle of New Orleans Reconsidered: Andrew Jackson and Martial Law," *Louisiana History* 39 (1998): 266.

62. James, 230; Warshauer, "The Battle of New Orleans Reconsidered," 266–68. Monroe had been acting secretary of war for a period of time in 1812–13, in addition to serving as secretary of state in the Madison administration. He had a strong influence on the president regarding war strategy.

63. Parton, 2:62–65.

64. Walker, *Jackson and New Orleans*, 150–51; James, 198–99, 206–17; Eaton, 256–57; Livingston to AJ, Dec. 25, 1814, PAJ, 3:220–21.

65. Walker, *Jackson and New Orleans*, 164–209; James, 218–26; Remini, 1:263–66. The report on Coffee's Tennesseans is consistent with the journal kept by a British soldier on the Ohio-Erie front, who noted of the western Americans he encountered that they "are nearly Indians, they use the Scalping knife and Tomahawk, and are merely a civilized Savage." See Donald E. Graves, ed., *Merry Hearts Make Light Days: The War of 1812 Journal of Lieutenant John Le Couteur, 104th Foot* (Ottawa, Canada, 1993), 146.

66. Parton, 2:110–11; Walker, *Jackson and New Orleans*, 297–304; Eaton, 306–7; Robert Butler to Robert Hays, Dec. 30, 1814, AJ Papers, LC, microfilm reel #71. Butler was the twenty-eight-year-old nephew of Jackson's friend, the late Thomas Butler, also the son-in-law of Rachel Jackson's brother-in-law Col. Robert Hays. He served with Jackson until Jackson's retirement from the army in 1821.

67. Parton, 2:102; General Orders, Jan. 1, 1815, AJ Papers, LC, microfilm reel #71; AJ to Monroe, Jan. 3, 1815, PAJ, 3:228–29.

68. Walker, *Jackson and New Orleans*, 156, 307–15.

69. Walker, *Jackson and New Orleans*, 321–33; Eaton, 312–23.

70. Walker, *Jackson and New Orleans*, 337–44; Parton, 2:213–17.

71. Remini, 1:285; Parton, 2:259–60.

72. C. Edward Skeen, *Citizen Soldiers in the War of 1812* (Lexington, Ky., 1999), 168–72; Clark and Guice, *The Old Southwest, 1795–1830*, 156–58; Eaton, 388–89; Remini, 1:273, 282–83; James, 248; Ward, 19–27. Ward's investigation of the legend of the riflemen's accuracy yields the most persuasive results; the actual descriptions of the enemy's casualties shows that cannon fire hurt the British more than individual marksmanship.

73. Eaton, 339; Jackson wrote Secretary of War James Monroe (concurrently secretary of state) on Jan. 19, 1815, of his concern that in spite of the "prodigious loss" on January 8, the enemy might "renew his efforts" at a later date, and thus there would be no "relaxation in the measures for resistance" (PAJ, 3:250–51).

74. Parton, 2:301–6.

75. Warshauer, "The Battle of New Orleans Reconsidered," 272–80; AJ to Claiborne, Jan. 18, 1815, PAJ, 3:248–49. In his private journal, Jackson wrote that Claiborne was "much better qualified for great pomp & show, and courting popularity in quiet life in civil walks— than military achievements amidst peril and danger."

76. Calendar, PAJ, 3:525; AJ to Thomas Beale, Mar. 6, 1815, PAJ, 3:301; Steven Watts, *The Republic Reborn: War and the Making of Liberal America, 1790–1820* (Baltimore, 1987), 283–89, quote at 285. Watts highlights several other religiously inspired pamphlets, as well as Presbyterian Alexander McLeod's *A Scriptural View of the Character, Causes, and Ends of the Present War*, presciently issued in January 1815, just before word of the Battle of New Orleans reached the public.

77. Monroe to AJ, Feb. 5, 1815, PAJ, 3:271; *Niles' Weekly Register*, Feb. 18, 1815.

78. "Song," by John M'Creery (of Petersburg, Virginia), composed on July 4, 1815, published in *Niles' Weekly Register*, Supplement to Vol. 9, Feb. 24, 1816.

Chapter Five. Political Instincts

1. David Young, *The Citizens' and Farmers' Almanac, For the Year of Our Lord 1826* (Morristown, N.J., 1825), n.p.

2. Parton, 2:323–24. The description of the pair dancing was provided by a member of the

committee of arrangements for that evening's ball, Vincent Nolte, whom Parton regarded as a reliable source.

3. Rachel Jackson to Hays, Mar. 5, 1815, PAJ, 3:297.

4. Parton, 2:308–20; Eaton, 353–69; PAJ, 3:321–36, 340–43, documenting Jackson's justification for maintaining martial law. Remini's recapitulation (1:315) is overtly sympathetic, stating that Jackson's courtroom performance demonstrated his dignity and reserve: "Jackson had style," he concludes, admiringly. "Always did have." This comes after the biographer's blanket declaration, at the conclusion of the chapter on the Battle of New Orleans: "Small wonder that Jackson's place in the pride and affection of the American people lasted until his death—and beyond. Small wonder that his popularity exceeded that of Washington, Jefferson, or Franklin." (1:295)

5. Parton, 2:327–28; James G. Barber, *Andrew Jackson: A Portrait Study* (Seattle, 1991), 36.

6. AJ to John Reid, May 11, 1815, AJ Papers, LC, microfilm reel #71; AJ to Livingston, May 17, 1815, PAJ, 3:357.

7. AJ to Livingston, July 5, 1815, PAJ, 3:370–71; Livingston to AJ, Sept. 15, 1815, AJ Papers, LC, microfilm reel #71. In a letter to Philadelphia publisher Mathew Carey (Aug. 28, 1815, PAJ, 3:379–80), Jackson conventionally declared the book to have been solicited by "the best Patriots of our country."

8. Rachel to AJ, Apr. 7, 1814, PAJ, 3:59.

9. Stokely to AJ, Feb. 13, 1815, PAJ, 3:277–78.

10. William C. Cook, "The Early Iconography of the Battle of New Orleans, 1815–1819," THQ 48 (1989): 218–37.

11. On Nov. 4, 1815, Jefferson wrote his daughter Martha from Poplar Forest: "I was most agreeably surprised to find that the party whom I thought to be merely curious visitants were General Jackson and his suite, who passing to Lynchburg did me the favor to call." Edwin Morris Betts and James Adam Bear, Jr., *The Family Letters of Thomas Jefferson* (Columbia, Mo., 1966), 411–12; *Niles' Weekly Register*, Nov. 25, 1815; John Reid to Elizabeth Reid, Nov. 18, 1815, PAJ, 3:391–92.

12. Parton, 2:351–52, citing Burr's letter to Alston of Nov. 20, 1815; on Monroe's qualities see especially Harry Ammon, *James Monroe: The Quest for National Identity* (New York, 1971).

13. Ward, 181–86; Barber, *Andrew Jackson: A Portrait Study*, 36–41; the miniature given to Livingston, painted by Jean François de Vallée, a French painter living in New Orleans, very much resembles Napoleon.

14. AJ to Robertson, Jan. 11, 1798, PAJ, 1:165; AJ to Livingston, May 17, 1815, PAJ, 3:357.

15. AJ to Butler, Dec. 31, 1815, PAJ, 3:397.

16. Burstein, *Sentimental Democracy*, 237–40; Harry L. Coles, *The War of 1812* (Chicago, 1965); J. C. A. Stagg, *Mr. Madison's War: Politics, Diplomacy and Welfare in the Early American Republic* (Princeton, 1982); Lewis, *The American Union and the Problem of Neighborhood*, 55; Watts, *The Republic Reborn*.

17. The definitive work on this subject is John Lauritz Larson, *Internal Improvement: National Public Works and the Promise of Popular Government in the Early United States* (Chapel Hill, N.C., 2001).

18. Lewis, *The American Union and the Problem of Neighborhood*, 76–94; AJ to Livingston, Oct. 24, 1816, PAJ, 4:71.

19. AJ to Coffee, Sept. 19, 1816, PAJ, 4:63–64.

20. AJ to Monroe, May 12, 1816, PAJ, 4:28–30.

21. AJ to Donelson, Feb. 24, 1817, PAJ, 4:91–92.

22. AJ to Monroe, Mar. 4, 1817, PAJ, 4:93–98.

23. AJ to Rachel, May 29, 1817; to Butler, Dec. 6, 1817; to Monroe, Dec. 20, 1817, PAJ, 4:117, 158, 162.

24. AJ to Butler, Dec. 6, 1817, PAJ, 4:158–59; on Crawford, see Chase C. Mooney, *William H. Crawford, 1772–1834* (Lexington, Ky., 1974), and Ammon, *James Monroe*, 360.

25. AJ to Scott, Dec. 3, 1817; to Butler, Dec. 6, 1817, PAJ, 4:156–59.

26. Calhoun to AJ, Dec. 26, 1817, PAJ, 4:163; AJ to Monroe, Jan. 6, 1818, PAJ, 4:166–67.

27. Parton, 2:463–86; Remini, 1:351–59; AJ to Calhoun, May 5, 1818; to Rachel, June 2, 1818, PAJ, 4:197–99, 212.

28. Lynn Hudson Parsons, *John Quincy Adams* (Madison, Wisc., 1998), 138–44.

29. Lewis, *The American Union and the Problem of Neighborhood*, 121–24; Remini, 1:367–68. In suggesting that Jackson might want incriminating letters altered, the president hinted: "Your letters to the dept. were written in haste, under the pressure of fatigue & infirmity. . . ." See Monroe to AJ, July 19, 1818, PAJ, 4:224–28. The details underlying the Spanish problem and Monroe's insecure position are given in Ammon, *James Monroe*, chaps. 23–24.

30. Parton, 2:382.

31. Sarah Harvey Porter, *The Life and Times of Anne Royall* (New York, 1972 [1909]), 50; Parton, 2:644.

32. House debate of Jan. 20–21, 1819, in *Annals of Congress*, 15th Congress, 2nd Session (Washington, D.C., 1855), 631–54. Margaret Bayard Smith, *The First Forty Years of Washington Society*, ed. Gaillard Hunt (New York, 1906), 145.

33. *Annals of Congress*, 15th Congress, 2nd Session, 654–58; Smith, *The First Forty Years of Washington Society*, 146; Merrill D. Peterson, *The Great Triumvirate: Webster, Clay and Calhoun* (New York, 1987), 56; *National Intelligencer*, Jan. 26 and 29, 1819. The Washington-based newspaper branded other papers for "fomenting into hostility of feeling" toward Jackson. In a similar spirit to Johnson of Kentucky, Representative John Holmes of Massachusetts said he understood what had prompted Jackson: "having crossed into Florida, for the purpose of meeting and fighting the Seminoles, what are his duties toward those who profess an allegiance to Spain?" Jackson had come upon Spanish who "were identified with the Indians . . . , [who] have conducted most treacherously, pretending to neutrality." The "right of discrimination," he said, had devolved upon the general. After Maine became a state in 1820, separating from Massachusetts, Holmes entered the U.S. Senate from Maine.

34. A Citizen of Tennessee [John Overton], *A Vindication of the Measures of the President and His Commanding Generals, in the Commencement & Termination of the Seminole War* (Nashville, 1819), esp. 42–43, 90–91. The principal international law cited is that of the Swiss-born Emmerich von Vattel (1714–1767).

35. Francis Walker Gilmer, *Sketches, Essays and Translations* (Baltimore, 1828), 41. The work was published posthumously, based on the author's writings not long after the War of 1812.

36. Smith, *The First Forty Years of Washington Society*, 285–86.

37. Parton, 2:572–73. Overton's address, as published in the *Nashville Whig* in April 1819; Monroe to Jefferson, Feb. 8, 1819, Thomas Jefferson Papers, LC.

38. Doherty, *Richard Keith Call*, 12–15.

39. Rachel to William Davenport (a Pennsylvanian and army officer who had earlier visited Nashville), Mar. 18, 1819, PAJ, 4:277; AJ to Donelson, May 17, 1819, and Sept. 17, 1819, PAJ, 4:299, 322; AJ to George Gibson, Sept. 7, 1819, PAJ, 4:318.

40. Parton, 2:643ff.

41. Barber, *Andrew Jackson: A Portrait Study*, 51–69.

42. Following up on the accounts of his frequent ailments during 1819, Jackson wrote again on his fifty-third birthday: "This is my birth day, but I am so aflicted with pains, that I have

some doubts whether I ought or ought not to rejoice, that I was born." AJ to George Gibson, Mar. 15, 1820, PAJ, 4:363.

43. AJ to James Gadsden, Aug. 1, 1819, PAJ, 4:307–11.

44. Not everyone was impressed with Eaton's literary accomplishment. Thomas Jefferson wrote John Adams that he had read the book with "great pleasure," but that "Reid's part is well written; Eaton's continuation is better for it's matter than style. The whole however is valuable." See Jefferson to Adams, Sept. 8, 1817, in *The Adams-Jefferson Letters*, ed. Lester J. Cappon (Chapel Hill, N.C., 1959), 520.

45. AJ to Call, Sept. 9, 1819, PAJ, 4:319–20. For a useful evaluation of the conduct of seconds, and the particular role of lawyers in nineteenth-century duels, see Douglas H. Yarn, "The Attorney as Duelist's Friend: Lessons from the Code Duello," *Case Western Reserve Law Review* 5 (Fall 2000): 69–113.

46. AJ to Monroe, Sept. 20, 1819, PAJ, 4:329–33.

47. M. K. Wisehart, *Sam Houston: American Giant* (Washington, 1962); Donald Day and Harry Herbert Ullom, eds., *The Autobiography of Sam Houston* (Norman, Okla., 1954), 18–22.

48. AJ to Coffee, Feb. 2, 1816, *Papers of John Coffee*, Dyas Collection, TSLA; also PAJ 4:6–8; AJ to Coffee, Feb 13, 1816, PAJ, 4:11. The unrelated James Jackson referred to in the Feb. 2 letter was Andrew Jackson's trusted friend, who loaned him large sums of money, and they invested together in land speculation in Tennessee and Alabama. James Jackson eventually moved to Florence, Alabama. See PAJ 2:22n, 354, and AJ to Coffee, Jan. 14, 1818, PAJ, 4:169–70. Jackson's prior relationship with Dr. Bedford is sketchy, though Bedford left a detailed journal of a voyage he took down the Mississippi River to New Orleans in the wake of Aaron Burr's flatboat adventure, in early 1807. The journal is held by TSLA.

49. Remini, 2:42–47; Ratner, *Andrew Jackson and His Tennessee Lieutenants*, 68; Goodstein, *Nashville, 1780–1860*, 41–42; AJ to John Coffee, Aug. 26, 1821, Bassett, 3:116. This letter, written from Pensacola, laments Carroll's election. Some of Carroll's political opponents felt that he lacked the personal wealth and social standing to represent Tennessee with appropriate dignity. Within two years of his election, however, he was honored when Carrollville and Carroll County, Tennessee, were named after him.

50. In 1822, Governor Carroll presented Jackson with a ceremonial sword in testimony of the state's gratitude for his military services. See *Niles' Register*, Aug. 3, 1822. The curious letter from Carroll to Clay is Oct. 1, 1823, in *Papers of Henry Clay*, ed. James F. Hopkins (Lexington, Ky., 1959), 3:492.

51. Wirt to Francis Walker Gilmer, Jan. 29, 1821, in *Gilmer Papers*, Manuscripts Division, University of Virginia Library.

52. AJ to the Officers and Soldiers Composing the Division of the South, May 31, 1821, PAJ, 5:75–76.

53. AJ to Monroe, Oct. 5, 1821, PAJ, 5:110–11. Though Jackson professed his intention to return at some point, this was his first step toward officially resigning the post.

54. "I remember nothing in early boyhood which gave much promise of future good or usefulness," Call wrote in a journal of later years, sounding much like Jackson's testimony concerning his own lack of social advantage. See Doherty, *Richard Keith Call*, 3.

55. AJ to Call, Nov. 15, 1821, PAJ, 5:114–15; Doherty, *Richard Keith Call*, 24–25; AJ to James C. Bronaugh, June 9, 1821, PAJ, 5:52–53. Jackson's former army surgeon, Bronaugh had become an unofficial adviser and trusted courier to Washington, who, like Call, established himself in Florida after Jackson's governorship there. He died of a fever that spread through Florida in 1822.

56. AJ to Call, Nov. 15, 1821, PAJ, 5:114–15.

57. Parton, 2:613–39; AJ to Secretary of State J. Q. Adams, Aug. 26, 1821, Bassett, 3:112–16; Rachel to John Donelson, Aug. 25, 1821, PAJ, 5:99.

58. "Friend" to AJ, Oct. 29, 1821, PAJ, 5:112–14.

59. AJ to James C. Bronaugh, Jan. 10, 1822, PAJ, 5:134.

60. Senator Eaton made this plain enough to Jackson at the end of 1822, when he wrote, none too subtly, of Monroe as "an old father" surrounded by sons who were seeking to inherit. Crawford and Monroe now got along poorly; Calhoun, of a "sanguine temper," maintained "pretensions"; but "Jno. Q. from the favours bestowed by the old man in his life time, has been deemed a favourite always." Eaton to AJ, Dec. 3, 1822, Bassett 3:179.

61. AJ to Bronough, Jan. 10, 1822, PAJ, 5:136, saying "I have confidence in the candeur of Mr Calhoun"; to James Gadsden, on Dec. 6, 1821, Jackson noted his preference for Calhoun over Adams, while praising Adams's "virtue, and integrity" and "first rate mind," and putting in his P.S.: "as to Wm H Crawford you know my opinion I would support the Devil first," PAJ, 5:120–21; AJ to Gibson, Jan. 29, 1822, PAJ, 5:139.

62. AJ to Coffee, Aug. 22, 1823, Bassett, 3:204.

63. Remini, 2:51–53, 56–57; James, 376–78. Jackson, Eaton, and Lewis had expressed support for the senatorial candidacy of John Rhea, but when it became apparent that Rhea could not muster the votes to defeat Williams, Jackson's name was substituted.

64. Peterson, *The Great Triumvirate,* 116–24.

65. Doherty, *Richard Keith Call,* 28.

66. John Somerville to AJ, Feb. 4, 1822; AJ to Jefferson, Feb. 6, 1822, PAJ, 5:142–44.

67. McNairy to AJ, Sept. 3, 1823, Bassett, 3:205–6; AJ to McNairy, Sept. 6, 1823, PAJ, 5:292–94.

68. Eaton to Rachel, Dec. 18, 1823, PAJ, 5:327–28.

69. AJ to Rachel, Mar. 16, 1824, PAJ, 5:375–76.

70. AJ to Livingston, Mar. 24, 1823, PAJ, 5:264–65; Calhoun to AJ, Mar. 30, 1823, PAJ, 5:266.

71. Houston to AJ, Aug. 3, 1822, PAJ, 5:211; as "Virginian," see *National Intelligencer,* Mar. 19, 1824; [Eaton], *The Letters of Wyoming, to the People of the United States, on the Presidential Election, and in Favor of Andrew Jackson* (Philadelphia, 1824); Ward, 44, 68–69; Robert P. Hay, "The Case for Andrew Jackson in 1824: Eaton's *Wyoming Letters,*" THQ 11 (1970): 139–51.

72. AJ to Rachel, Jan. 10 and Jan. 15, 1824, Bassett, 3:222–23; AJ to Kremer, May 6, 1824, PAJ, 5:402–3. Jackson's letters were reprinted in such papers as the Philadelphia *Columbian Observer* and Washington's *National Intelligencer.*

73. Calhoun to AJ, Mar. 30, 1823, PAJ, 5:266.

74. AJ to Lewis, May 7, 1824, PAJ, 5:404. Jackson was referring to the tariff bill then under discussion, in which he voted, as a nationalist, in favor of protectionism. It meant that he voted along with the manufacturing interests, rather than support the cotton producers of his own section. His pro-creditor, antibank perspective did not particularly hurt his chances, as economic recovery was under way. See AJ to L. H. Coleman, Apr. 26, 1824, Bassett 3:249–51. Similarly, he wrote to his wife on Apr. 12: "I regret to see no national feeling in the majority of congress. every one appears solely to be ingrossed with the interest alone of his own section of Country." Ibid., 247. A fragment in Jackson's hand, written either with respect to the election of 1824 or 1828, clarifies his position on the tariff: "one fourth of the amount of all the cotton raised in our country is consumed by the american manufacturers, creating a safe, sane, and permanent home market for the raw material." Ibid., 387.

75. Peterson, *The Great Triumvirate,* chap. 3; Burstein, *America's Jubilee,* chap. 9. For a good

overall treatment of the political environment, see George Dangerfield, *The Awakening of American Nationalism, 1815–1828* (New York, 1965).

76. Jesse Benton, "To All Candid and Reflecting Men," Sept. 1824, in AJ Papers, LC, microfilm reel #33.

77. Carroll to Donelson, Oct. 4, 1824, AJ Papers, LC, microfilm reel #33.

78. Henry A. Wise, *Seven Decades of the Union* (Philadelphia, 1872), 80; definition of lantern-jawed, or "lanthorn-jawed," from Francis Grose, *Lexicon Balatronicum. A Dictionary of Buckish Slang, University Wit, and Pickpocket Eloquence* (London, 1811 [Northfield, Ill., 1971]), n.p.

79. AJ to Coffee, Jan. 6, 1825, Bassett 3:273.

80. AJ to Lewis, Feb. 7 and Feb. 14, 1825, Bassett 3:275–76. To Richard K. Call, Jackson suggested that Clay had sold out to official Washington, in effect abandoning all allegiance to the western mind: "He will, as I believe, never return to Kentucky." AJ to Call, July 24, 1825, Call Family Papers, Florida State Archives.

81. Parton 3:68–70.

82. See Jeffrey L. Pasley, *"The Tyranny of Printers": Newspaper Politics in the Early American Republic* (Charlottesville, Va., 2001).

Chapter Six. The Avenging President

1. "Recollections of the Hermitage in 1828," unpublished manuscript of William R. Galt (1818–1892), in the Virginia Historical Society, Richmond.

2. Wise, *Seven Decades of the Union*, 80–81, 98–103. The theological argument concerned the validity of the teachings of Emmanuel Swedenborg (1688–1772). Jackson was curious about the concept of a mystical union among all people.

3. *Reminiscences of James A. Hamilton* (New York, 1869), 67–68.

4. Polk to AJ, Apr. 3, 1826, *Correspondence of James K. Polk,* ed. Herbert Weaver (Nashville, 1969), 1:38–39; AJ to Polk, May 3, 1826, ibid., 41–43.

5. Eastin Morris, *The Tennessee Gazetteer* (Nashville, 1834), lxxiv; advertisements from the *Nashville Republican* and *Nashville Whig,* 1826–27.

6. F. Garvin Davenport, *Cultural Life in Nashville on the Eve of the Civil War* (Chapel Hill, N.C., 1941), 3–11; Philip Lindsley, *An Address, Delivered in Nashville, January 12, 1825, at the Inauguration of the President of Cumberland College* (Nashville, 1825), 37, 40; Wisehart, *Sam Houston,* 31–32; AJ to Call, Sept. 30, 1826, Call Family Papers, Florida State Archives.

7. Crawford's infirmity made his candidacy impossible after 1824. On the state of political alignments after the election of 1824, see Andrew Burstein, *America's Jubilee.*

8. Charles Francis Adams, ed., *Memoirs of John Quincy Adams* (Freeport, N.Y., 1969), 7:345–46. "My own career is closed," he wrote a year and a half before the election of 1828. "My duties are to prepare for the end, with a grateful heart and unwavering mind."

9. "Address to the People of the Congressional District," Mar. 26, 1825, *The Papers of Henry Clay,* ed. James F. Hopkins (Lexington, Ky., 1959–92), 4:152–56. Other pertinent correspondence around this time includes Clay to Francis T. Brooke, Jan. 28 and Feb. 18, 1825; Clay to Francis P. Blair, Jan. 29, 1825, in ibid., 45–47, 73–74. For a sample of the Jackson camp's retort, see [Francis Baylies], *The Contrast; or, Military Chieftains and Political Chieftains* (Albany, N.Y., 1828).

10. *Liberty Hall & Cincinnati Gazette,* Aug. 1, 1826; [Charles Hammond], *View of General Jackson's Domestic Relations, in Reference to His Fitness for the Presidency* (Cincinnati, 1828), esp. 11–12, 18.

11. Catherine Allgor, *Parlor Politics: In Which the Ladies of Washington Help Build a City and a Government* (Charlottesville, Va., 2000), 172. The author of the quip on the Crawfords was Congressman Louis McLane of Delaware, a future Jackson cabinet appointee, writing to his wife.

12. Livingston to AJ, Mar. 7, 1828, in Hatcher, *Edward Livingston,* 317; [Harrisburg] *Pennsylvania Reporter,* Sept. 27, 1828, in *Edward Livingston Papers,* PUL; *Nashville Republican,* Nov. 24, 1828.

13. See especially Matthew Warshauer, "Andrew Jackson as a 'Military Chieftain' in the 1824 and 1828 Presidential Elections: The Ramifications of Martial Law on American Republicanism," THQ 57 (1998): 4–23.

14. Hayne to AJ, June 5, 1827, Bassett, 3:357–60; Houston to AJ, Jan. 5, 1827; Burstein, *Sentimental Democracy,* 315–16. This campaign strategy was later confirmed by John Eaton, writing: "I rejoice, that your firmness has borne you up, to leave all things in the hands of your friends, apart from any exercised feeling of your own." Eaton to AJ, Aug. 21, 1828, Bassett, 3:428.

15. Bassett, 3:455–62; Barber, *Andrew Jackson: A Portrait Study,* 153–54; James, center illustration.

16. Barber, *Andrew Jackson: A Portrait Study,* 162–63. The quote from *Richard III* is Act V, Scene 3, 216–17, and refers to the king's prior night's dream.

17. AJ to Branch, June 24, 1828, AJ Papers, LC, microfilm reel #35.

18. List of Jackson's library furnished by the Hermitage. It is always possible that he owned Shakespeare at an earlier date and that it was consumed by fire or otherwise destroyed. Theater ads from the author's survey of Nashville newspapers of the 1820s.

19. Parton, 3:147. The close Jackson confidant who had previously been Burr's loyal retainer was Samuel Swartwout, of New York. Swartwout had unsuccessfully eluded General Wilkinson in 1806, was arrested, and testified on Burr's behalf during the Richmond trial. It was at this time that he met Jackson. From their shared hatred of Wilkinson grew a close association, and in the mid-1820s Swartwout actively advanced Jackson in New York. See esp. B. R. Brunson, *The Adventures of Samuel Swartwout in the Age of Jefferson and Jackson* (Lewiston, N.Y., 1989).

20. AJ to Coffee, Dec. 11, 1828, Bassett, 3:452.

21. Rachel to AJ, Mar. 11, 1814, PAJ, 3:44.

22. *Reminiscences of James A. Hamilton,* 70.

23. AJ to Call, Dec. 22, 1828, unpublished letter owned by the Hermitage Association, Nashville. There is evidence in letters that Rachel, as much as her husband, treated Call like a son. On October 3, 1820, for instance, she expressed disappointment in not seeing Call before he set out from the Hermitage, noting: "I had maney things to say which I cann[ot] with this pen. Suffice it to say peace be with [you] going out and coming in is the of [sic] your friend." Letter in possession of the Virginia Historical Society, Richmond.

24. Wise, *Seven Decades of the Union,* 114–16; *United States Telegraph,* Jan. 12 and 18, 1829. The *Telegraph,* a Washington, D.C., pro-Jackson paper, was black-bordered, in mourning, on January 7, as the first intelligence of Rachel's death was received. Of the president-elect, it said, "He survives, and lives for his country."

25. Overton to Coffee, Apr. 11, 1829, *John Coffee Papers,* Dyas Collection, TSLA; *Reminiscences of James A. Hamilton,* 90.

26. Margaret Bayard Smith, *The First Forty Years of Washington Society,* ed. Gaillard Hunt (New York, 1906), 290–96; *United States Telegraph,* Mar. 5, 1829.

27. Jackson told James A. Hamilton that Eaton was the first or second cabinet appointment that he decided, "because he felt it was necessary for him to have in his Cabinet one old friend

upon whom he could always rely, and who well knew him." *Reminiscences of James A. Hamilton,* 89–90. Hugh Lawson White, a former Tennessee Supreme Court justice who had succeeded Jackson in the Senate in 1825, was also under consideration for the post. To some historians, Eaton's desire for the job, once known to the scrupulous White (who was highly competent and less emotionally bound to Jackson), led him to yield to Eaton. See Remini 2:161, 163; Lorman A. Ratner, *Andrew Jackson and His Tennessee Lieutenants* (Westport, Conn., 1997), 75–76. Jackson attested that Eaton had to be persuaded to accept the position, and did so "with great reluctance." See AJ to White, Apr. 9, 1831, Bassett, 4:258–59. Others weighed in as to their opposition to Eaton's appointment in 1829, in particular Virginians who were dismayed that for the first time there were no Virginians in the cabinet.

28. The most comprehensive treatment of the Eaton affair, in every particular, is John F. Marszalek, *The Petticoat Affair: Manners, Mutiny, and Sex in Andrew Jackson's White House* (New York, 1997). The conditions surrounding John Timberlake's death at sea are given on pp. 42–44. A glimpse of the rumors swirling about Washington as to Timberlake's circumstances and the widow's behavior appears in a letter from John Davis, a Massachusetts congressman, to his wife Elvira Davis, Dec. 11, 1829, *John Davis Papers,* American Antiquarian Society. The congressman calls Timberlake "an amorous swain" who was "deeply involved in debt" at the time he "procured the appointment [as navy purser] to extricate himself." Davis understood that Timberlake owed his job to the efforts of John Eaton, who Timberlake left behind as his wife's "protector."

29. John Niven, *John C. Calhoun and the Price of Union* (Baton Rouge, 1988), 167–68. For a recent interpretation of women's influence during the Eaton Affair, see Allgor, *Parlor Politics,* chap. 5.

30. Smith, *The First Forty Years of Washington Society,* 318.

31. *The Autobiography of Peggy Eaton* (New York, 1932), 14, 20–24.

32. Ibid., 35, 38, 48, 64–69, 147. "Whatever were his faults," she remarked of Jackson, years after his death, "his bitterest opponents never charged him with meanness. Where he trusted, he trusted; but let the world point to a bad man or woman he ever did trust." All he demanded of friends was that "he must have perfect confidence in them. He never had any half confidences."

33. Ibid., 67–73.

34. Henry Mackenzie, *The Man of Feeling* (London, 1793), quote at 81. The novel was first published in 1770, and was often reprinted in America well into the nineteenth century. It is in the context of such sentimental angst, of the female purpose to die with a virtuous name, that Rachel Jackson's tomb inscription tells the story of her bout with slander and proclaims her unsullied virtue: "A being so gentle and so virtuous, slander might wound but could not dishonor."

35. Doherty, *Richard Keith Call,* 30–34. Jackson revisited the incident in a memorandum of Sept. 1829, citing Call's "rudeness" to Mrs. Timberlake; see AJ to William B. Lewis, Sept. 10, 1829, Bassett, 4:72–73.

36. AJ to Call, Nov. 15, 1821, PAJ, 5:114–16; J. M. Glapell to AJ, Aug. 1, 1824, AJ Papers, LC, microfilm reel #33; Doherty, *Richard Keith Call,* 46. In 1821, Mary Kirkman (Call) expressed hope that her mother would "in a few years understand [Richard's] character better and at least allow him as much merit as he deserves." Mary Kirkman to Mrs. Kirkman, Nov. 7, 1821, Call Family Papers, Florida State Archives. Call's relationship with his mother-in-law finally became genial after Mary's death in 1836, when the Call children came to live with their grandmother. Dougherty, *Richard Keith Call,* 99.

37. AJ to Ely, Mar. 23, 1829, in Parton, 3:188.

38. Hatcher, *Edward Livingston,* 336–37; Parton, 3:188–89; Miscellaneous Diary of

Nashville events, Murdock Collection, TSLA. In another letter to Ely a few weeks later, Jackson repeated the Masonic injunction: Eaton, he assured, would never have betrayed the trust placed in him by his friend John Timberlake, who was overseas, by acting to "burst the bonds of masonry." The Masons were under fire from the newly formed anti-Masonic party, supported by ex-President Adams, which believed the Masons an antidemocratic society. Strongest in the Northeast, they would run a candidate, ex–Attorney General William Wirt, against Jackson in the election of 1832.

39. Call to AJ, Apr. 28, 1829, Bassett, 4:28–29; AJ to Call, July 5, 1829, Bassett, 4:50–53. According to his diary, John Quincy Adams believed that John Eaton had "lived very openly with" Margaret Timberlake "during the life of her former husband." He characterizes Jackson as "having, with all the violence of his temper, taken up the cause of Eaton and his wife as his own." See *Memoirs of John Quincy Adams*, 8:356.

40. Eaton to Emily Donelson, Apr. 8, 1829; A. J. Donelson to AJ, June 10, 1830; AJ to William B. Lewis, July 28, 1830, Bassett, 4:29, 145, 167. On the Donelson-Eaton relationship and its ramifications, see also Marszalek, *The Petticoat Affair*, 85–88, 131–48, 157–59, 176–78, 183–85, 193.

41. AJ to Ely, Mar. 23, 1829, in Parton, 3:187–91.

42. Rachel to Elizabeth Watson, July 18, 1828, Bassett, 3:415–16.

43. AJ to Call, May 3, 1827, and Aug. 16, 1828, Bassett, 3:354, 426. Confirmation that Rachel Jackson was fully aware of the attacks on her character is in John Eaton's letter to her of Dec. 7, 1828, which she did not live to read: "To prejudice your husband, you know well what envenomed slander has been aimed at both of you. . . ." See Bassett, 3:449. The reference to Jackson's mother is in AJ to Rev. Ezra Stiles Ely, Sept. 3, 1829, Bassett, 4:68.

44. AJ to William B. Lewis, Aug. 17, 1830, Bassett, 4:173.

45. Doherty, *Richard Keith Call*, 52–55, 82–83, 120–21. Not long after the Eatons' arrival in Florida, a judge there curiously noted in his diary: "Gov. E. is a rowdy—his wife drunk or crazy." John Eaton's drinking was talked about by others, especially later in his career. As curious is John Marszalek's suggestion that Margaret Eaton and Mary Call in fact enjoyed each other's company, though they were not able to spend much time together. See Marszalek, *The Petticoat Affair*, 211.

46. AJ to Rachel, Dec. 21, 1823, PAJ, 5:330–31.

47. AJ to John C. McLemore, May 3, 1829, Bassett, 4:30–31.

48. Kirsten E. Wood, " 'One Woman So Dangerous to the Public Morals': Gender and Power in the Eaton Affair," *Journal of the Early Republic* 17 (Summer 1997): 237–75, quote at 271. Writing John Coffee on May 30, 1829, Jackson again branded Clay, asserting, "There never was a more insidious attempt to intimidate me and to destroy a man." He further (and proudly) stated of John Eaton that "he will triumph over his enemies and become, if not already, one of the most popular members of the cabinet." Bassett, 4:38; AJ to Call, July 5, 1829, Bassett, 4:51–52.

49. Colonel Charles J. Love to AJ, Apr. 15, 1829, and Bassett's commentary, in Bassett, 4:23; Crane, *Life and Select Literary Remains of Sam Houston*, chaps. 4–5; Day and Ullom, eds., *The Autobiography of Sam Houston*, 45–55; Wisehart, *Sam Houston*, 41–51, 653n. The endnote provides a descendant's explanation of the dissolution of the marriage, based on oral history, which focuses on Houston's vulgarity as well as a repulsive "festering wound" from Indian fighting.

50. Houston to AJ, Sept. 19, 1829, Bassett, 4:74–75.

51. Jack Gregory and Rennard Strickland, *Sam Houston with the Cherokees, 1829–1833* (Austin, Tex., 1967).

52. Crane, *Life and Select Literary Remains of Sam Houston*, 42–44; Parton, 3:385–91.

53. Parton, 3:391; Jackson's handwritten notes on a conversation with Rev. Danforth, Apr. 30, 1832, Hurja Collection, TSLA.

54. Alexis de Tocqueville, *Democracy in America* (New York, 1945 [1835, 1840]), 1:264–65, 420–34, 2:146–47. On the nature of the Union, Tocqueville starts from the premise, in describing the federal system, that "The people in themselves are only individuals; and the special reason why they need to be united under one government is that they might appear to advantage before foreigners"—less so to manage the "internal affairs of society." See ibid., 1:120. On equality, compare Tocqueville's contemporary, the novelist Honoré de Balzac: "Equality may perhaps be accepted as a *right,* but no power on earth will convert it into a *fact.*" Balzac, *History of the Thirteen* (New York, 1974 [1833–34]), 180.

55. Michel Chevalier, *Society, Manners, and Politics in the United States* (New York, 1961 [1836]), 59, 97, 107, 184.

56. Frances Trollope, *Domestic Manners of the Americans* (New York, 1927 [1832]), 56, 101, 104.

57. Marvin Meyers, *The Jacksonian Persuasion* (Stanford, Calif., 1960), 122–25; Trollope, *Domestic Manners of the Americans,* 258–59.

58. Ward, 36–38; Remini, 2:227–28.

59. Curtis, 72–73; Ward, 41; Remini, 2:268–71; Rogin, *Fathers and Children,* 246–47.

60. AJ to Calhoun, Sept. 2, 1820, PAJ, 4:388.

61. Anthony F. C. Wallace, *The Long, Bitter Trail: Andrew Jackson and the Indians* (New York, 1993), chaps. 2–3. As a Mason, Cass was first master of the Grand Lodge of Michigan.

62. John Ehle, *Trail of Tears: The Rise and Fall of the Cherokee Nation* (New York, 1988), chaps. 14–15; Remini, 2:271–79, explaining Jackson's reluctance to irritate the Georgians in terms of South Carolina's nullification stand; for a good overview of Jackson's position with respect to the legal-constitutional aspects of Indian removal, see Leonard Baker, *John Marshall: A Life in Law* (New York, 1974), 731–46; [Associate Justice] Stephen Breyer, " 'For Their Own Good': The Cherokees, the Supreme Court, and the Early History of American Conscience," *New Republic,* Aug. 7, 2000. William Wirt ultimately received $500 for his efforts.

63. Bernard W. Sheehan, *Seeds of Extinction: Jeffersonian Philanthropy and the American Indian* (Chapel Hill, N.C., 1973), 150–52.

64. Smith, *The First Forty Years of Washington Society,* 283.

65. AJ to Coffee, June 18, 1824, Bassett, 3:255–56; Edmund Quincy, *Life of Josiah Quincy of Massachusetts* (Boston, 1869), 454; Smith, *The First Forty Years of Washington Society,* 289.

66. John Davis to Elvira Davis, Dec. 11, 1829, in *John Davis Papers,* American Antiquarian Society.

67. Rogin, *Fathers and Children,* 157–59, 206ff.

68. John Overton put it plainly in a letter to Jackson, just after the Jackson-Calhoun rupture: "He is aspiring we all know, and his eye has never been averted for a moment, from the presidency, since he became a member of Mr. Monroe's cabinet. This is not unnatural for talented men. Hence, no man saw with more pain (Mr Clay not excepted) the rise and elevation of your character, during the last War." Overton to AJ, June 16, 1830, Bassett, 4:151. James A. Hamilton (a Van Buren partisan) recorded in his later memoir: "The truth is—and that was well understood by General Jackson—that Calhoun and his friends made a desperate effort to induce the President to employ such men in his cabinet as would give them control of the Government." *Reminiscences of James A. Hamilton,* 91.

69. *Memoirs of John Quincy Adams,* 7:272–73.

70. On Van Buren's political rise, see John Niven, *Martin Van Buren: The Romantic Age of*

American Politics (New York, 1983). In chapter 14, Niven points to several early Jackson decisions that irked Van Buren who, being pragmatic, remained dutiful, though he had been moved to consider resignation in 1829. On Van Buren's relationship with Jackson from the mid-1820s to his own election as president in 1836, see also Thomas Brown, "From Old Hickory to Sly Fox: The Routinization of Charisma in the Early Democratic Party," *Journal of the Early Republic* 11 (Fall 1991): 339–69. John Quincy Adams took notice of Calhounite claims that Van Buren ingratiated himself with the Eatons while whispering to Jackson that "Calhoun's moral puritanism against Eaton's wife was only a political cant of hypocrisy, to head a party against the Administration." See *Memoirs of John Quincy Adams*, 8:356–57. Niven's characterization gives credence to Adams's comment. The historian writes of Van Buren's agreeable pose: "He could play the drawing room game to studied perfection." (Niven, *Martin Van Buren*, 249).

71. Calhoun to AJ, June 4, 1826, *Papers of John C. Calhoun*, eds. Clyde N. Wilson and W. Edwin Hemphill (Columbia, S.C., 1977), 10:111; Merrill D. Peterson, *The Great Triumvirate: Webster, Clay, and Calhoun* (New York, 1987), 185.

72. Parton, 3:310–20, reprinting the narrative of Jackson's confidant William B. Lewis.

73. Peterson, *The Great Triumvirate*, 170–80; William W. Freehling, *Prelude to Civil War: The Nullification Movement in South Carolina, 1816–1836* (New York, 1966). The most comprehensive analysis of the tariff question and nullification is Richard E. Ellis, *The Union at Risk: Jacksonian Democracy, States' Rights, and the Nullification Crisis* (Oxford, 1987).

74. Merrill D. Peterson, *The Jefferson Image in the American Mind* (Charlottesville, Va., 1998 [New York, 1960]), 70. The latter interpretation is that advanced by Richard R. Stenberg, "The Jefferson Birthday Dinner, 1830," *Journal of Southern History* 4 (Aug. 1938): 334–45. Stenberg believed that Jackson's persecution of Calhoun caused the latter to be backed into declaring his association with the nullifiers, and that Calhoun was far less committed to nullification than others in South Carolina. An instinct on the part of Jackson to avenge Calhoun's secret persecution of him in 1818, combined with Van Buren's own ambition to displace the vice president and succeed Jackson as president, make this scenario entirely plausible. However, this would also have to render Hayne, one of the event's arrangers, the dupe of Benton and Van Buren. See also John Niven's commentary on Stenberg's thesis in *Martin Van Buren*, 644–45n.

75. Benton, *Thirty Years View*, 1:148–49; Niven, *John C. Calhoun and the Price of Union*, 172–75; Remini, 2:234–36; Peterson, *The Great Triumvirate*, 185–86.

76. AJ to Calhoun, May 13 and May 30, 1830, Bassett, 4:136, 140–41; AJ to Calhoun, May 30, 1830, AJ Papers, LC, microfilm reel #73.

77. Remini, 2:204, 216, 239–40, 266, 322; A. J. Donelson to AJ, Oct. 25 and Oct. 30, 1830, Bassett, 4:189–97; AJ to A. J. Donelson, Oct. 26 (?), 1830, Oct. 30, 1830, Mar. 24, 1831, and May 5, 1831, Bassett, 4:191–96, 251–254, 273–78.

78. AJ to A. J. Donelson, Mar. 24, 1831, Bassett, 4:252.

79. Parton, 3:344–64; Peterson, *The Great Triumvirate*, 212–15. Livingston would have accepted the post of secretary of state in 1829, had Jackson offered; but when the honor was given to the ambitious Van Buren, Livingston chose to remain in the Senate rather than accept any lesser (as he conceived it) position.

80. Arthur M. Schlesinger, Jr., *The Age of Jackson* (Boston, 1945), 96; Parton, 3:466–67; AJ to Coffee, Dec. 14, 1832, Bassett, 4:499. Livingston had previewed the president's defense of the Union in the Senate of the United States in 1830, after the Webster-Hayne exchange. Referring to the new West as an "iron frontier," and his adopted state of Louisiana as "a race of independent, well-informed cultivators of the soil," he insisted that Union was ever strengthening, and was "happy unless corrupted by false corruptions or torn by mad and

ruinous resistance." There were no constitutional questions of such import or permanence, Livingston had averred, that need threaten the founders' federal system; the best argument against nullification was the obvious fact that no one's liberty was curtailed. In the original constitutional compact of 1787–88, he further reminded, the states had ceded certain powers to the general government, including "the right of enforcing obedience to the exercise of those powers." See *Register of Debates*, 21st Congress, First Session (Washington, D.C., 1830), 250–72.

81. Dusenbery, 371–88. On the concept of "Union" relative to Jackson's political program, see Richard P. McCormick, "The Jacksonian Strategy," *Journal of the Early Republic* 10 (Spring 1990): 1–17. On the nullification issue as an expression of Jackson's defense of "tradition," see Harry L. Watson, *Liberty and Power: The Politics of Jacksonian America* (New York, 1990), chap. 4.

82. Parton, 3:447; regarding the complexity of constitutional issues involved in the nullification crisis, see Ellis, *The Union at Risk*.

83. On Duff Green, Amos Kendall, and the other newspaper editors whose activities reshaped national politics, see Jeffrey L. Pasley, *"The Tyranny of Printers": Newspaper Politics in the Early American Republic* (Charlottesville, Va., 2001), esp. chap. 14; *Memoirs of John Quincy Adams*, 8:510–11.

84. Donald B. Cole, "A Yankee in Kentucky: The Early Years of Amos Kendall, 1789–1828," *Proceedings of the Massachusetts Historical Society* 109 (1997): 24–36; Cole, "Amos Kendall: The 'Moving Spring' of Andrew Jackson's Administration," paper presented at the Society for Historians of the Early American Republic annual meeting, Buffalo, New York, July 21, 2000; Kendall to AJ, Aug. 22, 1827, in Remini, 2:128; Remini, 2:326–30; Wise, *Seven Decades of the Union*, 117–18.

85. South Carolina's 11 electoral votes went, in protest, to Governor John Floyd of Virginia (Jackson won Virginia). Anti-Mason Wirt captured Vermont's 7 electoral votes. Jackson won approximately 55 percent of the popular vote.

86. Overton to Philip Barbour, May 30, 1831, Claybrooke Collection/Overton Papers, TSLA; Frances Clifton, "John Overton as Andrew Jackson's Friend," THQ 11 (1952): 40.

87. Marszalek, *The Petticoat Affair*, 184.

88. Gordon T. Chappell, "The Life and Activities of General John Coffee," THQ 1 (1942): 125–46.

89. Carroll to AJ, Dec. 2 and Dec. 18, 1832, AJ Papers, LC, microfilm reel #73. On the governor's support for Van Buren over Calhoun, see Carroll to AJ, May 6 and June 13, 1831, also in Jackson Papers, LC, microfilm reel #73.

90. Carroll to Clay, Oct. 1, 1823, *Papers of Henry Clay*, 3:492. This concerned Jackson's run against John Williams for a seat in the U.S. Senate. Curiously, Thomas Hart Benton, not yet having reconciled with Jackson, was cozying up to Clay around the same time, writing that he saw Jackson's chances for the presidency in 1824 as slim, and Clay Tennessee's second choice only because it would be "bad policy" in Nashville—from whence Benton was writing—not to support the local hero. See Benton to Clay, July 23, 1823, *ibid*, 460.

91. Ratner, *Andrew Jackson and His Tennessee Lieutenants*, 69–71; Wisehart, *Sam Houston*, 34–35, 46–50; Wise, *Seven Decades of the Union*, 147–48. The Tennessee state constitution required that the governor not serve more than three successive one-year terms; so when Carroll had served his first three, he yielded to Houston, expecting Houston to yield back after two years. When Houston left the governorship in 1829 and went to Arkansas Territory, Carroll wrote Jackson that he had always thought Houston emotionally unbalanced, "a man of weak and unsettled mind . . . incapable of manfully meeting reversal of fortune." Carroll to AJ, May 25, 1829, AJ Papers, LC, microfilm reel #37.

92. The preceding interpretation of the Bank War is largely informed by Watson, *Liberty and Power,* chap. 5; Meyers, *The Jacksonian Persuasion;* Schlesinger, *The Age of Jackson,* 88ff; Parton, 3:409–11, 415–16, 493–508, 537ff; Thomas P. Govan, *Nicholas Biddle: Nationalist and Public Banker* (Chicago, 1959); Remini, 3:142–78; Chevalier, *Society, Manners, and Politics in the United States,* 30, 37; Cole, "Amos Kendall: The 'Moving Spring' of Andrew Jackson's Administration." One scholar contends that there were factors in addition to Jackson's policy that caused changes in the money supply in 1834–35. See Peter Temin, "The Economic Consequences of the Bank War," *Journal of Political Economy* 76 (1968): 257–74.

93. Meriwether Lewis Randolph to Nicholas Trist, Jan. 31, 1835, *Nicholas Trist Papers,* LC. Trist was for a time President Jackson's private secretary, and was married to a granddaughter of Jefferson, making him Randolph's brother-in-law. Also see Benton, *Thirty Years View,* 1:521–24; Dusenbery, 104.

94. Parton, 3:583–84; Edwin A. Miles, "Andrew Jackson and Senator George Poindexter," *Journal of Southern History* 24 (1958): 51–66; Richard C. Rohrs, "Partisan Politics and the Attempted Assassination of Andrew Jackson," *Journal of the Early Republic* (Summer 1981): 149–63. Rohrs figures that the dampness of the weather was responsible for the two misfires, and that the scheme to make Poindexter look guilty of complicity was not Jackson's own idea but rather that of loyal followers who sought to embarrass a political defector.

95. The president became involved in 1834 in the French spoliation controversy. France was delaying an agreed-upon payment against claims due American shipping that had been damaged during the Napoleonic wars. By this time, Livingston (still much in favor, though he disagreed with Jackson on the bank issue) had left the State Department and was his minister to France. Livingston pressed forward in the president's interest, as Jackson used intimidating language in challenging the French to meet their obligation. Jackson's bullying nearly did irreparable harm to Franco-American relations, but the matter was finally resolved. Livingston's successor as secretary of state was, briefly, Louis McLane, and then John Forsyth, former senator from Georgia, who served from June 1834 until Jackson's term ended.

96. AJ to Col. Anthony Butler, Oct. 7, 1830, Bassett, 4:183–84; Curtis, 172–75; Remini, 2:218–20, 3:352–60. Jackson's denial of any improper collusion with Houston concerning his posture toward Mexico is found in AJ to Forsyth, Mar. 6, 1838, Bassett, 5:540–541n; even more clearly framed in AJ to William B. Lewis, Sept. 18, 1843, Bassett, 6:228–30. In the intervening five years between the two latter communications, events had led Jackson to drop his protective posture and more revealingly profess his desire for annexation.

97. Houston to AJ, Feb. 13, 1833, in Crane, *Life and Select Literary Remains of Sam Houston,* 46–47.

98. Notes of Henry D. Gilpin, a Van Buren cabinet appointee, in *Edward Livingston Papers,* PUL, Box 63.

99. *Letters of John Quincy Adams to Edward Livingston* (Boston, 1833), letter dated Apr. 10, 1833. In reply to Livingston's charge that the "honorable fraternity" was being unfairly criticized, Adams wrote acidly: "You, Mr. Livingston, are versed in the ways of ambition and ambitious men. You know their propensity to keep up excitements, and to direct them against political adversaries for their own elevation."

100. *Local Acts Passed at the First Session of the 21st General Assembly of the State of Tennessee* (Nashville, 1836), 269. In the same session of the state assembly, Coffee County was established, "in honor of the late General John Coffee" (p. 262).

101. Parton, *The Life and Times of Aaron Burr,* ix, 612, 633–36; Nathan Schachner, *Aaron Burr* (New York, 1937), chap. 29. The point worth making here is that we should be careful when we judge Burr in moral terms: just because he was less concerned than Hamilton, Jefferson, or Jackson with the fashioning of a legacy through a network of publicly vocal

friends does not make him necessarily less moral than they. As to Burr's sexual intrigues, these persisted in fictional accounts after his death, most dramatically in *The Amorous Adventures of Aaron Burr* (New York, 1859), which is pure pornography. The character of Burr is ennobled in the work, however: no matter how many women he seduced, he would never compromise a woman's reputation by speaking of his conquest. On Burr's sexuality and its importance in forming his public reputation, see Nancy Isenberg, "The Little Emperor: Aaron Burr, Dandyism, and the Treason Trial of 1807," in Pasley, Robertson, and Waldstreicher, eds., *Beyond the Founders* (forthcoming).

102. James, 712; Parton, 3:598.

103. Benton, *Thirty Years View*, 1:735.

Chapter Seven. Courting Posterity

1. AJ to Donelson, June 7, 1829; to Cryer, June 17, 1832, Bassett 4:41–42, 448.

2. J. Cunningham to Reuben Lewis, Apr. 9, 1837, in the Virginia Historical Society.

3. AJ to Van Buren, Mar. 30, 1837, Bassett, 5:466–68.

4. AJ to Poinsett, Oct. 19, 1837, Bassett, 5:516–17.

5. AJ to Louise Livingston, Nov. 12, 1840, Bassett, 6:82–83; Remini, 3:465–66.

6. Wise, *Seven Decades of the Union*, 154. This kind of critique emanated from other southern groups: "Citizens of Albemarle [County, Virginia] Opposed to the Re-election of the present President" circulated a petition in 1832, and declared of Jackson, "He has shown himself wanting in that frankness and fair dealing which his friends once claimed for him. . . . By studiously keeping his sentiments concealed . . . or rather, by affecting in each state the sentiments which chance to prevail there, he seeks to obtain popularity and votes with both parties." Original handwritten document at the Virginia Historical Society.

7. White's political shift led the way for an anti-Jackson faction in Tennessee to rise to new prominence. "How is it," Jackson wrote Polk, "that there is no man in the Republican ranks to take the stump, and relieve Tennessee from her degraded attitude of abandoning principle to sustain men who have apostatised . . . ?" AJ to Polk, May 12, 1835, Bassett, 5:345.

8. AJ to Kendall, May 15, 1841, Bassett, 6:112–13. Though Jackson always saw Van Buren as mannerly and consistent, many others believed this a façade. New Hampshire Democrat Benjamin Brown French, a lawyer and clerk in the House of Representatives in the 1830s, did not shift party loyalty, but he appeared to understand the phenomenon, explaining in his journal that he could not raise "one particle of affection" for Jackson's successor. "I never liked the character of Van Buren," he wrote in November 1840. "I believe him to be a cold-hearted *calculating* man, who cares more for his own personal aggrandizement than for anything else." Earlier in the campaign, French similarly remarked that while he had "rejoiced" in Van Buren's success, out of agreement with his principles, "I despise the man, for he is cold as an icicle & has no heart or soul." *Witness to the Young Republic: A Yankee's Journal, 1828–1870*, eds. Donald B. Cole and John J. McDonough (Hanover, N.H., 1989), 101, 104.

9. AJ to Francis P. Blair, Sept. 26, 1840, Bassett, 6:78.

10. Nancy N. Scott, ed., *A Memoir of Hugh Lawson White* (Philadelphia, 1856), 325.

11. Remini, 3:456–60.

12. AJ to Van Buren, Nov. 10, 1840, Bassett, 6:83.

13. J. Olney to AJ, Nov. 18, 1841; Lyman B. M.——to AJ, Nov. 20, 1841; David Lea to AJ, Nov. 22, 1841, AJ Papers, LC, microfilm reel #54.

14. Anonymous to AJ, June 10, 1841, AJ Papers, LC, microfilm reel #35.

15. Blair to AJ, May 3, 1842, Bassett, 6:151.

16. AJ to Kendall, Dec. 12, 1842, Jan. 9, 1844, Bassett, 6:179, 253–54; AJ to Kendall, Mar. 20, Mar. 24, and May 10, 1843, AJ Papers, LC, microfilm reel #78.

17. AJ to Call, Aug. 20, 1842, AJ Papers, LC, reel #35.

18. AJ to Call, Sept. 9, 1842, in *The Collector* (1905): 63. Call replied, "My best wishes for your health and happiness," presumably closing their once intimate, since troubled relationship, on a happy note. See Call to AJ, Oct. 18, 1842, AJ Papers, LC, reel #35.

19. AJ to Polk, Feb. 28 and May 2, 1845; to Blair, Mar. 18, and Apr. 7, 1845; to Maunsel White, Mar. 28, 1845, Bassett, 6:372–73, 386, 393, 395, 404.

20. AJ to Kendall, May 20, 1845, Bassett, 6:406–7; to Donelson, May 24, 1845, Bassett, 6:408.

21. On the language of loss, see, for instance, Lord Byron's epic poem *Childe Harold's Pilgrimage*; Washington Irving's short stories, "The Widow and Her Son" and "Rural Cemeteries" in his 1819 *Sketch Book*; Jan Lewis, *Pursuits of Happiness: Family and Values in Jefferson's Virginia* (Cambridge, 1983), chap. 3; Nancy Isenberg and Andrew Burstein, eds., *Mortal Remains: Death in Early America* (Philadelphia, 2003).

22. AJ to Polk, June 6, 1845, Bassett, 6:413–14.

23. "Old Hannah's Narrative of Jackson's Last Days"; Houston to Polk, June 8, 1845, Bassett, 6:415–16.

24. AJ to Lewis, Apr. 29, 1833, Bassett, 5:66. *Manes* is the Latin for spirit or ghost.

25. Dusenbery, 413–15.

26. Remini, 3:526.

27. *The Complete Essays of Montaigne*, ed. Donald Frame (Stanford, Calif., 1958), 471. Compare Jackson's comments on virtue to Commodore Elliott.

28. AJ to Rachel, June 2, 1818, PAJ, 4:212.

29. See Burstein, *The Inner Jefferson*, chap. 6; Freeman, *Affairs of Honor*.

30. On Washington's temperament, see especially John Ferling, *Setting the World Ablaze: Washington, Adams, Jefferson, and the American Revolution* (New York, 2000), 107, 172–73.

31. John E. Ferling, *The First of Men: A Life of George Washington* (Knoxville, Tenn., 1988), 253, 260–61; Benjamin Rush to John Adams, Feb. 12, 1812; Adams to Rush, Apr. 22, 1812 and June 12, 1812, in John A. Schutz and Douglas Adair, eds., *The Spur of Fame: Dialogues of John Adams and Benjamin Rush, 1805–1813* (San Marino, Calif., 1966), 209, 213, 225–26. Eulogists made a religious icon of Washington by drawing on messianic imagery. For example: "His countenance addressed us in a language more than human. . . . Earth he was not thine! He was the offspring of Virtue, the favourite of Heaven." See *Eulogies and Orations on the Life and Death of General George Washington, First President of the United States of America* (Boston, 1800), quote at 107. See also Paul K. Longmore, *The Invention of George Washington* (Berkeley, Calif., 1988), and Barry Schwartz, *George Washington: The Making of an American Symbol* (New York, 1987).

32. *Memoirs of General Andrew Jackson, Together with the Letter of Mr. Secretary Adams, in Vindication of the Execution of Arbuthnot and Ambrister* (New York, 1824); Burstein, *Sentimental Democracy*, 195–99; the modern study of the Washington image in this regard is Garry Wills, *Cincinnatus: George Washington and the Enlightenment* (Garden City, N.Y., 1984); see also Albert Furtwangler, *American Silhouettes: Rhetorical Identities of the Founders* (New Haven, Conn., 1987), chap. 4.

33. Dusenbery, 89–92, 104.

34. "Address to the People of the Congressional District," Mar. 26, 1825, *Papers of Henry Clay*, 4:153.

35. Ferling, *The First of Men*, 257; idem., *Setting the World Ablaze*, 173, quoting Adams and Jefferson.

36. [Horatio Hastings Weld], *Pictorial Life of George Washington* (Philadelphia, 1846), esp. 202–14; [John Frost], *Life of Jackson* (Philadelphia, 1845), quotes at iii–iv, 167, 172.

37. Robert P. Hay, "The Case for Andrew Jackson in 1824: Eaton's *Wyoming Letters,*" THQ 29 (1970): 149.

38. *United States Telegraph,* Jan. 18, 1829. On Jefferson and Jackson and the pastoral tradition, see Wallace Hettle, *The Peculiar Democracy* (Athens, Ga., 2001), chap. 1. More generally, see Leo Marx, *The Machine in the Garden: Technology and the Pastoral Ideal in America* (New York, 1964); Charles A. Miller, *Jefferson and Nature: An Interpretation* (Baltimore, 1988); John M. Grammer, *Pastoral and Politics in the Old South* (Baton Rouge, La., 1996).

39. Benton, *Thirty Years View,* 1:736, 738.

40. Any study of social authority or racial prejudice will find that power sharing, like trust, does not come easily. For one element in society to yield power to a less fortunate element for purely altruistic motives is an improbable event; thus slavery persisted over generations. Why else does the gap between rich and poor in the world continue to widen today? Human beings have proven many times over that possessing knowledge of the existence of an evil does not easily lead to its eradication. Isolating the activities of individual slave owners does not serve to explain, with any degree of significance, this kind of historical force.

41. David Ramsay, "An Oration," in *Eulogies and Orations on the Life and Death of General George Washington,* 89; George Bancroft's eulogy, in Dusenbery, 42–43.

42. First and Second Inaugural Addresses, Mar. 4, 1801, and March 4, 1805; Jefferson to John Breckinridge (U.S. senator from Kentucky), Aug. 12, 1803, *The Portable Thomas Jefferson,* 318, 495–97; Peter S. Onuf, *Jefferson's Empire: The Language of American Nationhood* (Charlottesville, Va., 2000), 15.

43. Norma Basch, "Marriage, Morals, and Politics in the Election of 1828," *The Journal of American History* 80 (Dec. 1993): 890–918, quote at 897.

44. Bertram Wyatt-Brown, "Andrew Jackson's Honor," *Journal of the Early Republic* 17 (Spring 1997): 34.

45. Doherty, *Richard Keith Call,* 137.

46. Wilkins Tannehill, *The Masonic Manual, or Freemasonry Illustrated* (Nashville, 1824), 70–73, 111–15. Interestingly, the text also seeks to encourage Masons to "abstain from all malice, slander and evil speaking; from all provoking, reproachful and ungodly language, keeping always a tongue of good report" (p. 73). It would have been difficult for Jackson, by any means of constructing his speech, to believe he had fulfilled this Masonic injunction, though his friends could easily retort that his patience had been tried more than any man in America in the heat of political warfare.

47. This particular extract is from AJ to James A. Hamilton, May 29, 1830, Bassett 4:140.

48. Meyers, *The Jacksonian Persuasion,* 12.

49. *Gen. Andrew Jackson and the Rev. Ezra Stiles Ely* (New York, 1828), 5.

50. Robert Walsh, *The Jackson Wreath* (Philadelphia, 1829), 54.

51. Houston, pseudonymously, as "Virginian," in *National Intelligencer,* Mar. 19, 1824.

52. Overton to White, Feb. 11, 1823, Murdock Collection/Overton Papers, TSLA.

53. Stephen Skowronek, *The Politics Presidents Make* (Cambridge, Mass., 1993), 130–52. Skowronek, a political scientist, compares Jackson's and Jefferson's common project of recasting political authority, but asserts that Jackson acted more forcefully in this regard "because his political authority was so much more directly besieged."

54. Hamilton to Timothy Pickering, July 3, 1828, in *Reminiscences of James A. Hamilton,* 76–77.

55. John Davis to George Nixon Briggs, Mar. 20, 1834, in *George Nixon Briggs Correspondence,* American Antiquarian Society. On the activities of Isaac Hill, see Pasley, *"The Tyranny of Printers,"* 352–56; also Donald B. Cole, *Jacksonian Democracy in New Hampshire, 1800–1851* (Cambridge, Mass., 1970).

56. Ward, 140.

57. This is my characterization of the Jackson of lore whom Robert Remini reconstructs. In his three-volume biography, Remini draws heavily on the anecdotal Parton, who in fact lived among Jacksonians and had a presumptive right to repeat what he heard. But Remini uncritically presents spoken utterances of Jackson, even when attribution is uncertain. He does so, apparently, in order to make Jackson colorful, and the result is a sympathetic portrait of the savior who blusters.

Remini's analysis of Jackson's passions is perplexing and incomplete. He allows key contradictions to stand, leaving readers with an irreconcilable set of attributes for his subject. While repeatedly depicting Jackson as the heroic progenitor of American democracy, he plainly charges his hero with an unforgivable disrespect for the highest law of the land. Of the Hall-Louaillier incident, Remini writes: "Jackson established a police state with no other authority but his own. He clearly overreached himself," and "The extent of Old Hickory's lunatic militarism had now reached comic proportions" (Remini, 1:311–12). In heralding Jackson's presidency, he insists that "Jackson's constitutional views proved untenable but they were genuinely democratic. . . . Central to the constitutional system was the notion of checks and balances, but Jackson made a shambles of that notion by insisting on his primacy as President in interpreting and executing the law because he—and he alone—represented all the people. Andrew Jackson was the great advocate of democracy. . . . But the democracy he practiced reduced to near ruin the kind of republic conceived by the Founding Fathers" (Remini, 3:317).

58. MacArthur openly clashed with President Harry Truman during the Korean War and was fired for his abrasiveness. Truman once privately referred to the general as "Mr. Prima Donna," one who presumed he could tell God what to do. See Michael Schaller, *Douglas MacArthur: The Far Eastern General* (New York, 1989) and Robert H. Ferrell, *Harry S Truman: A Life* (Columbia, Mo., 1994), chap. 15, quote at 330. I am grateful to Tom Buckley for our discussions of the Jackson-MacArthur comparison.

59. See Burstein, *Sentimental Democracy*, 284–87, 331–32.

60. Dusenbery, 389–405.

61. AJ to Taney, Oct. 13, 1836; Taney to AJ, Oct. 15 and Oct. 27, 1836, Bassett, 5:429–32.

62. Jackson did not appear to exhibit the complexity of thought that South Carolinian John C. Calhoun did, when he explained slavery to the erudite Adams partisan Edward Everett: "Scaffolding, scaffolding, Sir—it will come away when the building is finished." See Peterson, *The Great Triumvirate*, 257.

63. *Memoirs of John Quincy Adams*, 8:319, 546; Parsons, *John Quincy Adams*, 214–17, 223–28, 266.

64. Curtis, 134–37; Richard John, *Spreading the News: The American Postal System from Franklin to Morse* (Cambridge, Mass., 1995), chap. 7; Cole, "Amos Kendall: The 'Moving Spring' of Andrew Jackson's Administration." Curiously, in 1835–36 Jackson urged the candidacy of Van Buren's vice president, Kentuckian and Indian fighter Richard Mentor Johnson, over the objections of southern and western political allies who were revolted by Johnson's open relationship with a biracial woman with whom he had two daughters.

65. Overton's account of Burr's activities, Aug. 15, 1828, Murdock Collection/Overton Papers, TSLA.

66. Steven C. Bullock, *Revolutionary Brotherhood: Freemasonry and the Transformation of the American Social Order, 1730–1830* (Chapel Hill, N.C., 1996), 178–79.

67. John Tyler, "Eulogy, Pronounced at Richmond, Virginia, July 11, 1826," in *A Selection of Eulogies, Pronounced in the Several States, in Honor of Those Illustrious Patriots and Statesmen, John Adams and Thomas Jefferson* (Hartford, Conn., 1826), 15.

68. Dusenbery, 248; similarly a eulogy by John A. Bowles, Lowell, Mass., in ibid., 217.

Appendix. The Union of Andrew and Rachel Jackson

1. Parton, 1:151–52.

2. Remini, 1:xviii, 57–67; Remini, "Andrew Jackson's Adventures on the Natchez Trace," *Southern Quarterly* 29 (1991): 36–38. Remini cites G. Douglas Inglis, a graduate student, for unearthing the crucial information on Stark's and Jackson's early travels to Natchez; Harriet Chappell Owsley, "The Marriages of Rachel Donelson," THQ 36 (Winter 1977): 479–92; "Accounts with Melling Woolley" (Natchez merchant), Mar. 1 and July 1, 1790, PAJ, 1:21–22.

3. Cochran to AJ, Oct. 21, 1791, PAJ, 1:29–33. The Library of Congress had at one time dated the second part of Cochran's letter as 1794, but the editors of *The Papers of Andrew Jackson*, in 1980, reassigned the date to 1791.

4. PAJ, 1:425–27.

5. Robards had written to Robert Hays in January 1791, seeking to profit from Rachel's share of her late father's estate, and this suggests at least one direct source of information on Robards's activities in Kentucky.

6. PAJ, 1:424.

7. Curtis, 27–28. Another analyst of the chronology resists this conclusion. According to Harriet Chappell Owsley, Jackson did not have to know this aspect of the law because divorce was extremely rare, and he had studied the law in North Carolina rather than Virginia, from whence Kentucky law was drawn. However, this still does not explain the grounds of Robards's suit; nor does it explain the January 1791 document identifying "Rachel Jackson." Although that document was not officially filed until April 1791 (when, technically, enough time had passed to facilitate a wedding), it makes no sense that the January date was retained, and Rachel's surname suddenly altered in April. See Owsley, "The Marriages of Rachel Donelson."

8. Parton, 1:153.

9. This is consistent with the evidence of insignificant fines levied against convicted adulterers by early Nashville juries. See Goodstein, *Nashville, 1780–1860*, 14.

10. In eighteenth- and even nineteenth-century England, a protocol existed by which a wife could sometimes be "sold" by her erstwhile husband to her new mate for a simple fee. While this was not done in America, other informal procedures were in place, and they typically associated the cause of the action with adultery and desertion. Benjamin Franklin's *Pennsylvania Gazette* allowed advertisements from husbands disclaiming their wives' debts—one means of announcing the equivalent of a divorce. As newspapers sprouted in the trans-Appalachian West (including the *Nashville Republican* in the 1820s), similar ads persisted. Self-divorces were more common among the laboring classes but did occur, albeit with far less regularity, among elites. See Claire Anna Lyons, "Sex Among the 'Rabble': Gender Transitions in the Age of Revolution, 1750–1830," Ph.D. dissertation, Yale University, 1996, chap. 1. For comparable ads in Vermont, see Laurel Thatcher Ulrich, *The Age of Homespun* (New York, 2001), 367–68. Another important study shows that informal unions were recognized in various parts of the British isles at different times. In the border country of Scotland, among the poor, an exchange of promises before witnesses often constituted a marriage. Many thousands of these nonreligious border weddings were conducted during the early nineteenth century. To be "married in the Scotch form" was generally honorable. However, this practice also invited bigamy and such abuses as the easy wedding that merely facilitated seduction. Bigamy also occurred in reaction to a desertion. In sum, unorthodox divorces by mutual consent, or as a result of offensive actions by the husband, had a long history. While wife selling was a fairly common practice across England, it was less common in Scotland, because an older tradition of temporary marriage and extramari-

tal cohabitation made wife selling unnecessary. See Samuel Pyeatt Menefee, *Wives for Sale: An Ethnographic Study of British Popular Divorce* (New York, 1981), 9–16, 31–32.

11. [Charles Hammond], *General Jackson's Domestic Relations in Reference to His Fitness for the Presidency* (Cincinnati, 1828), 6–8.

12. Mary Dickson vs. John Dickson's Heirs, Supreme Court of Tennessee, Nashville. 9 Tenn. 110; 1826 Tenn. LEXIS 16. I thank Nancy Isenberg for bringing this case to my attention.

13. Remini, 1:65; John Buchanan's *Jackson's Way: Andrew Jackson and the People of the Western Waters* (New York, 2001), became available after research was completed on this book. Buchanan's careful analysis of Jackson's early years also calls into question Overton's dating and concludes that the Jacksons entered into a common-law relationship in the summer of 1790. He notes: "Rachel and Jackson were young, in love, and did what came naturally" (pp. 117–19). I take but slight issue with this interpretation, preferring to center the discussion around a strategically planned manipulation of the law and the custom of self-divorce. I find cultural explanations more convincing than the universal or "natural" power of love.

14. For the White House explanation, see Web site: *http://www.whitehouse.gov/history/firstladies/rj7.html.*

INDEX

Index

Indians (*continued*)
  Osage, 181
  Seminole, 4, 129, 131, 138, 185, 235
  Seneca, 4
  Shawnee, 90
  Waxhaw, 4
Irving, Washington, 75, 216

Jackson, Andrew
  elements of personality
  antagonism toward Indians, xiv, xix, 4,
    15–16, 23, 90–1, 100, 106, 120, 127–9
  compared to Indian, 5–7, 121, 187–8
  compared to Washington and Jefferson,
    122, 219–28, 233–4, 239–40
  domestic life, 121, 149, 159–62, 229
  and dueling, 17–19, 44–6, 52–60, 94–7,
    130–1, 140–3, 148–9, 155–6, 163
  espouses concept of "redress," 19, 53,
    67–9, 100
  as eulogized, xv, 10, 63–4, 87–8, 240
  heroic portrayals of, xiv, xviii, 98, 118–19,
    134, 138–9, 161, 234, 239
  humane gestures, 87, 93, 151–2, 157–8,
    160–2, 187–8, 230
  identified with Napoleon, 125–6, 169
  influence of frontier condition on, 15–16,
    21–5, 63, 188
  as moral absolutist, 37–8, 64–8, 76, 82–3,
    87–8, 101–2, 155, 168–9, 175, 218, 233
  paternalism, 47–8, 101–2, 147, 175–6
  perspective on death, 48, 104, 207, 215–17
  physical descriptions and health issues,
    5, 23, 101, 107, 116, 121, 122, 134, 137–9,
    148, 156, 160, 188, 189, 205, 207–8, 230
  political savvy, 84–5, 113, 191–2
  Scotch-Irish traits, 4, 10, 29, 32, 189
  sense of victimization, 58–9, 91–2, 101,
    144, 149–50, 170, 208, 217, 224
  Shakespearean comparisons, xiii, 59–60,
    74, 119, 168–70, 192, 217–18, 230
  as slave owner, 24, 26, 50, 51, 67, 86, 159,
    172
  unorthodox vocabulary, 7–8, 25, 40, 65,
    89, 160, 224
  vengefulness, 37–8, 44–6, 52–4, 60, 66–8,
    77–8, 90, 142–5, 166, 181–2, 211
  view of women, 28–9, 160, 170–80

letters to/from key figures
  Blount, Willie, *letters from*, 89, 91; *letters
    to*, 89–91, 103
  Burr, Aaron, *letters from*, 72, 73
  Call, Richard K., *letter from*, 178; *letters to*,
    140–2, 147–8, 163, 171–2, 176, 179, 207
  Calhoun, John C., *letters from*, 131, 154,
    189; *letters to*, 131, 192
  Carroll, William, *letter from*, 198
  Coffee, John, *letters to*, 50, 100, 127,
    144–6, 150, 156–7, 170, 187, 193
  Donelson, Andrew Jackson, *letter from*,
    178; *letters to*, 128–9, 137, 159, 192–3, 215
  Hays, Robert, *letters to*, 34–6, 40
  Houston, Sam, *letters from*, 153, 181, 203–4
  Jackson, Rachel Donelson, *letters from*,
    104, 124, 170; *letters to*, 32, 87, 100, 102,
    104, 129, 153, 170, 180, 218–19
  Jefferson, Thomas, *letter from*, 73; *letters
    to*, 22, 47, 65
  Kendall, Amos, *letter from*, 201; *letters to*,
    210, 215
  Lewis, William B., *letters to*, 154, 157, 217
  Livingston, Edward, *letter from*, 165;
    letters to, 123, 127
  Monroe, James, *letter from*, 118–19; *letters
    to*, 116, 128–31, 143
  Overton, John, *letters from*, 32–3, 60
  Polk, James K., *letters to*, 215, 216
  Robertson, James, *letters from*, 53, 97;
    letter to, 125
  Sevier, John, *letters from*, 42, 45; *letters to*,
    34, 42–5
  Van Buren, Martin, *letters to*, 208, 212–13
life on the frontier
  youth, 3–4, 7–11
  early Indian encounters, 5
  participates in Revolution, 8–9
  mother dies, 9
  studies law, 10–11
  named prosecutor, 11–12
  takes hard line on Indian diplomacy, 16
  challenges Waitstill Avery to duel, 17–19
  relates hair to independence, 22–3
  tolerates slavery, 24, 26
  arrives in Nashville, 25–6
  acquires law texts, 27
  controversial romance with Rachel
    Donelson, 28–33, 227–8, 235, 241–8